发刊词

强以华

  假如说人类的文化像一汪海洋，那么，在全球化的今天，各个国家、各个民族、各个地区的文化就像一条又一条河流那样，正在以汹涌澎湃之势从四面八方流入这汪海洋之中。它们相互冲撞、相互交融，在冲撞中交融，在交融中冲撞，汇成了当代世界文化竞争、对话、冲突、融合的交响乐。在这首交响乐中，不同国家、民族和地区的政治家和思想家发出不同的声音，并试图以自己的声音来影响甚至主宰这首交响乐。《世界文化发展论坛》正是试图提供一个平台，让来自世界各地的思想家尽情发出自己的声音，共同演奏出文化竞争与融合的交响乐的壮美篇章。

  早在人类世界逐步形成的蛮荒时代，由于高山的横亘、大海的阻隔，人类的祖先或渔或猎，或耕或种，往往局限于一隅之地。随着生产的发展和社会的进步，人类的祖先通过贸易和战争不断扩大自己的领域，形成了一个又一个国家，凝成了一个又一个民族。这些国家和民族又进一步形成了自己的文化，这些文化通常被称为民族文化。这些国家和民族由于生成地域的差异和成长道路的不同，它们的民族文化各具特色、千姿百态。正是这些各具特色、千姿百态的文化绘成了人类历史上的文明画卷。

  在很大程度上说，人类的历史就是随着生产发展、社会进步，不同的国家和民族在贸易和战争中相互分离、相互融合，并从总体上走向越来越大的融合的过程。在这一过程中，尽管有些小的国家和民族依然存在，甚至由于战争而变得更小，但是，一些大国和多民族国家逐渐形成，乃至一些跨地区的组织也逐渐形成，这些大国、多民族国家和跨地区的组织作为文化的载体支撑了特色各异的大国文化、多民族文化和跨地区文化。中国文化、印度文化、美国文化，以及中华文化、西亚文化、欧美文化、南美文化、非洲文化，等等，都是这些文化中的重要成员。

然而，尽管人类的历史从总体上说是大国、多民族国家和跨地区组织不断形成的历史，也是大国文化、多民族文化和跨地区文化不断形成的历史，但是，历史上的任何时候都没有像当今社会这样真正开始了经济全球化基础上的社会全球化和文化全球化，这种全球化使原本主要活动于不同区域（例如西方、南美、东亚、非洲）的国家、民族在真正的意义上聚拢起来，使它们真正相互"面对"。这样一来，原本构成人类共同的文明画卷并使这一画卷熠熠生辉的那些各具特色、千姿百态的民族文化反而成了不同国家和民族相互抵触乃至冲突的根源，人们都要固守自己的传统，可是这些传统又常常包含了某些难以兼容甚至互相反对的因素。问题在于，社会尤其是经济的全球化乃是一种人类无法阻挡的历史潮流，随着社会以及经济的全球化，不同国家和不同民族的文化不得不相互面对并且和平共处，因此，人类便面临着一个选择何种原则、采取何种方法来解决这些文化的冲突与兼容的问题。

在全球化的背景下，自诩本民族文化不可一世和哀叹本民族文化的昔日辉煌，或者拒其他文化于千里之外和把本民族文化强加于人都会显得感性有余而理性不足。作为有责任感、使命感的学者，我们应该静下心来，理性地面对全球化的事实，客观地评价各种文化的优劣，通过对话、讨论、争辩，探索一条文化全球化的道路，使不同的文化既能够在一些共同的原则下和平共处，又能够在人类文化的大家庭中各有位置。作为和平共处之基础的共同原则使人类文化真正能够成为人类共同的精神家园，人类文化大家庭中各具特色、千姿百态的不同民族文化又使人类的共同精神家园五彩缤纷、异香满园。湖北大学暨湖北大学高等人文研究院的《当代世界文化论坛》愿为有责任感、使命感的学者提供有责任感、使命感的理论平台，欢迎海内外的专家、学者来这一平台各抒己见，一起为丰富人类五彩缤纷、异香满园之共同精神家园贡献自己的智慧！

目录 CONTENTS

传统文化与现代文化 / Traditional Culture and Modern Culture

各国文化与世界文化 / Culture of Different Countries and World Culture

共同推进世界主流文化构建

——首届"世界文化发展论坛"（2013）武汉宣言*

Making Joint Efforts to Promote the Construction of World Mainstream Culture：Wuhan Declaration of the First World Culture Development Forum（2013）

2013 年 9 月 23 日，来自韩国、菲律宾、马来西亚、印度、泰国、以色列、澳大利亚、墨西哥、巴西、爱尔兰、美国、中国等 12 个国家的 25 位学者，相聚在中国武汉市湖北大学，共同讨论当代世界文化发展，其主题是"当代世界主流文化的现状与前景"。参加此次论坛的学者就世界文化发展特别是世界主流文化达成共识，并同意发表以下宣言：

On September 23rd, 2013, 25 scholars from South Korea, the Philippines, Malaysia, India, Thailand, Israel, Australia, Mexico, Brazil, Ireland, USA and China gathered at Hubei University, Wuhan, China, to discuss contemporary world culture development issues with the theme of "current situation and prospects of contemporary world mainstream culture". Scholars have reached a consensus concerning world culture development, especially the world mainstream culture, and agreed to make the following declaration：

人们普遍承认，当今的世界是文化多元化的世界。确实，与全球经济

---

* 编者按：2013 年 9 月 23 日，"世界文化发展论坛"（2013）在湖北武汉湖北大学召开，来自全球 12 个国家的 25 位学者齐聚沙湖湖畔，探讨世界主流文化发展的现状和前景问题，并根据江畅教授的提议，共同签署了《共同推进世界主流文化构建—— 首届"世界文化发展论坛"（2013）武汉宣言》。本宣言由江畅教授起草，由李家莲博士翻译成英文。

一体化趋势相反，今天的世界文化日益呈现出多元化的格局。很多学者、政治家乃至普通人都将这种多元化看作世界文化发展的必然趋势，并因而努力为这种多元化作论证和辩护。他们比较少地注意或思考在这种多元文化的世界新格局之下是否需要有世界的主流文化，是否需要有世界各国和世界人民普遍认同的共同价值观。我们认为，在全球经济一体化和世界文化多元化格局并存的今日世界，要构建世界主流文化和价值观，首先要对世界主流文化和价值观给予高度重视。世界主流文化和价值观是维护世界安全与和平的基本价值原则。在今天世界各国有政府而整个世界无政府的状况下，如果连这种起码的价值原则都没有，或者有了也可以完全无视，那么我们的世界将危在旦夕。

It is widely acknowledged that today's world is the world of cultural diversity. Indeed, being opposite to the trend of economic globalization, today's world culture increasingly shows a diverse pattern. Many scholars, politicians and even ordinary people regard this kind of diversity as an inevitable trend in world culture development, and therefore strive to prove and defend this diversity. They hardly think or notice whether the world needs its mainstream culture under the new pattern of cultural diversity and whether it needs the common values universally recognized by all countries and all people of the world. We believe that, in today's world where economic globalization and cultural diversity coexist, it is necessary to construct the world's mainstream culture, at least to give priority to it. Mainstream culture and values are the basic principles and values which safeguard peace and security of the world. Every country has its government but the world as a whole is in a state of anarchy. In this condition, if there is no basic value principles at all in the world, or although there is but completely neglected, our world would be at stake.

所谓主流文化，是指在社会生活中占据主导地位的、普遍流行的或者为公众普遍接受的文化。一种文化要成为主流文化，不仅必须代表大多数社会成员甚至全体社会成员的利益，反映社会成员的普遍愿望，而且必须比其他文化先进、更有公信力，并能不断地从非主流文化中吸收合理的成分，使自身不断丰富。因此，我们构建主流文化不是对文化多元化的否定和排斥，而是在承认非主流文化存在和共同发展的前提下，对它们起主导作用并得到它们的尊重和认同。主流文化是与非主流文化共存共荣的，是不断从非主流文化中吸取营养从而不断得到完善和发展的。世界主流文化更不是对各国主流文化的简单否定和排斥。它是在基本尊重各国文化的前提下形成的世界文化共识，以及建立在此基础上的最基本的共同原则。对于某一个具体国家来说，这些共同原则只是其价值体系和文化的底线原则，而不是其主要原则，更不是其全部原则。当然，这些原则也应当具有引导和规范作用，否则它们就不具有价值原则的意义。对于不尊重这些底线原则的国家可以而且应当进行世界舆论谴责。

What we call the mainstream culture refers to the culture which has a leading role and universal popularity accepted by the public in a society. If a kind of culture wants to be the mainstream culture, it must not only represent the interests and universal wishes of the majority or all member of a society, but also be much more advanced than all other cultures, and can always strengthen itself by accepting the reasonable constituents of all other non-mainstream cultures. Therefore, the mainstream culture we want to construct is not to deny and reject cultural diversity, but to regulate all the non-mainstream cultures and get respect and recognition from them with the pre-condition that the mainstream culture and non-mainstream cultures co-exist and co-develop with each other. It coexists with non-mainstream cultures and get continuously improved and developed by constantly studying from them. The mainstream culture of the world is not a simple denial and rejection to national mainstream culture. It is the universal consensus and common principles formed by respecting the culture of every country. For one particular country, these common principles represent only the bottom line in its value system and culture, not the dominant or the whole principles. Of course, these principles should have the function of guidance and regulation; otherwise they would lose the significance of value principles. To the country violating these regulations of bottom line, it will be disapproved by the world.

世界主流文化和价值观绝不是某个国家的文化和价值观，它是世界各国、世界人民普遍认同或达成共识的文化和价值观。一切将本国的价值观世界化或向外国输出的图谋，不仅无助于世界主流文化的构建，而且必将导致世界主流文化的损毁。在构建世界主流文化的过程中，我们要坚决反对这种图谋，真正使世界主流文化由世界各国和全世界人民共同构建、共同分享。

What we need to point out particularly is that, the mainstream culture and values of the world are definitely not the culture and values of a particular country, but the culture and values which are universally recognized and made consensus by all people of all countries in the world. Any attempt to globalize or output the value of one particular country, will not only make no contribution to the world's mainstream culture construction, but also result in the damage of it. During the process of world mainstream culture construction, we must resolutely oppose this kind of attempt, and make the world mainstream culture constructed and shared together by people of the world.

构建世界主流文化是世界各国、世界人民的共同责任，但首先是世界各国学者的共同责任。今天的世界是文明昌盛的世界，我们办任何事情都必须有思想理论的引导，必须有在理论上得到合理性论证的实施方案，构建世界主流文化和价值观这样事关世界前途和命运的生死攸关的重大问题更是如此。从理论上构建世界主流文化和价值观，或者说提供世界主流文化和价值观的理论构架并给予理论与实践结合上的论证，是当代世界各国学者的共同社会责任和重大历史使命。各国学者应当自觉地承担起这一共同社会责任和重大历史使命，为世界主流文化和价值观的理论构建做出自己应有的贡献。

It is the common duty of every country and all people of the world, but first of all, the duty of scholars, to construct the world mainstream culture. Today's world is a world of civilization and a world of prosperity. Anything we do must be guided by theories with implementation plans proved by theories, so must the world mainstream culture construction related to the future and the destiny of the world. It is the common social duty and historical commitment for scholars of various countries to provide theoretical framework or the theory with practical proof for world mainstream culture and values construction. Scholars from different countries should voluntarily take the common social duty and the great historical commitment to make the due contribution to the theoretical construction of the world mainstream culture and values.

要提供世界主流文化和价值观的理论，不仅需要各国学者个别的研究，更需要世界各国学者之间的交流、对话、合作。我们举办这一论坛，就是为了给世界各国学者共同研究世界文化提供交流、对话和合作的平台，建设研究世界文化发展的智库。这次论坛的主题是"当代世界主流文化的现状与未来"，我们今后还会共同探讨其他有关世界主流文化发展的重大问题。这次论坛的举办是世界各国学者共同研究世界文化的有重大历史意义的开端，它将翻开人类自觉地共同关注自己主流文化建设发展的崭新一页。我们希望这一论坛在世界各国长期举办，通过论坛的举办不仅扩大各国学者关于世界主流文化研究成果的世界影响，而且直接推动各国政府和人民重视世界主流文化的建设。

To provide theories for world mainstream culture and values not only needs individual studies of all the scholars from different countries, but also needs exchange, dialogue and cooperation among these scholars. The forum we host is to build up a platform for scholars studying world culture in various countries to make communication, dialogue and cooperation, and to set up the think tank for world culture development. The theme of this forum is "the current situation and future of mainstream world culture". We will explore together other great problems concerning world mainstream culture development in the future. The forum is a starting point with great historical significance for scholars of different countries to make joint research of world cultures. It will initiate the common concern of mainstream culture construction for the human being. We hope that the forum will be permanently held in different places of the world. We hope the forum will not only expand the influence of every scholar's academic study of world mainstream culture, but also directly promote the government of every country and the people of the world to do world mainstream culture construction.

为了使这一平台办下去，而且越来越宽广，我们同意建立"世界文化发展论坛"理事会，参加本次会议的各国代表作为首届理事会成员。理事会成员的责任主要有二：一是发展更多国家的更多学者参与这一论坛，大家共同为世界文化发展提供智力支持；二是力争在自己国家承办"世界文化发展论坛"。我们希望该论坛每年在不同国家举办，以扩大它的影响，并增强各国发展世界主流文化的意识和自觉性。

In order to have this platform permanently held and in order to make it more and more wide, I propose to establish the Council for "World Culture Development", and all representatives at this forum from different countries can be the member of the first Council if there is no objection. There are two duties for every member of the Council: one is to recommend more scholars to participate the forum in order to provide the joint intellectual support for world culture development; the other is to try to organize world culture development forum in his or her country. We hope that the forum could be held annually in different countries in order to expand its influence and enhance the awareness and consciousness for every country to develop world mainstream culture.

出席论坛并签署《武汉宣言》的与会学者名单：

江畅（湖北大学）、保尔·斯威夫特（布莱恩大学）、戴茂堂（湖北大学）、科拉松·多拉巴（菲律宾）、俞吾金（复旦大学）、麦尔·尼·罗根（爱尔兰）、万俊人（清华大学）、滕沙·屠雷尔·贝瑞（墨西哥）、张庆宗（湖北大学）、丹尼尔·维拉斯（巴西）、孙伟平（中国社会科学院）、韩康铉（韩国）、王忠欣（北美华人基督教学会）、萨米安（马来西亚）、吴向东（北京师范大学）、埃米尔·利迪亚（以色列）、刘文祥（湖北大学）、弗兰克·詹姆斯·乌辛斯基（美国）、李祥坤（湖北大学）、埃

拉克·左拉·维拉斯（巴西）、陈建华（湖北中医药大学）、强以华（湖北大学）、赵红梅（湖北大学）

Scholars who participate in the Forum and make signature：

Jiang Chang（Hubie University），Paul Swift（Bryant University），Dai Maotang（Hubei University），Corazon T. Toralba（Philippines），Yu Wujin（Fudna University），Mair Ni Lorcain（Ireland），Wan Junren（Qinghua University），Hortensia Cuéllar Pérez（Mexico），Zhang Qingzong（Hubei University），Daniel Veras（Brazil），Sun Weiping（Chinese Academy of Social Sciences），Han Gang-Hyen（South Korea），Wang Zhongxin（Chinese Christian Scholars Association of North America），A. L. Samian（Malaysia），Wu Xiangdong（Beijing Normal University），Lydia Amir（Israel），Liu Wenxiang（Hubei University），Frank James Wucinski（U. S. A），Li Xiangkun（Hubei University），Erika Zoeller Veras（Brazil），Chen Jianhua（Hubei University of Traditional Chinese Medicine），Qiang Yihua（Hubei University），Zhao Hongmei（Hubei University）

论坛综述

Forum Report Summary

"世界文化发展论坛"（2013）研究报告

强以华[*]

摘　要： 由湖北大学举办的"世界文化发展论坛"于 2013 年 9 月 23 日在武汉召开，来自世界各地的学者围绕会议"当代世界主流文化的现状和前景"这一主题进行了热烈研讨与交流。综合来看，会议有三个焦点问题，即文化与主流文化、各国主流文化以及各国文化与世界文化。本次研讨会观点富有创新性，成果较为丰硕。

关键词： 世界文化　主流文化　发展

文化的发展既是物质文明发展的结果，又是物质文明进一步发展的前提。正如中国社会的发展离不开中国（乃至世界）文化的发展一样，世界的发展也离不开世界文化的发展。鉴于文化发展对于当代世界发展的重要意义，2013 年 9 月 23 日，由湖北大学主办、湖北大学高等人文研究院、湖北大学哲学学院、湖北大学马克思主义学院协办的首届"世界文化发展论坛"（2013）在湖北省教育考试院沙湖基地隆重召开。来自美国、墨西哥、澳大利亚、爱尔兰、巴西、韩国、印度、以色列、菲律宾、马来西亚等国，以及中国社会科学院、清华大学、北京大学、复旦大学、北京师

---
* 强以华，湖北大学高等人文研究院世界文化发展研究中心主任，哲学学院教授、博士生导师。

范大学等国内院校或研究机构的专家参加了本次会议。会议以系列笔谈为基础，围绕当代世界文化发展的诸多问题展开了深入的探讨，取得了显著的成效。为了使讨论更为集中，我们把系列笔谈的相关内容同全部论文结合起来，纳入以下三个部分加以分析。

一 主流文化研究

会议探讨的一个重要主题是如何在文化的基础上理解主流文化以及各国主流文化。毫无疑问，文化是理解主流文化的基础，但是，理解主流文化作为理解文化的进一步提升，更能把握文化的实质，并且更能有效地帮助我们把握文化对于社会发展的作用。

1. 一般文化

文化，伴随着人类的诞生、成长与发展，从远古社会蹒跚而来，时至今日已蔚为大观。

那么，文化究竟是什么呢？在人们的生活中，文化有点像空气，它视之不见、嗅之不觉，却又或隐或显、或自觉或不自觉地无所不在、无时不在，始终以一种不可抗拒的力量左右着人们。正因为文化太广大、太深邃，并且太重要了，因而对它难以名状，难以下定义。文化成了定义最杂乱、界说最模糊的概念之一。正因为此，为了探讨文化的内涵，我们有必要进一步追寻文化这一概念的起源。中国社会中的文化概念最早见于《易经》。《易·贲卦》说："观乎天文，以察时变；观乎人文，以化成天下。"[1] 这里的"人文化成"便是最早出现的"文化"概念。具体到"人文化成"，则是指典籍和礼仪风俗。西汉时期，刘向在《说苑·指武》中说："圣人之治天下也，先文德而后武力。凡武之兴，为不服也，文化不改，然后加诛。"[2] 此处的"文化"指与武力相对的文治教化。西方社会中的"文化"概念从辞源上说，主要都来源于拉丁文的"cultura"，具有

---

[1] 参见金景芳、吕绍纲《周易全解》，吉林人民出版社，1989，第181页。

[2] 王英、王天海：《说苑全译》，贵州人民出版社，1992，第650页。

居住、留心、耕种、培养、敬神等含义，指的是生活方式和礼仪风俗。现代英文、法文和德文中的文化都从拉丁文演化而来，并且都保留了拉丁文的某些含义。因此，从起源上说，无论是中国的"文化"还是西方的"文化"，都包含了教化培育人的含义。就此而言，一切人化的东西（包含物质文明、精神文明、制度文明等）都应该属于文化的范围。所以，中国的《辞海》说，文化"从广义来说，指人类社会历史实践过程中所创造的物质财富和精神财富的总和"。[①] 然而，从教化培育人的角度看，精神或思想文化始终居于主导地位，因此，学者们更多是从精神或思想文化的角度来定义文化。文化的专门研究源于19世纪西方社会学和文化人类学对原始社会形态的探讨，而文化作为一个重要的范畴、一个中心概念则首次被英国人类学家爱德华·泰勒在其1871年出版的著作《原始文化》中提了出来。泰勒其实就是从精神或思想的角度给文化做了界定，他说：文化或者文明就其民族意义而言，指的是一个复杂的整体，包括知识、信仰、艺术、道德法律、风俗，以及作为社会成员的个人而获得的任何能力与习惯。[②]

在本次会议中，一些学者探讨了文化的含义。墨西哥学者霍藤沙·居雷尔·贝瑞（Hortensia Cuéllar Pérez）教授的研究更为深入。我们以贝瑞的观点为例来讨论会议对于一般文化的思考。在《文化与诸文化：对世界主流文化的简略反思》一文中，贝瑞也从文化一词的拉丁词源开始追溯，并且进一步指出，文化一词的拉丁语与动词 colere（培养或抚育）有关，它源自印欧语"变化或改变"。由此出发，他也把文化的基本意思理解成对人的培养，或者，个人、团体、民族或国家所经历的可能平静发生也可能充满艰辛的内在的"变化或改变"。因此，他说："文化一词，无论是东方的儒家学说还是西方的经典，都指的是对受教育者的塑造和培养。"贝瑞探讨一般文化含义的令人印象深刻之处表现在他把文化分为经典人文主义意义上的文化和现代人文主义意义上的文化，并描述了经典人

---

① 辞海编辑委员会：《辞海》（哲学分册），上海辞书出版社，1980，第112页。
② 〔英〕爱德华·泰勒：《原始文化》，连树声译，上海文艺出版社，1992，第1页。

文主义意义上的文化向现代人文主义意义上的文化之发展的内在逻辑。首先，他从西方的角度概括了经典人文主义意义上的文化的发展历程。在他看来，希腊人所谈论的希腊文化总是致力于把自由人的各种品格塑造得非常优异，古希腊人称之为同美德有关的内在塑造，这种塑造不仅针对个人，而且针对政治—社会或社区团体。这一观点的典范是亚里士多德的尼各马科伦理学中所表达出来的思想。基督教早期的文化继承了古希腊对人的培养，同时加入了宗教的成分，即信仰之光，也就是对上帝和基督的信仰，代表了有别于理性却不反对理性的另外一种知识的来源，从此，在智力的层面上开创了神圣的先河。从文艺复兴时代开始，强烈的科学理性得以发展，由此出发，诞生了工具理性。并且，在地理大发现时代里，世界在地理上得到了统一，从而直接导致了大陆与大陆之间、文化与文化之间的知识共享。然而，20世纪的两次世界大战引起了人们对于工具理性的反思，使人们意识到必须要限制工具理性和权力意志。最近，后现代运动及其文化和哲学的解构指出了理性的边界。现代人文主义意义上的文化正是这种反思的结果，它比经典人文主义意义上的文化更加尊重文化的多样性。其实，人文主义意味着某种综合性，它对不同团体开放，并且与之对话与合作。这就产生了一个问题：什么是文化？贝瑞说道：我们认为，在开始讨论"文化""文明"和"世界主流文化"之前，我们要理解复杂的世界，它与多种因素，例如历史语境、地理、政治、经济、社会、民族、地域、种族、语言、宗教、自然环境的丰富与否等有关。

2. 主流文化

文化（一般文化）一定是一个多层次的系统，它的多层次可以从时间和空间两个方面加以区分：其一，从时间的角度加以区分就是从历史发展的角度加以区分。在任何一个民族（国家）的历史发展中，文化都有主流与支流之分。例如，在中华民族（中国）的历史发展中，儒家文化始终是一种主流文化，它不仅相对于汉族文化中的诸如道家文化、法家文化、墨家文化、名家文化等是一种主流文化，而且相对于随着历史的发展后来加入中华民族的少数民族文化也是一种主流文化。其二，从空间的角度加以区分就是从一定范围内文化的现实横断面的角度加以区分。在任何一个民族（国家）的现实横断面上，文化也都有主流和支流之分。例如，在当代中华民族（中国）文化的横断面上，社会主义文化目前是一种主流文化，它不仅相对于中国传统文化和西方外来文化是一种主流文化，而且相对于其他大众文化也是一种主流文化。然而，尽管我们既可以从时间的角度也可以从空间的角度区分主流文化和非主流文化，甚至描述一个民族（例如中华民族）具体的主流文化究竟为何，但是，在如何具体定义一种主流文化方面依然存在着巨大的争议。在此方面，国内学者江畅教授的研究给人印象深刻。

江畅教授在本次会议上提交的论文为《主流文化存在的三种样态及我们的战略选择》。江畅教授从一个独特的视角亦即"价值"的视角来看待文化的实质，并且将其作为判定主流文化与非主流文化的标准。在他看来，价值观构成了文化的核心和灵魂，价值观的差异构成了文化之间的差异，这一情形不仅表现在不同的一般文化之间，而且表现在主流文化和非主流文化之间。从表面看来，"主流文化是在社会生活中占据主导地位的、普遍流行的或为公众普遍接受的文化，而非主流文化是在社会中不占主导地位、部分流行或为部分公众接受的文化"。但是，由于"无论主流文化还是非主流文化，都是指一定的价值系统的现实化"，所以，"从实质上看，两者之间的区别是价值观的区别，而不是某种风俗习惯、日常生活方式的区别：主流文化是其价值观占据主导地位并普遍流行，而非主流文化则是其价值观不占主导地位只为部分公众所接受"。既然主流文化区别于非主流文化的实质在于它的价值观，并且这是一种占据主导地位、普遍流行、得到公众普遍接受的价值观，那么，我们便可以得出结论：主流文化之所以是主流文化，乃在于它是一种包含了主流价值观或体现了主流价值观的文化。这样一来，江畅教授就从主流价值观的角度定义了主流文化。由此出发，江畅教授还进一步指出了主流文化的三种存在样态，并且根据这三种样态的理论提出了中国主流文化建设应有的战略选择。主流文化存在的三种样态包括：其一，主流价值文化一统天下的样态，在这种样态下，非主流文化完全被压制以致湮灭，社会看起来只存在着清一色的一统文化；其二，主流文化唯我独尊的样态，在这种样态下，非主流文化被边缘化乃至被排斥被否定，社会中存在着主流文化和非主流文化的对立与争斗；其三，主流文化兼收并蓄的样态，在这种样态下，主流文化吸收现实可能存在的非主流文化的合理成分，使自己真正强大，非主流文化则在有助于主流文化稳定繁荣的基础上与主流文化同时存在。在以上三种主流文化的存在样态中，第三种样态应该是最为值得推崇的样态，因此，选择主流文化的第三种样态也就是中国主流文化建设应有的战略选择。

会议不仅探讨了一般文化和主流文化，还进一步把探讨的触角深入具体的各国主流文化。

3. 各国主流文化

各国主流文化的探讨乃是本次会议的重点。除了国内学者关于中国主流文化的大量研究成果之外，北美华人基督教学会会长王忠欣博士和保罗·斯威夫特（Paul Swift）教授分析了美国的主流文化（参见王忠欣博士的论文《当代美国文化及其特征》和斯威夫特教授的论文《宽容作为美国核心价值观的优点与缺点》），马来西亚的萨米安（A. L. Samian）教授探讨了马来西亚的主流文化（参见他的论文《马来主流文化在世界上的现状与未来》），爱尔兰的摩尔·尼洛根（Mair Ni Lorcain）教授探讨了爱尔兰的主流文化（参见她的论文《爱尔兰主流文化的主流价值观》）。由于篇幅所限，本文仅以中国主流文化和美国主流文化的探讨为例进行阐述。

（1）中国主流文化

在本次会议上，有关中国主流文化的探讨呈现多样化的特点。这种多样化既表现为角度的多样化，又表现为观点的多样化。

从角度的多样化来看，学者们从诸多不同的角度探讨了中国主流文化方方面面的问题。复旦大学俞吾金教授的笔谈《世界文化还是世界文化多样模式》、北京师范大学吴向东教授的论文《为什么中国提出"社会主义核心价值观"的概念》、湖北大学强以华教授的论文《当代中国文化的源流思考》探讨了中国主流文化的内容和源流问题；中国社会科学院孙伟平研究员的笔谈《文化软实力》、湖北大学教授刘文祥的笔谈《从公共政策看中国公共服务体系的构建》和湖北大学张丽军副教授的论文《苏联主流文化边缘化的教训对当代中国主流文化构建的启示》探讨了中国主流文化与中国的发展战略问题。此外，还有一些学者围绕中国主流文化探讨了其他一些问题，如湖北大学赵红梅教授的论文《当代中国主流审美文化问题研究》探讨了中国的审美文化问题。

观点的多样化表现在两个方面：其一，角度的多样化所带来的观点的多样化；其二，同一角度之内观点的多样化。同样，我们不可能在一篇研究报告中探讨所有角度的多样化和同一角度内部所有观点的多样化，我们这里仅仅挑选两个角度，并在每一角度中选择一篇具有代表性的论文来窥视本次会议对中国主流文化的探讨。

第一，中国主流文化的内容和核心含义。在此方面，俞吾金教授深入地探讨了中国主流文化的核心内涵、基本特征和主导精神。在他看来，中国主流文化的核心内涵就是马克思主义，更为准确地说，就是"中国化的马克思主义"。为了避免误解，我们必须进一步理解中国化的马克思主义的具体含义。首先，在现、当代中国社会的语境中，必须区分两种不同类型的马克思主义主义，即以毛泽东为代表的"以阶级斗争为纲的马克思主义"和以邓小平为代表的"以经济建设为中心的马克思主义"；其次，在中国文化的语境中，"与谈话者同时代的'当代'"指涉的乃是以邓小平为代表的"以经济建设为中心的马克思主义"，亦即1978年以来的中国社会主流文化；最后，在马克思主义的语境中，以邓小平为代表的"以经济建设为中心的马克思主义"，实质上就是"中国特色的社会主义"，它不仅包含了邓小平的思想，也包含了邓小平之后继者的思想。根据中国主流文化的核心内涵是"中国特色的马克思主义"这一规定，我们还可以进一步概括当代中国主流文化的基本特征和主导精神。它的基本特征应该体现在四组张力之中，即中国共产党作为执政党与执政党自身建设之间的张力；物质文化建设与精神文明建设之间的张力；改革开放与坚持四项基本原则之间的张力；借鉴中国传统文化遗产与建设社会主义先进文化之间的张力。它的主导精神则可以概括为以下三组概念，即科学发展、公平和谐和民主法治。

第二，中国主流文化与中国的发展战略。在此方面，孙伟平研究员深入分析了文化作为软实力的内涵和构成要素，并分析了提升中国文化软实力的方略。他说："所谓文化软实力，是指一定的文化本身所内蕴或张扬出来的吸引力、感召力、凝聚力、竞争力、影响力等作用力的综合表达。这种'有方向'的软力量以相应的文化（包括物质文化、制度文化和精神文化）发展状况为基础，蕴藏在文化传统、价值观、意识形态、政策法规、科教活动、生活方式以及文化产品和服务之中。"这种文化软实力包含诸如"文化价值吸引力""文化知识创造力""文化产业竞争力""文化服务亲和力""文化传播影响力""文化体制引导力"等内在的构成要素，它以"教化""同化""感化""融化"等方式并带有"润物细无声"的特征发挥着巨大的作用。因此，发展文化软实力应该是中国发展战略的重要组成部分。为此，孙伟平研究员提出了提升中国文化软实力的方略。在他看来，提升中国文化软实力首先应该做好两件事：其一，探索和确立实事求是、合乎国情的中国特色社会主义文化发展道路；其二，坚定和确立人民大众的文化主体地位，依靠人民群众，促进大众创造力的充分涌现。在此基础上，他强调应该从文化软实力的内在结构出发，做好以下工作，即凝聚核心价值理念或核心价值观，增强文化价值的吸引力和凝聚力；树立科技立国和教育立国的发展战略，全方位提高全民科技水平、文化素养和道德素质，促进创新性的文化生产，稳步提升文化知识创造力；通过体制创新和技术创新推动文化产业和服务业快速发展，增强文化发展的竞争力和活力；大力开展对外文化交流与合作，以大众传媒为基础，打造全方位、覆盖广、有渗透力的传播平台和传播渠道，拓展中国的"文化边界""文化版图"，维护国家"文化主权"和文化安全；深化文化体制改革，转变政府职能，创新文化制度、内容和形式，提高文化体制的引导力和保障力。

（2）美国主流文化

在本次会议上，王忠欣博士清晰地勾画了当代美国文化及其特征。他首先回顾了美国文化的发展历史，指出美国文化早期接受的是来自欧洲殖民者的基督教文化，从19世纪中叶起，美国文化又深受欧洲的世俗文化和学术的影响，直到20世纪60年代，美国文化一直都被称为犹太—基督教文化。在回顾美国文化历史的基础上，他分析了当代美国文化的形成，并且指出了当代美国文化的核心内涵和特征。他说，20世纪60年代以后，随着大量非欧洲移民的涌入，美国逐渐从以基督教占压倒优势的文化转变成了纯粹的多元文化，美国是世界上文化最为多元的国家。那么，美国的多元文化究竟有无共同的核心内涵呢？有！根据王忠欣博士的分析，这种核心内涵就是有神、自由、平等。信仰上帝是美国文化之核心内涵的基础，追求自由是美国文化核心内涵的理想。崇尚平等作为美国文化之核心内涵就是强调人的平等，表现在"上帝面前人人平等""法律面前人人平等""机会面前人人平等"。这样看来，美国当代文化尽管走向了多元化，但是，它依然与美国传统文化一脉相承。尽管如此，它也表现出了一些新的特征，即多元性、开放性、宗教性（多元宗教）、大众性和创造性。

在《宽容作为美国核心价值观的优点与缺点》一文中，斯威夫特教授则深入探讨了作为美国核心价值观的宽容问题，即美国人与人之间赖以和睦共处的伦理原则和法律原则，亦即宽容以及宽容的意义。他说，美国是个移民国家，它的文化是国际性的多元文化，面对这样的多元文化，要想确定其核心价值观非常困难。在这样的情形下，宽容就显得十分必要，它有实用的功能，因为它可以使持有不同观点的人在某种程度上和平相处。特别重要的是：宽容作为一条基本原则，还与美国宪法第一条即保证言论自由相吻合。毫无疑问，这种宽容有好的一面，它的实用功能本身就意味着它有好的一面。它的好的一面在于：它使谈话保持开放的状态。然而，宽容也有不好的一面，它的不好的一面在于：它也会产生负面的效果。宽容是对差异的容忍，但是作为一种美德，宽容是有限度的，如果一个社会对所有的一切都持宽容态度，那么，它就没法反对毫不宽容的人。从底限上说，如果一个人想保持宽容，他必须对试图取消宽容的行为保持不宽容。美国保护言论自由，却不能宽容一个人在拥挤的剧院大喊"失火了"，因为这会直接导致伤害或踩踏。历史上的宗教迫害培养了宗教宽容的传统。在美国社会中，广泛存在着宗教宽容。即使今天的美国年轻人更愿意接受无神论，但是，与北欧相比，美国仍然是一个宗教气氛非常浓厚的国家。美国有很多宗教团体，其中有些宗教团体甚至对宗教进行恶搞，但没有人去惩罚它们，恶搞穆罕默德先知，虽然不受鼓励，却是允许的。伦理学中有伦理相对主义的争论，伦理相对主义有两种形式，即文化伦理相对主义和极端相对主义。文化伦理相对主义也就是传统相对主义，认为伦理因文化的不同而不同。极端的伦理相对主义也叫主观相对主义，认为人与人之间就基本的对与错都无法达成一致。从事实上看，文化伦理相对主义和极端相对主义的区别在于文化群体的大小。总之，美国文化内在的多样性使人难以对所有人认同的核心价值观做出介绍。但是，美国人的宽容，尤其是对不受欢迎的语言的宽容，表明美国不要求人与人相互认同，而是要求每个人都应该拥有宽容的耐心。

会议在一般文化和主流文化的基础上讨论了具体的各国主流文化，不仅如此，它还在此基础上深入讨论了传统文化和现代文化，以及各国（主流）文化与世界文化的关系问题。我们先来讨论传统文化和现代文化的问题。

二　传统文化与现代文化

传统文化与现代文化是本次会议的一个重要主题。围绕这一主题，学者们分别讨论了中外传统文化和现代文化。在传统文化的讨论中，学者们重点讨论了中国的传统文化，例如湖北大学吴成国教授的论文《论中华文化与中华民族血脉》、湖北经济学院肖春艳教授和刘冲冲的《孔子"性相近、习相远"思想的方法论及其现代价值》；在现代文化的讨论中，学者们重点讨论了西方文化，例如湖北大学副教授徐瑾的论文《位格与完整：马里坦人道主义思想探微》。在分别讨论中外传统文化和现代文化的基础上，学者们认真比较了中外文化（主要是中西文化），探讨了中外（中西）文化的传播方式。例如，湖北大学教授熊友华等的论文《中庸与中道——先秦儒家与亚里士多德伦理观之比较》比较了中西传统文化中的道德思想，湖北大学博士李家莲的论文《无为与守约：〈道德经〉与

〈创世纪〉处世方法之比较》比较了中西传统文化中的处世方法，同济大学张能博士的论文《德勒兹的"欲望机器"与王充的"气"的比较》则通过中西方两位著名的哲学家比较了中西文化的某个侧面，湖北大学教授张宗庆、郭熙煌的论文《文化传播中的中式英语媒介》巧妙利用了"中式英语"这一特殊现象分析了中西文化的传播。此外，在提交的涉及传统文化和现代文化的论文中，学者还就其他感兴趣的问题展开了广泛的讨论。例如，菲律宾学者柯拉松·多拉巴（Corazon T. Toralba）的《文化基础的哲学反思》从哲学的层面深入反思了文化的基础问题；温州大学方德志博士的论文《生态文明与儒家德性精神振兴》探讨了中国传统文化的现代价值问题；湖北大学舒红跃教授的论文《从"我"到"我们"——现代工业文化的批判与反思》则对现代工业文化和工程技术提出了批判与反思。

1. 传统文化的追寻

李家莲博士的论文《无为与守约：〈道德经〉与〈创世纪〉处世方法之比较》通过比较《道德经》和《创世纪》分析了中西传统文化中的处世方法。作者指出，《道德经》与《创世纪》以不同的名称共同阐释了哲学中相同的最高存在者——"God"与"道"，但是尽管如此，当中国哲人与西方哲人开始把宇宙最高存在者与"人"联系起来的时候，情况就发生了相当大的变化，这种文化源头的差异逐渐演变成为性格迥异的中西哲学内涵与文化传统。

在伦理思想上，相同的哲学最高存在者在《道德经》中对人的要求是"德"，而在《创世纪》中，对人的要求是"moral"，"德"与"moral"虽然中文译文大致相似，但二者在词语的文化内涵上是截然不同的，正是这种不同显示了《道德经》与《创世纪》对人的不同伦理要求。在伦理实践上，《道德经》的"德"要求人们做到"知常"，而《创世纪》却通过与人"立约"的方式要求人遵守约定。《道德经》与《创世纪》暗示的不同处世方式不仅体现了中西方民族对待哲学最高存在者的不同态度，而且体现了中西方"人"在哲学中的不同地位，更重要的是，还体现了中西方哲学基本思维方式的差异。

2. 中西文化的比较

熊友华、陈静文的论文《中庸与中道——先秦儒家与亚里士多德伦理观之比较》围绕中西传统文化的一个核心精神"中庸"和"中道"比较中西文化，试图发现先秦儒家思想的伦理观与亚里士多德的伦理观之间的联系和差异。

在比较中庸和中道之历史背景的基础上，作者分别比较了中庸和中道的基本内容、方法和目标。在内容上，作者指出，对于中庸和中道的思想内容，我们可以从以下几个方面加以比较：其一，过犹不及的思想。中庸的思想是过与不及的中间状态，所以过犹不及的思想是中庸的基本思想。儒家对中庸的这一理解与亚里士多德的中道思想基本相同。亚里士多德认为："人们应该选取中道，既不过度，也非不及。……中道就是过度与不及的居间者。"其二，时中的思想。孔子认为中并不是一成不变的，而应当是随着时间、环境、条件的变化而有所不同。对此，亚里士多德也曾有过相似论述，即相对中道思想。在他看来，除了绝对的中道之外，还有一种相对中道，它是随人随事、因地因时不断变化的，没有一个固定不变的尺度和标准来衡量。它只是对应该的对象，在应该的事件，于应该的地点和应该的时间，以应该的方式来行动。其三，中和的思想。"礼之用，和为贵"集中反映了孔子的中和思想。儒家中和思想的实质在于人伦关系的和谐，它以情感为纽带，强调温情脉脉的伦理道德，甚至将情感凌驾于理性之上。亚里士多德虽然也希望通过中道达到和谐的社会状态，但与儒家的感性主义原则不同，他所倡导的是理性主义原则。在方法上，作者也从几个方面来比较中庸和中道的方法。首先，中庸和中道都主张权衡适度法，也就是说，在他们看来，若是不能选择最好的方法，那就应该经过权衡去选择一种相对适度的方法。其次，先秦儒家的中庸和亚里士多德的中道根据各自的理论提出了各种不同的方法。儒家根据中庸中的时中思想提出权变的方法。所谓权变，就是根据事物发展的具体情况采取相应的措施。所以，儒家认为，我们在培养中庸思想时，要把握好实施中庸的应变能力，在不同形势下灵活应对。亚里士多德则提出感性怀疑法，即要警惕自身的感性欲望。所以，根据亚里士多德的观点，我们必须不断地对感性欲望提出质疑，用理性调控感性，将自己拽往相反的方向，才会避免失误，达到适中。在目标上，作者指出，无论是先秦儒家的中庸还是亚里士多德的中道，它们的核心思想都是在过与不及之间寻找中间，但这个中间的确定并不是随意而为的，需要有一定的标准。孔子明确指出，中庸的标准是"礼"。情感和行为只有合乎"礼"才可以称之为"中"。亚里士多德则认为，法律才是中道的标准，在他看来，只有法律才能遏制人性的恶欲，使人的生活合乎德性。他认为法律是没有感情的智慧，是合乎正义而毫无偏私的工具，所以他对人的品质要求是合法基础上的合德。在比较中庸和中道的基础上，作者还进一步讨论了先秦儒家的中庸思想和亚里士多德的中道思想对于后世的影响以及影响的特点。

三　各国文化与世界文化

万俊人教授关于《中国梦与世界梦》的演讲从一个基本角度把各国文化与世界文化相互关系的问题高屋建瓴地提了出来。他试图把中国梦与世界梦联系起来思考，从文化的角度来说，他是把中国文化的发展与世界文化的发展联系起来思考，试图找出一条中国文化与世界文化和谐发展的道路。在本次会议上，很多学者都探讨了各国文化与世界文化的关系问题，如墨西哥贝瑞教授的论文《文化与诸文化：对世界主流文化的简略反思》、韩国韩康铉教授的论文《一体哲学与新人类文化》、以色列李迪亚·爱弥尔（Lydia Amir）教授的论文《当代世界文化中的新怀疑主义世界观》、印度托马斯·门拉帕拉皮尔（Thomas Menamparampil）教授的论文《亚洲未来：受惠于世界伦理智慧》、湖北中医药大学陈建华教授的论文《中医药文化及其核心价值》，等等。湖北大学戴茂堂教授的论文《塑造我国主流文化的全球品质》则从另外一个角度把中国文化与全球文化联系起来。此外，美国学者弗兰·詹姆斯·吾辛斯基（Fran James Wucinski）教授的论文《美国和中国：关于教育之重要性的不同观点》和巴西学者丹尼尔·维拉斯（Daniel Veras）教授的论文《国与国之间的文化差异：巴西人与中国人经商的不同方式》还分别从教育的角度和经商的角度探讨了不同国家之间的文化差异问题。

1. 文化的多元化与世界化

当今世界是一个多元化的世界，那么，各国文化如何构成世界文化呢？贝瑞教授试图探讨多种文化如何共存的问题。贝瑞教授把文化区分为经典人文主义意义上的文化和现代人文主义意义上的文化，并且认为现代人文主义意义上的文化更加呈现出多元性和丰富性的特点。他充分论证了当代世界的文化多元性。他说：从社会政治学的角度而言，自从柏林墙倒下之后，世界上再也没有了两极分化的局面，而是呈现出大规模的政治、经济和文化的多元化格局，其中，从特定的角度出发，每种文化都提供了一种地缘意义上的政治文化身份，因此，产生了多种对于世界有重要影响的文化，例如欧共体的文化、包括中国和印度在内的东南亚国家的文化、以墨西哥和巴西为首的拉丁美洲的文化，以及以美国、英国和加拿大为代表的盎格鲁—撒克逊文化。这些情形说明，当今世界已成为多极化的世界。今天，已经没有任何伟大民族的身份特征或者文化能够保持不变，不管是西方的希腊文化、基督教文化，还是东方的印度文化、中国文化等，它们都不可避免地会接受发生在私人领域和公共领域之内的政治、经济和文化的改变。因此，贝瑞教授提出了这样的问题，即在今天的社会中，我们能说世界上存在着主流文化吗？他回答说：对于这个问题，我们难以给出肯定性的回答，因为这个问题隐含着另一个问题，即从什么角度说世界上存在主流文化？当今，世界权力的重心正在向东方和南方转移，2013年的联合国报告也表明了这一点。这样，我们面对的就是文化多元主义以及跨文化交流，但是，由于文化身份、认知身份、民族荣誉和尊严等思想的不同，跨文化交流是非常困难的，怎么办呢？解决问题的方式是进行以尊重多样性为前提的跨文化对话。由此出发，贝瑞教授提出了如何促进各国或者不同文化之间的交流和发展的设想。根据他的设想，我们可以采取两条路径来促进各国或者不同文化之间的交流和发展：首先，从动机层面上说，要具有进行开放性的对话与合作的态度，追求公平与和平；其次，从实践层面上说，每个国家都必须建立尊重其历史和传统的公共政策，以教育为途径，来提升其文化创造力，创造文化财富。在他看来，墨西哥就是这样一个多元文化并存的国家。

2. 文化的全球化与普世化

贝瑞教授讨论各国文化的多元共存，戴茂堂教授则在承认和坚持多元共存的同时讨论了各国文化的全球化与普世化问题。戴茂堂教授论文的主旨是探讨中国如何在全球化背景下塑造主流文化的问题，或者换句话说，其论文的主旨是探讨在全球化背景下如何塑造中国主流文化的全球品质问题。在围绕这一主旨的讨论中，他正好涉及了与贝瑞教授之观点具有互补关系乃至对立关系的观点，即各国文化的全球化与普世化问题。

戴茂堂教授首先讨论了全球化的历史过程和逻辑线索。他说：全球化原本是开放性和竞争性的商品流通，特别是市场经济高度发展的产物，因此，它的核心是经济全球化，包括资本、资源、金融、生产、贸易、服务的全球化。然而，社会的经济与社会的政治、文化等原本不可分割，经济的全球化不可能只是停留于经济领域，它虽然发端于经济领域，但不可避免地要辐射到社会的其他领域，尤其是政治领域和文化领域，因此，全球化不仅是经济的全球化，也是政治、文化等的全球化。"所以，全球化从时间上看大致还是经历了先经济再政治再文化的历史过程。"经济全球化是发端，文化全球化则是落脚。从本质上说，虽然人们把经济全球化作为全球化的核心，其实，文化的全球化才是全球化的真正核心。正如戴茂堂教授自己所说：经济全球化到政治全球化再到文化全球化"这一逻辑进程本身表明，经济和政治的全球化都有待于文化全球化的价值支持，全球化的核心、归宿和根本只能是文化的全球化"。在讨论全球化的历史过程和逻辑线索的基础上，戴茂堂教授进一步探讨了各国文化的全球化和普世化问题。他说："文化全球化要求不断超越本民族文化的国界并在人类的评价和取舍中获得文化的认同，不断将本民族的文化资源转变为人类共享、共有的资源。文化全球化依托信息革命，努力缩小、打破和消除了人民的文化界限，使知识信息在全球范围内自由流动。由于全球化作为一个整体首要的是一个社会文化系统，因此，全球化社会的关键在于多元社会文化构成的全球文化系统，全球化只能在既定的多元社会文化系统中进行整合。""全球化的最高境界就是走向对价值文化普世性的诉求，就是在文化上达成或完成价值共识或价值趋同。"在他看来，他所理解的这种文化全球化在实践上一直在进行，它既包含了 1993 年 8 月世界宗教会议第二次大会签署的《走向全球伦理宣言》，也包含了联合国的《世界人权宣言》，还包含了更多的相关组织的决议和报告。如今，珍重生命、正直公平、言行诚实、相敬互爱，以及人人享有生活、自由和人身安全的权利……这些伦理规范和价值追求越来越成为人们的共识。正是在这样的基础之上，戴茂堂教授才要求中国主流文化应该自觉对接于全球语境，并且通过增强文化自信来实现这一对接，构建中国具有全球品质的主流文化。

本届"世界文化发展论坛"作为湖北大学、湖北大学高等人文研究院等单位举办的高层次文化论坛，试图探幽发微，通过对文化以及主流文化的探讨，追寻走向当代世界的文化交流和整合之路，给学界留下了丰硕的成果。我们这里挑选一些论文结集发表，并且期待未来各届"世界文化发展论坛"能够取得更为丰硕的成果！

Research Report of the World Culture Development Forum

Qiang Yihua

Abstract：The Forum about the Development of the World Culture run by Hubei University and The higher the Humanities Research Institute of Hubei University is held in the Sha Lake Base of Hubei Examination Council in September 23, 2013. Scholars held heated discussions on the relevant theme. To sum up, their keynote speeches focus roughly on three questions, that is, research to mainstream culture, the traditional culture and the modern countries, and the relation between every country culture and the world culture. Their discussions and speeches contain a lot of creative opinions.

Keywords：world culture；mainstream culture；development

系列笔谈

*P*aper-Discussion

栏目主持人：江畅，湖北大学哲学学院教授，教育部长江学者，国家社会科学基金重大招标项目"构建我国主流价值文化研究"（项目编号：11&ZD021）首席专家。

Organizer：Jiang Chang, Professor of the School of Philosophy, Hubei University, the chief expert of National Grand Project "National Mainstream Culture Construction Research"（No.：11&ZD021）.

栏目主持人语：为了更好地理解当代世界文化与主流文化，我们邀请了几位国内外著名学者做了一个笔谈，深入探讨了文化以及世界主流文化的哲学基础、中国梦与世界梦的关系、文化软实力和公共文化服务体系。

Words of the organizer：In order to better understand contemporary world cultures and the mainstream culture, we invite several most eminent scholars in the world to make a paper-discussion about the concept of culture, the philosophical foundation of world mainstream culture, the relation between Chinese dream and the world's dream, the cultural soft power and the public cultural service system.

World Culture or Multiple Patterns of World Culture

Yu Wujin[*]

I am very interested in the topic of this international conference. However, I don't agree with its expressional mode. I would like to make a check on the two phrases – "world culture" and "mainstream cultures", in order to express the topic of this conference more rationally. I do so is just for arriving at an exact understanding on this topic.

World Culture or Multiple Patterns of World Culture

While one is going to use "world culture" as his research object , he or she will suddenly find out a surprising fact that there is no "world culture", and it is only an abstract concept, because any culture belongs to some pattern without exception. In other words, there is no culture which can transcend any patterns.

In his introduction of lectures to the history of philosophy, Hegel put forward a very interesting idea that if you want to send a fruit to another person, you will finally find it is impossible, because "fruit" is only an abstract concept which can't be sent to another. That is to say, what can be sent to another is only a concrete kind of fruit, such as apple, strawberry, banana and so on. However,

* Yu Wujin, Professor of Fudan University, Dean at the Center of Marxism Research Abroad.

"fruit" can't be sent to another.

In the similar manner, it is not possible for us to investigate "world culture", and the real objects we may make consideration on are multiple patterns of world culture, such as Asian culture, American culture, Arabian culture, African culture, and so on. Of course, more concrete patterns are Chinese culture, Indian culture, French culture, and so on.

Mainstream Cultures or Mainstream Culture

Obviously, as one uses the metaphor "mainstream cultures", he must be conscious that this metaphor comes from people's observations of the flowing of different streams. However, according to common sense, it is impossible for any stream to have two or three, even more mainstreams. In other words, a stream has only a unique mainstream. Of course, it is possible for any stream to have many tributaries. Like a stream, any pattern of culture also has only a unique mainstream, so I think we can't say "mainstream cultures", but we may say "mainstream culture". That is to say, the concept of culture here is only single, not plural.

Go without saying, there is no so-called united mainstream culture in the world either. In fact, different people always have different perspectives, and when they try to investigate culture, it is necessary for them to offer quite different answers to the question: "what is the mainstream culture in the world?" In this sense, it is absolutely impossible for us to debate on a mainstream culture approved by everybody, because there is no such united mainstream culture in the world.

Research Method: Speculative or Comparative?

If one talks about "culture" or "world culture", neglecting its concrete pattern, it is possible for him to see neither cultural multiplicity nor the significance of comparative method among different patterns of culture. As a matter of fact, the comparative method is a useful method in studies of contemporary cultures, because there is no abstract and general culture, but concrete culture belonging to a definite pattern, so what we really need isn't speculation on an abstract and general world culture, but comparison among different patterns of culture in the world.

By the way, comparative method can be divided into the following two different types: one is the dominant comparison, which means researchers openly announce in their papers, reports or books that they are investigating different patterns of culture, using the comparative method; the other is the recessive comparison, which means that researchers never mention such words as "comparison" or "comparative" in their papers, reports or books, but they still in fact use comparative methods, so long as their expressions have reference to different patterns of culture. In this sense, we may say that the comparative method is the only essential method in doing research on contemporary cultures.

Chinese Dream and the World's Dream

Wan Junren[*]

It is my pleasure to make a presentation on this symposium about contemporary mainstream culture. First of all, I would like to make an apology. Just a few days ago, something bad happened to me when I was in Europe. My suitcase was stolen and my presentation for this conference, together with my computer, cell phone and many other belongings disappeared. This morning, I will try to say something according to my memory. I would like to thank professor Jiang Chang for giving me the opportunity to make this presentation, with the title of China Dream and World Dream. This is a romantic metaphor and is a very difficult topic for me. I want to make the huge story a little bit brief and say something about the two dreams. Personally, I'd like to bridge rather than separate the two dreams. I have three points.

The first point is how to look at the two dreams. In this sense, there are two choices. One is to look at these two dreams from the perspective of particularism, and the other is from that of universalism. I prefer the latter. The reason lies in that in the age of globalization, the standard of universalism is much better for us to speculate our world. Then we come to another question: why do we have different dreams while we live in the same world. I'd like to borrow a traditional Chinese idiom—couples may have different dreams in the same bed. Here bed refers to the earth we live in. As for the answer, the national benefit and the national privilege separate our world and bring serious results, for

---

[*] Wan Junren, Professor of Philosophy, Dean of School of Humanities, Tsinghua University.

example, some countries trend to boost their economy by sacrificing other countries, which is very common. Can we change this situation? Although it may be difficult, we should take measures to make it. We should learn how to share something together rather than require something individually. This is my first point.

The second, in today's world, the more difficult and more important point, is that some developed countries should provide much more room for developing countries to achieve their modernization. The developed countries have gained lots of experience or models of modernity, and developing countries should learn from it, but we should realize that there is more than one model for us to speed up our modernization. Western model is a good way, but not the only way. Therefore, the developed country should help the developing country find their own way rather than follow the old one. Undoubtedly, it will take long time for most countries to catch up with the developed one. In this sense, I do hope the developed country can help in this process by giving much more room for them. Meanwhile, the country, taking the advanced position, should be more modesty. Fundamentally speaking, to keep our world on the right way in the age of globalization, I hope this point can make sense.

My third point is that the best way to bridge the two dreams is to open forums and tribunes, having a dialogue or trilogies between or among different countries. For this reason, I really appreciate the subject of this symposium. In the future, our world will develop in a democratic way, so that our development can go even further. Here I' like to borrow some words of professor John Rawls, my supervisor, the famous professor of politic philosophy from philosophy department of Harvard University. According to him, the principles of justice can be divided into two principles, one is the principle of liberal equality, and the other is the principle of difference. I speak highly of the latter. I suppose that the principle of difference in terms of John Rawls can work out something universal for our globalization, contributing to this world and to the world dialogue in particular. According to the principle of difference, the first thing we should do is to pay more attention to the benefit of the least developing country. In today's world, we should do everything we can for African countries and those impoverished people, helping them to be optimistic and improve their living standard. Therefore, I do agree with the theory of justice. Keeping the principle of difference in mind, a bridge can be built between the two dreams. For our Chinese people, we should focus on this point. Honestly speaking, there is still a long way to go for Chinese government and its people. Currently, China has got a great economic achievement and made great progress, with its national revenue increased, and its people's living standard being improved, but how can we break down the national boundary and contribute to the world? Maybe it is time for us to think about it.

Cultural Soft Power

Sun Weiping[*]

I am glad to attend this conference. Firstly, on behalf of contemporary culture society, I'd like to congratulate the opening of the first world culture development forum. Personally speaking, the forum is in due time, because culture becomes more and more important in contemporary world. There is a very important phrase—cultural soft power. The concept of cultural soft power is in fact a very obscure concept. As we know, we understand well the concept of hard power, such as economic power, military power, and political power etc. As to cultural soft power, what is its content? In other words, how should we define it? This is a very complex question. I will try my best to explain it. Firstly, I have to define the concept of cultural soft power. In my opinion, I consider cultural soft power as one kind of culture. To be specific, it refers to the attractiveness, emotional appeal, group cohesiveness, competitiveness, and influence expressed by one culture. The cultural soft power is embedded in the values, ideology, cultural tradition, policies and regulations, educational activities, the way of life, as well as cultural products and services. Cultural soft power has no fixed mode expressing its influence. An important way for cultural soft power to show its subtle influence is education and assimilation. What is cultural soft power? According to our research, we'd like to apply a quantifiable approach to understand it, in this sense; we suggest analyzing it from the perspective of structure and function. Roughly speaking, cultural soft power can

* Sun Weiping, Research Associate on Value Theory at Chinese Academy of Social Sciences.

be divided into the following several powers. The first one is the attractiveness of cultural value. The value of one culture reflects the interest and desire of relative cultural subjects, expresses the ideal and belief of them, and contains the overall blue print of the whole country. Therefore, it is the backbone of one country, the soul of one nation, the spiritual standpoint of the person involved. It is the essential part of the cultural system. On one hand, it is the power of education and passion; therefore the whole nation could have consensus to the common ideal proposed by the culture. It is the presupposition and basis for the nation to live together. On the other hand, it is the unique attraction recognized by other nations with its advanced spirit, rich contents, and inner charm. The cultural values in the world are always in the pattern of diversity and competition in human history. Although cold war has finished, the history continues. The competition of different cultural values is more and more intense. The input and output of values become the competitive stage for different cultural values. How to propose the universal values of democracy and human right distinguished from western ones? How to propose a national dream distinguished from American dream and eastern way of life? Which are the main tasks of China Dream? It is a challenge faced by contemporary Chinese culture. Secondly, I will discuss the creativity of cultural knowledge. Culture is neither born with nor a divine creation, but the practical product of the human being. The creativity of a culture is crucial to its soft power. The creativity of a culture is based on the production, spreading and application of knowledge. The knowledge production mainly depends on the academic research of natural and social science. The spread of knowledge depends mainly on education, mass media and the active learning of general public. The application of knowledge depends mainly on production research. The most important in the cultural production is to build a cultural system which encourages cultural creativity. Cultural creativity is an important factor which contributes to world culture and promotes national cultural production. Thirdly, I will discuss the competitiveness of cultural industry which is the connection between culture and economy. It covers a lot, including news service, book publication, copyright service, broadcasting, television, arts, internet cultural service, cultural leisure service, as well as the production and consumption of other cultural products. To some extend, it can be said that cultural values can be spread directly by cultural industry. The development of cultural industry has been the foundation of cultural competition. It has been an emerging industry in the information age with the characteristic of low-cost, high-output and great influence and has been an important force in economic development. For example, culture industry has become the number one industry leading the American economy in 1990s. It is very important for a country to own its independent intellectual property rights in international cultural competition. Fourthly, I will discuss the affinity of cultural service. It refers to the coverage ratio and quality of public cultural service. The right of culture is the innate basic right of the man. For some historical reasons, public cultural service has been not well developed in China, especially in the rural area. We should try to promote cultural service which is close to real life and ordinary public life. Finally, I think we should pay attention to cultural influence which is an important part in cultural soft power and cultural guide force for cultural system. All of the factors discussed above are very important for cultural soft power construction. We should respect our own cultural tradition and the diversity, as well as specific cultural needs while we construct our cultural soft power.

Construct Chinese Public Service System from the Perspective of Public Policy

Liu Wenxiang [*]

I will spend five minutes answering three questions. Question one, what is the goal of the policy? The 6th Plenary Session of the 17th Central Committee 2011 focused on cultural reform development and passed the second major decisions on the reform of the cultural system, promoting socialist cultural development and prosperity. The conference made a comprehensive plan for the future construction of public cultural system and put forward that the cultural field would be overall prosperous by 2020. Public cultural service system covering the whole society would be basically established and strive for achieving the basic public cultural service goal. This is the first question which concerns with the goal of the public cultural service. Second question is about the main content of the policy. What is public culture? Public culture, in simple terms, is to meet the basic needs of the people and establish a system of public culture services covering all groups in society. The main contents of public culture is to ensure people watching TV, listening to the radio, reading books and newspapers, appreciating public culture, and participating in public culture activities, as well as other basic cultural rights. The characteristics of public culture are public welfare, the fundamental equalization and convenience. Public service system includes public cultural goods, services, institutions and system. Public cultural

* Liu Wenxiang, Professor of Law, Dean at College of Politics, Law and Public Administration, Hubei University.

service system mainly includes five sub-systems, consisting of coverage network system, product and service supply system, technology support system, organizational support system, and assessment system. The third question concerns with the implications of future policy. There are three implications. One is that we have experienced the period of taking economy as our central task, and more attention in China now will be paid to social and cultural construction. In the past 30 years, our main focus is on economic construction. However, from then on, our attention will be paid to social and cultural construction. This is the first implication. The second implication is cultural service. It is part of our public service which requires our government to be service-oriented. The third implication is that the approach to realize the goal of public cultural service is government-led.

主流文化研究

Mainstream Culture

主流文化存在的三种样态及
我们的战略选择

江　畅[*]

摘　要： 主流文化与非主流文化话语中的文化，不是广泛意义上的文化，而是就社会文化体系而言的，指系统的价值观现实化意义上的文化。就与非主流文化的关系而言，主流文化有三种存在样态，即一统天下，唯我独尊和兼收并蓄。新中国成立后的主流文化建设虽然走过一些弯路，但改革开放以来，我国已经具备了构建可以解决目前多元文化对峙、冲突问题的最先进的"兼收并蓄"文化的现实条件，并正在作出实践上的努力。我们需要据此对我们主流文化建设的战略进行调整，更加自觉地构建具有中国特色的最先进的主流文化。

关键词： 主流文化　非主流文化　样态　社会主义文化　战略选择

无论从人类社会历史来看，还是从当代世界来看，在一定的以国家或民族为基本形式的社会，除非处于战乱或动荡时期，一般都同时存在着主流文化与非主流文化的情形。但是，主流文化与非主流文化之间的关系有不同的状况或样态，也可以说主流文化有不同的存在样态。在文化日益多元化的当代世界，任何一个社会都面临着处理主流文化与非主流文化之间

---

[*] 江畅，湖北大学高等人文研究院院长，哲学学院教授、博士生导师。

关系的问题。一个社会文化取向的选择不同，其主流文化存在的样态也不同，这种不同事关社会文化乃至整个社会的稳定和谐、繁荣发展，因而不能不引起社会管理者的高度注意。我国现阶段正致力于构建社会主义文化强国，以实现社会主义文化的大繁荣大发展。为了实现这一目的，我们有必要反思我国主流文化应当是一种什么样的文化，它与非主流文化应当是一种什么关系，从而作出我国文化建设发展的正确战略选择。

一　主流文化与非主流文化的概念及关系辨析

近年来，在文化日益多元化的背景下，人们越来越多地谈论主流文化和非主流文化。但究竟什么是主流文化，以及相应地什么是非主流文化，似乎并没有形成一个比较确切的共识。在当前我国同时存在着社会主义文化、西方文化、传统文化的新文化格局下，人们常常把社会主义文化看作是主流文化，而把西方文化、传统文化看作非主流文化。事实上，西方文化、传统文化也好，社会主义文化也好，都是不确定的概念，西方文化至少包括古代西方文化、中世纪西方文化、近现代西方文化，中国传统文化包括正统的、非正统的。就社会主义而言，也有传统意义上的、现代意义上的、一般意义上的、中国特色意义上的。那么，我们应该在什么意义上理解主流文化和非主流文化呢？

要回答这个问题，需要明确这里所说的"文化"的含义。正如亨廷顿所指出的，"'文化'一词，在不同的学科中和不同的背景之下，自然有着多重的含义"。① 大致上说，文化可以是严格意义上的文化，这种意义的文化指的是社会文化体系意义上的"文化"；文化也可以是宽泛意义上的"文化"，这种意义的文化不仅指严格意义上的文化，而且指风俗习惯、日常生活方式等。前者如"近现代资本主义文化""中国特色社会主义文化""基督教文化""佛教文化"等，这类文化的共同特点是：它们

① 〔美〕亨廷顿、哈里森主编《文化的重要作用——价值观如何影响人类进步》，程克雄译，新华出版社，2010年第3版，第8页。

是一定的系统价值观的对象化或现实化；后者则还包括并非系统价值观的现实化，如"岭南文化""服饰文化""饮食文化"等。前一类文化有两个要件：一是系统的价值观，二是这种价值观的对象化或现实化。在人类历史上，有许多思想家提出了系统的社会价值观，但它们并没有被现实化，这种价值观虽然也属于思想文化的范畴，但并不是我们这里所说的文化。只有当一种价值观变成了社会现实，成为了社会的价值体系，它才是严格意义上的文化（以下我们都是在这种严格意义上谈论文化）。

如果我们将现实化看作既定的，那么显然，不同的文化之间的区别就在于价值观。价值观是文化的核心、灵魂，价值观不同，文化也就不同。我们说"社会主义文化"与"资本主义文化"不同，就其实质而言，就在于它们所体现的价值观不同。系统的价值观是一种复杂的结构体系，它包括三个基本层次：终极价值目标、核心价值理念和基本价值原则。① 按照这种理解，同一类文化的不同具体文化之间也会因为价值观不尽相同而有所区别，尽管这种区别不一定是实质性的。例如，同属于资本主义文化范畴的近代资本主义文化、现代资本主义文化或美国资本主义文化、德国资本主义文化等不同资本主义国家的文化，也因为所体现的价值观不同而有所不同。

基于以上对文化范畴的辨析，不难看出，我们所说的"主流文化""非主流文化"不是宽泛意义上的文化，而是严格意义上的文化。无论主流价值还是非主流文化，都是指一定的系统价值观的现实化。一般来说，主流文化是在社会生活中占据主导地位的、普遍流行的或者为公众普遍接受的文化，而非主流文化则是在社会不占主导地位、部分流行或为部分公众接受的文化。例如，在美国社会，主流文化是美国资本主义文化，而天主教文化则是非主流文化。但是，从实质上看，两者之间的区别是价值观的区别，而不是某种风俗习惯、日常生活方式的区别：主流文化是其价值观占据主导地位并普遍流行，而非主流文化则是其价值观不占主导地位并只为部分公众所接受。正确认识这一区别是极其重要的。在现实生活中，

---

① 江畅：《论中国特色社会主义核心价值理念》，《社会科学战线》2012 年第 10 期。

不少人将一些与我国传统的或本土的生活方式（如语言、服饰、饮食等）有关的东西看作非主流的文化，这种看法不仅是表面的、肤浅的，而且是危险的、有害的。我们必须意识到，正因为主流文化与非主流文化的区别是不同价值观的区别，所以两者之间的关系一旦颠倒，就会导致整个社会制度乃至社会性质的根本变化。

关于主流文化与非主流文化的关系，有几点值得注意：

第一，主流文化与非主流文化总是就一定社会范围而言的，在一定社会范围内的文化与其外的文化不构成主流与非主流的关系。比如，美国国内的文化与中国国内的文化不能构成主流与非主流的关系。不过，当美国的资本主义文化渗透到中国而与中国的社会主义文化并存时，它们就存在着主流与非主流的关系。

第二，一个社会内部只有存在着不同的文化，才有可能出现主流文化与非主流文化的情形。如果一个社会范围内只存在一种文化，而不存在任何其他的文化，这个社会就不会发生主流文化与非主流文化并存的情形。但是，一个社会存在着多种文化并非意味着出现主流文化与非主流文化并存的局面。这里有两种不同的情形：一是在动荡不安、分裂割据的社会，即使有多种文化，但并没有一种成为主流文化；二是在一个相对稳定的社会，虽然统治者强制推行一种文化，但这种文化并没有现实化，没有为社会公众所普遍接受，相反，各种其他文化广泛流行。因此，多元文化格局是主流文化与非主流文化并存的必要条件，而非充分条件。

第三，主流文化并不等同于统治者推行的文化。统治者推行的文化可能没有成为主流文化，反之亦然。在历史上和在现实中都存在着这样的情形：统治者力图使自己倡导的价值观为社会公众普遍接受，但结果并非如此，充其量只为统治者内部成员所接受，甚至还存在统治者内部成员也不普遍接受的情形。例如，在西方中世纪后期，天主教会极力推行的价值观连教职人员都普遍阳奉阴违。这里的问题在于，统治者推行的文化和价值观是否体现了社会公众的普遍利益，是否顺应了人类历史发展的总趋势。如果体现了、顺应了，统治者的强力就有助于所推行的价值观迅速现实化，反之，则会适得其反。

第四，主流文化与非主流文化之间的区别可能是实质性的，也可能是非实质性的。前面我们已经提及，本质上相同的一类文化之间也存在着区别。这种区别有两个方面：一是新旧的区别。例如，西方资本主义文化存在着近代与现代的区别，近代的推行自由放任主义，而现代的则推行国家干预主义。由于多方面的原因（如文化的相对独立性、不同的价值观体现不同的利益等），在国家干预主义占主导地位的西方，自由放任主义为不少思想家所力主，并且在相当范围内流行。二是不同类型的区别。例如，美国市场经济是个人化的，而德国的市场经济则更倾向于社会化。我们不能排除在美国存在着市场经济社会化的情形。对这一点有清醒的认识也非常重要。这种复杂的情况告诉我们，在处理主流文化与非主流文化的关系时，不仅要注意处理异质的非主流文化，也要注意同质但与主流文化有重要区别的非主流文化的存在，并处理好两者之间的关系。

二　主流文化的三种样态

从历史和现实看，主流文化对非主流文化的关系存在着三种样态：其一，主流价值文化一统天下，非主流文化完全被压制，以致被湮灭，社会看起来只存在着清一色的文化；其二，主流文化唯我独尊，非主流文化被否定、被排斥、被边缘化，社会存在着主流文化与非主流文化的对立、争斗；其三，主流文化兼收并蓄，主流文化吸收现实和可能存在的非主流文化中的合理成分，使自己真正强大，非主流虽然存在，但不能与主流文化相抗衡，其存在有助于社会的稳定和繁荣。我们可以具体分析一下这三种样态各自产生的原因、利弊得失及其社会后果。

人类在进入文明社会的过程中，以及在文明社会发展的相当长一段历史时期，都是从分散的小群体逐渐走向大的共同体，其间又发生过无数的"分久必合、合久必分"的情形。如此，进入文明社会后建立的不同社会几乎都是由不同的小社会组成的。这些小社会有着自己的社会价值观（尽管可能是不自觉的），有着自己特殊的文化。由它们组成的新的社会因而客观上存在着不同的文化，存在着不尽相同的社会价值观。

历史上新社会的建立基本上都是通过武力的途径来实现的，取得战争胜利的统治者为了维护自己的统治并实现自己的利益，必然会将自己的价值观强加给全社会，构建体现其价值观的文化。他们在这样做的过程中，常常通过极端的手段（如秦始皇实行的"焚书坑儒"政策、中世纪天主教会的"火刑"）压制以至于剿灭一切与其不一致的文化及其价值观。当然，有时候统治者还会采取教化的政策，使被统治者心甘情愿地放弃自己的价值观和文化。其结果，社会就会形成一种文化一统天下的情形。一统天下的文化严格来说并不一种主流文化，但是从历史上看，真正实现文化完全一统的社会很少见，一个社会即使出现这种情形也是非常短暂的。从这种意义上看，文化一统的情形只是相对的，因而也可看作一种主流文化存在的样态。

历史事实表明，一种文化一统天下是一种弊多利少甚至是有害而无利的主流文化样态。首先，社会为了压制非主流文化、实现文化一统要花巨大的社会成本或代价。一种文化一旦形成，就具有其相对独立性并具有生命力，要使之完全泯灭，则要耗费大量的人力、物力和精力。其次，社会在压制非主流文化的同时，也压制了信奉其价值观的人对社会的认同，以及建设社会的积极性和热情，甚至导致严重的对立情绪和斗争。这对于社会的稳定和发展是有害的。最后，对非主流文化的过度压制必然导致社会文化缺乏活力以致衰败。历史上实行文化专制主义的社会，其结果都逃不出文化从单一走向枯萎的命运。更糟糕的是，尽管社会花费了巨大的成本，但非主流文化并不会因此而销声匿迹，相反会不同程度地存在，一有机会就会与主流文化相争斗、相抗衡，并力图取代主流文化。

不言而喻，传统社会采取这种形式常常是难以避免的。这是因为，传统社会的统治者都是通过暴力手段建立自己的统治的，而且这种统治的终极目的是实现统治者的利益。为此，他们必须压制反映被统治者利益的价值观和文化，使之无法在自己的统治下生存。

由于非主流文化不可能被完全剿灭，因而统治者可能会无可奈何地让其存在下去，当然也有些开明的统治者从自身的长远利益考虑采取一些宽容的或怀柔的政策，允许其存在。但是，其前提是对非主流文化进行种种限制、排挤，乃至干涉，严格限定其生存空间，不允许其发展，同时采取各种措施论证、宣扬主流价值观的合理性，扩大其影响，不断加强主流文化建设，以确保和不断增强主流文化的至尊地位。在这种情况下，社会虽然可能存在一些非主流文化及其价值观，但影响很小，有些只局限于极少数人的范围，几乎不可能发展，而且社会对这些人另眼相待，甚至视为洪水猛兽。欧洲中世纪早期的修道院所保存的一些希腊罗马文化，犹如沙漠里的绿洲，其情形就是如此。于是，社会就出现了主流文化唯我独尊的局面。这种局面是一种主流文化与非主流文化并存并敌对的局面，在通常的情况下，两者之间没有达到对峙的程度。

与一统天下的情形相比较，唯我独尊的情形是一种进步。至少，那些非主流的文化尚有一息生命，能够苟延残喘。更重要的是，由于有这些非主流文化的存在，主流文化始终面临不同的敌对势力，因而会保存一些活力，在一定程度上会注意从非主流文化中吸取一些内容以改进和完善自身。但是，唯我独尊的主流文化样态仍然是弊大于利的，只是其问题相对于文化一统天下的情形要轻一些而已。导致这种主流文化形态存在的原因较为复杂。一种原因可能还是为了维护统治者的利益，防止由于非主流文化的流行动摇政权的基础，损害统治者的利益。另一种原因可能是对统治者所推行的文化不自信，感到非主流文化流行势必冲击主流文化。这种不自信往往在很大程度上源于这种主流文化本身存在着问题，如果不强力推行主流文化，同时严格限制非主流文化，任由其自由生长发展，主流文化在与非主流文化的竞争中会败下阵来。当然，也有这样一种原因：主流文化本身是合理的，也有良好的社会基础，只是统治者没有认识到这一点，缺乏自信和气度，而不敢让其与非主流文化凭实力竞争。一般来说，在一个社会新建立的时候，统治者所推行的价值观及其文化势单力弱，对非主流文化采取措施是可以理解的，也是必要的。但是，如果长此以往，就说明这种推行的文化要么没有反映社会大多数成员的利益，要么其价值观本身缺乏合理性，不能为社会公众普遍接受。相比较而言，非主流文化可能更能反映大多数社会成员的利益，或者更具有合理性，因而更具有吸引力。在这种情况下，统治者不得不始终对非主流文化保持高压态势，使其不能与主流文化相抗衡。

与前两种主流文化样态不同的主流文化兼收并蓄的样态，从根本上改变了对非主流文化的态度。这种主流文化首先代表了大多数社会成员甚至全体社会成员的利益，而不只是代表统治者的利益，反映了社会成员的普遍愿望；其次，这种文化的价值观从根本上说是合理的，在理论得到了合法性论证，并进行了精心的顶层设计；最后，这种文化是开放的，能不断地从非主流文化中吸收合理的成分，使自己的实力不断强大，以至于非主流文化不足以与之相抗衡。显然，这种主流文化存在有三个条件：

其一，从根本上说，这种文化的基础是大多数社会成员的利益，而不是少数人的利益，或者是所有社会成员的非根本利益。一种文化只有代表社会成员的根本利益，成为了主流文化，才能有牢固的根基；一种文化只有代表大多数社会成员的利益，才能得到大多数社会成员的拥护和信奉。如此，其他一切代表一部分人利益或代表全体社会成员非根本利益的文化，就不可能与之相抗衡。这个条件是最重要的。历史上的那些主流文化之所以不能成为真正的主流，其根本原因就在于此。

其二，这种文化有科学的、合理的、可行的价值观。基于公众普遍利益的价值观必须是得到了理论论证和阐释的，它本身不仅应是科学合理的，而且应是采取可实施的形式。这一点在现代社会是非常重要的。如果社会的管理者确实是社会成员的代表，但并不能正确地反映其社会成员的心声，他们所致力推行的价值观还是不能为广大的社会成员所接受。在当代，反映社会成员愿望的价值观需要思想家来提供，思想家提供的价值观不正确，或者社会的管理者根本不让思想家提供，或思想家提供了也不采用，仍然我行我素，其价值观及其文化即使强力推行也仍然难以成为主流。这里的问题，一方面是要有科学、合理、可行的价值观，另一方面是采用了这种价值观后要自信。

其三，这种文化对非主流文化是宽容的、开放的，不仅允许其存在和发展，而且不断从中吸取营养。托克维尔在描述美国文明时就阐述了这种可能性。他说："这种文明是两种完全不同成分结合的产物，而这两种成分在别处总是互相排斥的，但在美国却几乎彼此融合起来，而且结合得非常之好。我们说的这两种成分，是指宗教精神和自由精神。"① 不言而喻，这两种精神是两种不同文化的精神。在利益多元格局的社会，不可避免地会存在着多元的价值观，任何一种价值观都不可能毫无遗漏地代表每一社会成员的利益和愿望。在这种情况下，允许不同的价值观及其文化存在，能够更好地反映社会成员的普遍利益。另外，那些代表部分人利益的文化的存在和发展，不仅使社会的文化更丰富多彩，更繁荣昌盛，而且也能够使代表大多数利益或所有成员根本利益的主流文化从其中吸其营养，使自己更强有力，也可以使自己始终保持竞争态势，从而充满生机和活力。要使主流文化对非主流文化宽容、开放，也需要社会管理者的自信和气度。缺乏这种自信和气度，主流价值文化也难成为兼容并蓄的文化。

三 兼收并蓄：我国主流文化建设应有的战略选择

中华人民共和国从成立到今天，不过 60 多年的历史，近几年中共中央提出要建设文化强国，深刻地表明了我国的文化尚处于建设之中。文化强国的文化无疑首要是主流文化，加强文化强国建设，当然首要是加强主流文化建设。那么，我们就面临究竟要建设什么样的主流文化的问题。虽然我们进行文化建设已有几十年，但这个问题并没有完全解决，而且走了一些弯路。在经过了 30 多年的改革开放的今天，特别是在中共中央提出了社会主义文化大繁荣大发展的当前，我们很有必要对我国过去走过的文化建设之路进行反思，对我国文化特别是主流文化发展的路向重新作出选择或进行必要的调整。

新中国成立之后，我国建立了社会主义制度，人民成为社会的主人，社会致力于建设代表广大人民群众根本利益的社会主义文化，并取得了巨大的成就。社会主义文化无疑是当代人类最先进的文化。但是在改革开放以前，我们一直认为建设社会主义文化就是要使社会主义文化不仅成为社

---

① 〔法〕托克维尔：《论美国的民主》上卷，董果良译，商务印书馆，1988，第 47～48 页。

会主流文化，而且要使其成为我国社会的唯一文化。在这种指导思想之下，我国运用政治的力量在全力推行社会主义文化的同时力图消灭一切非社会主义文化，特别是传统文化和资本主义文化。经过近三十年的努力，在封闭的社会条件下，我们达到了目的，形成了文化一统的局面。但是，由于这种文化是一种全新的文化，本身并不成熟，而且由于其他文化都被否定而不能从其中吸收有价值的内容，因而我国所致力于建设的文化内容越来越贫乏，严重影响了我国经济社会的发展和人民群众利益的实现。为此，我国实行了改革开放。伴随着改革开放的深入，过去文化一统的局面逐渐改变，无论我们的主观意愿如何，社会主义文化以外的各种文化竞相登场。在这种新的形势下，我们认可了文化多元的社会现实，并且对主流文化之外的文化采取了容忍的态度。同时，我们也不断地丰富和发展社会主义文化，于是有了中国特色社会主义的理论与实践。客观地说，改革开放以来，我国的主流文化已经吸收了许多非主流文化的内容，正因为如此，我国的主流文化正日益强大。但是，不可忽视的是，我们一直以来对一切非主流文化仍然主要持一种简单否定、排斥的态度，不能妥善处理主流文化与非主流文化的关系。从某种意义上说，我们对非主流文化的宽容态度并非出于自愿，而是因为我们要实行改革开放，而这是当代中国经济社会发展的唯一选择。由于对主流文化与非主流文化的关系在认识和处理上还存在一些问题，所以当前我国主流文化与一些非主流文化在相当大程度上处于对峙甚至冲突的状态。

那么，我国应当如何走出当前主流文化与非主流文化对峙、冲突的局面呢？笔者认为，我国需要调整对待非主流文化的战略，改变对非主流文化（无论是西方文化、传统文化，或是其他文化）简单否定、排斥的做法，在允许其存在和适度发展的前提下，充分地吸收其中的合理的、有价值的内容，为我所用，使我国主流文化成为包含当今人类一切文化中优秀内容的真正最先进的主流文化。具体地说，这种战略主要包括以下两方面的具体内容：第一，建构我国主流文化吸收、借鉴其他任何文化有价值内容的开放动态机制，使我国主流文化成为一种文化的"熔炉"。任何其他文化在与我国主流文化相接触的过程中，通过这种机制的过滤，其中有价值的内容都能融入我国的主流价值文化，我国主流文化的力量因而能日益强大，任何其他文化都不能与之相抗衡。主流文化不仅有宽宏的气度，而且有巨大的消化吸收能力。第二，对于那些在我国有一定市场的非主流文化，不仅允许其存在，而且支持其适度发展，同时，将其纳入主流文化引导和控制的范围，使其为主流文化服务，对主流文化做有益的补充，满足部分人群的文化需求和利益需求。这种控制包括两个方面：一是使非主流文化的存在和发展始终有利于主流文化乃至整个社会文化的发展繁荣；二是将这些文化的存在和发展限定于特定的人群。在这方面，西方近现代对待基督教文化以及我国唐代对待佛教文化的做法值得借鉴。

笔者曾谈及当代人类最先进的价值文化，提出："当代最先进的价值文化是集人类优秀价值文化之大成的最具竞争力的优势文化。它从根本上克服了其他价值文化的局限、缺陷和问题，尤其克服了其他价值文化的专制性、资本化、异化等问题；同时，它又吸收了这些价值文化中的合理内容和精华。当代先进价值文化是全体社会成员共建共享的民主文化，它的主体是人民，人民是价值文化的创制者、建设者、享有者。当代先进的价值文化是以社会成员幸福的普遍实现为终极价值追求并被法制化的完整价值体系，是谋求社会成员普遍幸福的幸福文化。它能充分体现社会成员根本的和总体的利益，能最好地满足人的生存发展需要。它是顺应人性的，是人情化、人道化的，具有感召力、凝聚力和亲和力。同时，先进的价值文化还能在引导和控制其他价值文化的同时与之共存共荣，它具有宏大的气魄和博大的胸怀，具有开放性、包容性和自我完善性，是具有竞争力、影响力和控制力的主流文化。"① 笔者认为，我国的主流文化从价值观的层面上看就应当是这种最先进的文化。

当代中国经过 60 多年的社会主义建设和 30 多年的改革发展而日益强大，完全有可能构建当今人类最先进的"兼收并蓄"的主流文化。首先，我国的社会主义制度为这种文化的建立奠定了坚实的社会政治基础。我国建立的社会主义制度是人类最先进的社会制度，在这种制度下，社会成员

---

① 江畅：《论社会主义价值文化的先进性》，《伦理学研究》2013 年第 2 期。

真正成为了社会的主人。社会主义制度和人民当家做主，为构建全体社会成员共建共享的社会主义文化提供了社会政治基础。同时，这种社会政治基础客观上也要求有代表全体社会成员根本利益和绝大多数社会成员共同利益的文化与之相适应。其次，中国特色社会主义事业建设取得的巨大成就为这种文化的建立提供了物质保障。中国特色社会主义建设取得的举世瞩目的成就，既证明了中国特色社会主义文化的强大力量，同时也为我国构建一种有竞争力、影响力和控制力的主流文化提供了物质条件。最后，近些年来，我国高度重视社会主义核心价值观和核心价值体系以及社会主义文化的研究，其成果将为我们构建人类最先进的主流文化提供理论论证和顶层设计。在各种文化并存并相互竞争、冲突、交融的当代，构建一种先进的主流文化，理论的支持是前提。没有理论上系统而深入的研究，即使其他条件具备，也不可能有理论的依据和辩护。改革开放以来，特别是近年来，党和政府以高度的理论自觉，组织理论界和学术界从不同角度和不同层次对我国的主流价值观和文化展开了研究，已经取得了并将不断取得许多理论的和具有实践操作意义的学术成果。这些成果不仅会为我们构建最先进的主流文化的必要性和可能性提供论证，而且会提供各种构建的方案供党和政府选择。此外，我国还具有构建"兼收并蓄"主流文化的传统和先例。比如，佛教的中国化、马克思主义的中国化、列宁主义的中国化，以及历史上一些入主中原的少数民族对汉文化的吸纳、认同和弘扬，等等。

　　以上所述表明，我国在构建先进的主流文化方面具备了各种必要条件，而且正在进行着伟大实践。我们相信，只要我们坚定不移地坚持下去，构建一种具有中国特色同时在世界上又是最先进的主流价值文化指日可待。这种主流文化构建起来之日，也就是中国特色社会主义文化大发展大繁荣、社会主义文化强国建成之时。那时中国的文化和价值观，将不仅具有中国特色、中国气派、中国风格，而且将形成"大中华及其共荣圈"①，对整个世界都具有影响力、辐射力和穿透力。

①〔美〕亨廷顿：《文明的冲突与世界秩序的重建》（修订版），周琪等译，新华出版社，2010，第146页。

Three Modes of Mainstream Cultures and Our Strategic Choice

Jiang Chang

Abstract: The culture in the context of mainstream culture and non-mainstream culture is not generally signified, but specifically signified in regards to the cultures in different social and cultural systems and the culture realized by systematic values. Comparing with non-mainstream cultures, there are three modes for mainstream culture: unity, superiority and mutual accommodation. The mainstream culture construction has met some difficulties after the founding of PRC; however, we have prepared to absorb other cultures after the reform and opening up policies. At present, we have to make strategic amendments while we construct our mainstream cultures with Chinese characteristics.

Keywords: mainstream culture; non-mainstream culture; modes; socialistic culture; strategic choice

The Vice and Virtue of Tolerance as a Core Value in America

Paul A. Swift[*]

Abstract: When one attempts to identify the core values of contemporary culture in America there is a difficulty in terms of making cultural generalizations. While one might argue that there is internal diversity in all peoples, there is more diversity within the United States due to its heritage as a "melting pot" of different people. Beginning with the concept of culture, this paper hopes to share some of the challenges American citizens share in trying to live together harmoniously, with commentary on the significance of tolerance as an ethical and legal concept.

Keywords: culture; diversity; tolerance; value

I would like to thank my generous hosts for inviting me here today. To contribute to the Forum for Contemporary World Culture Development I would like to offer some reflections about a core value of America and some brief comments about the nature of culture. In my presentation I hope to share with you some of the challenges American citizens share in trying to live together harmoniously, with commentary on the significance of tolerance as an ethical and legal concept.

---

* Paul A. Swift, Ph. D. , Professor of Philosophy, Bryant University, USA.

When one attempts to identify the core values of contemporary culture in America there is a difficulty in terms of making cultural generalizations. While one might argue that there is internal diversity in all peoples, there is more diversity within the United States due to its heritage as a "melting pot" of different people. James Clifford and others have pointed out how the concept of culture depends upon highlighting certain features and disregarding others, a point to which I shall return. Before I address some aspects of culture in America, it would be helpful for the purpose of clarifying some things about values to pose the questions: what kind of concept is culture? What kind of being does culture have?

In English the word culture is sometimes related to "the arts" as a term to describe a type of cultivation (often-but not always-associated with the distinction between high and low art). Many parents say they don't want their kids to grow up "uncultured" in the United States. The concept of *Bildung* in German is similar to this so a *lack of culture* means something like not having the ability to appreciate, have fluency in, or be able understand certain types of experiences. Sometimes those who pursue the development of this sense of culture are jokingly referred to as "culture vultures", persons who seek out an appreciation of art, classical music, etc.

However, there is also a distinct second definition of culture which is used to describe a pattern exhibited by a people, group, subgroup, etc. along the lines of what anthropologists study, often including the customs of the people, what foods they eat, what histories they tell about themselves, etc. This sense of culture would also include consideration of music, but in a descriptive sense, rather than music in the evaluative sense employed in the first definition of culture above. Anthropologists *describe* what styles of music occur rather than *evaluate* the aesthetic merits of music.

Additionally there is a third sense of culture as ethnicity and/or race: people refer to Black culture or Hispanic culture in the US, but also Asian culture as well. There is a fourth definition of culture which is used to describe any practice broadly defined—The Pittsburgh Steelers have a culture of winning, TV watching culture, media culture, rave culture, gaming culture, sports culture, biker culture, gun culture, gay culture, etc. These might be thought of better as subcultures, i. e. patterns of behavior. Not everyone participates in these types of cultures, but enough do to recognize a specific pattern of some group. It is not clear how big a group needs to be in order to be recognized as a culture, a point of ambiguity to be addressed further. The difference between a small group of deviant individuals and a subculture is murky, but at the very minimum, to have a culture or subculture, it must be made up of more than one person.

Identifying core values of the US poses a challenge since there is so much internal diversity about what people think is important in a nation of immigrants which is intentionally multi-cultural. It is difficult to make claims about core values when there is little consensus about fundamental values in general. There is less homogeneity in the US since there are virtually no rituals which everyone shares and there is no food everyone eats. As a general rule there is a lack of agreement about politics, religion, and the appropriate role of America in the world.

In the US, there is also in popular media the term "culture wars" which refer to the conflicts in the political arena where people argue about conservative vs. liberal values. These can be especially contentious disputes which require people who disagree with each other about fundamental values to at least listen to each other. There is widespread adoption of tolerance towards others' viewpoints in America, at least when it comes to speaking in the public space. This type of tolerance has a pragmatic function since it is a precondition for different people who have conflicting views to get along with some degree of harmony. It is undoubtedly related to the US Constitution's first amendment which guarantees freedom of expression.

There are good and bad things about this kind of tolerance. It is good in that it tries to keep open conversation with others and give everyone the space to voice their opinions about public policy, ethics, etc. However, there are downsides of it: US Secretary of State John Kerry told German students earlier this year that "Americans have a right to be stupid". Tolerance of stupidity and the accompanying perspective that all views are worthy of being heard can produce negative results.

There is a phrase, "we can agree to disagree" which reflects part of the challenge of tolerance. People often have different viewpoints and part of tolerance has to do with tolerating differences: it is ok if everyone does not agree on everything. However, there must be limits of tolerance to preserve itself as a virtue. If a society tolerates everything, it has no means to assert itself against those who want to eliminate tolerance itself. Philosophers like Anthony Appiah thus suggest that every form of tolerance requires some form of intolerance. [1] At the minimum, if one wants to preserve tolerance, one must be intolerant of those who want to eliminate tolerance.

The broad protection of speech in general in the US assumes that people will need to be both patient and tolerant for the good of the community. We cannot be tolerant of persons who yell "fire" in a crowded theatre since it is likely to cause immediately harm and injury through stampeding. There is tolerance of most other types of speech in the US, providing the speech does not do immediate physical harm. One of the difficulties which follows from this, however, is that there is tolerance for forms of extremely distasteful or offensive speech.

One example of this is that there is tolerance and legal protection of the activities of the Westboro Baptist Church, even though almost all Americans dislike this fringe group. One of their leaders, Reverend Phelps, obsessively protests against gay people in the United States. After the US military began to allow gay people to serve their country openly, Phelps orchestrated several protests of military funerals of those killed in combat. Because his group obeyed the letter of the law in terms of keeping the correct distance from funeral processions, they were legally able to do this, in spite of the increased emotional pain it causes grieving relatives who have lost their loved ones. Here we have a case where something is legally permitted but is ethically suspected.

The relationship between what is ethically permitted and what is legally permitted will always be a tricky issue, but there is a risk with tolerance where it creates a space for stupidity to flourish. In 2005 the Kansas Board of Education voted to include intelligent design theory to be taught in high school curricula

---

[1] Kwame Anthony Appiah, *Cosmopolitanism: Ethics in a World of Strangers* (New York: Penguin Books 2007).

alongside with Darwinian evolution, a move which tried to install a nonscientific theory to be included in Kansas schools with Darwinism: at bottom, intelligent design theory is basically creationism in disguise. President George W. Bush at the time stated, "I think that part of education is to expose people to different schools of thought.... You're asking me whether or not people ought to be exposed to different ideas, the answer is yes."[①] The problem here with staying open-minded is that some ideas are not worth taking seriously intellectually. So the idea of "open-mindedness" as a virtue can be rhetorically abused to defend stupidity. If one is too close-minded, one risks a type of stupidity, yet if one is too open-minded, one's brain may fall out of his head!

In America, there is a widespread tolerance for religion. The broader context of considering history's lessons that people can kill each other for theological reasons informs this tradition. Even if younger people are more accepting of atheism, America still remains a very religious country compared to northern Europe. It is difficult to make generalizations, but younger people have much to do with changing attitudes, many of which are resisted in the culture war with the older generation's values.

Like the civil rights movement of the 1960s, younger people were agents of change to reshape the next generation's attitude. There is always racism, but elimination of legalized racism helped to change attitudes, often couched in theological terms since Dr. Martin Luther King Jr. came from a background in theology which proclaimed that all citizens are equal in the eyes of God. Studies indicate that the most progressive advocates for change in values and public policy then (and now) were younger people, under the age of 30.

In the twenty first century a similar shift in attitudes has transpired which mirrors the struggle for civil rights in the 1960s, but has instead to do with granting equal status under the law for gay persons and the transgendered community. In some way the struggle for gay rights has been a much more difficult struggle to advance since the moral arguments are much harder to justify by appeals to Biblical views which specifically condemn homosexuality. It is not

---

① Bush: Schools Should Teach Intelligent Design, NBC News. 8/1/2005.

only Biblical teachings which account for the lack of equality for gay persons; after all, Russia is not religious at all but has anti-gay laws as well, a recent point of contention between Barack Obama and Vladimir Putin at the September, 2013 G20 summit.

Unpopular speech is protected in the United States, even toward religion. The US has many different religious groups and even if it is considered to be in bad taste to make fun of religion or religions in general, no one will be punished for it the way folks might be in theocratic states. Depicting the prophet Mohammed in a negative light is not encouraged, but it is permitted, just as there is tolerance for satire or criticism of other religious figures or doctrines.

There are practical, legal, and moral "oughts" of what one should do in the United States and speech is considered differently than action in terms of what one does. There are times when speech may become harmful but the broad protection of speech in general (even when it is unpopular) is a value held by most Americans, one which requires tolerance. There are limits for tolerance since there is no tolerance for child pornography in the United States because that is viewed as crossing the line of protected expression. Recipes for small pox are not viewed as a type of protected speech either.

There is an old saying, "Sticks and Stones may break my bones but names can never hurt me." Names and unpopular speech are not viewed as something which must culminate in violence. At this late date, America continues to have diverse cultural conflicts. Attitudes about equality under the law for gay people have undergone a shift, largely, but not exclusively, backed by young people. The legality of gay marriage is largely supported by people under the age of 30 but rejected by the majority of those over age 60.

America continues to be a fusion of diverse subcultures, making generalizations tricky. What is true of the whole is not necessarily true of every part. Contrary to most assessments, Carlin Romano has argued in *America the Philosophical* that America is actually more philosophical than most assessments which hold that Americans are anti-intellectual and anti-philosophical. There are many competing ideas of what America is and what goals she should aim for, but most of its citizenry still support a pragmatic tolerance for ideas of all kinds to be heard, even if they are unpopular. This allows everyone in principle to be considered in public discourse, but it also creates a space for unpopular expression which hopefully does no real harm.

AFTERWORD

Sometimes there is a dispute among ethicists about the status of ethical relativism, a position which takes two forms: there is cultural ethical relativism (also known as conventional relativism) which maintains that ethics vary fundamentally from culture to culture. There is also extreme ethical relativism (also known as subjective relativism), a position that maintains that what is right or wrong varies fundamentally from person to person. Many persons accept the former view of ethical relativism, but almost none accept the latter (extreme ethical relativism), since the latter seems like no moral theory at all. Somehow there is more respect for cultural ethical relativism, but not extreme ethical relativism. Louis Pojman has pointed out that this is strange since he claims that conventional ethical relativism ultimately boils down to extreme ethical relativism: the only real difference is that cultural ethical relativism has "cultural" before its name. As indicated in my introduction, the definition of culture at some level is somewhat arbitrarily reified. It depends ultimately on how big of a group one has before the group is recognized as a culture.

Anthropologists such as Isabel Fonseca have studied the Gypsy people: in Gypsy culture, many steal and lie to outsiders and it is accepted by the group as appropriate conduct. [1] Consider if you will whether that kind of behavior is ethically justified. If an individual steals and lies, he is usually considered unethical, deviant, and unworthy of respect. However, if a large enough group practices that same behavior, many persons are willing to accept it in the name of cultural tolerance. The Gypsies are a very unusual culture, but the point here is to raise the question, how large of a group does one need in order to have the group recognized as a culture? At what point does a deviant small group gain the

---

[1] Isabel Fonseca, *Bury Me Standing* (New York: Random House, 1997).

status of being a culture?

Pojman also points out that there are differences in cultures, independently of ethical issues. Different cultures have different customs and practices: this is the diversity thesis which is purely descriptive, based on anthropological observation. The question about ethics is whether ethics depends on those practices or not. Some thinkers claim that ethics depends on the culture: Pojman calls this the dependency thesis. If one accepts the proposition that ethics depends on the culture, then one is a cultural ethical relativist. However, one can be a cultural relativist without being an ethical relativist: cultural relativism in this view makes no claim about ethics, but merely recognizes that different cultures have different practices. Observing that these differences exist does not mean that one needs to adopt the position of cultural ethical relativism.

One argument against cultural ethical relativism is that if it is the case that whatever a culture claims is ethically correct actually is what is actually correct by definition, then there is no means to account for cultural reform. A similar problem exists for legalism as the basis of ethics: if whatever the law says is correct is identical to what is ethically correct, how can one account for any types of reform? Reform is based on being able to criticize the law or public policy. Having the tolerance for speech to consider how we can make our governing institutions more just indicates that we are able to change. If legalism were true as an ethical theory, by definition the law would be identical to what is ethically correct. Yet we know there have been reforms and this presupposes a space and tolerance for criticism. This tolerance can be used as a basis to make changes for the better, thus suggesting that what is legally permissible is not identical to what is ethically permissible.

Legalism and the position of conventional ethical relativism are similar in that neither of these theories can account for how reform of their position could be possible. In some ways Plato may have anticipated some of this in his *Euthyphro* dialogue where he asks, is it pious because the gods love it? Or do the gods love it because it is pious? A similar line of thought could ask: Is it right because the law says it is? (or) does the law say it because it is right?

It is tough to make claims about core values of America: to make generalizations requires one to selectively ignore those who do not fit into one's claims about culture. The internal diversity and multi-cultural identity of the US make it difficult to speak about what everyone values. However, there is a sense in which it is important to preserve the ability to speak, even if it means tolerating minority or unpopular speech. This value does not require everyone to agree which each other, but it does require the patience for tolerance.

宽容作为美国核心价值的优点与缺点

Paul A. Swift

摘　要：美国文化比世界上任何文化都更具多样性，美国自身就是一个不同文化的"大熔炉"，因此很难对当代美国文化的核心价值做出界定。本文认为，美国公民彼此和谐共处的原则是宽容，本文对宽容的伦理意义和法律意义进行了评价。

关键词：文化　多样性　宽容　价值

The Status and Future of Mainstream Malay Culture in the World

A. L. Samian[*]

Abstract: Malay Culture is part of the world culture. Currently the Malay language is spoken by 350 million people and is considered as the fifth language of the world. Malay society writ large could be found throughout South East Asia, predominantly in Malaysia and Indonesia. Malay culture by and large is influenced by "others" since the Malay Archipelago was colonized throughout history. In this article, the author examines the current status and future of the Malay culture in light of globalization. It is argued that the sustainability of this culture depends on its ability to be a significant part of virtual reality.

Keywords: Malay culture; South East Asia; future; sustainability

1. Introduction

Malaysia is a multicultural country. Since its independence in 1957, there are three main ethnics in West Malaysia, i. e. , Malay (60%), Chinese (25%) and Indian (8%). In East Malaysia, the main ethnics are Iban, Kadazan-Dusun, Melanau and Bidayuh. There are also the natives of Malaysia which are known as *orang asli*. Since it is a multicultural country, there is a diverse mélange

---

* A. L. Samian, Professor of Philosophy at the National University of Malaysia.

of different racial groups, not withstanding its variations by way of inter-marriages. There are always issues regarding unity, governance, sustainability and rights. The list of contestation of values, however, is not exhaustive.

In so far as unity is concerned, the paramount challenge is to ensure that despite the cultural differences, the *warga negara* or citizens could live together in a healthy manner. They must have the ability to share—sharing the difficulty as well as the wealth of developing the nation. This is no easy task because of the differences in values. One important step taken to overcome this challenge is promoting the *Rukun Negara*, or the National Principles, as the underpinning of national development. While we may not be able to unite strictly in the name of religion, we may be able to foster unity by sharing commonalities, similar values, that become the under grid of whatever national project that we might think of.

Unlike most modern countries in South East Asia, Malaysia has the most number of constitutional monarchs (nine altogether). While generally they don't have the legislative power with exceptions of matters regarding religion, they become symbols of unity whereby one of them is elected to be the Yang Di Pertuan Agung, or The King of Malaysia, on rotational basis as agreed by the Council of Rulers. The King officiates the Parliament, bestowing it's royal legitimacy. Thus "Kesetiaan kepada Raja dan Negara" or "Loyalty to the King and Nation" becomes one of the pillars of nation building. This brings us to the issues of governance.

The engine of growth in the public sector is the Malaysia Civil Service. With a staff of 1.3 million people serving a nation of 27 million, the civil service becomes the backbone of the government. It brings stability to the country in the sense that serving the country (*kerajaan*, as opposed to *negara* or state) is amounting to serving the King. The King then becomes the national symbol of unity and national ethos. Irrespective of what ethnicity one might belongs, they are the subjects of the King. So although the King does not have legislative power in the sense of a traditional kingdom, it endows a moral legitimacy to the elected representatives of the government, conferring them the right to implement the rule of the law, that is, the constitution. As a symbol of the status of the ruling monarch, the Prime Minister must take oath in front of the King before he is duly appointed as the Prime Minister of Malaysia. In short, the heart of governance, of serving the country, is in service of His Majesty Yang Di Pertuan Agong.

Religion is always an important part of culture in Malaysia since it is also a multi – religious country. While Islam is the official religion, the *warganegara*, citizens, could embrace and practice any religion that they prefer. 60% of the population are Muslims, around 20% are Buddhists and 10% are Christians. These are monotheistic religions. In view of these cultural *zeitgeist*, the foundation of Rukun Negara "To believe in God", precedes "Kesetiaan kepada Raja dan Negara" explicated earlier. So theoretically, to be a true Malaysians, each Malaysian must have a religion, any religion for that matter. As strange as it may sound, "Having a religion" is what unites Malaysians. Christians, Buddhists, Hindus and animists are, by and large, free to practice their religious beliefs. Multi-religiosity is then a critical component of Malaysian multiculturalism. (They are also multiculturalism that do not endorse religious belief in the sense that it does not require "believing in God" to be part of their doctrine of multiculturalism).

Surely a society could not prosper in the absence of the rule of the law, be it the constitution of the state or any other form of social contracts, social sanctions included. In as much as we like to do good, there are many kinds and degrees of goodness. Paraphrasing Rousseau, "People like to do good, it is in judging what is good that they go wrong." In the event that consent is not achieved, the rule of the law is to be pursued. No one is above the law. Therefore complementing the "keluhuran perlembagaan" or "the sanctity of the constitution" in the National Principles is the "kedaulatan undang-undang" or "the sovereignity of the rule of the law".

Last but certainly not the least of Malaysian National Principles are "Kesopanan dan Kesusilaan", to wit, "Ethics and Etiquettes". In the context of the National Principles, ethics and etiquettes mean the way we conduct ourselves, not so different from the Victorian concept of "the virtuoso" or the English "gentlemen". Paraphrasing Martin Luther King Jr, "Morality cannot be legislated but behavior can be regulated. " In tandem with the doctrine of the meaning, there is always a meaning in everything. Currently the government of Malaysia is embarking on the theme of 'moderation' which augurs well with the socio-politico-economics policies at the macro level or personal behavior at the micro level. The way forward is the way of moderation because it is by this way that we could attain a well balanced life, both the individual and the society as a whole.

So far I have elaborated the principles underlying multicultural Malaysia. The more detailed question is, what is the status and the future of the mainstream Malay culture in light of the national philosophy of holistic development and the wave of globalization?

2. The Malays

It is not easy to define what a Malaysian Malay is. Interracial marriage notwithstanding, Malays in neighboring Indonesia include the sub ethnic groups of Minangkabau, Bugis, Batak, Sunda *etcetra* irrespective of their religious beliefs. Malays are legally defined in Malaysia as those who are born in this country, a Muslim and lead a culturally Malay life, (food, lifestyle, language, etc.) It is obvious that this definition could not be applied to the Malay of Indonesia, Sri Langka, South Africa, Singapore and Philliphines. Evidently throughout history, Animism, Hinduism, Buddhism, Islam, and Christianity had made inroad into the Malay Society. For the purpose of the this paper, I will use the current Malaysian definition, i. e. , practicing the Malay culture, Muslim and speaking the Malay language while acknowledging the importance of other religious world views in shaping the Malay psychic. Ultimately, the reality is that all of us are part and parcel of the greater single family of humanity and are related by kinship.

Historically speaking, the ancient Malays believe that they are the subjects of the descendants of Alexander the Great. According to the two most important historical manuscripts, the 1612th *Sulalatus Salatin* (*Geneology of the Kings*), and *Tuhfat al-nafis* (*Significant Endeavor*) (1872). The Malay Kingdom in the Malay

Archipelago begins from the King Raja Sri Tri Buana governing Palembang, Indonesia including pre historic Temasik (modern day Singapore). This is the origin of the Malay Kingdom, which was temporarily shaken after the downfall of Kota Melaka in the reign of Sultan Mahmud, to the Portuguese (1511 – 1641). The Dutch replaced the Portuguese until 1824 before the colonial British "new imperialism" outmaneuvered the Dutch to generally govern the Malay Peninsula (1874 – 1946) interspersed with the Japanese occupation of the second world war (1941 – 1945), and again later, back to the British until the independence of Malaysia in 1957. There are other foreign forces such as the Siamese and Chinese. Interestingly China, at the time of Admiral Zheng He (Cheng Ho, 1371 – 1433), visited Malacca around 1414 with a massive fleet of twenty eight thousand people, sort of a floating palace, but it was not with an imperialist agenda, unlike the Western super powers, to the extent that the Sultan of Malacca (Sultan Mansur Shah) was married to one of the Princess of China by the name of Hang Li Po (Hang Liu) in 1459. So in this brief historical exegesis for the period under review, it is clear that the Malays in peninsula Malaya have engaged, at both the macro and micro levels, all kinds of European and Asian cultures. These interactions, which occured in the time of war and peace, shapes the present day Malay society in Malaysia. What is more, as a democratic country upholding the constitutional monarchy, Malaysia is governed by the majority ethnic groups which are the Malays. Accordingly in our assessment of the status and future of their culture, we have to examine the significant values which they subscribe.

3. Malay Values

Principles that we live by shape our values. Values are beliefs that guide us in our decisions, be it personal, societal, organizational, professional, public (as opposed to personal), in the cognitive, affective, sensory and spiritual domain. In addition to the national values underdetermined by the national code discussed earlier, values embraced by the Malays can further be gauged from their proverbs (peribahasa) in the Malay language, which is their mother tongue (bahasa ibunda). I am taking the philosophical position here that it is not possible to think in the absence of language and thus language determine values.

First and foremost, the Malays believe in religion as the overriding principle, as a regulative principle, as entrenched in the maxim "hidup bersendi adat, adat bersendi syarak". "*Adat*" in the Malay culture refers to the accepted normative behavior of the individual and society. There are four kinds of *adat*. *Adat nan sebeno adat* (the law of nature), *adat nan diadatkan* (the proposed norms), *adat nan teradat* (the agreed norms) and *adat istiadat* (ceremonies, rites, festivals). Underlying the construction of these norms is the Malays deep seated belief that man proposes, God disposes, or in other words, man has the innate propensity to create but ultimately it is The Divine that make it possible.

Man acts of creativity—*air setitik jadikan lautan* (From a drop of water we create the sea) and *tanah segengam jadikan gunung* (From a handful of earth we create a mountain) show the need to create from the two basic elements of the cosmos-earth and water (the absence of air and fire). It is the earth that needs to be recreated. "Created" implies "extension", a kind of Descartesian extension. The extension of water—that is from a drop to an ocean, requires not a meagre theoretical and practical creativity. It is the destiny of man to create. The worthiness of a man lies in his ability to create. Hence, again, from "alam terkembang jadi guru" (phenomena of nature be your teacher), they have the traditional code of value:

Penakik pisau diraut

Seludang jadikan nyiru

Cacang kayu jadikan ukiran

Air setitik jadikan lautan

Tanah sekepal jadikan gunung

Not everything is absolute. Relativism has its space and time, spatial and temporal value. The Malays are pragmatic in the sense that:

Di mana pokok bergulung di sana cendawan tumbuh

Di mana ranting dipatah di sana air disauk

Di mana bumi dipijak di sana langit dijunjung

Di mana negeri diduduk di sana adat dipakai

In other words, in the hierarchy of values, Malays believe that relativism is part of the cosmos and to be relativistic is "to live according to the teaching of nature".

Malays like communal life more compared to Westerners. The proverbs *bukit sama didaki*, *lurah sama dituruni*, *lautan sama direnangi*, and *terendam sama basah*, *terapung sama hanyut*, *terampai sama kering*, *berat sama dipikul*, *ringan sama dijinjing* point to the significance of togetherness. It is perfectly natural "to treat others as you wish to be treated" on the moral ground that all men are created equal.

The problem is, with some of these universal values and with the advent of globalization that all of us are currently facing, how would the Malay mainstream culture fare? Is it sustainable or will it be overshadowed, and worst still, eliminated, by Western culture?

4. The Impact of Globalization

Malay culture is part of world culture. In the advent of globalization, or rather the ongoing Westernization which is happening at an unprecedented scale in front of our very eyes, people benchmark *everything* globally *everyday*. With the ubiquity of the internet, people are more aware of similarities and differences, on the meaning about being human, on the definition of success and failures, justice and injustice, the down trodden and the *nouveau* rich. An offshoot of globalization is what I called "internetism", for a lack of better word. Under the Kuhnian paradigm of Cartesian mechanical philosophy, the world is mechanically connected like a clock; in internetism, the world is digitally connected. What is more, epistemologically speaking, our knowledge is digitally constructed; what is mirrored is more real than what is. The internet is now neither a tool nor a technology- it is more than that. "Internetism" is a paradigm by itself. We don't really exist unless we exist in the internet.

"Internetism" (as distinguished from the internet as a mere technology) has significantly shaped the future of the mainstream Malay Cultures. I have elaborated the status of the Malay Cultures in the aforementioned paragraph. Obviously there are similarities with other cultures. In more specific term, no human being likes to be mistreated. Thus the value of " treating others like yourself to be treated" is quite trans culture, quite homogenous, and universally acceptable. The same goes with the value of "togetherness", in facing difficulty and in ease, in defeat and in victory. Values such as equal distribution of wealth, (berat sama dipikul, ringan sama dijinjing) certainly bodes well with humanity *writ large*. Equality in hardship has a global appeal. Whether the good is the vision of God, self realization, pleasure, the object of positive interest or axiological pluralism, people globally are in the pursuit of the The Good. Irrespective of our theories of moral value, whether it is consequences or intention which is more fundamental, we want to be moral rather than immoral. Regardless of our persuasion of what moral knowledge is, whether it is skepticism, relativism, scientism ..., globally we are concerned about the importance of moral knowledge- that it is imperative for *any* human being to acquire moral knowledge and to be morally correct.

All of the above point to the significance of universal values. Cultural norms that are shared by humanity will, more often than not, survive better than those norms that are subscribed only by a particular culture. For example, gender discrimination has less chance of global acceptability compared to competency. A person is hired more so because of his ability than his or her sexuality. A culture with the norms of promoting competency has a better future than one that promotes gender before anything else. Ditto for Malay mainstream culture.

In the case of multicultural Malaysia, those common values shared by the different ethnicities will prevail in the sense that it will be more nationally and globally acceptable. Most of these values are subsumed under "professional values" or rather "professional ethics" —punctuality, integrity, honesty and credibility in addition to effectiveness and trustworthiness. These common values that are embedded in the Malay culture will enhance the sustainability of the latter. Values that are localized to geographical and climatic parameters, for example kinds of food, textiles and fashions, which are by and large seasonally defined, will ensure the enduring differences of a particular culture. In so far as these values could complement those universal Malay values, the future of the Malay culture is bright. Otherwise, under the wave of globalization,

Malay culture in particular will lose its malayness in lieu of the western global values.

5. Conclusion

In conclusion, I submit that the destiny of mainstream Malay culture by and large depend on the Malays themselves. They have to chart their own future. They were colonized by the Portuguese, Dutch, British and Japanese and yet they still exist. It is more challenging to live as a colony, under the imperial power, than under the pervasive Westernization if we look it from the perspective of governance and accessibility to our natural resources. If we examine further from the angle of trans-national globalization, it is even more difficult today because *everything* is connected globally *everyday* with the internet. For cultural and practical purposes, nothing is inaccessible anymore. Our thoughts are no longer very privy to us. A better option is to ensure that the virtual is the real, that what is real must *exist* in the virtual; there must be "cultural thinking in the virtual" or rather "cultural thinking on line". The best scenario is to have our own virtual reality. In short, Malay culture, with all its strength and weakness, uniqueness and similarities, differences and commonalities, must be available on line. If this could be done, then the status, development and future of the Malay Culture is as good as any.

马来主流文化在世界上的现状与未来

A. L. Samian

摘　要: 马来语是世界上第五大语言, 马来文化是世界文化的一部分。整个东南亚国家, 尤以马来西亚和印度尼西亚为甚, 都具有马来社会的特征。马来文化在很大程度上受其他文化的影响而形成, 因为马来群岛曾有过相当长时期的殖民地历史。作者把马来文化置于全球化的背景下, 审视了这种文化的现状和未来, 认为能否在道德现实中扮演有意义的角色，决定了这种文化能否具有可持续发展的未来。

关键词：马来文化　东南亚　未来　可持续性

Peferences

［1］Batuah, A. dan Madjoindo, A. 1957. *Tambo Minangkabau.* Jakarta: Balai Pustaka.

［2］Dewan Bahasa dan Pustaka. 1999. *Ensiklopedia Sejarah dan Kebudayaan Melayu.* Kuala Lumpur.

［3］Jeong Chun Hai et al. 2012. *Principles of Public Administration: Malaysian Perspectives.* Kuala Lumpur: Pearson.

［4］Junjiro Takakusu. 1896. *A Record of the Buddhist Religion as Practised in India and The Malay Archipelago AD 671 – 695 by I-tsing.* Oxford; London.

［5］Khaled Hussain (ed.). 1966. *Taj-Us-Salatin* (The Kings' Crown). Kuala Lumpur.

［6］Matheson, Virginia (ed.). 1982. *Tuhfat Al-Nafis* (Significant Endeavor). Kuala Lumpur.

［7］M. Nazri, R. Ibrahim, A. L. Samian et al. 2012. The Discrimination of protection in the federal constitution from the perspective of ethnic relations in Malaysia. *International Journal of Learning.* 18 (9): 305 – 320.

［8］Samad, Said, A. 1986. *Sulalatus Salatin* (Geneology of the Kings). Kuala Lumpur: Dewan Bahasa dan Pustaka.

［9］Tenas Effendy. 2010. *Ungkapan Melayu Pemahaman dan Masalahnya.* Yayasan Tenas Effendy: Pekan Baru.

［10］Thomas L. Friedman. 2006. *The World is Flat: A Brief History of Twenty first Century.* New York: Garrar, Straus & Giroux.

The Main Values of Mainstream Culture in Ireland

Mair Ni Lorcain[*]

Abstract: We are seeing this speed of cultural change increase all round the globe at present. In regard to Ireland, as the phenomenon of globalisation forces change on cultures around the globe, it is notable that mainstream culture in Ireland is changing faster than many. The paper will introduce the changes concerning the mainstream cultures in Ireland.

Keywords: cultural change; Ireland; globalization; mainstream culture

At one point in F. Scott Fitzgerald's 1934 novel *Tender is the Night*, the main character rides a ski lift. He sees valleys and small towns laid out as if for inspection beneath him, and thinks, in what constitutes a fair warning to intellectuals "This is how town planners and retired people see the world".

Here at this seminar we are trying to decipher patterns, to impose generalisations and to deduce future probabilities from the flux of being that is caught for fleeting moments in the human societies in which we live.

The originators of the patterns labelled culture create them not with intent but instead in response to the exigencies of everyday living; in attempting to fulfil the human needs to enjoy, to love, to laugh, to make and to survive they create

* Mair Ni Lorcain, teaching English at Hubei University at present.

patterns of behaviour which often evolve before they can be classified by sociologists or noticed or by the historians of culture.

We are seeing this speed of cultural change increase all round the globe at present. In regard to Ireland, as the phenomenon of globalisation forces change on cultures around the globe, it is notable that mainstream culture in Ireland is changing faster than many.

Culture in Ireland was quite monolithic through most of the 20th century. There was a universal consensus on what constituted a proper republic, and these shared ideas were broadly based on Christian values. Irish culture rewarded idealism and altruism with public recognition and reinforcement. The idea of helping others was admired; and the pursuit of money was of secondary importance. For example thousands of young men and women joined religious orders to spend their lives working in education or health without any monetary reward; in high school the brighter students studied the classics while business studies and accounting was reserved for those deemed less than clever.

Increasing the Irishness of the country was a generally received aim; the united States were called "the next parish" and the US was considered to have a special status as a friendly nation; it was accepted that Ireland would one day be united.

This basic consensus has changed, due to the interplay of both outside influences and internal events. Some of the factors driving change acted very slowly and stealthily on the culture; others had a surprisingly immediate impact.

Until the advent of the Internet, Ireland had the highest consumption of newspapers in the world. Until approximately 1975, newspapers from England had a very limited circulation in Ireland. After Ireland joined the Common Market—the precursor of the European Union—in 1973, trade barriers were no longer possible and the Irish market was opened up to English papers. They differed in tone and content from the newspapers in Ireland and they would slowly bring about widespread changes in cultural assumptions.

The Irish papers tended to be conservative, the English papers led with full page spreads of girls who forgot to put on their underwear. Their lower prices led to the current situation where they produce Irish editions, and are a significant factor in bringing about cultural change, particularly in the area of sexual habits. On their introduction 40 years ago they had little circulation and were examples of a totally foreign culture; the situation has evolved now to the stage where they have become mainstream papers in Ireland.

Television also played a part in changing culture slowly in Ireland. It was always a strong part of the culture to go visit other people's houses in the evening, to chat about the events of the day and to play cards. The establishment of Irish TV in 1963 changed that immediately. People wanted to follow TV stories and those who went visiting were suddenly expected to watch TV with the people they were visiting, instead of talking with them.

The advent of TV also put an end to the practice of children going back to school in the evenings to do extra study or to prepare dramas.

But culturally, it was the purchase of two English TV series by an Irish channel which made even more difference. "Coronation Street" and "Eastenders" exercised the fascination of another world on Irish viewers. After a few months of dedicated watching, most Irish people were able to penetrate the accents—the two series chronicle the love lives of unemployed people in Manchester and Inner London respectively and the two series proceeded to greatly raise peoples' tolerance of permissive lifestyles and thus to produce fundamental changes in Irish attitudes and practice.

In conjunction with those factors bringing about cultural changes slowly other factors came into play more recently.

These cultural changes which had a more immediate impact came about with the arrival of economic immigrants who flocked to Ireland during the economic boom of the early 21st century. The majority came from Eastern Europe. Their habit was to drink at home, thereby saving money as the cost of alcohol was higher in the pub.

The pub had been traditionally a hub of cultural and social activity all over Ireland, but the example of the new arrivals showed that other ways of conviviality were possible. As the economy swung downwards, pub culture came under increasing pressure. This was also due to the high cost charged by the public houses

The effect of misbehaviour by priests of the Catholic Church cannot be overstated when we are examining the vast changes that have occurred in mainstream culture in Ireland. The population were 95% Catholic but this has fallen to the point in the last census (2011) where 84% describe themselves as Catholic. Although we still have the highest percentage of church attendance in Europe, it fell dramatically after these scandals became common knowledge. There is some truth in the argument that people used outrage at these offences to excuse lifestyle changes which they had already made.

Changes to life style were enabled by the economic growth which was continued steadily after the Good Friday Peace Agreements of 1995. These lifestyle changes percolated even further into the fabric of society with the boom which the economy experienced after 2000. Amongst this writers acquaintances, hairdressers went to New York to buy Christmas presents; Physical Education teachers brought their shop assistant wives to Lapland to meet Santa on December 23rd; a journalist took out a 1.5 million Yuan loan to build an extension to his house; a high school teacher bought 7 houses; a bricklayer bought a second home in the sun in Turkey; university car parks were crowded when students got their own cars.

The days when only the slow learners were interested in economics and accounting were now long gone-farmers of this writer's acquaintance formed investment clubs and traded on the stock exchange. Conspicuous consumption became frequent—a student I knew took out a bank loan worth 5,000 Yuan to buy a designer winter jacket.

That was fun; and it was enjoyable to see the new expensive cars lined up in each town. But when the bubble burst it burst more than bank accounts—it burst many fundamental cultural assumptions about life in the republic.

Political life suffered-politicians were blamed for the economic crimes of the bankers, blamed for not keeping a tighter rein on them. Belief in democracy has been deeply undermined to the point where the present government was elected only as a protest against the former government—not in support of their policies.

The election of this present government has brought more fundamental changes in the culture of the country. The former government was part of an ineffective conservative minority in The EU. This new government is allied in the EU to both the Socialist bloc and to Angela Merkel's centrist group. The result is that not only are they committed to implementing massive spending cuts, which any government in the current post crisis situation would be, but they are also committed to implementing cultural changes.

One of these is to abolish the Seanad, the second house of parliament. The possibility of implementing this diminution of democracy is allowed by the new found disdain for all things political which pervades the electorate.

Amongst the cultural changes being pushed by the EU partners of the present government is the introduction of abortion to Ireland. Despite a referendum where 83% of the voters opposed this practice in Ireland, the present government is bringing in laws to force hospitals to do this operation. Only the great shift in political attitudes caused by the economic crisis could have enabled the introduction of this new cultural element to the country.

Chairman Mao Tse Dong said that "Power comes from the mouth of a gun", in reference to military power. Political power flows from assuring the economic needs of the people; fundamental changes in the economy have deep cultural impact.

The impact of economic changes has led to changes in the psychological orientation of the populace. The media, victims themselves of purchasing property at too high a price, are leading the people's attitude now. The Irish culture metamorphosed has from the point where people asked "How can I create a good life for myself?" to the present point where people ask "Why are the politicians not punished for taking the good life away from me?" despite the fact that this "Good Life" was being funded by loans.

Pessimism and cynicism are the rule of the day now, and the effects of the economic crisis of 2008 exercise a huge influence on the prevailing culture.

Only the areas of sport, writing, poetry, installation art and caring for the family flourish unaffected by this pervasive psychological woe.

However, hen we are examining such weighty topics as culture, it is wise to remind ourselves frequently that culture is like Heraclitus' constantly changing river—never static. Where these changes will bring us we never know in advance, but the tendency of humanity is to self preservation. It follows thus that wallowing in self pity cannot last long in Ireland—it is only a matter of time before life nurturing elements breathe life back into the political system and into many fields of cultural life in Ireland.

爱尔兰主流文化的主流价值

Mair Ni Lorcain

摘　要：当代全球范围内的文化正在迅速改变。对爱尔兰而言，正如全球化的力量使全球文化都发生了改变一样，爱尔兰文化也在迅速改变。本文对爱尔兰主流文化的变化做了简要介绍。

关键词：文化变迁　爱尔兰　全球化　主流文化

Culture and Cultures: Brief Reflections about the Mainstream Cultures in the World

Hortensia Cuéllar Pérez [*]

Abstract: Is it currently possible to say that mainstream cultures exist in the world? An affirmative answer is complex because it implies a second question: From which standpoint? Nevertheless, it is roughly true that, at least at a sociopolitical level, we no longer find the bipolarity prevailing before the fall of Berlin Wall, but a large-scale refitting, a cultural, political and economic mosaic made up by different nation blocks where each one, within its particularism, offers an unquestionable geopolitical and thus cultural-identity. A brief analysis of some of the great cultures that have an influence on the configuration of the world we live in is presented here.

Keywords: culture; mainstream culture; geopolitics

First of all, I want to express my greetings to authorities and colleagues attending this Forum, and to express my gratitude to Prof. Dr. Jiang Chang for his kind invitation to participate in this First Forum "The Status and Future of Mainstream Cultures in the World", as the inaugural event of The Advanced Institute for Humanistic Studies, at the prestigious University of Hubei. It is a great honor for me, and I am very happy to be here, once more in China. Thank you very much, Prof. Dr. Jiang Chang, and congratulations for this

* Hortensia Cuéllar Pérez, Professor of Philosophy, TEC de Monterrey Campus Ciudad de México.

Advanced Institute for Humanistic Studies.

Given the interesting subject of this First Forum the question is inevitable: What will be the standpoint where I will focus the subject from? Philosophical? Sociological? Political-economic? This is a subject title wide enough to allow for the development of anything. But the official invitation to the event gives a key for its treatment: This Forum is thought "in order to promote the communication and development of cultures in different nations of the world".

This indicates – if I am plausibly interpreting it – that work will be about the subject of interculturality, multiculturalism and transculturality, taking as a starting point for the Forum – maybe the revision of various national cultures about which a few features will be described that will enable us to know them, appreciate them and/or recall their impact and contributions to our present day world, in order that they become a part of humanity's universal cultural legacy.

Why? Because the world of culture – of cultures, of their reciprocal communication and enrichment in the intercultural environment, is the field of what is human, where nobody can remain alien or isolated, because it represents one of the purest expressions of man's own identity, in its immense versatility. This shows that the world of culture – or of cultures – is complex and plural, but immensely rich. This is why it is worth the while to reflect about the following basic questions, and place them on the discussion table: What do we mean by culture? What do we mean by cultures? What can we do to promote their communication and development, which imply a diversity of novelties and problems arising from the contemplation of culture, and cultures? And this, from a synchronic or diachronic i. e. historical but at the same time contextual-perspective, within a given time and a given space, with a development and richness of their own. I will briefly pose these three aspects, which are interrelated.

1. What Does Culture Mean?

The word "culture" comes from Latin *cultura*, meaning cultivation, linked to the Latin verb *colere*, referring to cultivation or breeding. Edward A. Robert and Barbara Pastor (1996, 89), point out also that the verb *colere* comes from Indoeuropean *kwl*, meaning "to change, to revolve", so that when we talk about "culture", we refer to the cultivation of somebody, *to the inner change or revolution, either peaceful or with a great effort*, experienced by a person, a community, an ethnic group, or a nation when being cultivated. This cultivation necessarily implies education, in some of its meanings[1]. This is why Cicero (106 – 43 B. C.), the great Roman philosopher, in *Tusculanas* (2, 13), when talking about "*cultura animi*", meant "spiritual education", as different from "*cultura corporis*", or from other types of cultivation such as that of land, which is agriculture.

The Greeks, in turn, as we are told by Werner Jaeger in *Paideia: The Ideals of Greek Culture* used the expression *paideia* referring to the *education of excellence* in the several aspects of the personality of free men. By this they meant, as we are told by Gadamer, *Bildung*, i. e. integral formation, linked to *cultivation of virtue* (*arete*), not only at an individual level, but also at a political-social or communitarian level. A sample of this is found at the *Ethica Nicomachea* and at the *Politica*, where Aristotle develops the classical doctrine of intellectual and moral virtues, and the citizen's ideal, focused on the *polis*, a model, with all applicable nuances, to our present day, Republicanism.

We then found that the expression, in its original and classical meanings, at least in the West, and I also think that in Confucius teaching, means formation, education of virtues of those being cultivated, and an individual so cultivated is said to be educated, to have culture, to be a cultivated person or better, a wise person, where the moral dimension of a person who, because of his/her *life wisdom*, is a good person.

---

① Education, as an anthropological and social reality, has at least these meanings: a) As a *process*, because it implies movement (*kinesis*), and in this sense it implies a never-ending task. We can be educated all our life long. (b) As *instruction*, when mnemonic and cognitive education is privileged over human formation. Information is awarded primacy, without a critical discrimination. (c) As an *art*, when a good educator (such as Confucius or Socrates) looks for a better way of teaching, of educating, of cultivating his disciples, and this action has a consequence *the dimension which is most proper of human education, which is formation* (Cuellar, H. , 2012).

In the early Christian era, the Greek *paideia* was called *humanitas*, an expression which is very rich in meaning: as a continuation of the Greek heritage of formation of the human being in accordance with *the requirements of its own nature*, as the education of intellectual and moral faculties (hence the importance of subjects such as logics and moral formation), it adds an element with a fundamental novelty that confers its cultural and religious identity profile: *the light of faith*, the belief in God, alive and incarnate in Jesus Christ, representing another source of knowledge which is distinct from reason but not opposite to it, as Thomas Aquinas undertook the task of demonstrating in the 13th Century. This nuance is very important, because it opens the knowledge of what is divine and, at an intercultural level, links it to the Jewish people.

This relationship between faith and reason as distinct but complementary sources of knowledge was worked on in a systematic way in the incipient *Universitas*, whose foundation occurs between the Ninth and Thirteenth centuries of Christian era. In these first Occidental universities such as Bologne, Paris, Oxford, Salamanca, fundamental wisdoms of Greek and Roman formation agglutinated around what was called Liberal Arts (*trivium* and *quadrivium*) which, together with Philosophy and Theology, made up their basic curriculum. Roman influence was clearly perceived in the use of Latin as the official language.

It is important to highlight the following information, which is relevant about interculturality and transculturality: even from those days, the university is considered as the preeminent institution of higher education, a natural source of irradiation and promotion of culture. As implied by its very name (*unus-versus-alia*), the university as an institution encloses a strong humanistic profile, besides the scientific profile, linked to the opening and cultivation of all types of knowledge in the search of truth, good, and a harmonious, just, solidary, cooperative and peaceful life, which in no way renders it less critical in the assessment of its own work and its contributions to society.

Because of its objective, and because of the freedom of framework derived from fertile research, the University's actions and fields of knowledge (science, philosophy, art, politics, economics, among others) should be oriented towards the enhancement of the civilization and culture of countries where universities are established and, consequently, towards the service of humanity, which is the sign of their universal dimension. This is why we, who work at a university, have a serious social responsibility.

And all of this is *humanitas*, the life of spirit, concretized in actions for the service of the human being, as has been shown by the great university teachers of the East and the West who, through their teachings and their wisdom, have ushered us into the universe of culture, to generate it, enjoy it and spread it.

A behavior against the promotion of what is truly human, from the university or outside of it, is unworthy, and is somewhat or utterly irrational and unfair because it offers countercultural proposals in the disguise of a tolerance accepting, for instance, "the culture of violence" of terrorist groups, or extols "the bloodiest powers", as was the case of those who looked approvingly upon Hitler's or Stalin's actions, or those who present "legalization of drugs" as a "cultural advance", when what they really look for is doing business at any rate.

One additional comment on this subject, now referred to the Renaissance (15th Century). Turning back to look at the ideals of classical Greek culture, and concretizing through arts and literature its Christian soul (as shown, among others, by Dante, Michelangelo and Leonardo da Vinci with their magnificent works), the Renaissance begins to develop a strong "scientific rationality" which, in the age of discoveries and trans-oceanic travels, led to the geographical unity of the world and to the mutual knowledge between continents and cultures.

Thus, the birth of *instrumental rationality* takes place, whose summit in Kant's *autonomous reason*, expressed as the famous motto *Sapere aude*!, "Dare knowing!" which becomes the center of the Aufklärung, the Enlightenment which, with the French Revolution, declares "equality, fraternity and liberty" for all men, with a strong humanistic wisdom. But also, paradoxically, this movement pays a limitless worship to human reason and to the power of science. Is this latter positive? Or negative?

In the 20th Century, with the terrible experience of both World Wars and all their atrocities, the reply comes out: It is necessary to put limits to instrumental reason and to the will of power, because not everything human reason can conceive is the best for humanity and culture. UN proclaims this with the Universal Declaration of Human Rights, in 1948. Dr. Peng Chung Chang, then Director of the Human Rights Division of United Nations, was among signers of this Declaration (UN, 2012). Eleanor Roosevelt, in her memoirs, recalls: "Dr. Chang was a pluralist and claimed, in a charming manner, that more than one type of conclusive reality existed." (UN, 2012).

More recently, post-modern movements and their cultural and philosophical deconstructionism point out to the limits of the illustrated reasons. Contemporary humanism does the same: Without despising advances of science it rather extols them, it warns that achievements of scientific knowledge have a concrete objective: being at the service of human beings, and not being used for their destruction or for global unbalance. Besides, it aims at promoting and raising human development indexes in the world, by raising cultural and economic life levels, by fighting against diseases and famine, by promoting social justice and the solidary respect to everybody's human rights, in order to build a society that is more just, egalitarian and peaceful. All these are expressions of culture and preoccupation about human beings.

2. What Do We Mean by "Cultures"?

Neither classical nor contemporaneous humanism is homogenizing or segregating, because it respects cultural diversity and richness of expressions of such diversity. Humanism, in any of its expressions, is comprehensive, open to dialogue and collaboration among different parties. This leads us into the question: What are cultures? Do they represent the objective and civilized expression of human spirit, as Hegel said? We think they do, and therefore we can talk about "cultures", "civilization", "mainstream cultures in the world", and not only about a "worldwide culture", because this is impossible, utopic, considering human diversity.

With this assertion, we get into the world of complexity, human self-understanding in the diversity of its cultural expressions linked to many factors of a historical, contextual, geopolitical, economic, social, ethnographic, racial, linguistic and religious type, and even factors of richness or non-richness of natural environment where cultural expressions of the various people and nations are born and displayed. By this I mean that it is not the same thing living among Eskimos, in the Equatorial forest, in Central Africa, in Mexico or in Beijing.

This is why I consider that one of the reflection and discussion approaches in the Wuhan Forum is focusing on getting closer to several national cultures. We will outline a few features that will enable us to know these cultures and to appreciate or recall their impact and contributions to our present day world, and its future projection. Because the world of culture, of cultures, is the universe of what is human, where nobody can remain alien or isolated, at least not in the dynamics of a time like ours, characterized by telecommunications, Internet, social networks and a number of other factors existing in the Global Village or at the "Big Screen", as expressed by McLuhan and Lipovetsky. This does not guarantee – it is plausible to state it – an in-depth knowledge about the news we receive, which may be superficial or biased, but not failing to contribute data because of such superficiality or bias.

Nowadays, hardly any person or any set of cultural or identity features of a given nation can remain in anonymity. This is even truer for great cultural trends that have an impact, at a global level on lives of persons, as it has occurred with cultural movements derived from Greek thinking, Christian culture and Illustration, in the West. As to the East, the current day influence of India, and particularly from China, as a millenary culture and a great emerging power, is evident. China is a hardly avoidable political, economic and cultural benchmark, both at public and private levels.

This is why I pose the question: Could we currently say that mainstream cultures exist in the world? An affirmative answer becomes complex, because then the new question would be "from which standpoint?" Notwithstanding this, it is roughly true that, at least at a geopolitical level, we no longer find the bipolarity that existed between the United States and the Soviet Union before the fall of the Berlin Wall in 1989 with its extremely strong political and cultural influences and with the Capitalist and Communist weltanschauungs.

What we observe in the 21ˢᵗ Century is a large-scale refitting, a cultural, political and economic mosaic made up by distinct blocks of nations, each within its particularism, offering an unquestionable geopolitical and hence cultural identity. I am talking among the most relevant about the European Community, the East and South East Asiatic countries, with China and India as essential model references, Latin America where leaders are Mexico and Brazil, and, on the Anglo-Saxon side, the United States, the United Kingdom and Canada.

This shows deep changes in world's physiognomy and in global equilibrium. Bipolarity has been replaced by multipolarity, where, as per the opinion of several analysts such as Carlos Westendorp (2011, p. 9), the axis of gravity of global power looks like it could shift towards East and South. It's true as is shown in the latest U. N. Report about Human Development for 2013.

This Report asserts that, in last ten years, besides China as the huge emerging power, other countries such as India, Brazil, South Africa and Turkey have had great and fast advancements at a *different level.* If this trend holds, their growth could keep as a solid one, and expectations for reduction of poverty of their populations would be encouraging.

On the other hand, the European Community seems like tottering when failing to completely overcome its current economic and cultural prostration. This is illustrated by Spain and Greece cases. On the American side, United States keeps having the largest economy in the world, despite its big internal problems and the challenges being faced by its global influence.

This shows that if these trends hold the cultural influence of some of these actors will become evident. On the American side, its models and ways of life will keep being a paradigm at a global level; for instance, the worship for freedom and democracy, the search for wellbeing, and the defense of human rights, which in several occasions has become a double speech, if judged by recent historical events such as the invasion of Irak.

As to China, this country, with its millenary culture, has become the center of attention of the world because of its political economic ①, social and philosophical② model, which led it to becoming the "great world's factory". What is appreciated is its efforts towards a "Socialism with Chinese features", as expressed by the President of the Popular Republic of China, Mr. Xi Jinping in late 2012, meaning "to work in favor a modestly fluent society in a generalized form, to improve the population's level of life", "to create (sources of) work and to promote exportations by the State", "to increase leadership capability at a global level", and to "fight corruption and moral degeneration" (Source: Spanish. news. cn/ especiales/ 2012 – 11/19c_ 131983198. htm). All this within the parameters of China's strong cultural roots and its "political-cultural outpour" towards contemporaneity which, with its openness to our present-day world, shows the indefatigable work of their inhabitants and Government, who – it seems to me – offer friendship, harmony and peace.

Thus, we are talking about phenomena such as multiculturalism and interculturality, due to communication channels which may be either sought for or spontaneous, ransom or politically planned found in the world of culture, cultures and life. But these processes, in a variety of occasions, are not simple,

---

① Justin Yifu Lin, former senior vice president and chief economist of the World Bank, tell us China's economy has potential to sustain fast growth. He proposes that emerging markets have been impacted by shrinking demand from high-income economies since the global financial crisis erupted in 2008. However, China's huge deposit and foreign exchange reserves will provide the world"second-largest economy with great potential for realizing industrial upgrading and infrastructure improvements that could sustain fast economic growth, according to Lin's analysis. China's gross domestic product (GDP) growth slowed to 7. 6 percent in the January-June period of 2013, the weakest first-half performance in three years, but it was in line with market expectations and above the government's full-year target of 7. 5 percent, data from the National Bureau of Statistics (NBS) show. In: http: // english. peopledaily. com. cn/90778/8361397. html (Retrieved September 10th, 2013).

② According the Chinese Academy of Social Sciences' annual Yellow Paper of World Socialism says that the "China's success in the past 60 years, specially after the opening-up, has surpassed the achievements of Britain during the Industrial Revolution and the US's progress in the 19th century". Cfr. http: //english. cpc. people. com. cn/7305104. html (Retrieved September 14th, 2013) What is the key for this progress? I believe the combination between its own millenary tradition in order to achieve the common good, to learn lessons from the collapse of communist rule 24 years ago in the former Soviet Union, to review the balance between political stability and socio-economic development, besides a good and hard organization. For Chinese leaders the "Socialism with Chinese features" is a combination of the basic theories of Marxism and China's reality.

but imply elements of shared complexity posing problems such as "cultural identity", "recognition policies", "national honor and human rights", "dignity and equality for all", which makes this issue a conflictive one. What is then to be done?

One way is intercultural dialogue and policies of reciprocal respect within diversity. In this regard, Dora E. García, following Raúl Fornet Betancourt, says that interculturality "is achieved starting with a concrete praxis of life where the relationship with the other is cultivated in an enclosing way, i. e. not limited to a possible rational relationship through concepts, but rather seated on letting oneself be affected, or "touched" by the other, in our day-by-day dealings" (2011, 64). I find this proposal reasonable. The fact must be considered, furthermore, that interculturality talks about exchange, interrelation, mutual enrichment in values and conceptions about the world and the life, knowledge and respect of traditions between diverse cultures. Hence the subject of identity of cultures. Are not different Chinese culture, the Teotihuacan culture and the Greek culture? Yes, indeed, in many aspects, including their cultural productions: the Great Wall of China is not the same as the Parthenon or the Pyramid of Sun in the Anahuac plateau.

When admired and shared, these cultural productions become a part of humanity's cultural wealth. They become a global heritage upon showing a universal identity full of meaning for their people and for humanity as a whole. Another category becomes apparent here, more linked to the world of culture: *transculturality*. What is *eternal at a cultural level* is transcultural, even though it has an origin in a determined space and time. Its historicity does not suppress its value because it shows, with a great purity, the very soul of people.

3. What Can We Do to Promote Communication and Development?

Culture, and movements linked to it or derived from it are, as we know, expansive, communicating, public – to a greater or smaller extent – both in the private scope and in the public scope. In the private scope, because refinement and manners of a cultivated, educated person are easily perceived. In the public scope, this is so because of the influence exerted by cultural movements among their followers or detractors. This is why I applaud the Forum's initiative, which becomes a good occasion for thinking about what is obvious without being so.

If the Forum's fundamental goal is the promotion and development of cultures in today's world – maybe after getting to know them and having a first approach in several cases – the questions would be: How can we face this gigantic endeavor? Is it our responsibility? Isn't it a direct responsibility of each country's government? Or maybe the protagonists of their own national cultures (multicultures) who should promote their reciprocal communication and development in order to make them appreciated and recognized by the world?

Or yet other alternative: Is it not perchance the State with the people (the State with other distinct organizations such as universities, enterprises, market and civil society), who, in their reciprocal work relationship, should create, favor, promote, respect, *not hinder*, better living conditions of the citizens living in their territory?

Shouldn't the State promote the development of the respective cultures (or multicultures) within a given country? Can this be seen as a contribution to our present world? But, what about immigrants? Would they be offered the same opportunities? This pathway, as it can be appreciated, is not exempt from labyrinths and problems. But Confucius said: "Men can expand the way. The way cannot expand men." (*The Lun Yü in English*, Chapter Fifteen, 28)

This shows that an intense work is required, in order to look for new paths in everything that seems irreconcilable, to set up a "policy of recognition" of the different actors in the several orders of attention. How? In a first stage, through an open dialogue and a cooperative attitude regarding fundamental human rights, and the search and instauration of justice and peace. We are aware, however, that the answer is not easy. What is indeed obvious is that we are dealing with a strategic issue requiring common sense and imagination, citizen and State contribution, as well as participation of pro-culture agencies of international institutions such as UN.

On a practical way, in each nation, public policies must be set up, or tuned up, that are respectful of its history and traditions, and promote its natural and cultural creations and wealth. It is imperative to encourage creative people, inventors, artists, cultural promoters and persons who, as philosophers and other social actors, are forging through ideas the profiles of the great movements of humanity, known as "culture", "cultures" and civilization. All this is education, a personal and politic-social task, poured into actions. What is sterile is remaining idle, failing to find out problems and opportunities to try to solve them.

In order to illustrate with a historical example what has been said up to now, I will briefly talk about my country – Mexico, trying to give an overview of its features and its multicultural and intercultural development since its inception, seven centuries ago (1325 A. D.), up to present day. This time span shows that Mexican history and culture are too recent as compared with millenary cultures coming from old ages, such as Chinese, Hebrew, Greek, Hindu and Egyptian cultures.

Mexico's historical and cultural tradition is recent: we only have seven centuries of existence. But this history is rich in multiculturalism. Those who know Mexico, its history, its culture and its way of thinking, know that this is not a country with a homogeneous face, but rather very heterogeneous. It is even spoken about "many Mexicos". This profile corresponds to its history as a nation integrated by different stages of its own development, as well as a diversity of ethnicities, races, cultures, languages, mythical conceptions, religious beliefs, and a self-awareness of its own historicity, its past, its present and its future.

Our origin is historically placed in 1325, with the foundation of the Great City of Tenochtitlan, which on time became the commercial, cultural and religious center of the Aztec Empire. Tradition tells that this Mesoamerican culture was built in the center of a lagoon where its first settlers were to find as a signal an eagle standing on a nopal cactus, devouring a snake. This sign is kept as a symbol in our national flag. That immense lagoon was placed at the Anahuac plateau, where the large city of Mexico is presently seated[1].

Aztecs are not the sole protagonists of that pre-Hispanic past. In other zones of the present national territory, we found the great Mayan culture, the Olmecas, Toltecas, Zapotecas, Xochimilcas, Tlaxcalans, etc. But Mexico's historical and cultural memory does not end here.

With the discovery of America in 1492, and the Spanish conquest of the Aztec Empire between 1521 and 1525, we get into the Colonial period and the Spanish Domain, lasting for three centuries. It ends up with the declaration of the War of Independence, in 1810, by Don Miguel Hidalgo y Costilla, the Father of the Country, and the consummation of national independence in 1821.

So we enter the period of the independent Mexico, with its highs and lows, up to our day. From the political, social, cultural, education, economic standpoints, we have been building up our own identity as a nation[2].

This shows that at three great influences are found in the identity configuration of the Mexican nation in our days: pre-Hispanic influence, Colonial influence, and that of the independent Mexico. This triple influence is translated as various world and life visions; modes and ways of life according to times and places where one lives, running parallel to the upcoming of models of political, economic, social, and cultural-educational organization of one's State/Nation. This results in a mixture that renders very complex the analysis of the Nation's specific cultural categories.

For instance, with consummation of Mexican independence, the question became: who are true Mexicans? Were they Spaniards born in Mexico? Or were

---

[1]   Here are some minimum data for the socio-cultural contextualization of my country. Its official name is Estados Unidos Mexicanos (Mexican United States), also known as Mexico, or the Mexican Republic. It has a territorial extension of 1,964,373 km^2, with a population of 120 million as per last Government census. Official language is Spanish. Majority religion is Roman Catholicism (90%). There are multiple indigenous groups speaking multiple languages and dialects. These groups are given schooling in their own languages. At an ethnical level, most Mexicans are mestizo. (Cfr. Secretaría de la Función Pública, 25 de agosto del 2013)

[2]   All these events have been gathered by intellectuals, writers and people of action, including Fray Bartolomé de las Casas (1484 – 1566), José Vasconcelos (1882 – 1959), Miguel León Portilla (1926 –), Octavio Paz (1914 – 1988), Enrique Krauze (1947 –), etc.

they mestizos, children of a Spaniard and an Indian? I believe that now we have the answer: A Mexican is any person born within the Mexican territory or adopts the Mexican nationality, without any kind of distinction. But this identity is not only political, but also cultural, in its broadest sense, because, in general, Mexicans love their own traditions, their national history. We feel proud about our country, and we want that everybody's conditions of life improve.

What is very clear for us is that we are individual subjects of a given country, and we have a specific identity ("being Mexican"). With this identity we project a "symbiotic relationship" in phrase of Gilberto Giménez (2012), with the cultural dimension of our nation, expressed in several instances through folklore, art, singing, dancing, typical costumes, gastronomy, but not only these. Mexican culture goes beyond, up to the point of wishing to offer other people, as a sign of friendship en recognition, the open doors of its home and its very heart.

Our form of political organization is that of a representative republic, democratic and liberal, with several structural failures due to the very recent transition to political democracy, the corruption of several persons in Government, and the lack of consolidation of a strong project of a nation by those who govern us. Even so, we love our country and wish to get interculturally with other countries in the world, offering them our friendship and desires for justice, concord and peace in the reciprocal relationship. We have deeply rooted values, such as love for family and children, love for our land and traditions, and deep appreciation for our friends, for our religious beliefs and for any worthy cultural expression coming from other nations and latitudes. We are open to anything that could make us better persons sharing as well the values we have.

References

[1] Edward A. y Bárbara Pastor. 1996. *Diccionario etimológico indoeuropeo de la lengua espa? ola*. Madrid: Alianza Editorial.

[2] Ciceron. 2010. *Tusculanas*. Madrid: Alianza Editorial.

[3] Confucius. *The Lun Yü in English*. Hong Kong: Confucius Publishing Co. , Ltd.

[4] Cuéllar, H. 2012. *Qué es la Filosofía de la educación?* México：Trillas.

[5] García D. E. Coord. 2011. *Filosofía de la cultura. Reflexiones contemporáneas. Horizontes y encrucijadas.* México：Editorial Porrúa/UNESCO/Tecnológico de Monterrey.

[6] Gimenez, G. "La cultura como identidad y la identidad como cultura". In：http：// perio. unlp. edu. ar/teorias2/textos/articulos/gimenez. pdf.

[7] Jaeger, W. 1945. *Paideia：The Ideals of Greek Culture*, vols. I-III, trans. Gilbert Highet. Oxford University Press.

[8] Westendorp, C. 2011. "Las potencias emergentes hoy：Hacia un nuevo orden mundial". Introducción. En *Cuadernos de Estrategia*. Barcelona：Ministerio de Defensa Instituto Espa"ñol de Estudios Estratégicos. In：www. bibliotecavirtualdefensa. es/ BVMDefensa/i18n/catalog.

[9] Li Jialian. 2012. *The Sentimental Origin of Virtue：An Inquiry into Thoughts of Moral Sentiments*. Hang Zhou：Zhejiang University Press.

文化与诸文化：对世界主流文化的简略反思

Hortensia Cuéllar Pérez

摘　要：当今世界有可能存在主流文化吗？对此我们难以给出肯定性的回答，因为其中隐含着第二个问题，即从什么角度而言？不过，至少在社会政治层面，我们不再能看到柏林墙倒塌之前的政治两极对立，但是，每个民族在其特殊性之内所构建的文化、政治和经济结构构成了其地缘政治身份以及文化身份。本文对当今世界有影响的文化进行了简单的分析。

关键词：文化　主流文化　地缘政治

Why Does China Propose the Concept of "Socialist Core Values"?

Wu Xiangdong[*]

Abstract: It is of great significance for us to understand the reason for presenting the concept of "socialist core values" in both delineating the connotation of the concept and understanding the tendency of China's historical movements and contemporary social praxis. The paper holds that there are three reasons for China to propose the concept of "socialist core values": one is the self-understanding and self-construction of socialism with Chinese characteristics, the other is to guide and construct the value order of contemporary Chinese society, and the third is to establish the national image and promote the national cultural soft power.

Keywords: socialist core values; socialism with Chinese characteristics; cultural soft power

Socialist core values have become a concept of importance in present political culture of China. Early in 1990s, along with the establishment and development of market economy system, people had begun to discuss corresponding issues of socialist core values. In October, 2006, the Sixth Plenum of the 16th CPC Central Committee presented for the first time the "socialist core values system" and

---

[*] Wu Xiangdong, Professor of Philosophy, Beijing Normal University.

delineated its connotation. In October, 2007, the report of the 17th CPC National Congress presented the strategic mission of "vigorously build the socialist core values system". Ever since then, consensus has been increasingly reached in Chinese academic sphere, namely, to condense the core values with more definite direction, more concentration and more ease to communicate and observe, and discussions with respect to the corresponding condensing has been unfolded in consistent fashion, which has led to a great upsurge of studies. In the discussions, scholars have presented more than 60 formulations with regard to the socialist core values, concerning more than 90 specific categories (or judgments). Due to the differences on perspective, train of thought and method, there are multitudinous cases which seem hard to agree on. In November, 2012, the report of the 18th CPC National Congress presented three promotes, i. e., "promote prosperity, democracy, civility, and harmony, promote freedom, equality, justice and the rule of law, and promote patriotism, dedication, integrity, and friendship so as to cultivate and observe socialist core values."

Albeit this formulation has yet clearly pointed out what socialist core values are, the concept as such is by no means an empty or decorative political term. The presentation of it is an event of importance in contemporary Chinese political life and will surely exert important and far-reaching impact on the political, social and cultural life of China. It is of great significance for us to understand the reason for presenting the concept in both delineating the connotation of the concept and understanding the tendency of China's historical movements and contemporary social praxis.

1. The Self-understanding and Self-construction of Socialism with Chinese Characteristics

It is a consensus to take the path of socialism with Chinese characteristics. For the building of socialism with Chinese characteristics, "What socialism is" is undoubtedly the primal fundamental theoretical issue. Nonetheless, history often shows some strangeness. Although socialism has experienced nearly five hundred years' theoretical development and practical movement, socialisms of various forms have emerged, and socialism genealogy and different socialism traditions have been formed, we failed to gain a clear idea as to the question of "What socialism is" in the past. As regards the history of socialist thought, there are two different traditions when it comes to the understanding of "socialism": "scientific" socialism and ethical socialism. In "scientific" socialism, people like Kautsky, Althusser, etc. positivized and systemized socialism, ignoring and denying the value factors of socialism; in ethical socialism, Bernstein, social democratic party, some western Marxists, etc. constrained socialism to ethics and values. They separate, from their own stances, the interconnections between the values and system of socialism, having made one-sided understandings of the essence of socialism. In our praxis of socialism building before the reform and opening up, the decline of socialism values had once been brought about due to the improper grasping of the relationship between goals on the one hand and means, values and ideals and practical paths on the other. At the same time, due to the influence from the USSR mode and the thinking mode of scientism caused by understanding Marxism in scientific fashion, in the mind's eye of most people, socialism is systemized again and its dimension of value has been ignored. As has once been said by Zhou Enlai, "What is socialism? The most fundamental thing of socialism is the fulfillment of socialism reformations, the private capitalist ownership of means of production having been canceled and then transformed to state ownership, and the collectivization of agriculture and handicraft industry." We failed to form reasonable socialist values, to see clearly the significance of socialist value and that of socialist values to socialism, and hence were unclear about what socialism is. This unclarity has caused severe faults, and even brought about severe consequences in our socialism praxis. Deng Xiaoping has once forthrightly pointed out, from the hight of history and with the keenness and wisdom of a politician, "The crux lies in what socialism is and how to build it. We have many experiences and lessons, the most important of which is to make clear about this question."

The proposing of socialist core values highlights the value dimension of socialism. Since the reform and opening up, we have been paying stress to recognizing and understanding socialism from the perspective of values. Deng

Xiaoping has pointed out once and again that poverty is not socialism, egalitarianism is not socialism, polarization is not socialism, there is no socialism without democracy, there is no socialism without legality, and so on. He presented at last, "The essence of socialism is emancipating productivity, developing productivity, annihilating exploitation, eliminating polarization and ultimately achieving common prosperity." In this argument, he treated common prosperity as the essential goal of socialism and introduced, in clear-cut fashion, socialist value into the essential stipulations and judging criteria of socialism and hence rectified the previous positivistic and systemized understanding of socialism. Under the new historical conditions of building a well-off society in all respects, Jiang Zemin presented that promoting one's all-round development is the essential requirement of building a new socialist society, Hu Jintao pointed out that social equity and justice is the essential requirement of socialist system and social harmony is the essential attribute of socialism with Chinese characteristics, and the forth. This has indicated that we will go on understanding socialism from the perspective of values, and that the recognition with respect to socialist value is being increasingly deepened. The presentation of "socialist core values system" and "socialist core values", on the other hand, reflects in full fashion that our recognition as regards socialist values and the relationship between them and the essence of socialism has reached a sort of rational consciousness.

Socialist core values are the fundamental value ideals and value principles of socialism and the essential content of socialism, and they answer, at the level of values, "What socialism is and how to build it". During the practice of over thirty years of reform and opening up, we have paved the path of socialism with Chinese characteristics, formed the theoretical system with Chinese characteristics, and improved socialist system. Socialist core values are the soul of the path, theoretical system and socialist system. The path of socialism with Chinese characteristics is a practical process unfolded around socialist core values. The core values as such determines the direction of the practice of socialism with Chinese characteristics, stipulates its process, measures its results, and promotes the practice itself to constantly develop. The theory of socialism with Chinese characteristics is the ideological system constructed around socialist core values, and it is the discussion and elucidation with regard to the conditions, means and path of realizing socialist values. Chinese socialist system is the arrangement of system to be realized around socialist core values. Socialist core values guides the foundation of socialist system, performs legitimacy defense for it, instills value goals and direction in its reform, and guides the changes and innovations of socialist system itself. As to socialism with Chinese characteristics, the socialist core value is the soul of its life and expresses its particular spirit. Without the consciousness of the socialist core values, there would not be the consciousnesses of the path, theories and systems of socialism with Chinese characteristics. In addition, since the socialist core values guides the developing direction of the path of socialism with Chinese characteristics, promotes the development of the socialist theoretical system and guides the further improvement of socialist system, the consciousness of the socialist core values means not only the self-understanding of socialism with Chinese characteristics but also its self-construction.

2. Guide and Construct the Value Order of Contemporary Chinese Society

People always live in a certain social order. Any sound society is of steady and harmonious economic, political and social orders, and value order as well. Value order not only reflects the economic and political orders of a society, but also constructs, via itself, ordered meaningful world for people, promoting the steadiness and harmony of the society. Order needs a core. Just like a wonderful music will merely become a clutter of notes without the theme, to form a value order in the authentic sense of the word, a sort of core values is necessarily needed to adjust and integrate the intension and conflicts between the multiple values, and to govern the value life. On this account, any mature society and culture whatsoever will be engaged in constructing and constantly strengthening its core values. Guan Zhong, the politician of the Spring and Autumn Period of China, left the following political instructions: there are four dimensions of a state—

Propriety (*li* 礼), Righteousness (*yi* 义), Integrity (*lian* 廉), Honor (*chi* 耻)." "If the four dimensions cannot be upheld, the state will ruin." That is to say, propriety, righteousness, integrity and honor are the four criteria of a state without which the latter will ruin. Guan Zhong treats the core values at the level of the survival of a state.

Since the reform and opening up of China, along with the sharp transformation of the society and the profound adjustment of the interests structure caused by the establishment and development of market economy, people's values have also experienced great changes and hence showed the traits of being multiple, diverse and changeable. Economic globalization and the rapid development of modern scientific technologies with information technology as the core have all the more strengthened the agitations and collisions amidst the multiple cultures and values in the same space and time, various trends of thought ebbing and flowing, and various ideas overlapping one another. To be sure, the historical advancement of the reform determines and demonstrates the advancement of the change of people's values, and the diversity and variety of values have broken the monotonous, closed and rigid statement of traditional social values, enabled people's value life to reveal a colorful and lively situation, and reinforced the vitality and energy of the society.

Meanwhile, the change of value order is also filled with intension, conflicts, and even disarrays to a certain extent. The diversity of values has caused and brought about relevant conflicts manifested in the fact that different even opposite ideas and choices appear between individuals, groups and different social subjects at the level of a series of important value issues such as efficiency and equity, interests and morality, freedom and equality, and the like. The same subject also shows, as a rule, diversity and contradiction on value orientation in different spheres and aspects. The contradictions and conflicts as such are also the series of contradictions and conflicts between values of different forms, say, those between traditional and modern, local and alien, religious and mundane, elite and secular values. In the conflicts and contradictions as such, we also see that there are materialism, relativism and nihilism of values to a certain extent. To some people, money, property and the obtainment of them are their primal even unique goals, and are a sort of their life style. They identify materialized logic and believe in money worship, consumerism and hedonism. The values of some people are of obscurity for they take the relativity of things as the excuse and confuse right with wrong, being unable to distinguish between beauty and ugliness, honor and disgrace. This sort of relativism will often convert into philistine pragmatism with nihilism qua the extreme. Some people are short of belief and are blurred spiritually without any reliance as the result of which they get enmeshed in meaningless anxiety and loneliness and move towards nihility, banality and indifference. That's why we often see that in daily life the moral bottom line frequently falls, the dregs of feudal superstition reappear, and ridiculous events incessantly occur, e. g. , the series of food-safety scandals like gutter oil, poisonous capsules, clenbuterol etc. ; events like old people falling down or young children being crushed to which people showed indifference and coldness; the officials' " Erotic-photo Gate ", " Famous-cigarette Gate ", "Smiling Gate", among others.

Socialist core values shoulders the historic mission of guiding and constructing social value order. The contradictions and conflicts and the disarray to a certain extent during the changing of value order reflect the contradictions and conflicts of interests among the relations of social economy and, in the meanwhile, highlight by way of questions the recourse to core values. The presentation of the concept of socialist core values expresses the consciousness of the recourse as such. In virtue of condensing and highlighting socialist core values, people may perform critical integration with respect to multiple values, mediate the conflicts between values and, on the ground of this, understand and govern social life and dispel the materialism, relativism and nihilism in values so as to efficiently construct spiritual home and settle their mind in the clamor of multiple values. The society may also hence find the most possible common divisor among the whole social members at the level of value identification, obtain in the broadest sense the value consensus as to the specific contradictions of interests and various thought differences, efficiently guide the integration of the complicated social ideologies, effectively avoid the contradictions and confusions of thought brought about by social separation, and establish a steady and efficient value order.

3. Establish the National Image and Promote the National Cultural Soft Power

Any nation and state whatsoever has its own culture and the rise of any nation-state whatever is accompanied by both economic prosperity and cultural flourishing. At present time, culture is increasingly becoming the important source of national cohesion and creativity and the important factor of the competition of overall national strength, which is called soft power. He who occupies the high ground of cultural development and owns powerful cultural soft power will gain the initiative in the fierce international competitions. More and more countries in the world are taking improving cultural soft power as an important content of their developing strategies. The core of culture is values whereas the strength of culture comes, in the final analysis, from the influence and attraction of the core value condensed therein. The competition of cultural soft power is in essence that of core values represented by different cultures. The presentation of the concept of socialist core values means a sort of consciousness of modern China with regard to promoting the national cultural soft power.

Socialist core values may strengthen national cohesion and cultivate national sense of identity. National cultural soft power is first and foremost manifested in cultural cohesion which mainly comes from people's identification and pursuit of core values. History and practice have indicated once and again that each social community needs its particular core values and by dint of the common values as such it may perform demonstrations of reason and legitimacy for its existence, shape and rally its members, and unite the members of the community so as to produce a sense of unity and form a sort of affinity, charisma and cohesion. The production of them is due to the fact that the core values as such offers common value ideal and value norms to its members, enabling people to have common goals and pursuit in terms of their own long-term and fundamental interests, to reach value consensus and hence to form a strong centripetal force. Contemporary China needs to offer common ideal believes and value goals to people by virtue of socialist core values so as to help people go beyond the differences in terms of nation, kinship, language and territory etc. , and of class, industry, profession, interests etc. , and strengthen the centripetal force and sense of belonging of the big family of Chinese nation. At the same time, it is exactly by virtue of socialist core values that contemporary Chinese society is performing self-identity, putting self-confirmation into practice, answering the question of "Who we are" and showing its own particularity, difference and identity therein.

Socialist core values promote the influence of Chinese culture. The socialist core value in our terminology is that with Chinese characteristics and it is the core of contemporary Chinese culture. This core value is the reply of the significance of world history given at the level of values to the issues of the development of contemporary China under the circumstances of globalization. The practice of socialism with Chinese characteristics that settles the developmental issues of China is performed both on the basis of Chinese cultural tradition and history and in the background of economic globalization and world history. It needs to employ capital and market mechanism to the maximum extent, but it also needs to strive for eliminating the various predicaments and crises brought about by capitalist modernity. In this connection, socialist core values cannot be detached from the reasonable inheritance and absorption of Chinese traditional culture and western capitalist values, but it also needs to make criticisms of and transcendence over them. In the criticism and transcendence as such, the defect and crisis of modernity values should be overcome and dispelled for the sake of finding a new path and direction for the development of human civilization. In this sense, socialist core values is both with Chinese characteristics and of the significance of world history. On this account, if socialism with Chinese characteristics is the creative answer to the historical riddle of "Where China is heading for" since modern time, socialist core values with Chinese characteristics is then the creative answer to the disputes of value between China and the West, ancient and modern since modern time of China. The values as such is not only the cultural sign of contemporary China which shows the cultural images of the state and nation outward and constitutes the solid foundation for international cultural conversations, communications and interactions, but also the particular contribution of contemporary China to human civilization, and hence is of particular value.

4. Conclusion

Socialist core values offer answers to "What socialism with Chinese characteristics is and how to build it" at the level of values, and socialism with Chinese characteristics needs the core values to perform self-understanding and self-construction. The contradictions and conflicts and disarray to a certain extent during the changes of the value order of contemporary Chinese society need the guidance and norms offered by socialist core values so as to dispel the materialism, relativism and nihilism of values, settle people's mind and remold social value order. Under the circumstances wherein culture becomes a soft power and an important factor of the competition of overall national strength, contemporary China needs, in virtue of socialist core values, to reinforce national cohesion, cultivate the sense of national identity, delineate national image and establish the cultural soft power corresponding to China's economic status. The presentation of the concept of socialist core values is exactly based on a sort of consciousness as regards the various aspects mentioned above.

为什么中国提出"社会主义核心价值观"的概念？

吴向东

摘　要：理解"社会主义核心价值观"提出的理由，对于理解这个概念以及中国的文化历史与社会实践，具有重要意义。本文认为，提出"社会主义核心价值观"有三个理由，一是为了中国特色社会主义的自我理解与自我构建，二是为了引导中国社会价值秩序的构建，三是为了树立国家形象并提升国家文化软实力。

关键词：社会主义核心价值观　中国特色社会主义　文化软实力

当代美国文化及其特性

王忠欣[*]

摘　要：美国文化是世界上影响最大的文化。美国的政治理想、价值观、语言、饮食、大众娱乐以及生活方式，无时无刻不在影响着世界上亿万的民众。本文探讨了美国文化的形成、当代美国文化的核心内涵、特性以及面临的挑战。

关键词：美国　文化　特性　挑战

今天世界上影响最大的文化，当数美国文化。美国的政治理想、价值观、语言、饮食、大众娱乐以及生活方式，无时无刻不在影响着世界上亿万的民众。全球文化的发展在很大程度上也仰赖美国文化所提供的理念和资源。故此，了解当代美国文化的内涵、发展进程以及特性，对于任何希望与时俱进的人群都具有非同寻常的意义。

泛泛地说，反映人的思想、由人所创造出来的东西都称为文化。再具体一点讲，文化是一个群体形成的思想、理想、情感、价值等内在的、精神性的东西。如果把一个群体比喻为一个人，那么文化就相当于一个人的灵魂。一个群体与另一个群体本质上的区别是文化上的区别，是内在的、精神性的区别，表现在思维方式、价值观、情感的表述、理想、宗教等方面。

---
* 王忠欣，美国波士顿大学全球基督教研究中心研究员。

居住在一个地方的人群会产生自己的文化。产生在自己中间的这个文化就成为这个地方的人群的主体文化或原色文化。然而，文化并不是静止的，它是可以传播的、流动的。一个地方的文化可以被另一个地方的人群所接受，甚至成为另一个地方的主要文化。所以，文化的传播、流动和渗透是文化本身所具有的特性。当代美国文化的形成很大程度上得益于文化本身所具有的传播、流动和渗透的本性。

一　当代美国文化的形成

美国文化是一个相对来说还很年轻的文化，这与美国国家形成的时间有关。美国18世纪下半叶从英国统治下独立，美国建国以前的北美英国殖民地是17世纪初开始建立的。美国的文化应该是在北美殖民地时期开始产生的。

在欧洲殖民者来到北美新大陆以前，土著印第安人已经在这里生活了很久，他们有自己的文化，然而，印第安人的文化在后来形成的美国文化中并没有多大影响。在北美洲这块土地上后来发展出的美国文化，主要来自欧洲殖民者在欧洲所接受的文化。也就是说，早期的美国文化主要是从欧洲流动过来或殖民者从欧洲带过来的文化。这种文化主要就是基督教。

宗教与文化有着密切的联系。著名神学家田立克一针见血地指出，宗教是文化的内核，文化是宗教的形式。美国的文化完美地诠释了宗教与文化的这种关系。

在17世纪初，欧洲殖民者来到北美大陆时，欧洲的主流文化是基督教。基督教产生于1世纪，是从犹太教中发展出来的，与犹太教有着千丝万缕的联系。基督教相信存在独一的上帝，上帝是宇宙万物的创造者；人是由上帝照着上帝的形象创造的；人由于受撒旦的引诱堕落在罪中，背离了上帝；处于罪中的人无法自救，上帝道成肉身，来到世上拯救人类。这是最基本的基督教信念，是当时每个基督徒都相信的。

16世纪初欧洲大陆进行宗教改革，从当时欧洲的主流基督教即天主教中分裂出了基督新教。基督新教与天主教在基本信仰上没有很大的区别，但基督新教毕竟提出了一些新的信念。德国改教领袖马丁·路德提出，信仰最高的权威唯有圣经，人成为义人唯有信心，人获得拯救唯有恩典，并且人人是祭司。马丁·路德为基督新教奠定的信仰要义突破了天主教神职人员所掌控的信仰权威，使得所有的基督教都可以直面上帝，与上帝直接交通，并在上帝之下人人平等。这一革命性的信念极大地影响了日后的美国文化。

路德之后的另一位改教领袖约翰·加尔文系统地整理和阐述了基督新教的信仰体系，其最著名的思想就是上帝主权的思想。加尔文认为上帝是无所不在、无所不知和无所不能的，宇宙万物都是在上帝的掌管之下；人的所思所想、所作所为以及是否能够得到救赎都是在上帝的掌握中。加尔文的上帝主权的思想又被称为"预定论"，即一个人的堕落和拯救都是上帝预定好的，被预定获得拯救的人就成为上帝的选民；成为上帝选民的人，在地上也是很出色的；他们取得成就，遵守上帝的诫命，过道德的生活；一个人获得救赎成为上帝选民的证据，就是在世上的工作和生活上得到上帝的祝福。加尔文的神学思想影响了很多英国的基督徒。英国 16 世纪宗教改革期间，一些基督徒来到加尔文所在的日内瓦学习、取经，接受了加尔文的新教神学观。他们回到英国后，就大力推动在英国的国教会中清除天主教的痕迹，故被称为清教徒。清教徒的宗教改革做法不为英国国教会所容，国教会就对这些清教徒进行迫害。为了躲避迫害、寻求宗教信仰自由，很多清教徒于 17 世纪初越过大西洋来到了北美洲殖民地，这样，加尔文的思想就开始在北美殖民地落地开花，成为那个时期殖民地的一个主流文化。清教徒对宗教信仰的虔诚、对工作的刻苦态度、对教育的重视，塑造了早期美国的文化。

北美最早的 13 个殖民地都有自己的宗教信仰，主要以基督新教为主。基督新教包括众多各自独立的宗派。当时北美殖民地的北部地区以继承清教徒传统的公理会为主，中部地区为贵格会、路德宗和荷兰改革宗等，南部地区主要是圣公会。大多数的居民都是不同教会的成员，教会作为最基本的社会团体为殖民地的居民提供了世界观、价值观和道德准则，而这些正是构成文化的最基本要素。

　　基督新教对美国文化的影响还表现在殖民地时期和后来的美国教育和出版上。1647 年马萨诸塞殖民地规定，每个有 50 个家庭的城镇要建立一所小学，每个有 100 个家庭的城镇要建立一所中学，建立这些学校的目的是要确保清教徒的子女能够学会读圣经、接受加尔文主义信仰的基本要义。其他殖民地的不同宗派的教会也成为当地开办教育的主力。当时学校主要的教科书就是圣经，祷告也是学习的内容之一。人们普遍相信，阅读圣经可以拯救灵魂。

　　被誉为"美国学术和教育之父"的诺亚·韦伯斯特（Noah Webster，1758 – 1843）是一位虔诚的基督徒，也是一位加尔文主义者，他认为美国需要被基督教化。他一生出版了很多书，包括好几本很有影响力的教科书。1825 年他完成了《韦氏大词典》的出版，该书是英语世界中最大的词典，成为美式英语的标准词典。在这部大辞典中，韦伯斯特引用圣经来解释和定义大量的英语单词。透过他的词典，韦伯斯特逐渐把圣经观念灌输到美国英语中，其影响超越了过去任何一个人，也塑造了美国人的世界观。他的其他著作，如《拼字书》《文法书》等也通过无数引自圣经的格言和谚语，将圣经的道德伦理反复传递给读者，其中《拼字书》的发行量超过一亿本，影响巨大。韦伯斯特认为，离开圣经，教育将是毫无用处的。

　　另一位担任过弗吉尼亚大学教授和俄亥俄大学校长的美国学者威廉·麦高菲（William McGuffey，1800 – 1873）也是一位加尔文主义者，曾在长老会教会传道。他对美国文化最大的贡献就是撰写出版了《麦高菲读本》。该套读本 1836 年出版，是美国第一套和使用最广的教科书，在1836 至 1960 年间售出了一亿两千多万本，与圣经和《韦氏大辞典》同为发行量最多的书籍。麦高菲在编写这套读本时引用了许多不同的资料，但圣经及其神学构成了该书内容的基础，圣经经文常常出现在该书中。麦高菲相信上帝的道可以应用在生活的每一个层面，他的著作真实地反映了他的信念。他在书中的道德教导，背后的根据都来自圣经神学。圣经、《韦氏大辞典》和《麦高菲读本》深深影响了美国的教育与文化，使美国文化与基督教产生了密不可分的联系。

基督教信仰对美国文化影响巨大。虽然从 19 世纪中叶开始，欧洲世俗的思想和学术对美国文化的影响逐渐加强，但直到 20 世纪 60 年代，美国一直都被称为犹太—基督教文化的国家。美国人的身份认同也与基督教有密切的关系。谁是美国人？美国人就是热心宣教的白人基督新教教徒。

美国是一个移民组成的国家。20 世纪中叶以前，受移民配额的限制，美国的移民主要来自欧洲，来自世界其他地区的很少，而欧洲的主流文化是基督教，所以来自欧洲的移民在文化上并没有为美国带来很大的变化。当代美国文化的一个重要转变发生在 20 世纪 60 年代，与美国移民法的修改有关。1965 年美国修改了移民法，新的移民法规定，世界各地区每年移民美国的配额相等，这一移民政策极大地改变了美国的人口结构。新法通过后，来自亚洲、非洲、南美洲的移民大大超过欧洲的移民。在 20 世纪 50 年代，一半以上的移民来自欧洲，亚洲的移民只占 6%；到了 20 世纪 90 年代，欧洲的移民只有 16%，而亚洲的移民猛增到 31%。大量非欧洲移民的进入，使美国的文化景观产生了巨变。

我们知道，移民不仅是身体的转移，也是每个移民本身所承载的文化的转移。当非欧洲的移民来到美国时，他们同时也把非基督教的文化带入了美国。这些非基督教的文化通常也表现在宗教上。来自阿拉伯世界的移民带来了伊斯兰教，来自亚洲如泰国、缅甸、斯里兰卡、越南、中国等地的移民带来了佛教，来自印度的移民带来了印度教，此外，流传在世界各地形形色色的宗教也都在美国找到了安身之地。这些宗教所推崇的世界观、价值观和道德规范不仅影响着信仰这些宗教的新移民，并且也对美国的主流文化产生一定程度的影响。所以，当代美国文化很难再用以往所说的犹太—基督教文化来描述和概括了，美国文化也从以往基督教占压倒优势的文化转变为多元文化，美国已成为世界上文化最多元的国家。

二　当代美国文化的核心内涵

当代美国文化与传统美国文化有着密不可分的联系。当代文化是由传统文化发展而来的，并且继承了传统文化最核心的价值，这些价值理念仍然是当代文化的核心内涵。当代美国文化的涵盖面广，内容丰富多彩，本文仅就其核心内涵做一讨论。

纵观美国文化发展的进程，我们可以清楚地看到美国文化中的一个重要思想，那就是有神论。美国的早期居民主要是来自欧洲的殖民者，他们大多信仰基督教。基督教是最典型的有神论，相信有一位全能的上帝，创造了宇宙万物。美国的基督徒深受加尔文主义的影响，不仅相信上帝创造了世界，而且也相信上帝继续守护着世界，人类的历史发展、宇宙的千变万化都在上帝的引导和守护（Providence）之下。与欧洲的基督徒相比，美国的基督徒更强调上帝是世界的守护者，特别是美国的历史，从殖民开荒，到独立战争，到西进发展，再到"二战"后的世界第一强国，一直都有上帝的守护与引领，美国是蒙受上帝特别祝福的国家。这种上帝与美国同在的思想在美国文化中有着非常深厚的影响。美国国家最重要的历史文献之一——《独立宣言》，向全世界表明北美英属殖民地从英国统治下独立出来是依赖上帝的保佑。《独立宣言》的最后一段这样宣告："我们坚定地信赖上帝的保佑，同时以我们的生命、财产和神圣的名誉共同宣誓来支持这一宣言。"对于美国人来说，如果没有上帝的引导和守护、没有上帝的干预，当初他们从世界超级大国英国的统治之下独立出来几乎是不可能的。

美国建国之后，这种对上帝信赖的思想延续至今，一直都没有中断，并且在经历各种危机时都成为美国人的精神依靠。美国独立后，与英国的关系一直处于敌对状态中，终于在1812年爆发了美英战争。在战争期间，美国现在使用的国歌《星条旗永不落》被创作出来，四段歌词的最后一段写道："正义属于我方，我们一定得胜，'上帝是我们的信靠'，此语永矢不忘。""上帝是我们的信靠"逐渐演变为"我们信仰上帝"，成为了美国的国家格言，并被刻印在美国的货币上。美国南北内战时期，民众的宗教热情高涨，美国国会于1864年通过法案，允许财政部和铸币局把"我们信仰上帝"刻在美国的硬币上。1956年在冷战时期，为了与信奉无神论的前苏联区分开来，美国国会通过一项决议，宣告"我们信仰上帝"是美国的国家格言。随后，这个格言被印在了美国的纸币上。今天我们在各种面值的美钞和硬币上都能看到"我们信仰上帝"。2001年美国遭受"9·11"恐怖袭击后，美国各地的公立学校的教室、图书馆和餐厅里都张贴了"我们信仰上帝"的标语牌，许多公共建筑上和高速公路旁都竖起了"上帝保佑美国"的巨型标语，这一切都表明了在美国人的心灵深处的有神论信仰。2003年，美国的各大媒体和民意调查机构所做的民意调查显示，90%的美国民众支持把"我们信仰上帝"刻印在美国货币上。2006年和2011年，美国参众两院再次确定"我们信仰上帝"是美国的国家格言。今天，在一个文化多元化的美国，"我们信仰上帝"已经突破了原本基督教的语境，为其他宗教所接受。伊斯兰教的可兰经中有类似的教导，如"信靠你的主，信仰上帝、信仰祂的天使"等。印度教认为"我们信仰上帝"的格言提醒我们，"不管我们是否意识到，上帝都是无所不在的"，这正是印度教的信念。

美国文化的另一个核心内涵是对自由的追求。美国人常常把美国称为自由的国家或自由的土地，把自由看作人类的最高理想。美国国歌《星条旗永不落》的最后一句，把美国称为"自由之地，勇者之家"。在美国，到处都可以看到自由的字眼，人们用各种方式来表达对自由的推崇。提起美国，大家都会想起一些标志性的建筑，其中之一就是位于纽约的自由女神。为什么叫自由女神？为什么不叫理性女神？智慧女神？慈善女神？这与美国的历史，特别是追求自由的传统密切相关。17世纪初，最早从欧洲移民到北美大陆的殖民者中，有相当一部分的人是为了躲避欧洲的宗教战争和宗教迫害，到美洲大陆寻求宗教自由的。欧洲宗教改革期间，从欧洲各国的国教天主教中分离出来的基督新教各宗派都在不同程度上与天主教发生了冲突；在一些国家，比较激进的宗教改革者也与已成为国教的新教宗派发生了冲突。这些在欧洲各国没有取得合法地位且不为官方宗教所容忍的基督新教宗派，只能远走他乡去寻求宗教自由，其中不少受到迫害的宗派都来到了北美大陆。在最初北美的13个殖民地中，受到英国国教圣公会迫害的清教徒来到了东北部的新英格兰地区，同样受到英国圣公会迫害的贵格会来到了宾夕法尼亚和新泽西，在法国受到天主教迫害的胡格诺派来到了南卡罗来纳，在欧洲大陆受到天主教和其他新教宗派迫害的摩拉维亚弟兄会、门诺会和阿米什人来到了宾夕法尼亚。最有意思的是，在英国受到新教迫害的天主教也来到了马里兰。北美殖民地开始之初就充满了对自由的追求，"自由"这一理念深深地嵌入美国的文化和传统中。

与美国文化中的有神论密切相关，美国人认为人的自由是上帝所给予的，因此是神圣的。美国《独立宣言》写到，造物主赋予了人不可剥夺的权利，这些权利包括生存权、自由权、追求幸福的权利。位于洛杉矶的"森林草地"墓园中，有一面描绘美国历史的巨型壁画，上面写着一行大字："上帝给我们自由，离弃上帝的人失去他们的自由。"自由的神圣性在这里得到彰显。美国人非常崇尚和珍惜自由，甚至把自由看得比生命还重要，美国东北部的新罕布什尔州的机动车牌上的法定格言是"不自由毋宁死"（live free or die），正是这种文化传统的写照。18世纪下半叶，在遭受英国的压迫后，北美殖民地的人民认为他们的自由受到了侵害，如果不进行反抗，他们就会逐渐失去自由沦为英国的奴隶。为了捍卫自由，北美殖民地的人民不惜与英国一战，最终脱离了英国，获得了政治自由。美国建国之初，人们心中最大的恐惧就是新建立的美国联邦又成为欧洲各国那样的专制政权，人们离开欧洲来到新大陆千辛万苦争取到的自由又被剥夺。所以为了最大限度地保护人民的自由，美国建国时在设计政府框架时就最大限度地限制政府的权力，这就是美国实行三权分立的缘由。在美国，人民享有的受到保护的自由有时超出我们的想象，比如人民有拥有枪支的自由。虽然美国有时会发生滥用拥枪自由的枪击案，但拥枪自由的这项权利始终不能被取消或限制，究其原因就在于美国人认识到自由是要付出代价的，为了享有自由，付出代价也是值得的。

在讨论美国文化时，人们常常也把个人主义作为美国文化的内涵。实际上，美国人所说的个人主义指的主要是个性自由，以及对个人权利的追求和保护，与中国语境中所意指的追求个人利益的自私自利有着天壤之别。

美国文化还有一个非常重要的核心内涵，这就是平等。美国人所理解和崇尚的平等主要是在三个方面：上帝面前人人平等，法律面前人人平等，机会面前人人平等。美国《独立宣言》开宗明义：我们认为下述真理是不言而喻的：人人生而平等，造物主赋予他们若干不可剥夺的权利，包括生存权、自由权和追求幸福的权利。为什么人人生而平等？因为人是由上帝创造的，具有上帝的形象，应该受到尊重。我们前面提到过，美国文化中有强烈的有神论倾向，所以美国很多的重要理想和价值理念都与基督教信仰有关。基督教认为，上帝是宇宙万物包括人的创造者，人作为被创造者与创造者有着本质的差别。人与上帝是不可能平等的，因为一个是创造者，一个是被创造者。然而，作为被创造者的人在面对上帝时，面对超越者时，彼此之间却获得了一种平等，即大家都是被创造者，这就产生了一个非常重要且有意义的观念，即上帝之下人人平等。在这里，上帝的存在成为人人平等的参照坐标和基石，离开了上帝，人与人之间的平等就无从谈起。欧洲宗教改革运动期间，马丁·路德提出信徒人人皆祭司，每个人都可以直面上帝。这就使基督新教更在实践的层面落实了上帝面前人人平等的信念。早期从欧洲移民到北美大陆的主要是新教的信徒，基督教关于平等，特别是经由马丁·路德倡导的上帝面前人人平等的观念也就自然而然地植根于北美大陆了。

北美殖民地的人民大多经历过欧洲的专制统治，他们厌倦了那种反复无常的人治社会，所以在建立美国时努力把美国建设成一个法治的国家。在美国，统治这个国家的不是总统，不是国会，也不是任何党派，而是法律。宪法和法律具有崇高的尊严，每个人都要遵守法律，任何人包括总统和政府官员都不得超越法律之上，这样在法律面前就杜绝了特权阶级，实现了人人平等。法治社会的一个重要特点就是法律面前人人平等，不管一个人的种族、性别、肤色、宗教、身份、地位、健康怎样，在法律面前都是平等的，每个人的个人权利都受到平等的保护。美国法治社会的建立受到英国很大的影响。英国在1215年签署了《大宪章》，规定国王像所有的人一样都要遵守法律，不能凌驾于法律之上。这一法治的传统被早期的移民从英国带到了北美。

在美国，平等也表现为机会的平等，机会面前人人平等，这也是美国梦的主要内涵。美国梦是美国《独立宣言》宣告的"人人生而平等"的进一步表述,强调任何人都有平等的机会,通过自己的刻苦努力获得富足、成功和社会地位的提升。上帝之下的人人平等是一种起点上的平等,是一种基础性的表述,在美国的经验中则表现为每个人都可获得相同的机会和公共资源去拼搏和发展。机会平等在美国社会的一个重要表现就是就业机会的平等。几乎所有的美国公司、机构、学校、政府部门招聘,都要表明种族、性别、年龄上的平等,没有任何的歧视。如果在招聘空中服务人员的广告中出现只招收 25 岁以下的女性,一定会被人以年龄歧视和性别歧视告上法庭。机会的平等与发展结果的平均是不一样的概念。虽然大家都是站在同一条起跑线上,但由于每个人的能力、天赋、勤奋程度不同,最后的结果必然会不同,这个结果在很大程度上表现在财富和社会地位上。在美国,结果的不同主要是由个人因素造成的,并不是机会的不平等造成的。正像大家参加 100 米田径比赛,大家的起点和起跑时间是一致的、平等的,但比赛的结果必然不同,对于这个结果大家没有道理不接受,因为每个人都被给予了一个平等的机会。正是由于机会平等,在美国,很少有人会有仇富心理,大家都能接受通过自己的努力所取得的结果。

三　当代美国文化的特性

美国文化到 20 世纪 60 年代还是用犹太—基督文化来概括。1965 年美国移民法修改以后,随着欧洲以外地区移民的大量涌入,美国的人口结构开始发生重大改变,美国的文化也有了新的发展和变化。当代的美国文化虽然在核心内涵上与传统文化一脉相承,但也表现出了一些新的特性,这些特性主要有以下几个方面。

1. 多元性。当代美国文化的一个主要特点就是文化的多元性。美国从 20 世纪下半叶起,已经从一个基督教文化的国家进入一个多元文化的国家。这种变化的根本原因是美国人口结构的变化,即欧洲以外非基督教传统的移民的大量增加。非基督教传统的移民自然就把基督教以外的文化带入美国，这些文化的进入和存在使得美国的文化逐渐从基督教一种文化变为多种文化并存。目前在美国社会比较有影响的文化除了基督教文化外，还包括南美与墨西哥文化、伊斯兰教文化、佛教文化，以及印度教文化。饮食是文化的一种外在表现，如果从饮食上去观察，美国的多元文化就更为显著。在美国许多城镇的商业街上，你都能看到中餐馆、泰国餐馆、印度餐馆、意大利餐馆、墨西哥餐馆、日本餐馆……从 1780 年到 1970 年的近 200 年间，美国强调文化的大熔炉（melting pot），要求其他的文化都要与主流的基督新教文化相融合，使其他文化为基督新教文化所同化。从 1970 年开始，随着多元文化的出现，美国放弃了大熔炉的说法，转而使用沙拉碗（salad bowl）或马赛克的概念，即各种不同的文化在社会中都有自己独特的价值，应该保存自己的文化特色。虽然不同的文化混合在一起，但彼此保持自己的特性。就要一碗沙拉一样，虽然都在一个碗中，但不同的蔬菜仍然保持自己的形式和特色。

2. 开放性。当代美国文化表现出宽厚的开放性和包容性，如果没有这种开放性，文化的多元性是不可能的。美国文化的开放性与美国文化的核心价值—自由、平等，以及美国社会的法治精神有着密切的关系。建国之初，美国宪法第一修正案明确规定：国会不能立法去支持一种官方宗教，也不能阻止宗教的自由实践。这样，掌握公权力的政府就被排除在文化，特别是思想的自由运作之外。即政府不能去推广一种文化，也不能去禁止一种文化，这就为多元文化在美国的发展提供了肥沃的土壤。在欧洲的历史上，很多与各国的国教在信仰上有冲突的基督教小教派都被视为异端，受到国教（天主教或新教）和政权的迫害，这种情况在美国却很少发生。当今世界上基督教内影响最大的几个异端派别都产生在美国，如摩门教、耶和华见证人、基督教科学派，虽然他们遭受过其他基督教宗派的冲击，但政府都没有介入。在殖民地时期，新英格兰地区的一些基督新教人士如约翰·温斯罗普（John Winthrop）、罗杰·威廉姆斯（Roger Williams）都呼吁过宗教宽容，他们的呐喊和鼓吹，在思想上为美国文化的包容性打下了基础。美国文化的开放性也与美国对世界各地难民的人道主义庇护有关。美国是一个移民的国家，除了早期寻求宗教自由、政治自由的移民外，还有很多人由于天灾人祸、战乱动荡不得不逃离家乡到异国他乡寻求庇护，美国接纳了大量世界各地的难民。19 世纪时，爱尔兰人由于饥荒来到美国，德国人由于国内的革命逃到美国，亚美尼亚的基督徒为躲避伊斯兰教的迫害来到美国，墨西哥人也因着国内革命的动乱逃到美国，俄国的犹太人受到反犹主义的迫害来到美国。20 世纪中叶以后，由于战乱，难民从东南亚地区特别是越南和柬埔寨涌入美国，非洲的饥荒和战乱也把大量的难民送到了美国。美国接纳了来自不同文化的难民，也就要包容难民带来的不同文化。接纳难民的道义与勇气强化了美国文化的包容性。

3. 宗教性。当代美国多元文化实际上是美国多元宗教的表现，美国文化带有很强的宗教情结，各种文化现象的背后几乎都能看到宗教的影响。很多美国的文学作品、电影、动画、音乐、绘画、雕塑等，或包含宗教的内容，或受到宗教信仰的影响。宗教为美国的文学艺术既提供素材，又提供创作的灵感，彼此间有着千丝万缕的联系。塑造美国文化的宗教既包括传统的基督教，也包括伊斯兰教、佛教、印度教、新兴宗教，以及源自世界各地的形形色色的宗教。在思想、思维方式、价值观的层面上，多元宗教是多元文化的基础。在言论自由的美国，你会听到人们对各种事情的看法和评论，这些看法和评论基本上都与人们的宗教信仰有关，同时也是他们宗教信仰的表达。美国文化强烈的宗教性，与美国人口中信仰宗教的人数占压倒性的多数有关。美国著名的民意调查机构皮尤研究中心 2013 年的宗教信仰调查显示，美国各种宗教的信仰者占总人口的 88.9%，其中基督教的信仰者占总人口的 78.4%。庞大的宗教人口必然会把他们的宗教信念带入文化，在语音、思想、价值观、思维方式、生活方式等各个层面显示出来，这就使得美国的文化带有很强的宗教性。

4. 大众性。当代美国文化具有全民参与的大众性，也可以说，美国文化是一种全民参与的大众文化。这既与自由和平等的理念在美国被充分地张扬有关，也与早期欧洲移民的成分有关。17 世纪从欧洲特别是英国移民到北美新大陆的殖民者，或是在宗教上受到迫害的基督徒，或是在当地没有多少经济发展机会的普罗大众。从阶级上看，大部分都是社会上无权无势的平民阶层，或用今天的话说，草根阶层，很少有皇族、贵族移民到北美。这一背景，就使早期的移民没有多少等级的观念，大家都是新大陆的殖民者，都有相同的命运。美国建国时，为了避免重复欧洲的专制体制，创立了自治的民主政体，其基础就是平等，这在《独立宣言》中已经表述得非常清楚。所以在美国没有帝王的概念、没有贵族的概念，更多的是平民草根的气息。美国文化的大众性，在政治上表现为全民的政治参与，其典型就是以总统选举为主的各种选举，每一个人都有一张选票来影响国家的政治。美国的音乐很少像欧洲的音乐那样表现为精英音乐，如歌剧、宫廷音乐等，更多的是民众中的音乐，或草根风味的音乐，如爵士乐、摇滚乐、乡村音乐。美国文化大众性最明显的表现是在体育运动上，美国的体育运动是大众广泛参与的体育运动，而非集中训练极少数人的精英体育运动。在美国，每个学校、每个城镇都有众多的体育俱乐部，每个学生在读书期间都会参与一种以上的体育运动。任何的美国体育运动和比赛都是有众多粉丝参与的嘉年华，美国大众对体育运动的喜爱和参与达到了令人发狂的地步，这一点是每一个到过美国的人都会深深地感受到的。

5. 创造性。美国文化是一种鼓励创新和创造的文化，这一点在美国的科技创新和影视作品的创作上表现得最突出。美国的科技一直在世界上处于领先的地位，每年诺贝尔科学奖的奖项多数为美国科学家所得。美国科技创新的专利在世界上也是名列第一，遥遥领先于其他国家。以计算机为代表的当代科技成果中很多也是在美国发明创造的，如微软、英特尔等。近几年，苹果电脑和手机异军崛起，小小的一部苹果手机改变了全世界的生活方式。苹果的创意和理念都与美国文化的创造性有关。在影视作品中，美国一直不拘泥于历史和现实的题材，而是凭借丰富的想象和创造构思未来的场景。美国的银幕（屏幕）上很少出现历史古装剧，更多的是像《2012》《阿凡达》《后天》这样前瞻性的作品。在动画作品中，这种基于丰富想象力的创造性的作品就更多了，《猫和老鼠》《玩具总动员》《海底总动员》都是典型的范例。如果文化不具备创造性，这些经典的作品是根本无法构思出来的。美国文化深受基督教信仰的影响，基督教信仰中的一个重要教义就是创造论，认为上帝是宇宙万物的创造者，祂从无到有创造了世界，包括人；人具有上帝的形象，也具有创造的潜力。这种思想鼓励人去创造，因为创造的能力是上帝所赋予的。美国文化崇尚自由，自由也给予了每个人更大的空间去发挥自己的想象，这种不受约束的想象正是创造的基础。美国的历史比较短，也使美国人没有历史的包袱和羁绊，而把目光投向前方，培养出一种向前看的思维方式，而前方一无所有，需要的就是去创造。

四 美国文化面临的挑战

当代美国文化发展到今天，虽然在接纳和尊重外来文化、欣赏文化多元、促进种族和睦、构建和谐社会等方面都取得了很大的成就，但也遇到了前所未有的挑战。这些挑战也正是美国接纳、包容外来文化、倡导多元文化带来的。多元文化就像一把双刃剑，既对美国文化的丰富和繁荣有帮助，也会对原有的文化和社会结构带来损害。目前来看，当代美国文化遇到的挑战主要是在两个方面：

一是道德方面。美国社会的人际关系、公共秩序、信用制度等都是建立在基督教信仰的道德基础上，靠的是自觉和自律来维持。我们谈到美国是一个法治社会，统治这个国家的不是总统、国会或任何党派，而是法律。法律只是写在纸上的一些文字，怎么会有权威和效力呢？法律要产生作用必须要有人愿意去遵守。愿意自觉地遵守法律是一种道德，在美国主要为基督教道德。美国整个政治、社会体系的运转都是建立在基督教道德的基础上。美国第二任总统约翰·亚当斯认为美国的宪法只是为有道德和宗教信仰的民族制定的，它远远不足以管理任何其他民族。20世纪下半叶从欧洲以外的地区移民到美国的人大多没有基督教的信仰，很多人到了美国以后也没有认同和尊重基督教的价值观，将他们的文化与基督教文化进行必要的调整与适应，这样，他们的一些行为就对美国原有的道德造成了损害。比如，美国的报纸都是放在自动售报箱中出售，你投入一元钱，就可以打开报箱取出报纸。但有的新移民打开报箱后却取出两份，甚至更多份的报纸，拿去送给自己的朋友。这种做法就对美国长期以来行之有效的信用制度带来了伤害，也迫使售报方采取不信任人的方式来售报，人际关系被扭曲。在美国很多快餐店都是把饮料机放在餐厅里，向顾客敞开，由顾客自助取饮料，但有些新移民并没有在餐厅买饮料，却用自己带来的杯子装餐厅的饮料，引起大家的哗然。

二是社会安全方面。美国是一个崇尚自由的国家，也是一块自由的土地。在美国，自由的取得和维持也与基督教信仰有关。约翰·亚当斯认为基督教是维持美国自由体制的根基，他说：除非美国公民的道德行为以基督教的信条为引导，否则美国将难于维持自由体制。有些移民到美国的非基督教信仰者，不仅没有认同美国的主流价值，还利用美国自由、包容的环境从事一些恐怖活动，对美国社会的安全造成严重的危害，使个人和社会都付出了沉重的代价。2001年"9·11"事件以前，美国的机场是没有现在这样严格的安检程序和规定的，接送旅客的人可以直接到达登机口，旅客也可以把刀具、饮料带上飞机。但是恐怖分子利用美国自由与宽松的环境，劫持飞机制造恐怖，迫使政府不得不使用严格的安检方法检查每一个旅客，这一方面使个人的自由受到限制，另一方面也要多收纳税人的钱来维持安检，使个人和社会都造成了损失。2013年4月波士顿马拉松比赛时，两个来自俄罗斯的移民在人群中引爆自制炸弹，当场炸死3人、炸伤100多人，制造了震惊世界的恐怖事件。这两人都是车臣战乱的难民，受到美国人道主义的庇护，在美国已经生活了很多年，其中一人还宣誓成为美国公民。然而这两个人并不认同和尊重美国的价值观，反而恩将仇报，在社会上制造恐怖。这一事件让很多美国人开始检讨和反思他们的移民政策与推动文化多元的做法，对新移民也采取更加怀疑的态度，加剧了新老移民关系的紧张。

自由就像一个美丽但易碎的玻璃花瓶，如果没有精心的呵护，随时都可能被打碎。

参考文献

[1] 戴德理：《迟延的盼望：基督教与美国文化之探讨》，沈裕民译，台北：中福出

版有限公司，2003。

［2］于歌：《美国的本质：基督新教支配的国家和外交》，北京：当代中国出版社，2006。

［3］约翰·范泰尔：《良心的自由：从清教徒到美国宪法第一修正案》，张大军译，贵阳：贵州大学出版社，2011。

［4］彼特·里尔巴克：《自由钟与美国精神》，黄剑波、高民贵译，南昌：江西人民出版社，2010。

［5］道格拉斯·凯利：《自由的崛起：16~18世纪，加尔文主义和五个政府的形成》，王怡、李玉臻译，南昌：江西人民出版社，2008。

［6］布鲁斯·雪莱：《基督教会史》，刘平译，北京：北京大学出版社，2004。

［7］Nancy Koester, *The History of Christianity in the United States*. Minneapolis：Fortress Press, 2007.

［8］Douglas A. Sweeney, *The American Evangelical Story*. Grand Rapids：Baker Academic, 2005.

［9］Diana Eck, *New Religious America：How A " Christian Country" Has Become The World's Most Religiously Diverse Nation*. Harper San Francisco, 2002.

［10］Bruce David Forbes ed. , *Religion and Popular Culture in America*. Berkeley：University of California Press, 2000.

［11］John Berthrong, *The Divine Deli：Religious Identity in North American Cultural Mosaic*. New York：Orbis Books, 1999.

［12］Robert T. Handy, *A Christian America：Protestant Hope and Historical Realities*. Oxford University Press, 1984.

Contemporary American Culture and Its Characteristics

Wang Zhongxin

Abstract：American culture is the culture with greatest influence in the world. American culture influences the world with its political ideal, language, food and daring, entertainment and the way of life. The paper inquires the formation of American culture, its core value, characteristics and the challenge faced by it.

Keywords：America；culture；characteristics；challenge

当代中国文化的源流思考

强以华*

摘　要：中国当代文化有马克思主义文化、中国传统文化（主要是儒家文化）和市场经济文化三个源流。从客观描述的角度看，这三个源流经过一定时期的磨合虽然已经初步被整合成了统一的当代中国文化，但是，它们之间依然存在明显的妨碍整合的差异乃至矛盾；若是不能更好地整合当代中国文化的三个源流，必然不利于当代中国文化的进一步发展。为了更好地为整合当代中国文化的三个源流打下基础，我们必须从主观评价（价值判断）的角度分析当代中国文化的三个源流在整合中应该具有的不同地位，即从马克思主义文化到中国传统文化再到市场经济文化之重要性依次递减的地位顺序。

关键词：当代　中国文化　源流　整合

随着中国经济的快速发展并且在世界经济体系中的地位越来越高，中国文化发展的问题便越来越被提到更为显著的位置。为了更好地发展中国文化，除了采取各种更为有效的发展文化的措施之外，进一步加强当代中国文化自身的研究也是必不可少的题中应有之义，其中，一个十分重要的方面就是，我们必须弄清楚当代中国文化具有哪些主要源流，它们之间存在着什么关系，以及我们应该如何整合它们以使当代中国文化能够成为一种更为合理因而也更有生命力的文化。

---

* 强以华，湖北大学哲学学院教授、博士生导师。

一　源流

为了思考当代中国文化的源流，我们必须大致界定何谓当代中国文化。为此，我们首先应该界定何谓文化。从广义上说，一切人化的东西或者说一切打上了人的烙印的东西都是文化。从狭义上说，文化应是社会诸多系统中的一个子系统。我们可以从两个层面来看这一定义：其一，我们若把社会看成一个通过社会分工形成的"整合系统"，认为它由社会政治系统、社会经济系统、社会文化系统、社会军事系统等子系统组合而成，那么，文化便是这一整体社会系统中的一个由哲学、宗教、文学、艺术等在内的精神性的学科以及人们的精神活动构成的子系统；其二，我们若把社会看成一个通过物质文明系统、精神文明系统、制度文明系统和行为文明系统组成的"整合系统"，那么，文化便是这一整体文明系统中的一个由哲学、宗教、文学、艺术等在内的精神性的学科以及人们的精神活动构成的子系统。其实，广义的文化作为一切人化的东西，是狭义的精神性文化的体现与展开。这就是说，尽管广义的文化和狭义的文化属于两个层次的文化，但是，它们却有着内在的一致性，即狭义的文化是广义的文化之精髓，广义的文化乃是狭义的文化精神体现。文化作为一个重要的范畴、作为一个中心概念首次被英国人类学家爱德华·泰勒在其 1871 年出版的著作《原始文化》中提了出来。泰勒把文化解释为一个复杂的整体，认为它包括了知识、信仰、艺术、道德法律、风俗，以及作为社会成员的个人而获得的任何能力与习惯。这里，他的文化定义其实就是狭义的文化定义。在本文中，我们也从狭义的角度理解文化。其次，在我们确定了何谓文化之后，进一步通过加上"当代"和"中国"两个定语来界定当代中国文化。当代是一个时间概念，我们把当代理解为 20 世纪中叶以后尤其是改革开放以后。需要注意的是，当代作为一个时代概念必须受到另外一个空间概念"中国"的限制，以便表明它是"中国的"当代；中国则是一个空间概念，我们把中国理解成为中华人民共和国，它是一个以汉民族为中心的由多民族组成的属于中华民族的地域。需要注意的是，中国作为一个空间概念必须受到时间的限制，以便表明中国是"当代的"中国。因此，当代中国文化就是 20 世纪中叶以后尤其是改革开放以后逐渐形成并且蓬勃发展的中华民族的精神文化（文明）系统，它主要由包括哲学、宗教、文学、艺术等在内的精神性的学科以及人们的精神活动构成。

从本文所讨论的当代中国文化的定义出发，当代中国文化究竟包含了哪些主要源流呢？大致来说，当代中国文化包含了三个方面的主要源流：其一，马克思主义文化。马克思主义文化是一个发展的概念，它在以马克思主义经典文化为主要内容的基础上演变成了一种中国化了的马克思主义文化。这就是说，在当代中国文化中，马克思主义文化虽然指的是传统（即马恩列斯时代）的马克思主义文化并且确实保留了传统的马克思主义文化的基本原理，但是，它更包含了中国共产党根据中国社会发展的具体情况，以及当代世界演变的具体情况对于这些基本原理所进行的补充、发挥，乃至必要的修正和删除。其二，中国传统文化。中国传统文化是一个笼统的概念，它主要指的是儒家文化。在中国的历史上，儒家文化的主流文化地位并不影响其他一些文化特别是与儒家文化具有互补作用（儒道互补）的道家文化和外内关系（外儒内法）的法家文化在中华民族文化中的重要而显赫的地位，但是，在当代，道家文化和法家文化的地位大为逊色，并且不能成为当代中国文化的主要源流。究其原因，除了当代中国文化的成分发生了巨大变化之外，道家文化和法家文化自身的文化特征也受到挑战。在中国的历史上，道家文化主要体现在私人亦即非统治者的文化中，尤其体现在失意文人和官僚阶层地位弱化之后的私人生活中，它表达了顺其自然、伴山乐水、自然悠闲的生活态度，但是，当代中国社会是市场经济社会，节奏快，竞争激烈，道家的那种生活态度已经不能适应这种社会的发展需要。至于法家文化，由于当代中国的性质所决定的法制与作为一种封建社会的法制完全不同，所以，当代的法制文化必然要淘汰法家文化。正因为如此，作为当代中国文化源流的传统文化主要就是儒家文化。其三，市场经济文化。市场经济文化是在经济改革中从发达市场经济国家引入并经过发挥的文化概念。市场经济作为一种自由竞争的经济运行方式，在传统上与资本主义制度相联系，但是，当引入中国后，它也成了一种属于社会主义制度的文化，亦即社会主义市场经济文化。尽管根据中国的理解，社会主义市场经济和资本主义市场经济不同，但是，由于都是市场经济，并且社会主义的市场经济总要借鉴西方资本主义国家发达的市场经济的发展经验，所以，社会主义市场经济与资本主义市场经济总有一致之处。相应的，社会主义市场经济文化与资本主义市场经济文化也有一致之处。

我们确定当代中国文化的源流，并非对当代中国文化的价值取舍，而是一种客观判断。这就是说，在确定当代中国文化的源流时，我们并不出于任何好恶对不同的文化源流进行选择，而仅仅是从客观上描述当代中国文化中哪些文化因素"事实上"属于主要成分，并且指出它们来自何处。

二 描述

"描述"指不带任何主观价值情感的客观描述。我们这里要描述的是当代中国文化的三种主要源流之间的差异关系。毫无疑问，马克思主义文化作为从西方引进的文化与中国传统文化已经过了长达100多年的磨合，并且市场经济文化随着中国社会的改革开放也和马克思主义文化（作为中国化了的马克思主义文化）以及中国传统文化经过了几十年的磨合，它们之间肯定存在着一致性，但是，我们认为，尽管如此，它们之间依然存在着很大的不一致性，如果对这种不一致性（差异）没有十分清晰的认识，不能对其进行厘清、辨别和判断，以便更好地将其整合为有机统一的当代中国文化，那么，我们就难以更为有效地发展当代中国文化，提升当代中国文化建设的水平。

首先，我们描述马克思主义文化与中国传统文化（主要指儒家文化）之间的差异。从起源的角度说，马克思主义文化诞生于近代西方工业社会，中国传统文化诞生于古代中国农业社会，这种诞生地点、时间以及由时间（时代）所决定的社会性质的不同导致了它们之间产生了三点主要差异。其一，民族的差异。民族的差异是指中华民族的文化和西方社会的文化之间的差异。其二，发展程度的差异。发展程度的差异是指工业社会的文化和农业社会的文化的差异。其三，性质的差异。性质的差异是指社会主义的文化和封建主义的文化的差异。当然，以上三种区别仅仅局限于文化起源的角度，其中，民族的差异属于最大的差异，其次是发展程度的差异，至于性质的差异则比较复杂。中国已经进入了社会主义社会，就此而言，中国传统文化已经具有了社会主义文化的特征。另外，由于中国社会正处于农业社会向工业社会的过渡之中，有些地方还有很强的农业社会文化的痕迹，农业社会文化或多或少都会夹杂某些寓于传统文化中的封建文化因素。所以，这里需要关注的恰好是与马克思主义文化有所差别的中国传统文化中的某些封建文化的因素。我们认为，在当代中国文化中，以上以不同的程度存在着的三种差异相互交织，并以发展程度的差异亦即工业社会的文化和农业社会的文化的差异影响最大。从马克思主义文化的角度看，马克思主义文化产生于工业社会，当代中国社会正在快速地日益从农业社会走向工业社会甚至后工业社会，尽管农业社会和后工业社会的因素在当代中国或多或少地依然存在，但是，从总体来看，当代中国社会应该属于工业社会。从农业社会的因素看，它属于正在被工业社会超越的因素，相对于这些因素，马克思主义文化作为诞生于工业社会的文化体现了它的先进性。从后工业社会的因素看，它属于超越工业社会的因素，由于中国的马克思主义文化一直自觉地随着社会的发展而发展，所以，相对于这一情况，马克思主义文化作为诞生于工业社会的文化体现了它的发展性。从中国传统文化的角度看，中国传统文化产生于农业社会，尽管中国传统文化一直随着社会的发展而发展，但是，中国从农业社会向工业社会过渡主要还是改革开放以后的情况，尽管这一过渡速度很快并且接近甚至已经完成，但是它的过渡时间很短。文化作为一种精神现象它的相对稳定性要远远大于物质现象，再加上迄今为止学界很少认真系统地探讨过中国传统文化如何由农业社会的文化向工业社会的文化转型的问题，所以，在很大程度上说，中国传统文化主要还是农业社会的文化。由此可见，就发展程度而言，马克思主义文化与中国传统文化有着很大的差异，并且这些差异与民族的差异和性质的差异相互交织，进一步增加了整合它们使之成为一种有机的当代中国文化的难度。

其次，我们描述马克思主义文化与市场经济文化之间的差异。马克思主义文化与市场经济文化之间的最大差异是意识形态差异。从传统（马克思主义创始人）的观点来看，马克思主义文化属于一种无产阶级的意识形态，市场经济文化则由于市场经济属于资本主义意识形态下的产物而在一定的意义上可以视为资产阶级的意识形态。具体地说，在马克思主义文化的创始人看来，资本主义社会是生产资料私人所有制社会，在这种社会制度下，占有生产资料的人（通常通过企业）成为生产什么、如何生产以及生产多少的决定者，他们根据在市场竞争中形成的价格因素做出自己生产什么、如何生产和生产多少的决定。这样一来，马克思主义文化的创始人把市场经济看成资本主义社会制度下特有的东西，从而使得市场经济文化带有了意识形态特征。马克思主义文化创始人进一步认为，资本主义的生产资料私有制以及与其相关的市场经济带来了局部生产的有计划性和整个生产的无政府状态之间的矛盾，正是这种矛盾的存在，才导致资本主义周期性的经济危机，并且正是由于这种矛盾无法克服，才需要社会主义乃至共产主义代替资本主义，社会主义乃至共产主义之所以必然代替资本主义的理由在于：社会主义社会能以基于生产资料公有制形式下的计划经济取代资本主义社会基于生产资料私有制形式下的市场经济从而达到消除资本主义社会生产资料私有制所导致的局部生产有计划性和整个社会生产无政府状态之间的矛盾，促进生产力的发展。然而，在改革开放的实践中，中国提出了社会主义市场经济这一概念，把社会主义与市场经济联系起来，从而修正了市场经济为资本主义所特有的经济运行方式的传统说法，并且使得市场经济成为社会主义经济运行方式的一个部分。这一修正使得市场经济文化不能简单地被看成资本主义意识形态的一个部分。然而，中国社会依然在一定意义上把市场经济文化打上了意识形态烙印，这种烙印的表现形式就是它把自己的市场经济称为社会主义市场经济，意在表明自己的市场经济与资本主义的市场经济之间存在着某种区别。但是，社会主义市场经济与资本主义市场经济作为"市场经济"，它们依然存在着本质上的一致性，既然如此，那么，马克思主义文化作为社会主义的文化，它就或多或少与市场经济文化有着差异，若不能区别并且有效弥补这种差异，那么，中国就难以真正建立"中国的社会主义市场经济文化"并且把它有机地融入包括马克思主义文化在内的当代中国文化。

最后，我们描述中国传统文化与市场经济文化之间的差异。市场经济作为一种经济运行方式，诞生于工业社会（也是资本主义社会），它是工业社会乃至后工业社会中显示效率的一种经济运行方式，与其相应，市场经济文化也是工业社会（也是资本主义社会）乃至后工业社会所特有的文化。中国传统文化诞生于中国传统的农业社会，如前所述，它并未随着中国由农业社会向工业社会转型而自觉地随之转型，而是还带有很强的农业社会的痕迹，所以，中国传统文化与市场经济文化依然有着十分巨大的差异。例如，自由放任（即让生产者决定生产什么、如何生产、生产多少）是市场经济的基本特征，它要求参与市场活动的人都是独立、自由、平等的人，它鼓励人的自由竞争，并且通过法律制度、互订契约来保证市场竞争的有序进行，由此出发，市场经济文化衍生出了诸如独立精神、自由精神、平等精神，以及竞争精神、法制精神、契约精神等一系列体现近现代社会特征的人文精神。显然，带有农业社会痕迹的中国传统文化在此方面有所欠缺，即使在表面上有时零散地表现出其中的某种精神，也缺乏现代意义。

三　分析

"分析"指带有主观价值判断的分析。我们曾说，若要当代中国文化能够更好地发展，我们必须更好地整合当代中国文化的主要源流，使之成为更为融洽的有机整体。在既定的框架内——亦即仅在我们以上客观描述的在事实上已经主要存在的当代中国文化三种主要源流的范围之内——进行思考，我们试图为这三种主要源流理出价值地位的顺序，以便能够更为有效地发展当代中国文化，我们必须在厘清当代中国文化三种源流的基础上更好地整合当代中国文化的不同源流，使之成为有机整体。然而，这是一项十分巨大的工程，我们这里并不想去从事这一巨大的工程，我们只想对既定（强调"既定"就是我们暂且把当代中国文化的已有源流看成一个封闭系统，这丝毫不意味着我们排斥其他优秀的文化源流的注入）的当代中国文化的三种主要源流进行价值分析和价值评估，确定它们的价值顺序，以便为它们更好的整合提供基础。

为了能够更合理地为马克思主义文化、中国传统文化和市场经济文化三种主要文化源流进行价值排序，我们首先必须明确当代中国社会的现实定位，看看这些文化源流在当代中国的现实定位中占有何种位置，以便为这些文化源流的价值排序提供思考依据。中国的领导者把当代中国社会定位为"具有中国特色的社会主义社会"。这里，我们发现了两个关键词，一个是"中国特色"，另外一个则是"社会主义社会"。如果认真辨析，中国特色这一关键词还可进一步分为"中国"和"特色"两个关键词。我们知道，社会主义三大改造以后，中国社会开始进入社会主义时期。这时，中国所理解的社会主义是一种"一般的社会主义"，也就是说，它所理解的社会主义是源自马克思主义创始人并且与其他社会主义国家（例如苏联）的社会主义没有区别的社会主义；改革开放以后，中国为了强调中国的社会主义与一般的社会主义的区别，或者说为了强调中国的社会主义是"一般的社会主义"在中国的"特殊"体现，在中国的社会主义之前加上了"中国特色"的字样。"中国特色"主要强调的是中国的社会主义区别于其他国家的社会主义的特殊之处。就此而言，"中国特色"仅仅与中国的社会主义性质相关。但是，细究起来，我们可以从两个方面来理解"中国特色"，即一方面，我们把中国特色理解成中国的社会主义具有"中国"的特点，这里，中国的特点侧重强调的是中国传统的特点，从文化的角度看，这里的中国特色应该具有中国传统文化之意，并且"中国"二字更能表达这一意思；另一方面，我们把中国特色理解成中国的社会主义具有"市场经济"的特点，因为中国改革开放以后提出"中国特色的社会主义"的主要原因就是中国当时要在计划经济体制中引入市场经济体制，从而建立中国的社会主义市场经济体系，它有别于一般（传统）乃至其他一些社会主义国家关于社会主义的理解，因此，市场经济应是中国特色的题中应有之义。从文化的角度看，这里的中国特色应该具有市场经济文化之意，并且"特色"

二字更能表达这一意思。因此，我们若把"马克思主义文化"看成与"社会主义社会"相对应的文化的话，那么，我们就把"中国传统文化"和"市场经济文化"看成与"中国特色"相对应的文化。更细致地说，我们还可以把"中国传统文化"与"中国特色"中的"中国"二字对应起来，并把"市场经济文化"与"中国特色"中的"特色"二字对应起来。这样一来，从当代中国的现实定位（"具有中国特色的社会主义社会"）出发，恰好包含了当代中国的三种主要文化源流，即马克思主义文化、中国传统文化和市场经济文化。

根据我们对当代中国社会现实的定位，我们可以从形式和内容两个方面来为当代中国文化的三种主要源流亦即马克思主义文化、中国传统文化和市场经济文化作价值排序。

首先，从形式上来分析。所谓从形式上分析，就是从"具有中国特色的社会主义社会"这一当代中国的现实定位之"表述形式"来进行分析。我们发现，在"具有中国特色的社会主义社会"这一表述中，如果将这一表述理解成包含两个关键词即"中国特色"和"社会主义社会"的表述的话，那么，"中国特色"仅仅是一个定语，只有"社会主义社会"才是被修饰的中心词，它构成了这一定位的核心。因此，从形式上看，与"社会主义社会"相连的"马克思主义文化"应该属于价值地位最高的文化。此外，我们还可以把"中国特色"这一关键词拆分为"中国"和"特色"两个关键词，对于"当代中国文化"来说，尽管中国应该是特色的定语，但是，该词的重心在中国上，"特色"所表达的仅仅是附着于"中国"的一种特色，"中国"这一概念显然比"特色"这一概念具有更加重要的价值地位。这一情形表明：与"中国"相连的"中国传统文化"在价值地位上应该高于与"特色"相连的"市场经济文化"。

其次，从内容上来分析。所谓从内容上分析，就是从当代中国文化的三种主要文化源流在当代中国文化中的重要程度来进行分析。毫无疑问，从内容上进行分析的基本依据依然是当代中国现实社会的定位亦即"具有中国特色的社会主义社会"的规定。从内容上说，社会主义和中国传统都是涉及一个社会整体的规定，它们关涉到一个国家人民的整体生活，能从整体上将人民的生活变成美好的生活或者不好的生活。就此而言，它们对于人民的美好生活应该具有目的价值。"马克思主义文化"和"中国传统文化"分别作为与"社会主义"和"中国传统"相连的文化，它们也是涉及社会和人民之生活整体的具有目的价值的文化。市场经济并不涉及一个社会的整体规定，尽管市场经济会渗透到社会整体的各个方面，但是，就其自身来说，依然只涉及社会整体的一个方面亦即经济运行方式方面，它主要（并不局限于）从社会物质福利方面有助于人民的美好生活。就此而言，它对于人民的美好生活应该只有工具价值。据此，我们便可以说，市场经济文化作为一种主要涉及社会和人民生活局部方面的文化，只是一种具有工具价值的文化。毫无疑问，目的价值高于工具价值，因此，在更好地整合当代中国文化的三种主要源流的时候，应该以马克思主义文化和中国传统文化为主导。此外，尽管马克思主义文化和中国传统文化都是涉及社会与人民生活整体的具有目的价值的文化，但是，在它们之间也同样具有价值程度区分。根据"具有中国特色的社会主义社会"的现代社会定位，社会主义决定了中国现实社会的性质，所以，社会主义以及与社会主义相连的马克思主义文化"应该"具有更高的价值地位。但是，尽管如此，中国社会主义社会依然是"中国的"社会主义社会，从逻辑上说，"中国"应是一个比社会主义更基本的概念，并且，从历史延续的角度看，正是中国传统文化使中国成为中国，并使中国人成了中国人。那么，在当代中国社会中，究竟马克思主义文化具有最为重要的价值地位还是中国传统文化具有最高的价值地位呢？我们认为，中国传统文化确是中国文化之根，但是，中国传统文化作为中国文化之根，只有随着时代的进步而不断进步才能保持自己的活力，也才能具有成为中国文化之根的资格。在既定的当代中国文化的框架内，马克思主义文化是一种更新的时代文化（市场经济文化也是如此），只有把这种更新的时代养料注入中国传统文化才能为中国传统文化引进新的时代养料，确保中国传统文化具有"传统"地位。因此，在当代中国社会中，马克思主义应该具有更为重要的价值地位。从长远看，若是马克思主义文化彻底融入中国传统文化，那么，马克思主义文化或许将成为中国传统文化的一个有机部分。

有了当代中国文化三种主要源流的价值排序，我们就有了更好地整合这三种主要文化源流的良好基础，最终也就有了更好地发展当代中国文化的良好基础。当然，我们对当代中国文化三种主要源流进行价值排序一点儿也不意味着我们认为排在后面的文化源流是不重要的源流。恰恰相反，我们依然十分重视它们的价值地位。例如，在当代中国文化中，"市场经济文化"作为一种在价值排序中处于最后的文化源流，我们依然认为它是一种地位十分重要的文化。其实，马克思主义在当代的发展和中国传统文化在当代的革新一点儿也不能离开市场经济的文化，市场经济文化所包含的一些特有的人文精神（法制精神、契约精神等）应该是马克思主义文化发展和中国传统文化革新不得不借鉴和吸纳的宝贵财富。

The Origins of Contemporary Chinese Culture

Qiang Yihua

Abstract：Contemporary Chinese culture has three origins as Marxism, traditional culture and the culture of market economy. Objectively speaking, the three origins have been intergrated into one current Chinese culture. However, there are still differences and contradictions among them and they need to be further united. We should analyze the different positions of different origins from the perspective of value judgement, i. e. , the order of importance is decreasing from Marxism to traditional culture and the culture of market economy.

Keywords：contemporary；Chinese culture；origin；intergration

当代中国主流审美文化问题研究

赵红梅[*]

摘　要： 当代中国主流审美文化是对传统主流审美文化的一种反叛与否定，在把握当代中国主流审美文化概念的基础上，本文指出了当代中国主流审美文化存在的主要问题，并在此基础上，尝试提出了化解当代主流审美文化问题的策略。

关键词： 当代中国　审美文化　策略

戴维·斯沃茨认为："文化为人类的交流与互动提供了基础，它同时也是统治的一个根源。艺术、科学以及宗教——实际上，所有的符号系统，包括语言本身——不仅塑造着我们对于现实的理解、构成人类交往的基础，而且帮助确立并维持社会等级。"[①] 一句话，国家文化是国家权力的体现。作为四大文明古国之一的传统中国，通过伦理型的家国一体文化——"君君、臣臣、父父、子子"，向世界展示了中国的封建等级制度及金字塔式的权力结构。传统中国审美文化同样注重等级尊卑的言说。宗白华先生认为，中国古代艺术的"第一个方向是礼教的、伦理的方向。三代钟鼎和玉器都联系于礼教，而它的图案画发展为具有教育及道德意义

---

* 赵红梅，湖北大学政法与公共管理学院教授。

① 〔美〕戴维·斯沃茨：《文化与权力——布尔迪厄的社会学》，陶东风译，上海世纪出版集团，2012，第1页。

的汉代壁画（如武梁祠壁画等），东晋顾恺之的女史箴，也还是属于这范畴"。① 中国的居住文化更多与伦理道德有关。同是讲中轴线，在西方人那里是几何图形，法国的凡尔赛宫就是追求"数的和谐"的典范，而北京故宫，午门和太和、中和、保和三殿序列就是为了在朝贺时表现统治者在"万人之上"的尊严而设计的。

当代中国主流审美文化是对传统主流审美文化的一种反叛与否定。本文的目的是：通过审美文化的体验与研究，通过直面各种"非主流"，细观主流与"非主流"的交融与碰撞，将渗透于现实生活中的个体审美情绪提升为群体审美情感，判别当代中国审美文化主流取向，剥离出当代中国审美文化主流新内核，铸就转型期中国人的审美理性。也就是说从感性世界入手、从基层说起，凝练中国主流审美文化价值取向，并在一定程度上从思维方式的角度回归中国审美文化传统。本文的内容主要包括：遍观当代中国主流审美文化诸现象，拿捏当代中国审美文化的主要问题，提出中国审美文化病症的解决策略。

一　当代中国主流审美文化概念的把握

（一）审美文化

改革开放之后，中国人致力于小康社会建设。如今，中国人的温饱问题基本得到解决。古人云：饥寒起盗心，饱暖思淫欲。按照马斯洛的需要层次论，人在生理需要满足后，就会欲求自我设计、自我实现等自由境界，就会寻求自我的精神皈依。在中国，物质欲求基本得到满足之后，安身立命之学成了文化研究的至高目的，修身齐家治国平天下的文化传统与文化治国策略在一定程度上也决定了文化研究热的诞生。学者周宪指出："现在国内不少大学开设了文化研究课程，也出版了不少文化研究方面的译著、专著和教材。从总体上说，文化研究的中国语境早

---

① 宗白华：《美学与意境》，人民出版社，2009，第241页。

已形成，但文化研究的中国问题和中国视角似乎还没有得到深入的讨论。"① 其实，文化研究的中国化就是现实化，文化研究的中国问题和中国视角就是指文化研究要从具体文化现象、从具体文化问题切入，走向现实，踏地而生。

20 世纪 90 年代，中国掀起了审美文化热。审美文化的厘定成了文人学者首先要讨论的话题。有学者认为，审美文化即大众文化；有学者认为，审美文化即当代文化；有学者认为，审美文化是具有审美属性或审美价值的文化；有学者认为，审美文化是整个文化发展的高级形式，是把审美原则贯穿于人们的社会日常生活的产物；有学者认为，审美文化是文化系统中的审美层面。笔者认为，审美文化，即通过审美现象体现出来的文化精神，或文化品位通过审美现象呈现出来。

审美文化的兴起是时代前进的一种必然，是工具人、经济人、理性人走向审美人、道德人的一种标志。新中国成立后，国内阶段斗争突出，狠抓私字一闪念。20 世纪五六十年代，人的个性被束缚，美学讨论成为阶段斗争的场所，美在现实生活中成为一种被规避或嘲弄的对象，活下来成为许多人的梦想。20 世纪 80 年代，随着改革开放的到来，全国上下以经济建设为中心，人的本性在一定程度上复苏，逐利基础上人的性格的复杂性被认可，人物性格复合论成为学术讨论的时尚话题。美学迎来了学术上的大开放，中西美学观念交锋与碰撞激烈。20 世纪 90 年代后，受金钱主义、消费主义的影响，文化产业规模日益扩大，美走下神坛来到现实生活中，审美文化逐渐成为经济发展的一大亮点。21 世纪伊始，国内有关审美文化的书迭出。美学生活化或生活美学化日益成为中上层的鹄的。

（二）主流审美文化

主流审美文化是相对于"非主流"审美文化而言的，主流审美文化的标志是占据时代前台，成为公认的、达成共识的主旋律的审美文化。主流审美文化立足于基本价值观念，如高贵典雅、古拙自然、里仁为美。但

---

① 陶东风、周宪：《文化研究》（第 8 辑），广西师范大学出版社，2008。

一个时代的主流审美文化必有其价值核心。20 世纪五六十年代的中国主流审美文化推崇崇高和英雄主义，"那是一种极其亢奋的、狂飙突进式的崇高审美心态，是一种真诚、热烈、夸张和'万众同声'时代审美风尚"。① 随着 20 世纪 80 年代的改革开放，欧风美雨再次倾泻在中国大地上，伴随着暴风雨式启蒙的是"痛苦、艰巨、危难、严峻、动荡、恐怖以及挫折、斗争、反抗"。② 受市场经济大潮的影响，20 世纪 90 年代的中国主流审美文化走向对物质的崇拜，长期以来居于文化正堂（政治晕轮下）的高雅、严肃的审美文化日益通俗化、大众化，经济尺度导向下的消费主义逐渐崭露头角。21 世纪伊始，审美文化左冲右突，竭力摆脱市场这双"大手"，在以政治为中心、以经济为中心之后走向"以文化为中心"的痛苦剥离、回归文化本位的征程。审美文化再次觉醒！人性解放再次被提到前台！

主流审美文化诞生有其标识物：其一，审美文化教材进高校，学校通过审美普及教育，培养与铸就中国人的审美情趣、审美意识；其二，出版一系列审美文化方面的研究成果，通过权威期刊及研究专著占据宣传"制高点"；其三，举办有关主流审美文化的国际国内研讨会，吸引更多学者关注主流审美文化。目前，有关主流审美文化的研究文章及专著并不丰盛，再次形成主流审美文化（审美迷失后）还要假以时日。

（三）当代中国主流审美文化

当代中国，计划经济与市场经济的碰撞、社会的转型再一次引发了文化上的"地震"。当代中国主流审美文化从审美的角度展现了中国人文化情趣的演变。可以说，当代中国主流审美文化正处于重建与整合中，经过 30 余年的震荡，以崇高为主流的中国审美文化、审美理想和审美趣味裂为碎片，曾经经典的不再经典，曾经流行的不再流行，三无作品压倒中心人物、中心情节、中心主题，调侃、戏谑、反讽成为"周末大餐"。"脑

---

① 陶东风、金元浦：《从碎片走向建设》，《文艺研究》1994 年第 5 期。
② 陶东风、金元浦：《从碎片走向建设》，《文艺研究》1994 年第 5 期。

震荡"就是当代中国主流审美文化的观感印象。

目前，各种审美现象繁盛，"非主流"与主流并存争锋。消费文化空前繁荣，政治文化极度萎缩。"大众消费文化或娱乐文化一头独大，占据了文化地盘的至少一半以上。"[①] 一个是精英领导的推崇崇高的英雄主义走悲剧路线，一个是大众引领的推崇快适的快乐主义走喜剧路线。尤其是网络世界的到来，传媒文化的网络化使大众参与进入狂热与非理性阶段。20世纪80年代流行的审美——道德主义批判话语和批判范式明显"out"了，而新的审美与批评范式在形成中。

在一个"Let it be"的世界里，网络成了人们最亲密的伙伴，"网络文化/文学的积极面是大众化与民主化，但它的消极面就是泥沙俱下，所谓'网络排泄'"。[②]"无思想""无主体""无灵魂"的计算机、手机及其思维模式逐渐渗透到人的生活的方方面面。而计算机的美学精神在于娱乐大众、提供便利与消费。"进门易、出门难"（易进入，难辨别）的网络世界牢牢地控制与影响着审美理念刚刚萌生的青春期孩子，网络世界的虚拟性及网络世界的种种缺失其实是在"拿青春做赌注"。本性天然的学生群的自由审美理念受控于计算机编程世界的干扰，中国审美文化原有的十分明显的正统亦"主线"受到世俗网络世界的冲击，化为斑驳陆离的审美取向。

当代中国主流审美文化重建于危难之时，多途径恢复人的丰富感性是其重要一环，而审美正在途中。

二　当代中国主流审美文化存在的主要问题

当代审美文化的产生与时代的进步、美学的泛化密切相关，当代中国审美文化关注审美理论与现实生活的"融合点"，立足于人的感性生活领

[①]　陶东风：《无聊的嬉戏：去精英化时代的大众娱乐文化》，载陶东风、和磊著《文化研究》，广西师范大学出版社，2008，第9页。

[②]　陶东风：《无聊的嬉戏：去精英化时代的大众娱乐文化》，载陶东风、和磊著《文化研究》，广西师范大学出版社，2008，第12页。

域，着眼于人的衣食住行，追求审美生活化。也就是说从美学的维度引导人的现实生活、提升人的审美品位，使人成为审美的人、道德的人。当代中国审美文化主流与传统审美文化主流的最大不同，是当代中国审美文化主流正处于与"非主流"纠绞的转型期，当代中国审美文化呈现出一种裂变无主的状态。

其一，去精英化、去政治化，追逐娱乐文化。

公民社会注重公共精神与公共道德，公民社会注重价值观念的普世性与一致性。公民是当代中国实现法治、德治的人性基础。而大众则不同，大众指的是大多数人，大众以数量取胜，他们在价值观念上推崇"无争辩"。由大众到公民需要严格的启蒙与教化，面对审美活动，"大众社会需要的不是文化，而是娱乐"。[①] 当下中国社会是大众狂欢的时代，娱乐文化应时而生，娱乐文化迎合大众的需要，竭力释放人的种种欲望。娱乐文化的兴盛在一定程度上消解了政治至上的审美文化的严肃性、权威性，政治化、道德化的审美文化与娱乐文化分道扬镳，大众娱乐文化盛行一时。娱乐文化在给我们带来诸种快感时如"潘多拉"盒子一样给人类社会的治理带来了破坏性因素。"'去精英化'的趋势是和'去政治化'的趋势同时出现、齐头并进的……大众传播媒介的普及和文化活动的'去精英化'虽然极大地降低了公共文化空间的准入门槛，却没有能够提升公共文化空间的政治质量。"[②] "去政治化"在一定意义上就是"去精英化"。"学而优则仕"的政治文化其实就是贵族精英文化。"去精英化"是对传统审美文化的极大反动，当然也是对传统政治主导的审美文化的一种批驳。官方—精英—大众"三分天下"的审美文化格局被娱乐文化所强逼，审美文化面临范式的转换。

其二，从"去个性化"到"个性化"。

在西方传统审美文化中，"文人成为占据领导地位的政治人物，因为

---

① Hannah Arendt：*Between Past and Future：Eight Exercises in Political Thought*，New York：Penguin Books，1977，p. 205.

② 陶东风：《无聊的嬉戏：去精英化时代的大众娱乐文化》，载陶东风、和磊著《文化研究》，广西师范大学出版社，2008，第 13 页。

他们说话带有权威性，尽管他们事实上没有在政府中担任职务"。① 在中国，天地君亲师、尊师重教成为一种美德。20 世纪 80 年代以后，随着国门的打开以及市场经济的繁荣，中国人的文化口味也逐渐发生了变化。

西方文化、港台文化、日本文化等文化浪潮汹涌，"花式文化大餐"不断呈现于中国文化的表演舞台，中国传统审美文化中占据统治地位的集体主义、整体主义、权威主义不断萎缩与后退。崇高的受到嘲弄、严肃的被边缘化、步调一致被"一半是海水、一半是火焰"所冲刷。审美大军由 20 世纪 80 年代的"我想唱歌可不敢唱，小声哼哼还得东张西望"到 21 世纪的超女超男"我的地盘我做主""我是流氓我怕谁"！想说就说、我行我素、标新立异的"新新人类"（New New People）的审美偏好独步一时。萨顶顶的"自语"表演登峰造极、街头动漫稀奇古怪、语言上哲学与无厘头相结合的蔡世忠漫画成了大人与孩子的"开心果"。服装的自我化、语言的自我化、性格的自我化展示于公共空间的结果是审美领域的一片混乱。有学者认为，私人生活及其话语的公共化，实际上造成了一种虚假的公共性，并没有实现公共领域理性交往的原则，理性商谈意义上的公共文化空间的急剧萎缩和蜕化②，反倒引发了一系列复杂的伦理和社会问题。个人主义盛行于公共文化领域，导致洪水滔天式的沉渣文化泛起。从"去个性化"到"个性化"的阶段，个性所需要的宽容被忽略，个性张扬的边界被僭越。在审美的世界，各为其主、各自为战，群体认同与民主公共性缺乏。

其三，"去真善"，求唯美。

在西方，《少年维特之烦恼》演绎出唯美主义对"物质至上""唯利是图"时代风尚的反驳。戈蒂叶的"为艺术而艺术"与波德莱尔的"恶之花"主张艺术的使命在于为人类提供感观上的愉悦，而非传递某种道德或情感上的信息。他们拒绝接受约翰·罗斯金和马修·阿诺德。无论是

---

① 〔美〕戴维·斯沃茨：《文化与权力——布尔迪厄的社会学》，陶东风译，上海世纪出版集团，2012，第 249 页。

② 陶东风：《无聊的嬉戏：去精英化时代的大众娱乐文化》，载陶东风、和磊著《文化研究》，广西师范大学出版社，2008，第 13 页。

绘画还是建筑，唯美主义者都追求单纯形式上的美感，"符号美学"是对这种"小愤青"式的审美爱好的一种理性批驳。

在中国，一方面，市场经济的"初潮"让许多国人"跳海"，许多高校知识分子弃教从商甚至街头摊大饼，许多名牌高校生弃学从商甚至回乡养"生态猪"，"重义轻利"的传统价值观念受到严重挑战，不谙市场经济"潮水"的中国人"崇洋媚外"，西方经济学几乎成了大学课堂的"唯一"经济学，"经济人"几乎成了唯一"人性假设"。过劳奔波、急功近利的一代冲突于社会各个领域，"真善"成为了他们实现目的的障碍物。"文化产业以经济利益为现实目的……苦行僧式的禁欲性的观念被抛弃了，代之以享乐的原则甚至感官的解放；理想主义奉献精神被弱化了，代之以时尚的追求和及时的享乐。"① 传统审美理想受到冲击和否定。

另一方面，网络世界的虚拟性与诱惑性使很多人沉迷于虚幻世界而不能自拔，现实的失意变本加厉地促使他们"远离尘嚣躲进网络自成一统"。在此背景下，"文以载道"的老传统和"去虚妄，求真实"的审美趣味被弃之一旁，"信言不美，美言不信"的古训演化成了"去信求美"的妄念信条。传统的意象艺术走向仿像艺术，就是唯美、唯形式的一种具体体现。传统的书法艺术被"线条""色彩""墨艺"各霸一方；传统的绘画艺术被"拷贝""缠扎""杜尚艺术事件"所切割；传统的寓伦理道德于自身的建筑走进形式主义的死胡同；传统的叙事电影原生态的演员被淹没于华美的服装、美艳的肉身、绝美的必杀技等"艺伎"风格中。

唯美主义之后就是批判现实主义，"郭敬明的小清新之后就是韩寒的回归现实主义的路"。只有走向现实，回归日常生活，我们才可以在一定程度上拯救仿像艺术盛行的时代缺陷②。

三　化解当代中国主流审美文化问题的策略

"文化大革命"激情澎湃式的阶级斗争引发的是知识分子对官本位、

---

① 许共城：《中国当代审美文化发展的新趋向》，《哲学动态》2008 年第 6 期。
② 黄卫星：《当代中国审美文化的负面价值观语境》，《云南社会科学》2010 年第 3 期。

官方价值观念的隔膜；市场经济大潮带来的是知识分子地位的衰落与精英贵族精神的贬损。内外交困的知识分子在引领大众前行的道路上不断跋涉、心力交瘁。富有良知的知识分子开始了再次的文化启蒙，他们不断地传播中国传统文化经典、引进西方文化精粹。近几年，书店里的儿童读物不可胜数，许多家庭的购物车成了购书车。"合久必分，分久必合"，裂为碎片的审美文化的整合及当代中国主流审美文化问题症结的化解成为可能。

其一，审美文化重心下移，回归日常生活。

"去政治化""去精英化"等"去去去"的审美心态是对传统审美文化的极度不满、不耐烦、呵斥和否定。文化研究者指出，由于"公共政治的世界被视作'他人的'世界，一个无奈的、自己不能做主的世界，而且无法参与这个世界的游戏规则的制定，只能听命于别人确立的规划的世界"。[①] 审美文化在转型期表现出一种"青春期"式的狂躁不安："去精英化""去政治化"和对娱乐文化的"熊抱"。审美文化"娱乐化"是长期紧张后的一种暂时释放。如果"娱乐化"的审美文化长期立于前台，国人审美的"精、气、神"甚至国人的生命力就会在哈哈大笑中被耗散。大众对传统审美文化的抗拒只是一种姿态，精英及政治权威层必须下移，俗众与精英互融渗透后才能相互提升与包容。

一方面，对于那种精神贵族、时代的精英、公共知识分子，市民应该尊重有加，抱着"移动大驾，请帝王出行"的姿态，为那些敢为民生请命的人提供支持。我们知道，经济大潮下，"百无一用是书生"的观念顿生，"笑贫不笑娼"的社会风气曾经冷落了很多知识分子的心。过优雅生活，走文化审美之路，市民还需要知识分子——"白衣卿相"的引领。

另一方面，当代中国审美文化主流要超越原有的二元对立的审美文化结构（大众与精英、先锋与保守、生活与艺术），成为 21 世纪的价值"中枢"强有力的感性表现，必须关注当下"百舸争流"的各种审美现象。如果说传统审美文化主流偏重于形而上的哲学、伦理学及艺术等

---

① 陶东风：《无聊的嬉戏：去精英化时代的大众娱乐文化》，载陶东风、和磊著《文化研究》，广西师范大学出版社，2008，第13页。

"远离尘嚣"的领域，大领风骚的是精英先锋派，那么当代中国审美文化主流则逐渐向下扩张于小说、服装、饮食、建筑、网络及环境等现实领域，广被喝彩的是世俗味极浓的流行文化，体现出一种浓浓的"踏地"倾向。"占据大众文化生活中心的已经不是小说、诗歌、散文、戏剧、绘画、雕塑等经典的艺术门类，而是一些新兴的泛审美、艺术活动，如广告、流行歌曲、时装、美容、健身、电视连续剧、居室装修等，艺术活动的场所也已经远远逸出与大众的日常生活严重隔离的高雅艺术场馆，深入到日常生活空间。"① 有学者分析指出，"日常生活进入了审美的理论视野，美学所讨论的纯粹理论问题被日常生活的审美体验所代替。审美理论所关心的是当代大众的日常生活对人的文化精神的价值建构的意义，是对当下日常生活生存意义的体验。日常生活进入审美的主要视野，有两个方面的前提，一方面是市场化冲淡了传统的审美理想观念，精英文化的理想主义受到世俗的实用主义的极大冲击，审美理论由热衷于对范畴的推演和对概念的解析转向对现世生活的当下体验，艺术越来越生活化了。另一方面是人民大众以审美的态度来看待周围的日常生活，扩大了美的视野，审美现象更为丰富。审美活动走出了经典的美学追求，进入了更现实、更直接的审美感觉中。"②

如果人的日常生活不能被保证，人性的解放就是难题。③ 在审美泛化、世俗化以至于媚俗的今天，我们应该"躬身"回归生活、从现实的角度近距离地关注各种审美文化，去其糟粕、吸取精华，为更好地引导当代中国审美文化、迎接审美文化主流的正向"蜕变"提供理论支撑，迎来人性的大解放。

其二，政治、精英、大众三元共生。

人与动物的区别之一在于人类有识有情有义有文化。文化的类型多种多样，如体悟型、规范型等。文化之为文化不仅来源于个人的深刻体悟，更是广为人所接受并深刻影响着个人。文化与政治紧密相关，"文化不能

① 陶东风：《日常生活审美化与文化研究的兴起》，《浙江社会科学》2002 年第 1 期。
② 许共城：《中国当代审美文化发展的新趋向》，《哲学动态》2008 年第 6 期。
③ 王福民：《论马克思哲学的日常生活维度及其当代价值》，《教学与研究》2008 年第 5 期。

免于政治的内容，而是政治的一种表达"。① "学而优则仕"的中国传统文化在一定程度上规定着知识分子的责任与使命，政治与精英的融合在一定程度上侵蚀了知识分子的独立性，知识分子的独立品格及其飘逸神韵难以显现。其实，政治文化、精英文化、民众文化三元共生、三足鼎立更符合后现代多元化的时代吁求。以和谐为中心，立足于传统与现实，标榜个性与宽容成为新的审美原则。

首先，确立审美文化政治导向的威信。君子之德如风，风行草上，小人必偃。有学者指出："官方希望把民族主义当成一种社会整合的工具。"② 也就是说，通过回归传统文化，吸取传统政治审美文化的精髓与力量，强调本土文化传统，打造具有中国特色的审美文化，影响并提升大众的审美抉择。

其次，确立知识分子专业化的审美文化生产者与传播者的地位。文化商人是市场经济体制改革中教育与经济的"合谋"，文化产业的繁盛与知识分子的广泛参与有关，知识分子文化品位的高低影响并决定着中国审美文化的精神气质。知识精英、公共知识分子的地位必须得到尊重。

最后，打通精英、政治与大众间的文化壁垒。审美文化的创新离不开受众，审美文化的接受者同样重要。当代中国审美文化主流是"合力"下的产物，无论是审美文化的创作者及其居住的世界环境，还是审美文化的欣赏者，都是当代中国审美文化新主流的推动者。关注审美文化的诠释与传播，尽可能地消除审美文化新主流被误读的现象，可以为新的审美文化的生存提供健康的"土壤"。

19 世纪的西方，有些作家对"公众"的不满凸显。诗人济慈说："我对公众丝毫没有谦卑之感。"③ 尼采主张远离尘世六千英尺。目前，中国娱乐文化的流行并不能代表精英政治文化的无意义，服务型政府的建设、

---

① 〔美〕戴维·斯沃茨：《文化与权力——布尔迪厄的社会学》，陶东风译，上海译文出版社，2006，第 7 页。

② 陈国战：《新世纪以来中国大众文化中的民族主义》，载《文化研究》，广西师范大学出版社，2012，第 220 页。

③ John Keats：*Selected Letters of John Keats*，Edited by Grant F. Scott（Cambridge：Harrard University Prers，2002），p. 113.

公民社会的铸就需要公共伦理精神与公共审美理想。公共知识分子参与的意义在于促进政治精英与普通大众的交流与沟通！现在"强调避免使用与理论紧密相关的艰深的'行话'，目的就是要促进与'普通群众'的交流与沟通"。①

其三，凝练新的审美文化精神。

当代中国主流审美文化在与非主流审美文化的拉扯中形成了自己新的核心价值观念，通过主流审美文化价值观念的重新凝练，引导大众的审美情趣与高雅生活。当代主流审美文化价值观念的主要精神表现为：

第一，回归现实，返璞归真。"哲学走向荒野""美学走向荒野""美学走向自然""美学走向现实环境"为当代中国审美文化主流取向提供哲学基础与美学基础。见素抱朴、烂漫天真成了新的审美趣味。服装美学向传统回溯，主导功能主义，健身、舒适、美观成为新的设计原则，"第一夫人"彭丽媛出访各国的服装完美地展示了这一点。小说、电影等文化出现强有力的"穿越波"。各色人物在时空中不断穿越，多角色中体验自己的"前身后世"，彰显出一种新的寻根意识和"归元"心态。

第二，多元并存，多声部共鸣。"作为世俗化时代文化主流、以消遣娱乐为本位的大众文化，在中国特定的转型期，客观上具有消解政治文化与正统意识形态的功能。②""一切皆有可能"的民主观念不断消解审美文化中的话语霸权，新的审美偏好层出不穷。满眼异族情调、满街都是"百搭"式的审美文化。"孩子式"的猎奇、搞怪和"智者"的调侃、幽默为"中正"的审美文化提供了新鲜血液，形成了一种调皮、活泼、生机盎然的多元审美世界。

第三，生态趣味凸显，钢筋水泥式的科技世界被弱化。无论是动漫文化、公园文化、网络文化，还是饮食文化，科技成为被人把控利用的工具而不再是至上的主宰，生态环境成为最受欢迎的关心对象与创作主题。生生不已的生态文化不断撞击科技理性，几何式的规整还原于生命的本然状态。

---

① 〔英〕加里·霍尔、克莱尔·伯查尔：《新文化研究的理论探险》，杨建国译，载《文化研究》，广西师范大学出版社，2008，第195页。

② 陶东风：《文学理论的公共性》，福建教育出版社，2008，第173页。

The Inquiry Concerning Contemporary Chinese Aesthetic Culture

Zhao Hongmei

Abstract: Contemporary aesthetic culture in China is the rebellion against traditional mainstream aesthetic culture. The paper begins with the understanding of concept of contemporary aesthetic culture, points out the main problems in contemporary aesthetic cultural acitivities, and then tries to find the ways to solve the problems.

Keywords: contemporary China; aesthetic culture; strategy

苏联主流文化边缘化的教训对当代中国主流文化构建的启示[*]

张丽君^{**}

摘　要： 苏联社会主义主流文化在苏联解体后成为边缘文化。这一演变过程给当代中国主流文化构建提供了一些有益的启示：继承和发展民族的文化传统非常重要；要处理好主流文化内部的意见分歧；恰当地对历史做出评价对于社会的健康发展非常重要；要恰当地处理好学术性和政治性、艺术性与政治性的关系；要尽力弥合"官"文化和大众文化之间的裂痕；要处理好经济和文化的关系；要引导知识分子和大众舆论朝着健全理性的方向发展等。

关键词： 苏联　主流文化　边缘化　启示

"十月革命"诞生了苏联社会主义。"1917 年 10 月布尔什维克在俄国掌握政权不仅意味着一场社会变革，也是一场政治革命。'伟大十月'之后的几十年见证了俄国向苏联社会的转变，也见证了一种全新的苏联模式文化的出现和发展。"① 这种全新的苏联模式文化是一种新的文化现象和

---

   *　本文系湖北省社会科学基金项目"十二五"规划资助课题的研究成果。

  **　张丽君，博士，湖北大学马克思主义学院副教授。

  ①　〔美〕尼古拉·梁赞诺夫斯基、马克·斯坦伯格：《俄罗斯史》，杨烨、卿文辉译，上海人民出版社，2007，第 545 页。

文化类型。这种文化的类型凸显了意识形态的特征，或者说打上了浓厚的意识形态的烙印。1989 年 5～6 月苏联第一次人民代表大会决定改变国家权力机构，人民代表大会成为最高国家权力机关，最高苏维埃成为常设机关——议会。1990 年苏共中央二月全会还提出在苏联设立总统职位的问题，同年 3 月召开的苏联第三次非常人民代表大会，通过了苏联总统职位法，戈尔巴乔夫当选苏联第一任总统。1991 年 12 月，苏联彻底瓦解。苏联的主流文化逐渐被边缘化。

一　对苏联主流文化的批评声音

社会转型给俄罗斯哲学带来了困境，苏联解体后马克思主义由意识形态的地位跌落成一般的学术研究，甚至受到了某种压制。莫斯科大学副校长米洛诺夫教授在《马克思主义的哲学遗产在当代俄罗斯的地位和作用》中指出，在俄历史上理解马克思主义有如下几种模式：英雄神话模式；意识形态化、万能化模式；回到经典马克思模式；严肃对待马克思主义模式；反马克思主义思潮。波波夫认为马克思主义是一个严肃的学说，具有理论的整体性，需要补充而不是否定。

苏联社会主义自诞生以来，就伴随着对苏联社会主义意识形态的批评声音。随着苏联解体，在俄罗斯国内也出现了对马克思主义尖锐的批判声音。"在俄罗斯，我们可以听到对马克思主义和社会主义最刺耳、最粗鲁的评价，而且对马克思主义批评最狠的人恰恰是以前马克思主义的颂扬者。还是那位齐普科，他曾多年颂扬并宣传过马克思主义，现在他断定，马克思的学说在逻辑上自相矛盾，在学术上站不住脚，甚至在道德上是危险的。"[1] 在马克思的价值视野中，也包含自由—权利—平等（公平、正义）这一基本的逻辑结构。不过马克思主义是从唯物史观的角度来理解这些范畴的内涵。"在道德上是公平的甚至在法律上是公平的，从社会

---

[1] 〔俄〕罗伊·麦德维杰夫：《俄罗斯向何处去——俄罗斯能搞社会主义吗?》，关贵海、王晓玉译，当代世界出版社，2003，第 137～138 页。

上来看可能远不是公平的。社会的公平或不公平，只能用一门科学来断定，那就是研究生产和交换这种与物质有关的事实的科学——政治经济学。"① 除了从道德上批评以外，也有从阶级立场角度来批评的。"著名导演马克·扎哈罗夫感慨道：'我们为什么曾经那么喜欢卡尔·马克思呢？因为这位受教育不良的德国边缘人物思考出的科学结果，是给流浪汉、流氓、社会弃儿的，最终也就是给无赖和败类的，也就是给那些终生未做任何让人喜欢或让人不肯释手之事的人的。'"② 科学社会主义的确是关于无产阶级解放的学说，不过马克思所说的无产阶级并不仅仅是流浪汉，还包括那些在资本主义大工厂中工作的有较高的技术和文化水平的工人，恰恰是这些工人代表了人类社会历史发展的未来。齐普科还说："马克思……在自己的行文中从来没有认真地、至少是公开地考虑过一个至关重要的问题：关于人、关于他的灵魂、欲望和深藏内心深处的隐秘想法。"③ 马克思主义关心人和人的命运，不过是从社会历史的角度来关心人的命运的。

另外一种声音来自托派。欧内斯特·曼德尔（1923～1995）是 20 世纪下半叶在马克思主义研究方面最重要的经济学家和政治学家之一，生前曾为布鲁塞尔自由大学教授，1946 年以后长期担任托派"第四国际"的领导人。曼德尔把斯大林主义看成对官僚制所做的特殊的意识形态的辩护，没有很好地反映工人、青年、农民、妇女和少数民族的利益。"他们为官僚制所做的特殊的意识形态的辩护，掩盖了社会现实，滋长了'虚假意识'。"④ 在曼德尔看来，"在官僚制的意识形态中，国家拜物教是与经典的商品拜物教结合在一起的"。⑤ 在曼德尔看来，国家拜物教和商品

---

① 《马克思恩格斯全集》第 25 卷，人民出版社，2001，第 488 页。
② 〔俄〕罗伊·麦德维杰夫：《俄罗斯向何处去——俄罗斯能搞社会主义吗?》，关贵海、王晓玉译，当代世界出版社，2003，第 138 页。
③ 〔俄〕罗伊·麦德维杰夫：《俄罗斯向何处去——俄罗斯能搞社会主义吗?》，关贵海、王晓玉译，当代世界出版社，2003，第 154 页。
④ 〔比利时〕曼德尔：《权力与货币——马克思主义的官僚理论》，孟捷译，中央编译出版社，2002，第 18 页。
⑤ 〔比利时〕曼德尔：《权力与货币——马克思主义的官僚理论》，孟捷译，中央编译出版社，2002，第 57 页。

拜物教的混合体采取了一种特殊形式对官僚制的作用和职能做辩护。官僚制的意识形态缺乏逻辑的一贯性。"其另一重要方面是不能形成自我意识并公开地自我确认，不能形成逻辑上一贯的、真正为它自己特有的世界观。"① 官僚集团就把科学变成了具体政策以及他们所维护利益的婢女。在曼德尔看来，官僚制的意识形态对工人阶级的一般觉悟有灾难性的伤害，而这一点带来的消极后果是长远的。"官僚集团篡夺权力以及工人的原子化和非政治化长期累积的效果是导致共产主义、马克思主义和社会主义在群众中严重丧失声誉。"② 曼德尔的看法也有其局限性。对于社会主义意识形态的评价需要结合理论和实践两个角度来考虑。在不同的国家和时代背景下，会形成不同的社会主义意识形态。这些意识形态都具有自己的历史合理性。另外，从历史发展过程的角度来看，无产阶级先是进行反对资产阶级的斗争，然后是组织自己的国家，并维护国家政权，然后是利用政权的力量逐步消灭自身，从而解放全人类。对社会主义的评价可以立足于无产阶级，也可以立足于社会主义政权和社会主义国家，也可以立足于全人类的视角。立足于哪个视角更具有合理性，要根据具体国情和历史发展阶段来判断。任何超前或者滞后的评价视角都会带来一定的偏颇。

另外一个视角就是俄罗斯思想传统的视角。别尔嘉耶夫就开始用这一视角审视苏联社会主义。别尔嘉耶夫在"第三罗马说"中找到俄罗斯共产主义的渊源："俄罗斯人民没能实现莫斯科作为第三罗马的理念。17世纪的宗教分裂表明，莫斯科王国并不是第三罗马。当然，彼得的帝国更没有实现第三罗马……"③ 然而，随着十月革命一声炮响，"俄罗斯人的命运发生了惊人的变化。在俄罗斯，取代第三罗马的是第三国际的实现。而且，第三罗马的诸多特点转移到了第三国际身上。第三国际也是神圣的王

---

① 〔比利时〕曼德尔：《权力与货币——马克思主义的官僚理论》，孟捷译，中央编译出版社，2002，第109页。
② 〔比利时〕曼德尔：《权力与货币——马克思主义的官僚理论》，孟捷译，中央编译出版社，2002，第94页。
③ Н. А. Бердяев. Истоки и смысл русского коммунизма. Москва. , 1997. С. 371.

国，同样建立在一个正宗的信仰基础之上。西方人不懂，第三国际其实并不是共产国际，而是俄罗斯的民族思想"。① 别尔嘉耶夫继而明确指出俄罗斯共产主义的内涵和起源："俄罗斯共产主义比大家习惯上所想的更具传统性，是古老的俄罗斯弥赛亚意识的转化和变形。"② 安德兰尼克·米格拉尼扬也采取了这一视角。安德兰尼克·米格拉尼扬认为，从苏联到俄罗斯意识形态演变的第一个阶段可以叫作"革命救世论的意识形态"。③ 这个意识形态信奉超民族的国际主义原则。他认为苏联展示了 20 世纪较为彻底的、清晰的和完整的国家意识形态。"早期的苏联是一个真正的意识形态帝国：官方意识形态不是从社会、社会的组织结构和价值观的土壤里产生出来的，而是发端于一种强加给社会的先验原则；布尔什维主义追求的目标是掌握最终的真理，而且用囊括一切和渗透一切的意识形态（极权主义）来强化这种追求。"④ 他说："然而，布尔什维主义之所以能取得胜利，是因为它正是俄罗斯的马克思主义。也就是说，我国的政治文化不仅吸收了欧洲的意识形态公式，而且对它进行了加工，注入了具有民族特色的内容。存在于布尔什维主义和苏维埃制度的声势浩大的社会发展的基础中的是俄罗斯民族文化中老一套的传统思想：救世主说、世界末日论、自我牺牲精神、禁欲主义和追求公平、村社主义和国家主义。"⑤

对于"十月革命"有偏向东方或者偏向西方两种解读的冲突。强调"十月革命"继承了俄罗斯传统的观点认为"十月革命"是村社制传统的延续。这种传统强调集体主义、直接民主、社会保护和平均主义的社会公正。一些俄罗斯学者认为"十月革命"没有改变亚细亚社会的传统。虽然布尔什维克的主观意图是要达到社会主义的目标，但在政策上却符合亚

---

① Н. А. Бердяев. Истоки и смысл русского коммунизма. Москва. , 1997. С. 371.

② Н. А. Бердяев. Истоки и смысл русского коммунизма. Москва. , 1997. С. 411.

③ 〔俄〕安德兰尼克·米格拉尼扬：《俄罗斯现代化与公民社会》，徐葵等译，新华出版社，2003，第 264 页。

④ 〔俄〕安德兰尼克·米格拉尼扬：《俄罗斯现代化与公民社会》，徐葵等译，新华出版社，2003，第 263 页。

⑤ 〔俄〕安德兰尼克·米格拉尼扬：《俄罗斯现代化与公民社会》，徐葵等译，新华出版社，2003，第 263 ~ 264 页。

细亚社会的传统，主要表现为公有制的原则。有的学者认为"十月革命"是知识分子的革命，是俄罗斯激进主义传统的延续。还有的强调"十月革命"是俄罗斯救世传统的延续。"有人更为明确地指出，共产主义具有其救世的学说：其弥赛亚（救世主）就是无产阶级；天堂就是无阶级的社会；教堂就是政党；而经书就是马克思、恩格斯、列宁和多年来斯大林的著作。"① 俄罗斯传统的救世学说和共产主义在本质上是不同的，共产主义是建立在唯物史观基础上的一种现实的学说，而传统的救世学说不是建立在对历史的科学论述的基础上。也有人强调布尔什维克的领导人有西方生活的经历，他们来自多个民族，而马克思主义诞生在西方，从而强调"十月革命"的西方性。总体上看，从融合性和马克思主义的俄国化来理解是比较恰当的。"这就是列宁的一代，尽管他们每个人的命运各不相同，可他们既是俄罗斯'道德追求'、绝对的伦理观等传统的继承者，也是吸收了他们所处时代欧洲文明的各种观点的人，他们的个人经历都体现出了东西方相互融合性、不同文化、不同思想、学派观点和思潮的互融性。"②

安德兰尼克·米格拉尼扬认为，作为官方意识形态的保守主义是苏联意识形态演变过程的第二个阶段（从赫鲁晓夫到契尔年科时期），它从进化保守主义形态过渡到20世纪80年代上半期的顽固保守主义形态。这一阶段是"势力范围"论的意识形态。革命的遗产只是用来做宣传和使制度合法化。从革命性到保守性的转变过程中，苏联官方意识形态具有了软化和"人性化"的特点，直接的意识形态强制已完全被人们遗忘了，只要遵循固定的已仪式化的规章，就可以保留精神和思想上的某些自主性。苏联权势阶层中政治和思想见解不一（类似有限的多元化）的状况被容许，这一切为意识形态的进一步转变提供了前提条件。而且，由于苏共对政权的垄断及其对政治经济领域的控制，这种转变必然是朝着非革命性

---

① 〔美〕尼古拉·梁赞诺夫斯基、马克·斯坦伯格：《俄罗斯史》，杨烨、卿文辉译，上海人民出版社，2007，第449页。

② 〔俄〕T. C. 格奥尔吉耶娃：《俄罗斯文化史——历史与现代》，焦东建、董茉莉译，商务印书馆，2006，第465页。

的、自由主义的、"温和的"（社会民主主义的、"人性的"）马克思主义的方向走的。改变意识形态尝试失败在很大程度上是由于俄国知识分子根深蒂固的历史性急躁情绪。使苏联马克思主义适应现实，逐渐和谨慎地把它改变成社会民主主义的尝试，被自由主义的扩张浪潮冲垮了。"自由主义的革命主义，针对保守主义和进化主义的布尔什维主义，这大致就是80年代和90年代之交的意识形态上的两种选择。"①

从俄罗斯思想传统的角度来审视苏联社会主义意识形态同样有局限性。无产阶级联合起来解放全人类完全不同于俄罗斯传统的救世论，如果有相似之处的话，也仅仅是从民族的心理上来说的，民族心理具有一定的稳定性。苏联所实施的农村政策完全不同于村社主义。

二 苏联主流文化应对挑战的启迪

苏联社会主义诞生后面临一系列的挑战。有来自国内的，主要是部分公务人员的抵制，部分农民的叛乱和工人骚动，一些知识分子离开俄国，左翼社会革命党人的决裂，以及少数民族的独立运动。外部则是协约国的干涉等。"反革命势力常被模糊并不无误导地称为'白卫运动'，对苏维埃政权构成最大的威胁。'白卫运动'势力包括波兰和各边境少数民族以及协约国的干涉部队，前者的目标仅限于俄国特定地区，后者没有明确的目的。"②

要建立一种全新的苏维埃文化，自然就面临如何处理好和传统文化的关系问题。在这个方面，苏维埃文化采取了用马克思主义世界观对旧知识分子和旧文化进行改造的办法。苏维埃官方还用驱逐出境的办法对待一些有不同意见的旧式知识分子。如1922年的哲学船事件，结果是在俄罗斯文化史上出现了一种特殊移民文化现象。其中也有支持苏维埃政权的知识

---

① 〔俄〕安德兰尼克·米格拉尼扬：《俄罗斯现代化与公民社会》，徐葵等译，新华出版社，2003，第266页。

② 〔美〕尼古拉·梁赞诺夫斯基、马克·斯坦伯格：《俄罗斯史》，杨烨、卿文辉译，上海人民出版社，2007，第458页。

分子及报纸如《社会主义导报》，有持中立态度的知识分子和报纸如《最近新闻报》。但在移民知识分子中，持有反对布尔什维克和苏维埃政权观点的报纸和杂志较多，如《复兴》《舵手》《革命俄罗斯》《道路》等。这部分报刊所聚集的知识分子把自己看成俄罗斯精神的代言人，关心俄罗斯的发展道路，否定苏联社会主义。从文化角度来看，这造成了文化上两个"俄罗斯"的情况。"只是到了 20 年代后半期，由于苏维埃政权加强对国内文化的意识形态控制，在俄罗斯本土文化和俄罗斯侨民文化之间才渐渐竖起了一座意识形态高墙。此后，俄罗斯侨民杂志和出版物无法达到俄罗斯国内读者手中，俄罗斯国内知识分子也无法与俄罗斯侨民知识分子进行文化交流和沟通。这样一来，俄罗斯侨民文化隔断了与俄罗斯国内的文化联系，才在与俄罗斯本土文化的对峙中渐渐地形成一种文化本体形式和文化形态，作为 20 世纪俄罗斯文化的一个强大层面，凸显在欧洲、亚洲或其他地区的民族文化背景上。"[1] 而后来在 20 世纪 80 年代后半期苏维埃文坛出现与"回归文学"相伴随的侨民文化回归，对加速苏联社会主义的解体起到了精神上的推动作用。苏维埃文化遇到的这一问题的启迪意义是：政治中心本身应努力成为文化的中心，在政治生活中，人们能够获得充分的关于人生意义和民族使命的答案。政治活动的文化意义越丰富，越充分，越有吸引力，越能够最大限度地吸引民众，文化生命和民族生命、政治生活之间越是高度地统一，这个社会越具有可持续发展的可能性。而要达成这一目标，继承和发展民族的文化传统就显得非常重要。随着时间的推移，如何才能使得苏维埃文化健康发展，如何才能清除文化发展中的不良现象？很多知识分子重新拿起传统的武器，力求从弘扬俄罗斯文化传统中焕发苏维埃文化的活力，由此又激发了新的保守和自由的争论。"这场捍卫俄罗斯文化与反俄罗斯文化的斗争，实际上是 20 世纪60～70 年代文化界保守派和自由派斗争的继续，是文化发展中继承俄罗斯民族文化传统的新'斯拉夫主义'与走西方文化之路的新'西方派'的论争。"[2]

---

① 任光宣：《俄罗斯文化十五讲》，北京大学出版社，2007，第 203 页。
② 任光宣：《俄罗斯文化十五讲》，北京大学出版社，2007，第 283 页。

另外，苏联社会主义的挑战还来自党内。一些共产党人感到革命的崇高目标被人们淡忘，从而提出批评的意见；一些共产党人和工人反对使用沙俄时代的军官和资产阶级专家管理工厂；一些"民主中间分子"批评官僚化。党内的不同声音集中体现在党内的"左""右"两种倾向中。以托洛茨基为代表的左派强调通过强化党和国家的坚强领导迅速改变俄国的经济和文化的落后现状，以布哈林为代表的"右派"强调用和平的道路通往社会主义。显然，苏联主流文化的另一个启迪是要处理好主流文化内部的意见分歧。

1924 年 1 月 21 日，列宁逝世，斯大林继任苏联领导人的职务，从此以后领导苏联近 30 年。在列宁、斯大林的领导下，苏联成功地克服了困难。"斯大林的苏维埃体制于 20 世纪 30 年代就开始显现其清晰的轮廓。此后不久，它就要经受第二次世界大战的残酷考验。"① 1953 年斯大林去世后，赫鲁晓夫开始担任苏共总书记直到 1964 年。在这一时期，列宁和斯大林遇到的问题有了新的表现形式，除此之外苏联还面临一个如何对以往苏联社会主义进行评估的问题。尤其是 1956 年以后，"此后数十年间，斯大林问题始终是苏联政治生活中的核心问题。"② 从苏联的历史经验来看，恰当地对历史做出评价对于社会的健康发展是很重要的。"人们习惯地把赫鲁晓夫统治苏联的十年左右时间称为一个转型时期，这个时期也是苏联所达到的一个巅峰期的标志。"③

从 20 世纪 30 年代开始，苏维埃文化取得了一定的成效，艺术和文学表达比以前更加统一和遵循常规，同质化倾向得到了很大的发展。从官方的立场来看，苏联社会只有一种意识形态，不同的社会层面和社会阶层的不同之处只是在于他们体现这种意识形态的程度。同质化带来的一个结果是部分知识分子出现了"双重思想"现象。"所谓知识分子的'双重思

---

① 〔美〕尼古拉·梁赞诺夫斯基、马克·斯坦伯格：《俄罗斯史》，杨烨、卿文辉译，上海人民出版社，2007，第 492 页。
② 〔美〕沃尔特·G. 莫斯：《俄国史（1855～1996）》，张冰译，海南出版社，2008，第 356 页。
③ 〔美〕尼古拉·梁赞诺夫斯基、马克·斯坦伯格：《俄罗斯史》，杨烨、卿文辉译，上海人民出版社，2007，第 523 页。

想'，就是一方面知识分子对苏维埃政权的某些文化法令、政策和措施有不同的看法，在思想上产生不满情绪，在行动上有抗议的表现，并且在自己创作的作品里表现出来。另一方面知识分子又畏惧苏维埃官方的政治高压和迫害，他们的不满是有克制的，抗议是有局限的。因此，在知识分子身上产生一种双重思想，甚至产生了政治的归顺心理，导致了他们个性的分裂和创作的矛盾。"① 文化法令如何深入文化的内核、深入人心是一个很大的历史难题。对官方思维模式、审美风格的疏远，本身就包含着对制度疏远的意味，这种疏远动摇了社会主义制度的心理基础。

另外，苏维埃文化比较强调用文化的"党性"和"社会主义现实主义"两个标准来衡量学术和文艺创作。这两个标准和艺术的审美标准之间往往会发生冲突。这种情况导致了"地下文化"的出现。"'地下文化'是一种非官方文化，在苏联'地下'流行，与官方文化同时存在。'地下文化'与官方文化一起构成那个时期文化发展的总体图像。"② "地下文化"吸引了部分民众，对官方文化起到了某种侵蚀的作用。恰当地处理好学术性和政治性、艺术性与政治性的关系，让二者相得益彰，既保持一定的分界，又不互相伤害，对于文化的健康发展是非常有意义的。

布尔什维克们相信他们能够创造出一种新文化，并取得对旧文化的胜利。在创造新的苏维埃文化的过程中，遇到的另一个难题是如何处理和通俗文化的关系。无论在城市还是在乡村，人们的闲暇时光是在与家人、邻里、朋友的闲谈和交流中度过的。民众间闲谈、喝酒、舞蹈、唱歌、游戏等通俗文化形式本身包含了一定的价值取向，同时也会以特定的形式反映国家大事。如何让通俗文化为苏维埃文化服务是一个涉及面更广也更为复杂的问题。以体育为例，苏维埃文化本身就遇到了一定的挑战。"但总体而言，这一旨在使苏联运动员更有'文化'的宣传运动收效甚微。国家有在体育方面的优先考虑，而运动员和体育爱好者们则有自己的优先考

---

① 任光宣：《俄罗斯文化十五讲》，北京大学出版社，2007，第227页。
② 任光宣：《俄罗斯文化十五讲》，北京大学出版社，2007，第281页。

虑。和其他通俗文化领域里的情形一样，两者的优先性并不总是那么吻合。"① 在以赛亚·伯林的眼中，苏联形成了统治者和被统治者之间文化上的裂痕，"苏联社会中最深刻的裂痕是统治者与被统治者之间的差异"。② 他感受到的俄罗斯的普通老百姓是性情温和、彬彬有礼、柔弱温顺、谨小慎微、充满想象力而又天性淳朴的人，他们身上体现着某些俄罗斯传统的性格特征。他感受到统治者则是另外一番模样："另一方面，你也能从其粗俗的话语，虚伪的温情，每次党的表述发生重大变化时表现在他们脸上的特有表情，以及明显的玩世不恭和机会主义，瞟一眼就能明白上司实际需要的能力上分辨出谁属于统治阶级，不管他是哪个层次的。"③ 在以赛亚·伯林的眼中，各级官员往往仿效最高领导人的口气讲话，讨厌文雅，讨厌知识分子阶层，同时又要求知识分子发明创造。这种情况影响了知识分子创造力的发挥。从历史经验来看，在民众日常生活中缔造一种文化传统需要更长的时间和更系统的努力。并且，缔造的过程要能够和大众的生活密切相关，反映大众的基本需求才能得到成功。而缔造大众文化的成功又会在很大程度上有利于国家和民族的长治久安。

苏维埃文化在形成新的俄罗斯民族认同方面发挥了重要的作用，但也潜藏着一些挑战。苏维埃文化按照"形式上是民族的，内容上是社会主义的"这一原则来处理各民族文化和苏维埃文化的关系。苏联政府很注意推动各民族地区教育的发展，包括当地知识分子基层组织的创立，为当地各民族的个体创造机会去承担在当地具有影响力的职位，虽不承认各个民族在意识形态上有自己的独立性，但也允许当地人保留自己的语言和文化。"但是，这种对各民族的双重做法证明在实践中很难推行下去。文化自治很容易就变成了文化民族主义，接着将会导致分立主义。"④ 民族独立的身份意识和身份意愿并没有消失，民族主义的威力最终成为摧毁苏联

① 〔美〕沃尔特·G. 莫斯：《俄国史（1855～1996）》，张冰译，海南出版社，2008，第355页。

② 〔英〕以赛亚·伯林：《苏联的心灵》，潘永强、刘北成译，译林出版社，2010，第117页。

③ 〔英〕以赛亚·伯林：《苏联的心灵》，潘永强、刘北成译，译林出版社，2010，第122页。

④ 〔美〕尼古拉·梁赞诺夫斯基、马克·斯坦伯格：《俄罗斯史》，杨烨、卿文辉译，上海人民出版社，2007，第556页。

的重要力量之一。

1954 年 12 月 15～26 日，在莫斯科召开苏联作家第二次代表大会，大会允许作家进行相对自由的文学创作。从此以后，苏维埃文化出现了一些新现象和新特征，即"文化的'解冻'和'封冻'交替出现甚至并存"。① 这种情况在很长一段时间保证了文化沿着苏维埃文化既定的发展轨道进行。但是一旦出现了特殊的历史情况，这种平衡被破坏了，文化发展就会偏离既定的意识形态轨道。寻找到化解文化领域中存在的矛盾的有效办法才能更好地促进社会主义文化的发展和繁荣。

1964 年赫鲁晓夫从党和政府的领导岗位上退了下来，苏联进入了勃列日涅夫领导的时期。对于一个社会的健康发展来说，社会的经济结构、政治结构和文化结构之间保持一定的张力和协调发展也是至关重要的。苏共二十三大"提出了教条主义式的反对帝国主义的外交纲领，并强调要在意识形态和文化领域内执行强硬路线。另一方面，大会对某种程度上的'经济自由化'表示支持。而且，与赫鲁晓夫时期的传统相比，大会对经济和社会发展以及苏联的潜在力量采取了更为现实的态度。用一些评论家的话说，苏联当局选择了经济发展而没有考虑其后果"。② 在一些学者看来，勃列日涅夫时期把满足大多数人对日益增长的福利需求当成国内政治的核心和政治稳定的关键，取得了成效，但试图用快速见效的方法来解决长期存在的问题，却把其他一些问题掩盖了下来。

三　苏联晚期意识形态危机及其启示

戈尔巴乔夫当选为苏联共产党总书记以后，改变了苏共领导人和苏维埃政权对资产阶级社会及其民主观念的看法，他们把资产阶级的民主、人权、法治国家、权力分配和议会制度等视为全人类的观念，并将之引入苏维埃社会之中，这表明苏维埃官方在意识形态领域的重大变化。苏联放松

---

① 任光宣：《俄罗斯文化十五讲》，北京大学出版社，2007，第 259 页。
② 〔美〕尼古拉·梁赞诺夫斯基、马克·斯坦伯格：《俄罗斯史》，杨烨、卿文辉译，上海人民出版社，2007，第 524 页。

了对广播电台的控制，电影、音乐等领域都发生了很大的变化。在这个过程中出现了一些对政权非常不利的思维模式和话语体系。苏联政府对这些流行的思维模式缺乏有效的解读和反击，进一步加深了社会主义意识形态的危机。

苏联晚期意识形态危机的启示之一是：具有健全理性和精神追求的知识分子群体对社会的健康发展非常重要。"苏联知识分子特别是经济学家的观点日益转向拥护资本主义，是国家社会主义最终终结、亲资本主义联盟最终取得政治胜利的一个重要因素。"① 苏联知识分子有着良好的待遇，为什么他们会加入推翻给自己带来巨大物质利益的社会制度呢？在《来自上层的革命——苏联体制的终结》这本书看来，原因之一是苏联知识分子认为他们的物质生活远比西方资本主义世界的知识分子的物质生活糟糕。另外一个原因就是苏联的部分知识分子对官方意识形态的实际信仰并不坚定。"改革之前就有一些持不同政见的人，但绝大部分还是官方意识形态积极的倡导者。因为这样做，他们就能得到舒适的生活，也能得到事业追求上的满足。"② 在知识分子中有独立发表见解、学术和审美追求与政治要求之间的紧张感和冲突感，以及由此带来的缺乏尊严感和安全感。当社会环境发生变化的时候，一些知识分子变成社会主义制度的颠覆力量是有其心理和思想根源的。

苏联晚期意识形态危机的启示之二是：必须结合国情、民众的心理和社会习惯准确把握一些概念范畴在公众中的实际内涵。从理论和实践两个角度来看意识形态，理论概念的内涵和现实生活中公众的理解可能并不一致。弄清楚实践中的概念内涵及其起到的实际社会作用就显得非常重要。"我们发现，'民主派'一词现已完全习以为常地意味着拥护叶利钦—丘拜斯体制的人，没有人再去深究它的内涵。"③ 如"个人权利"概念在一

---

① 〔美〕大卫·科兹等：《来自上层的革命——苏联体制的终结》，曹荣湘、孟鸣岐等译，中国人民大学出版社，2002，第94页。

② 〔美〕大卫·科兹等：《来自上层的革命——苏联体制的终结》，曹荣湘、孟鸣岐等译，中国人民大学出版社，2002，第88页。

③ 〔俄〕谢·卡拉·穆尔扎：《论意识操纵》下，徐昌翰等译，社会科学文献出版社，2004，第502页。

些人的实践那里变成了"无法无天"。如用"合作社"概念来说那些非股份制的私有企业。显然，仅仅从学术上看一些概念的内涵无法有效地了解这些概念内涵的实践内容，以及相应的社会后果。

苏联晚期意识形态危机的启示之三是：公共舆论健全的理性的培养和培育非常重要。这种健全的理性要求尊重事实，能够全面地、辩证地看待问题，能够历史地看待问题，能够从他人的视角看待问题，能够合理地推理。如俄罗斯的市场主义者们经常使用的一个隐喻是：怀孕是不能部分怀孕的。意思是说要完全实行市场经济，要彻底摆脱计划经济。但从对比的角度来看，二者具有可比较的逻辑基础。没有健全理性的公共舆论往往会忽略事实，或者夸大社会的污点，或者盲目相信实现某些措施后，社会就会奇迹般地变好。

苏联晚期意识形态危机的启示之四是：要正确地对待历史，保持恰当的历史记忆是形成民族凝聚力和认同感的重要条件。扩大公开性是十月革命胜利后列宁提出过的口号，目的是扩大群众的知情权，防止官僚主义。1988 年初，戈尔巴乔夫在苏联宣传舆论负责人会议上主张"毫无保留、毫无限制的公开性"。1990 年 6 月 12 日，《苏联出版法》正式颁布，苏联允许反对派和私人办报。在公开性运动中，苏联社会掀起了"历史反思热"。这股"历史反思热"集中在"揭露苏联历史上的阴暗面"。这场运动混淆了民众的身份认同，使得民众丧失了生活在社会主义制度下的荣誉感。在这场运动中，出现了很多伤害苏维埃象征符号的现象。"由于苏维埃国家是思想统治型的国家，所以要保持它的合法化及其领导地位，就要靠各种象征和神圣观念的权威，而不是靠个人头投票的戏剧表演（政治市场）。"① 如把 5 月 1 日改为"春天与劳动节"，把 11 月 7 日改为"和睦节"。如 1992 年 6 月 22 日，在红场举行摇滚音乐会，电视播音员竟然宣称："我们将在全国名气最大的这座墓地纵情欢舞。"② 这一运动动摇了苏

---

① 〔俄〕谢·卡拉·穆尔扎：《论意识操纵》下，徐昌翰等译，社会科学文献出版社，2004，第 634 页。

② 〔俄〕谢·卡拉·穆尔扎：《论意识操纵》下，徐昌翰等译，社会科学文献出版社，2004，第 640 页。

联共产党和社会主义制度的思想政治基础。

苏联晚期意识形态危机的启示之五是：要全面地理解意识形态，对意识形态主要领域内的变化要有清醒的认识。意识形态由一定的政治、法律、哲学、道德、艺术和宗教等社会学说组成。法律、道德、艺术等领域都会在某种特定的情况下成为意识形态斗争的主战场。20 世纪 80 年代以后，苏联社会的道德生活发生了很大的变化，人们开始对一些道德规范进行反思，出现了道德规范相对化，甚至取消或者突破原有道德规范的现象。如"戈尔巴乔改革末期，卖淫的直接宣传开始了。改革的意识形态干部们不但把卖淫辩解为一种不可避免的社会恶行，而且还把它说成是一种近乎高尚的行业，定位为一种对苏维埃制度诸般不公平的社会抗议形式"。[1]

苏联晚期意识形态危机的启示之六是：意识形态工作要直面社会舆论，引导社会舆论，及时澄清社会舆论中存在的误区。在苏联晚期，干部集团搞特权、腐败现象普遍，一提到干部，人们就认为他一定是腐败的，这种情况导致了人们对干部的仇视心理。"我们可以看到，这件事成功了：人们仇恨乘坐'伏尔加'汽车的区委书记。但是同样是这个人，摇身一变当上银行家以后，就不会引起人们的任何反感。"[2] 在苏联晚期，一些人数较少的民族被"吃亏的民族"的思维范式所鼓动，"他们的特殊纲领是唆使小民族反对苏维埃制度。"[3] 谢·卡拉·穆尔扎认为，由苏联到俄罗斯意识形态演变过程中的 1991 年 8 月的事件，"这是一出规模巨大的政治戏剧，它不仅在演出过程中完全操纵了'观众'的意识，而且还为紧随其后出台的长期操纵意识的节目创造了条件"。[4]

---

① 〔俄〕谢·卡拉·穆尔扎：《论意识操纵》下，徐昌翰等译，社会科学文献出版社，2004，第 663 页。

② 〔俄〕谢·卡拉·穆尔扎：《论意识操纵》下，徐昌翰等译，社会科学文献出版社，2004，第 757 页。

③ 〔俄〕谢·卡拉·穆尔扎：《论意识操纵》下，徐昌翰等译，社会科学文献出版社，2004，第 764 页。

④ 〔俄〕谢·卡拉·穆尔扎：《论意识操纵》下，徐昌翰等译，社会科学文献出版社，2004，第 938 页。

"任何统治都企图唤起并维持对它的'合法性'的信仰。"① 显然，意识形态对于社会统治秩序的建立具有十分重要的意义。意识形态是人们认识世界、描绘世界、评价社会的一种重要力量。意识形态"赋予社会状态以意义——而非如此社会情势便无法被理解，并由此解析社会状态，以便有可能在其中采取有目的的行动"。② 意识形态，特别是统治阶级的意识形态具有极强的整合功能。在保持整个社会集团的统一中，意识形态起着凝聚的作用。另外，意识形态在国际交往中也起着很大的作用。美国前总统尼克松说："如果我们在意识形态领域的斗争中失利，我们所有的武器、条约、贸易、外援和文化交流将毫无意义。"③ 鉴于此，"意识形态因素下降""意识形态的终结""淡化意识形态"等说法是不科学的。但把一切都打上政治的标签也不利于意识形态的健康发展。恰当地处理政治性和学术性的关系，恰当地处理政治性和娱乐性的关系，对意识形态的健康发展是非常重要的。

Lessons from Mainstream Culture Marginalization of the Soviet Union

Zhang Lijun

Abstract：The mainstream culture of the socialism of the Soviet Union becomes the marginal culture. The change can provid some lessons to China's mainstream culture construction. It is important to develop national cultural tradition, and it is also important to deal with the disagreement within mainstream culture.

Keywords：the Soviet Union；mainstream culture；marginalization；lesson

---

① 〔德〕马克斯·韦伯：《经济与社会》上卷，林荣远译，商务印书馆，1997，第239页。
② 〔美〕雷迅马：《作为意识形态的现代化——社会科学与美国对第三世界政策》，牛可译，中央编译出版社，2003，第21~22页。
③ 屈全绳等：《和平演变战略及其对策》，知识出版社，1990，第67~68页。

塑造我国主流文化的全球品质

戴茂堂[*]

摘　要：全球化既是构建我国主流文化的背景，也是我国构建主流文化的机遇。我国主流文化对全球语境的自觉对接只能是在全球化与中国化、全球基本价值观与中国特色价值观之间，保持必要的张力。面对西方强势文化的压力，我们只有自强不息，不断提高对外文化交流和传播能力，牢牢掌握我国主流文化的自主权和话语权，才能有效维护国家安全：这是中国人的精神家园建设问题，是中国人的人文世界的建构问题，是中国文化的复兴、繁荣与发展问题。如果我国主流文化能更多地吸纳人类业已达成普遍共识的价值文化，具有最大可能的全球品质，那么我国主流文化将更有国际影响力和竞争力。

关键词：主流文化　对接　全球品质

近些年来，不断发生的高新技术革命，尤其是交通与通信领域的网络化和一体化，极大地改变了整个人类的生产方式、生活方式、价值观念以及思维方式，使整个世界最大限度地趋同，使全球化成为一种不可回避的现实。孙伟平先生指出："生存环境、生存状况特别是相互交往的这种社

---

* 戴茂堂，湖北大学哲学学院、高等人文研究院教授、博士生导师。

会化、全球化，极大地突破了人们的狭隘视野、地方意识和封闭情结，突出了人类文化精神中的'类意识'、整体精神，要求不同民族、文化的不同群体、个人，摆脱既有的各种限制，真正作为'社会人''世界公民''普遍价值的主体'思考问题。在这种情况下，人们之间的封闭、对抗意味着代价、落后，而开放、合作则可能意味着双赢、共赢。这一切要求人们在相互交往过程中，必须超越种族、国别、地区、宗教、文化等等的不同，超越具体主体的个性化需要和多样性诉求，在诸多共同的、统一的目的和需要导引下，从整体、全局的视角来看待问题，特别注意相互之间的关系、利益的协调一致。因此，在开放性、多样化的具体主体的价值取向之间，也必然存在着社会的、历史的统一性或一致趋势。"①

全球化是全球的全球化、全世界的全球化。全球化规定并强化了世界的相互依存性，也给中国提出了站在整体和全局的高度思考和解决文化发展问题的要求，特别是提出了要在世界不同文化相互碰撞、相互交融、相互竞争的背景下去确认和定位主流文化的发展方向的要求。在全球化时代，构建我国主流文化，不仅要立足于国情，也要立足于全球。无论愿意还是不愿意，全球化作为当今世界不可阻挡的大潮流，已经构成了我国主流价值文化构建的国际语境。如果全球化不可阻挡，那么我们唯一可以做的就是，自觉地将我国主流文化纳入全球化背景下来构建。否则，我国主流文化只能孤立于世界。

一　全球化对文化普世性的诉求

全球化本来是开放性和竞争性的商品流通特别是市场经济高度发展的产物，核心是经济全球化，包括资本、资源、金融、生产、贸易、服务等的全球化。但是，全球化发端于经济领域，但没有停滞在经济领域，而是很快就辐射到政治、文化领域②。这是因为经济生活的同质化，要求和期

---

① 孙伟平：《价值差异与社会和谐——全球化与东亚价值观》，湖南师范大学出版社，2008，第34页。

② 〔美〕塞缪尔·亨廷顿：《文明的冲突与世界秩序的重建》，新华出版社，2010。

待不同制度、不同发展水平的国家也必须遵循共同的游戏规则和制度安排，从而进一步加强和加深不同文化、不同国家之间的政治接触，有力地推动不同文化集团之间的交流与融合。事实上，当今时代，一方面，政治、文化和经济一样，存在着全球共同利益，政治、文化自身当然也就有全球化的内在渴求。另一方面，"经济发展是一个文化过程"①，经济形势也与政治密切关联，如果不理会政治、文化层面的全球化，经济全球化根本就不可能实现。经济、政治和文化的全球化从来就是相互交织、难分彼此的。

当今世界经济发展趋势表明，人类在满足基本的物质需要后，必然向满足文化需求的方向迈进。世界发达国家文化产业的崛起，既体现了产业演进的客观规律，更体现了人类从获取自然资源以满足物质需求走向发挥文化创造力、实现人的全面发展、实现人与自然和谐共存的伟大文明进程。世界范围内产业结构转变趋势表明，文化正在同土地、劳动和资本融合在一起，成为新的重要生产要素。所以，全球化从时间上看大致还是经历了先经济再政治再文化的历史过程。这一逻辑进程本身表明，经济和政治的全球化都有待于文化全球化的价值支持，全球化的核心、归宿和根本只能是文化的全球化。文化全球化是指不同民族的价值观、思想意识、风俗习惯、伦理道德在全球范围内交流、碰撞、理解和融合，并不断达成共识的历史过程。文化全球化要求不断超越本民族文化的国界并在人类的评判和取舍中获得文化的认同，不断将本民族的文化资源转变为人类共享、共有的资源。文化全球化依托信息革命，努力缩小、打破和消除了人们的文化界限，使知识信息在全球范围自由流动。由于全球作为一个整体首要的是一个社会文化系统，因此，全球化社会关键在于多元社会文化构成的全球文化系统，全球化只能在既定的多元社会文化系统中进行整合。所以，英国学者汤姆林森说："全球化处于现代文化的中心地位；文化实践处于全球化的中心地位。"② 他还说："文化对全球化是至关重要的，因为

---

① 〔美〕塞缪尔·亨廷顿、劳伦斯·哈里森主编《文化的重要作用——价值观如何影响人类进步》，新华出版社，2012，第89页。
② 汤姆林森：《全球化与文化》，南京大学出版社，2002，第1页。

它是复杂的联结整个进程的一个内在的方面。"① 全球化的最高境界就是走向对价值文化普世性的诉求，就是在文化上达成或完成价值共识或价值趋同。从价值文化层面看，全球化可以视为超越本土文化的狭隘性而逐步达到文化认同和价值认同的过程。

事实上，近代资本主义自产生以来，就一直在努力进行着超越民族和国家的狭隘限制，并促进民族历史向世界历史转变的实践。民族历史向世界历史的转变，使社会和人类作为一个有机的整体而生存、活动和发展，作为共时态意义上的类主体面对自然、整治社会和正视自身。在这种相关、相似甚至共同的生活实践经验的基础上，有些局部利益也正在整合而为人类的共同利益。当今世界已经产生了影响极大的寻求普世价值的伦理实践，人们期望通过这样的实践在价值文化上来完成全球伦理构建。1993 年 8 月世界宗教议会第二次大会签署的《走向全球伦理宣言》，提出了全人类都应当遵循的一项基本要求——每个人都应受到符合人性的对待，提出了珍重生命、正直公平、言行诚实、相敬互爱四项不可取消的规则。1995 年由德国前总理勃兰特领导的"全球政治管理委员会"发表了《全球是邻居》的报告，倡议以"全球性公民伦理"作为不同国家和文化之间合作解决全球性问题的基础。同年，由联合国前秘书长德奎利亚尔领导的"世界文化与发展委员会"发表了《文化多样性与人类全面发展》的报告，呼吁建立一种"适用于整个世界的全球伦理"。1996 年，"相互促进委员会"在维也纳召开会议，通过"寻求全球伦理标准"报告书，呼吁制定一套全球伦理标准，应对 21 世纪人类所面临的全球性问题。1997 年，又通过了"世界人类责任宣言"，旨在确立一种推动人类进步和保证人类追求完善的普世性价值标准。显然，全球伦理、普遍价值已经成为一个不断成长着的不可逆转的历史趋势。联合国《世界人权宣言》规定：人人享有生活、自由和人身安全的权利，享有言论和信仰的自由，法律面前人人平等，人人有权得到无任何歧视的同等保护，人人有权直接地或通过自由选择的代表参与自己国家的治理，人人有权得到相当的生活水平，以保证其本人及其家人的健康

---

① 汤姆林森：《全球化与文化》，南京大学出版社，2002，第 30 页。

和福祉，包括食、衣、住房和医疗照顾及必需的社会服务，人人享有受教育的权利……今天，全人类的共同文化财产和共同价值观念比以往任何一个时代都多。应该说，世界上各个民族、国家、地区，各种不同的文明体系，在全球一体化、统一化的力量面前，正在主动或被动地、自觉或不自觉地趋同或走向共识。寻求普世价值的全球伦理实践植根于人类共同利益和人类精神的深层需要，是一种立足于人类整体的视角，在全球化背景下，理性、主动、积极地构建全球主流价值文化的努力，对于构建我国主流文化具有特别的启示意义①。中国作为世界大家庭中的一员，中国的发展离不开世界，世界的发展也离不开中国。全球化既是构建我国主流文化的背景，也是我国构建主流文化的机遇。作为背景，我国主流文化构建必须充分考虑全球化带来的世界经济、政治、文化一体化趋势，必须充分考虑文化软实力在世界经济和政治中的核心作用。作为机遇，我国主流文化构建恰好可以借助全球资源和世界平台来推进。

二 我国主流文化与全球语境的自觉对接

伴随全球化浪潮席卷世界各地，伴随一系列全球问题的凸显，具有全球品质的普遍价值的追寻，也理所当然地成为了当代中国主流文化构建的重要话题和实际行动。全球化所凸显出来的相互依存关系，所强化的共同利益，要求当代中国构建主流文化必须认同相应的普遍价值。全球化使得离开世界谈论特殊的价值文化失去了原有的意义，有时甚至不可能。全球化必然突破局限于民族和国家的狭隘视野，要求人们站在世界公民的立场上，以一种新的全球性视角构建我国主流文化。对于全球化大潮，我们既无须全面迎合，也无须逃离与回避，更不能一味抵制和抗拒。面对全球化，如果无动于衷、无所作为，结果只能是"被全球化"，至多也只是等待西方提出价值文化建设方案，我们再来被动地发表意见，做出非常有限的修改

---

① 孙伟平：《价值差异与社会和谐——全球化与东亚价值观》，湖南师范大学出版社，2008，第39~41页。

和补充。既然全球化是大势所趋,那么,正确的选择只能是主动融入、自觉对接,只能是从世界发展大势中来定位和把握我国主流文化的发展前景,主动地与包括西方在内的世界各价值主体进行平等的对话,对于全球伦理、普世价值提出建设性的主张。

唯有自觉对接,才能真正让世界了解中国主流文化。在主流文化交流方面,应该说中国对别国的价值文化的了解要多于别国对中国的价值文化的了解,这里有着一种极大的不平衡。如果不能让世界了解中国主流文化,一方面就不能展现中国主流文化的特色与魅力,另一方面,也就不能化解这种交流中的不平衡性。经过30多年来的飞速发展,中国已经由世界舞台的边缘走到中心,中国境内发生的事情必然影响世界,就像世界发生的事情必然影响中国一样。当有人别有用心妖魔化中国主流文化的时候,当我们寄希望于追求一个好的国际环境的时候,就更加有必要向世界说明中国主流文化的真实情况,就更加有必要向世界实事求是地对自己的形象做出解读。

也唯有自觉对接,才能真正让中国主流文化走向世界。世界的变化发展为我国文化的繁荣兴盛提供了历史性机遇和广阔舞台。在全球化的国际语境下,让中国主流文化走向世界,从表面上看,就是让中国主流文化"走出去",从深层次上看,就是尽一个发展中大国的责任。让中国主流文化走向世界,目的不是把自己的主流文化强加于别国,更不是用中国主流文化取代别国主流文化,只是让不同的价值文化从相互交流、相互碰撞到相互融通、相互欣赏。

历史上,中华民族曾经表现出自我中心情结。这种自我中心情结,一言以蔽之,就是自认为,中华民族是礼仪之邦,是世界的中心,以"天朝上国"自命,而视域外的一切民族都为夷狄,域外的一切文化为雕虫小技,域外的一切人为穴居土人。这种自我中心情结,从地理上看,就是断言:中国处于天下之中,占据着世界的中心位置,而四夷居天地之偏;这种自我中心情结,从文化上看,就是断言:中国之所以位于天之正中而得天独厚,是因为在九州之内,人们享有君臣、父子、夫妻、兄弟、宾客之三纲五常的伦理,享有礼乐、教化、衣冠、祭祀之文明,而四夷之所以居天地之偏，恰好是因为他们缺乏这样的文明。梁启超在《新民说》中谈到，中国人往往以为"中国环列皆小蛮夷，其文明程度，无一不在我数等，……纵横四顾，常觉有上天下地唯我独尊之概"。林语堂也指出："在中国的古人眼里，中国的文明不是一种文明，而是唯一的文明；而中国的生活方式也不是一种生活方式，而是唯一的生活方式，是人类心力所及的唯一的文明和生活方式。'中国'一词，在古代课本里意为世界的文明部分，余者皆为蛮族。"① 这种自我中心情结，在近代中国社会运演出"中体西用"论。"中体"就是坚持形而上的中国孔孟之道，坚守孔儒之学的文化正宗地位，"西用"就是采纳形而下的西方科技之器。中体西用论强调，中国孔孟之道作为主流文化具有绝对优越性，即所谓"中国学术精微，纲常名教以及经世大法无不具备"，器用技术只是"卫吾尧舜禹汤文武周孔之道"之工具。这种自我中心情结，在近代中国社会还运演出与"中体西用"论相配套的"西学中源"论。在西学中源论者看来，不仅西方政教出于中国，而且西方学术文化也俱出自中国。如西学的格物就是《中庸》所讲的尽物之性，西方的上议院就是《洪范》所讲之卿士、《孟子》所讲之诸大夫，西方的下议院就是《洪范》所讲之庶人、《孟子》所讲之国人，等等。

正是这种自我中心情结构筑了一道坚固的屏障，阻碍了中国文化与世界的自觉对接，延缓了中国社会和观念从古代向近代的转型步伐，一度导致了以坚强的本土化心态来抵御全球化，"不是锐意进取，而是被动防御，甚至惯于以空洞的口号、说教（如'物质文明落后，精神文明领先'）来遮蔽理论上的落伍和空虚，以曾经的辉煌来逃避现实中的尴尬与失落，从而在很大程度上偏离了全球主流文化价值观。因此，承认现实，直面现实，勇敢地走向世界，迎接全球化时代的挑战，建构性地发展自己，……并在世界文化、文明的大视野、大格局中，理智地进行自我定位，寻找自己的角色，争取自己的地位，发挥自己的作用，是新时代的使

---

① 林语堂：《中国人》，学林出版社，1994，第337页。

命与当务之急"。①

今天，构建我国主流文化不能局限于自我实践和自说自话，而应主动融入国际语境和世界大潮，展开价值文化间的对话，提振我国主流文化的辐射力。全球语境下，构建我国主流文化不需要徒劳地去复兴一个古老的文明，而是应该自觉地选择"国际接轨"，拥抱一个全球化的现代文明。这直接关涉我国主流价值文化的普世效应和国际地位。在全球化背景下，全球利益、国际标准、国际惯例、国际公约将让任何主体无法抗拒。与世界同步、与国际接轨，必然成为每个要求进步的国家的行动口号。最自信的文化最勇于反思自己的文化弱点，也最善于吸收和尊重人类创造的一切优秀文明成果。一个国家，如果过于强调文化的个性特征，否定其文化与人类文化的共性，只能使其主流文化建设远离人类政治文明而停滞不前。这种共性的东西，实际上体现了人类和人类社会对于政治法则、政治规范、普世价值的认同和遵从②。如果执意背离人类政治文明的共性，就会造成人类文明的中断甚至倒退。全球化背景下我国主流文化的构建，不能满足于一厢情愿的自恋自爱，只能按照人类文化的普遍规律加以推进和拓展。我国主流文化不仅应该是民族的，而且应该是世界的，不仅应该是自赏的，而且应该是共享的。这种主流文化所蕴含的价值观不是与世隔绝、自我封闭的价值观，不是拒绝和排斥人类普遍、基本价值的价值观，而是与现代文明相适应的共同价值理想、价值取向。它也不否定全球业已取得的价值实践成果，而是强调把自己主动纳入全球化的进程之中，在与世界的充分联系、交往互动中，吸取全球基本价值（科学、民主、人权、法治等）并以之作为中国价值观的基础。因此，我国主流文化对全球语境的自觉对接，就只能是在全球化与中国化、全球基本价值观与中国特色价值观之间，保持必要的张力。③

---

① 孙伟平：《价值差异与社会和谐——全球化与东亚价值观》，湖南师范大学出版社，2008，第265~266页。

② 罗金远、戴茂堂：《伦理学讲座》，人民出版社，2012，第27~32页。

③ 李家莲：《道德的情感之源——弗兰西斯·哈奇森道德情感思想研究》，浙江大学出版社，2012，第322页。

三　文化自信与我国主流文化构建

当全球化走向由发达国家主导游戏规则的时候，全球化就可能异化为国家经济实力和军事实力的博弈并助长文化霸权主义。这种情况表现为：只有发达国家，才更有可能拓展自己的文化市场，更有可能输出自己的文化产品，更有可能发出自己的响亮声音。发达国家借助强大的经济实力和军事力量，在全球范围内推广其价值理念和文化信仰，给不发达国家带来巨大的文化冲击，导致发达国家的文化殖民，导致不发达国家的文化流失或被同化，甚至文化主权的丧失。尤其是伴随着西方国家的商品、货币、人、图像、技术、知识和思想等在全世界范围内的大面积扩散和加速度流动，文化从强势的西方国家向发展中国家传播，诱导发展中国家及非西方国家的民众接受其文化并淡忘甚至放弃自己的传统文化，从而形成了事实上的文化殖民主义或文化帝国主义格局。恰如孙伟平先生所言："伴随着全球化的进程，强势文化能够轻易地、'自然而然'地闯入经济发展滞后、文化相对'落后'的地区，而弱势文化则很难真正挤入强势文化的地盘。强势文化必对弱势文化形成压迫、挤压，令弱势文化感觉到前所未有的威胁，感觉到尖锐的生存危机。"①

毋庸讳言，一百多年来，西方文化在世界文化中一直占据着强势地位。当前，世界范围内各种思想文化交流、交融、交锋更加频繁，"西强我弱"的国际舆论格局没有根本改变。今天，西方文化特别是美国文化在全球处于霸主地位，西方发达国家依然掌控着今日世界文化的主导权，拥有最大影响力的文化品牌（如以好莱坞为代表的影视文化、以圣诞节为代表的节庆文化）。现在，世界文化市场的80%由欧美占据，传播于世界各地的新闻90%以上由西方七国垄断，美国出产的影片占全球总放映时间的50%以上、电影总票房的2/3。这些文化品牌正是西方发达国家输

---

① 孙伟平：《价值差异与社会和谐——全球化与东亚价值观》，湖南师范大学出版社，2008，第25页。

出它们文化观的绝好工具。国际社会借助于各种方式进行"西化""分化"的活动一刻也没有停止，西方国家四处推销自己的意识形态、社会制度、发展模式，总是想在全球化的名义下，把其他非西方国家的价值文化发展导入符合西方利益的轨道，使其主流文化更符合西方的价值观。当下世界文化的全球发展，在看似差异化、多元化的表象下，实际上面临趋同乃至死亡的"灰质化"结局，而这和强势的西方文化、资本逻辑是分不开的。走入异化的全球化往往在"同一"与"全球"的表象背后将既存的不平等的世界经济体系合理化和强化，并赋予强权随意界定和解读国家利益的自由，从而片面保护发达国家的特殊利益，全面牺牲不发达国家的特殊利益。走入异化的全球化往往在权力垄断的背后把"全球自由贸易"包装和修饰成利益共享的大同世界和华丽口号，倡导的其实只是强者的自由，而对发展中国家而言，这却是一个失去自由的过程。这就是有学者所说的："自由的世界市场的预言家在全球的活动愈是成功（这意味着民族国家和领土国家的结构遭到侵蚀），受世界主义观念驱动的威胁就变得越大。西方的'人道主义干预'将威胁越来越多的世界居民。人们在推行新自由主义的世界政策的过程中，鼓吹并创造一种弱国家世界体系。在这样的世界体系中，帝国主义滥用世界主义使命将不再有任何障碍。"① 全球化的到来，一方面增加了发展中国家经济发展的机遇和空间；另一方面，资本的全球化会加剧一些发展中国家的分配不公，放大国内矛盾，增大执政风险。这或许是全球化进程中不可避免的二律背反。这就特别要求我们具有一种文化自信，要看到中国改革开放的巨大成绩，看到中华民族伟大复兴的光辉前景，积极抵御西方化和美国化的压倒性冲击，而不可以消极地走向反全球化。

面对西方强势文化的压力，我们只有自强不息，不断提高对外文化交流和传播能力，牢牢掌握我国主流文化的自主权和话语权，才能有效维护国家安全。这个问题是中国人的精神家园建设问题，是中国人的人文世界的建构问题，是中国文化的复兴、繁荣与发展问题。如果我们对全球化可

---

① 乌尔里希·贝克、哈贝马斯：《全球化与政治》，中央编译出版社，2000，第44~45页。

能产生的异化没有足够的警觉，我们就很难在全球化进程中趋利避害，我们的文化甚至会面临被融化、被改变的危险。

我们必须坚决地拒绝任何形式的全盘西化，反对任何形式的西方中心主义和霸权主义，旗帜鲜明地保持中国主流文化的特色，并通过把中国主流文化发扬光大来提升其国际影响力和竞争力。从本质上讲，捍卫民族文化个性，是一种历史责任，因为它关系到一个民族和国家的生存根据。坚守民族文化发展的个性，是维护民族文化的心理认同的首要前提。一种文化形态生生不息向前发展的最持久动力来源于该文化的内在精神及其个性。同时，也正是这种内在精神及其个性，使该文化区别于其他文化形态并在世界文化之林中展示其独特的魅力。越是具有民族性的文化，往往越具有个性和生命力，因而也就越能走向世界，从而获得全球品质。郭齐勇先生指出："21世纪的人类历史告诉我们：'世界性''现代性'与'民族性''根源性'并不是相互排斥的，而是同时并存、健康互动并可以整合在一起的。世界思潮与民族精神、现代性与民族本己性、普遍原则与特殊道路、东亚价值与全球价值，都是可以而且必须互动、整合的。"①

在全球化背景下，一个民族、国家，特别是像中国这样历史悠久、文化独特的大国，是不可能简单照搬世界上任何一种现成的发展模式的，我们必须自主探索自己的发展道路，相信并扩大自己文化的实力和魅力。所谓扩大自己文化的实力和魅力，就是充满自信地将自己的文化普遍化地推向世界，并将能否普遍化地推向世界作为考察自己的文化是否有实力和魅力的试金石。这就要求我们要有强烈的文化自强意识。文化必须通过它的实力和魅力来赢得最大的普遍性。优秀的文化往往扎根于民族的特有土壤，但又能够超越狭隘的民族利益，具有高度的开放性和绝对的普遍性，具有最大的普世价值。文化价值观上的独立与自强，是一个民族、国家自信、自立、自强的根本。一方面必须在全国形成统一的精神坐标、共同的理想信念，另一方面又必须大力推进文化"走出去""送出去""融出去"战略，大力推进对外文化交流、对外文化传播和对外文化贸易，让

---

① 郭齐勇：《守先待后：文化与人生随笔》，北京师范大学出版社，2011，第10页。

中国文化影响世界，打造我国良好的国家文化形象和世界级文化品牌。塑造一个良好的国家文化形象，是实现"和平崛起"大国战略的重要一环。中华民族要实现自己的伟大复兴，就必须高扬自己的文化理想，高举自己的文化旗帜，树立自己的文化形象，反对民族虚无主义。唯有如此，我们才能在国内增强我国主流文化的凝聚力、震撼力、感召力，在国际上形成和扩大我国主流文化的世界竞争力、影响力，以及知名度和认可度。当然，我国主流文化的构建要有自强意识，不是说一定得拒绝人类已经达成普遍共识的价值文化。从历史进化的角度看，全球交融、世界共存是大趋势，一个民族、一个国家总是有必要在坚持自我特质的同时，向其他民族、其他国家吸取异质文化的养分，从而与时俱进，发展壮大。如果我国主流文化能更多地吸纳人类业已达成普遍共识的价值文化，具有最大可能的全球品质，那么我国主流文化将更有国际影响力和竞争力。

Cultivate Global Quality of Our Mainstream Culture

Dai Maotang

Abstract：Globalization is the background and opportunity of our mainstream culture construction. The consciousness of globalization in our mainstream culture can be formed only in the tension between globalization and the values with Chinese characteristic. Facing western pressing cultural pressure, what we can do is only to guard the security of our country by improving the ability of cultural exchange and grasping the language power of our mainstream culture. This is the issue of Chinese spiritual home construction, the construction of Chinese humanistic world, and the issue of revitalization of Chinese culture. If our mainstream culture has the quality of globalization and has been universally acknowledged by the world, it will have more international influence.

Keywords：mainstream culture；the quality of globalization

传统文化与现代文化

Traditional Culture and Modern Culture

China English as the Linguistic Medium in Cultural Translation

Zhang Qingzong; Guo Xihuang*

Abstract: Language and cultural transmission constitutes an important part of international exchanges and co-operations for China with other countries, and it is also an important approach to realizing its soft and smart power. Along with the considerable growth of China's overall national strength and the steady rise of its international standing, the country's cultural soft power should be improved significantly, and the international influence of Chinese language & culture will steadily increase. Against this background, Chinese language & culture will play a significant role in the international exchanges. This paper deals mainly with the impact of China English, embodiment of Chinese cultures, upon the international media and Westerners.

Keywords: language; culture; soft power; international exchange

1. Introduction

Language and cultural transmission constitutes an important part of international exchanges and co-operations for China with other countries, and it is also an

* Zhang Qingzong, Professor, Dean of the School of Foreign Languages, Hubei University; Guo Xihuang, Professor of the School of Foreign Languages, Hubei University.

important approach to realizing its soft and smart power. Along with the considerable growth of China's overall national strength and the steady rise of its international standing, the country's cultural soft power should be improved significantly, and the international influence of Chinese language & culture will steadily increase. Against this background, Chinese language & culture will play a significant role in the international exchanges. Just as President Xi Jinping said, the Chinese leadership has recognized the importance of soft power in achieving comprehensive national power, and has accepted the mainstream academic view that the core of soft power is culture. Culture is emerging as an important part of the country's comprehensive competitiveness in today's world, and China is feeling the urgency of enhancing its soft power and the international influence of its own culture. This paper deals mainly with the impact of China English, embodiment of Chinese cultures, upon the international media and Westerners.

2. Language and Culture

It is generally believed that there are two sharply contrasting points of views as to whether or not language and culture are interrelated. Does the language we speak shape or influence the way we think or does it merely convey thoughts, emotions or desires? There are many ways in which the phenomena of language and culture are intimately related. These phenomena are unique and have been the focal subject of the linguistic, anthropological, sociological, methodological and even memetic study in the past decades.

The question about whether languages influence the way we think even dates back to *The Allegory of the Cave* by the Greek philosopher Plato in *The Republic*, one of his most well known works, in which a group of people are trapped in a cave and are tricked into thinking that the shadows on the wall are reality. It implies that the power and capacity of learning exists in the soul already. About one thousand years later, Charlemagne, also known as Charles the Great and Father of Europe, a medieval emperor who once ruled much of Western Europe, once said: To have a second language is to have a second soul. That is to say, each language has its own cognitive toolkit. Typological studies show that different languages handle verbs, distinctions, gender, time, space, metaphor, and agency differently, and that these differences make people think and act differently. [1] Just as an old Czech proverb goes, those who know many languages live as many lives as the languages you know.

About the influence of language on culture, Humboldt, German philosopher & linguist has been credited as an originator of the linguistic relativity and as being the founder of the term *worldview*. [2] Humboldt contended that language is an activity the character and structure of which express the culture and individuality of the speaker, and he also asserted that man perceives the world essentially through the medium of language, that language is tightly connected to thinking and people who speak different languages would think differently. So language is seen as the expression of the spirit of a nation. He thus foreshadowed the modern development of ethno-linguistics, which explores the interrelationship of language and culture.

His prophetic seminal ideas lead to the well-known linguistic relativity principle, or the Sapir-Whorf hypothesis, the idea that the structure of a language affects the perceptions of reality of its speakers and thus influences their thought patterns and worldviews. In terms of the hypothesis, the differences in the way languages encode cultural and cognitive categories affect the way people think, so that speakers of different languages will tend to think and behave differently depending on the language they use. For example, in Indo-European language family, a "*dragon*" is a legendary creature, typically with serpentine traits, that features in Greek mythology, and being a symbol of the devil or monster. So now the English word "*dragon*" derived from Greek means a ferocious serpent of huge size, monster-like water snake. It is a derogatory term.

Interestingly, in Sino-Tibetan language family (including Japan, Korea and other East Asian countries), a *dragon* is a token of totem, an incarnation of monarch, signifying the paramount majesty. So *dragon* is a commendatory term. In different cultural backgrounds the word denoting the same concept conjures

---

① L. Boroditsky, Lost in Translation. *The Wall Street Journal.* July 24, 2010.
② J. Underhill, *Humboldt, Worldview and Language* (Edinburg: Edinburgh University Press, 2009).

up the different images, and consequently involves the different semantic associations. The language one speaks will definitely influence the way one thinks, acts and behaves.

Based upon the discussions, it may be concluded that language is a nation's cultural gene, and that language is culturally but not genetically transmitted. Language, any language, has a dual character: it is both a means of communication and a carrier of culture. Language and culture are closely related.

3. China English and Chinese Cultural Transmission

China has witnessed a continuous economic booming growth in the past three decades. As a result of the considerable growth of China's overall national strength, China's international standing ascends steadily and its international exchanges with other countries sharply increase. Language, as a means of cultural transmission, takes a momentous role in the international exchanges. China English, used by a tremendous number of Chinese people learning and speaking in the Mainland China, as a distinctive Chinese variety of English worldwide, can be regarded as a media or a window of Chinese cultural transmission in the international exchanges and co-operations.

3.1 What is China English?

Generally, there are several terms that have been used to refer to the English written or spoken by mainland Chinese, such as Chinese English, Chinglish, Sinicized English and China English. Traditionally, the first three terms are different from the fourth one (China English) in that the former is ungrammatical or not standard while the latter is grammatical.

Chinese English and Chinglish, somewhat derogatory terms loaded with social stigma, are usually regarded as a blend or a hybrid of both Chinese and English due to the interference of mother tongue in the aspects of morphology, syntax or pragmatic discourse. So they are usually viewed as bad English, beginner's English, or an interlanguage which needs to be improved.

Sinicized English is a term first proposed by Jia Delin①, who suggested that sinicized English is more appropriate and can best describe the linguistic and cultural features of Chinese English. Unlike other scholars, Jia points out that despite its ungrammaticality, the use of sinicized English will help facilitate the communication and cultural transmission in the international exchanges.

China English, a term first put forward by Ge Chuangui②, who believed that China English was entirely different from Chinese English, that the former is normative and the latter is not, is defined as a variety of English which has the international normative English as its core and which facilitates the transmission of Chinese-specific cultures, linguistic expressions, ideologies, and traditions in international settings. According to Ge, each language or nation has its peculiar ways to express thoughts and concepts. If no equivalents or counterparts can be found in one language, new expressions with normative language as its core have to be employed in the other. For example, the Chinese-specific expressions "三个代表" "双百方针" "精神文明" can be rendered into *Three Represents*, *Two Hundreds Policy*, *Spiritual Civilization* respectively. All these expressions are normative English with Chinese characteristics.

In recent years, however, China English is used in its broad sense to cover all the varieties, including Chinese English, Chinglish, Sinicized English and China English.

3. 2　What are the salient linguistic features?

Numerous studies have been done of China English by scholars and netizens (internet citizen). In terms of the linguistic features of China English, they are essentially centered on four levels: phonology, lexicology, syntax and pragmatics. In this paper the emphasis is laid on the lexicological aspect which is one of the defining features of China English.

One important feature of China English is characterized by its unique lexicon

---

① Jia Delin. Thinking Model and Linear Sequence: The Salient Features of the Word Order in Sincized English. *Journal of Foreign Languages*, 1990, (5), pp. 12 – 16.

② Ge Chuangui. Random Thoughts on Some Problems in Chinese-English Translation. *Chinese Translator's Journal*. 1980, (2), pp. 1 – 8.

and syntactic structures, words or phrases that are native or peculiar to China. A vast number of China-specific words and expressions are rendered into English through one of these two ways: *transliteration* and *loan translation*.

Transliteration is a way in which one system of writing is mapped onto another, word by word, or letter by letter, that is, the spelling of a word in one language with the alphabet of another language. For example, *Fuerdai* (the second generation of the rich, 富二代), *Ernai* (little second wife, 二奶), *Changhong Dahei* (singing red and striking black, 唱红打黑), *fenqing* (angry youth, shit-youth, 愤青), *fangnu* (mortgage slave, 房奴), etc.

Loan translation, also called calque in linguistics, refers to the adoption by one language of a phrase or compound word whose components are literal translations of the components of a corresponding phrase or compound in a foreign language. By this way, a large number of Chinese lexical items are formed by translating them literally into English, e. g. *the Great Cultural Revolution* ("文化大革命"), *paper tiger* (纸老虎), *iron rice bowl* (铁饭碗), *dragon well tea* (龙井茶), *snakehead* (蛇头), *beggar's chicken* (叫化鸡), *Eight-legged Essay* (八股文), etc.

3.3 Developmental stages of China English

From a diachronic perspective, China English has undergone the changes from Pidgin English to Chinese English, then to China English. From the perspective of social development, China English has undergone a shift from English globalization to English localization. Such changes represent the steady rise of China's overall national strength and its influence on the international community, a sign of its soft power.

Historically speaking, cuisine and traditional cultures have made up a fair chunk of English vocabularies of Chinese origin, such as *tea*, *dim sum*, *kung fu*, *moutai*, *tofu*, etc. Therefore, China English found its way into English language. A frequently quoted example is *Long time no see* (好久不见). *Long time no see* (好久不见) is an English expression used as a greeting by people who have not seen each other for a while. Its origins in American English can be traced back to broken or Pidgin English in 1900, and despite its ungrammaticality it is widely accepted as a fixed expression. The phrase is a multiword expression that cannot be explained by the usual rules of English grammar due to the irregular syntax. It may derive ultimately from an English pidgin such as that spoken by Native American Indians or Chinese, but there is no conclusive evidence for either. Many scholars tend to believe that the expression is derived from Chinese. But such type of China English is very rare in English even if it is developed from Chinese, indicating that China didn't enjoy a high international status at that time.

As China's influence expands in recent years, China English, or the Chinese-English hybrid language grows larger. According to the Global Language Monitor (GLM), an Austin, Texas-based institution that collectively analyzes and tracks trends in language usage worldwide, with a particular emphasis on the English language, China English accounts for about 20% of all buzzwords and usages in English language. That means China English plays an increasingly important role in English language, or on the world stage.

4. Case Study of Words and Phrases in China English

China English is a very fascinating topic in linguistics because it offers a special perspective on the study of China's social issues and Mandarin. As more and more China English words and expressions come into being, we are wondering what makes it popular and accessible. For example, when the Chinese movie *People Mountain People Sea* (人山人海) directed by Cai Shangjun won the Silver Lion award for best direction at the 68th Venice Film Festival in September 2011, the title of the movie, a typical Chinese English title, has been an interesting topic and been accessible to the Westerners. As is known, the phrase is the literal translation of the Chinese original, and irregular in English syntax, thus making no sense. But, interestingly, it does make sense now. According to Urban Dictionary, a Web-based dictionary, this phrase is from a Chinese idiom, just like "long time no see". It means there are a lot of people in a place, which is very crowded. It is usually used to describe a big event or a scene, e. g. :

The parade is great; there is people mountain people sea.

The phrase *people mountain people sea* conjures up the image of a scene or event which teems with people. As a matter of fact, Chinese movies, especially the title translations, exert a very important influence on the world. For example, the influential movies 《卧虎藏龙》 and 《色戒》 directed by Li An are rendered into *Crouching Tiger*, *Hidden Dragon* and *Lust & Caution* respectively. 《霸王别姬》 directed by Chen Kaige is put into *Farewell My Concubine*, and 《赤壁》 is translated into *Red Cliff*. All these English translations are characterized by China English. In addition, many such phrases have been coined by Chinese people and included in GLM and some dictionaries, e. g. *good good study*, *day day up*（好好学习，天天向上）. It seems that the extensive employment of China English as the movie titles proves accessible to both natives and foreigners. What's more important, it implies that the ever-increasing popularity of Chinese cultures is proportional to China's clout, or its influence on the world affairs.

Heaven Is High, *the Emperor Faraway*（天高皇帝远）is the title of a book by Valery Garret, a British writer, published by Oxford University Press in 2009. Surprisingly, China English is used as the title. The book tells us that as capital of the powerful Nan Yue kingdom and the largest city in southern China, Guangzhou has been one of Asia's most important commercial, political and cultural centers. Due to the fact that it is far away from Beijing, capital of China, beyond its reign, Guangzhou has developed its unique and distinctive regional culture. The China English title best describes the relationship between Beijing, representing the northern cultures and Guangzhou, symbolizing the southern cultures.

Dama（大妈）is a word created by *The Wall Street Journal* in 2013, which reports that hordes of Chinese aunties have stampeded into jewelry shops, gobbled up glitzy metals and are striving to strike gold amid lackluster economy. As Chinese married female buyers are very sensitive to the gold price down, to seize this opportunity to buy a lot of gold jewelry, they have become the powerful main force to uplift the gold price. For this reason, the Wall Street Journal specially created "dama" that come with the *pinyin* word. Chinese Dama, which means something akin to "big mama" in Chinese, conjures in China an image of a middle-aged woman who keeps a tight grip on the family purse and an eagle eye on gold prices in jewelry shops. The creation of Dama by the western media indicates that China's economic prosperity and stability gives a push to the booming of the world economy.

Guanxi (关 系) is a general Chinese term which literally means "relationships" and represents any type of relationship, but it is quite different in meaning from "relationship". In Chinese society, guanxi describes the basic dynamic in personalized networks of influence, and deals with the study of the art of relationship, so it is usually understood as the network of relationships among various parties that cooperate together and support one another. Because of such differences, the word *guanxi* was used in English media. For example, in 2002, Cambridge University Press published a book *Social Connections in China: Institutions, Culture and the Changing Nature of Guanxi* by Gold, Thomas, Douglas Guthrie, and David Wank. In 2007, the textbook *Guanxi and Business Strategy: Theory and Implications for Multinational Companies in China* by Eike Langenberg (Contributions to Management Science) was published by Springer. The book discusses the issue of paramount importance to those people doing business in China: the impact of personal relationships (guanxi) on business affairs. It shows that the commercial utilization of guanxi with suppliers, customers and authorities yields significant sustainable competitive advantages.

On August 19, 2013, Michael Tyson, American boxer, wrote on his Sina Weibo, a twitter-like micro-blogging service, "Who is the best fighter in China?" The post quickly received hundreds of comments, but one comment stood out in particular. A netizen answered with "Chengguan" to which Tyson replied "Who is Chengguan? A tough man? I've never heard it. " Next day, American GlobalPost published the article *Boxing: Mike Tyson confused by Chinese web humor.* The word *Chengguan* (China's widely despised enforcers of urban management officers, who have a reputation for brutality.) was repeatedly used in the article. In fact, "Chengguan" was widely used in the British media, the most influential *Times*, and America's *New York Times* several years ago, as reported in *New York Times: . . . the beatings repeatedly continued in a nearby chengguan office.*

In the eyes of the western media, *Chengguan* is defined as either Urban Administrators in charge of enforcing local bylaws or a shadowy urban-management force that operates with startling impunity across the nation. Such definitions reflect the problems with which the Chinese society is being confronted at present. On the one hand, *chengguan* officers do exist throughout the country, but on the other, some of them do have a reputation for brutality. In this sense, China English is a window to acquiring the knowledge and a better understanding of China.

5. Cultural Phenomena Underlying China English

The fact that the buzzwords & usages of China English have gained acceptance in the Western mainstream media reflects some interesting social and cultural phenomena. What underlies China English is that some words with Chinese-specific cultures seem to be untranslatable, or no counterparts in English, but on the other hand, language transmission signifies China's more frequent contact with other countries, the steady rise of its international influence and soft power. In this sense, China English symbolizes the increase of China's national strength. Small wonder that Mandarin Chinese is to challenge English globally. It does imply that China's clout in the international affairs is growing large.

In general, the more financially powerful a country is, the more appealing the language spoken in the country will be, the greater influence the country will exert on the world affairs. In the history of mankind, when Roman Empire was in its heyday, at a period of power and splendor, Latin language was popularized. Similarly, English has become a global language after British Empire on which the sun never sets, was the foremost global power.

China English is the image of a social kaleidoscope reflecting variegated social and cultural phenomena or problems in Chinese society. It has been fully realized that of all China English usages, some convey quite positive connotations and some negative. In recent years, a number of derogatory terms (Brother Watch 表哥; Uncle House 房叔) have been widely used in the news report by the Western mainstream media (*CNN*, *Reuters*, *ABC*, *The New Yorker*, *The Daily Telegraph*, *Sky News*, *The Japan Times*). Such cases are most probably related to Chinese social problems. For example,

China's 'Brother Watch' sentenced to 14 years in prison

A Chinese official who became known as "Brother Watch" because of his taste for luxury timepieces was convicted of corruption and sentenced to 14 years in prison on Thursday, according to reports. (The Daily Telegraph, Sept. 5, 2013)

It can be assumed from the examples that the booming of China English reflects many social problems or phenomena that widely exist in China, but on the other hand, it shows clearly that China's international positions steadily rise. In addition, learners and users of China English at home and abroad stand to gain from the social, cultural and linguistic perspectives. It will also help promote a strong sense of ownership among the users, especially among the Chinese users. We are looking forward to the day when more positive terms with Chinese-specific cultures will be a basic component of English language.

References:

[1] Boroditsky, L. 2010. Lost in Translation. *The Wall Street Journal.* July 24.

[2] Ge Chuangui. 1980. Random Thoughts on Some Problems in Chinese-English Translation. *Chinese Translator's Journal.* (2), 1 – 8.

[3] Humboldt, A. 1999. *On the Diversity of Human Language Construction and Its Influence on the Mental Development of the Human Species.* Cambridge: Cambridge University Press.

[4] Jia, Delin. 1990. Thinking Model and Linear Sequence: The Salient Features of the Word Order in Sincized English. *Journal of Foreign Languages* (5), 12 – 16.

[5] Underhill, J. 2009. *Humboldt, Worldview and Language.* Edinburg: Edinburgh University Press.

文化传播中的中式英语媒介

张庆宗　郭熙煌

摘　要：语言和文化传播是国际交流以及中国与其他国家合作的重要

内容。随着中国综合国力以及国际地位的日益提升，我国文化软实力也会得到明显改善，中国语言与文化的国际影响力会持续增强。在这种背景下，中国语言与文化将在国际交流中扮演重要角色。本文主要探讨了蕴含中国文化的中式英语对国际媒体和西方人产生的影响。

关键词： 语言　文化　软实力　国际交流

Philosophical Reflections on the
Foundations of Culture

Corazon T. Toralba[*]

Abstract: Using philosophical anthropology, this paper puts forward the case that culture is created by man through his work. In the process of culture formation, he transforms what he inherited from the past as a legacy for the future while he himself simultaneously undergoes self-transformation. The culture he creates and that has created him is influenced by the understanding of *who* and *what* he is. The claim is proven through a discussion on what culture is and how it develops, followed by a reflection on the notion of person and work, and, lastly, a discussion on the future of mainstream culture emphasizing the importance of the humanities in preparing this future. The paper spins off from Joel Stein and Josh Sanburn's article in *Time* magazine about "the new greatest generation" —the narcissistic, net savvy, earnest, and optimistic millennials. I will also rely on Karol Wojtyla's notion of the person, education, and community.

Keywords: culture; philosophy; foundation; work

* Corazon T. Toralba, Ph. D. at the University of Asia and the Pacific, Philippines.

I

In a controversial article in *Time* magazine, Joel Stein and Josh Sanburn dubbed the millennials as "The New Greatest Generation". [①] The authors described those born in the early 1980s to early 2000s as narcissistic, net savvy, placid, forever connected through their mobile devices, ambivalent with respect to authority, and proud in the belief that they are an entitled class. Stein and Sanburn added that part of the qualities that make these young people the greatest are their earnestness and optimism, pragmatic idealism, realism, and pro-activism. One may think that the authors simply described the youth from affluent societies or from the West. Such was not the case; the description fits any youth that has access to the Web. The article belies such misconception because globalization has flattened the once hierarchical structure. The Filipino youths' behaviour, in particular, has similarities with their American counterparts. [②] If we believe in the adage that the youth is the hope of the future, then it is worth reflecting on the future that this "me, me, me generation" will breed.

This paper will address today's theme of "The Status and Future of Mainstream Cultures in the World", using philosophical anthropology, and argue that man, through his work, creates the culture that he leaves as a legacy to the future and is created by the culture he inherited from the past. However, the culture he creates and that has created him is influenced by the understanding of *who* and *what* he is. To establish my stand, I will start with a discussion on what culture is and how it develops. It will be followed by a reflection on the notion of the person and work, and, lastly, a discussion on the future of mainstream culture emphasizing the importance of the humanities in preparing this future. This paper

---

[①] Joel Stein and Josh Sanburn, "The New Greatest Generation", *Time Magazine*, 181. 19 (2013).

[②] See David Watkins and Andes Gerong, "Culture and Spontaneous Self-Concept among Filipino College Students", *The Journal of Social Psychology*, 137 (1997): 480 – 488, and Timothy Church et al., "Culture and the Behavioural Manifestations of Traits: An Application of the Act Frequency Approach," *European Journal of Personality*, 21 (2007), pp. 389 – 417.

will take off from the article quoted above and use Karol Wojtyla's ideas on person,① education, and community. ②

II

Today's youth are products of nature and nurture in the same way that all persons of all ages have been. Just as nature abhors vacuum, nurture does not take place in a vacuum. While the family, where the parents are the primary and principal educators of their children, is still the immediate milieu that influences the kind of persons that these children are and will become, society is also largely co-responsible. The youth, especially the adolescents, are the most vulnerable because at that point in their lives they want to forge their distinct identity and establish their independence from their family. Ironically, they also seek acceptance from outside the family home; hence, they easily fall prey to peer influences. Together, as idealistic youths, they create their sub-culture within existing ones.

Culture has various meanings. The term itself originates from two Latin words: *cultus* and *colere.* The former refers to worship, while the latter to the act of cultivation. Contemporary understanding of culture includes (1) the general state of the mind, having close relations with the idea of perfection; (2) the general state of intellectual development in a society as a whole; (3) the general

---

① Wojtyla defines the person as "an objective entity which as a definite subject has the closest contacts with the whole (external) world and is most intimately involved with it precisely because of its inwardness, its interior life. " —Karol Wojtyla, *Love and Responsibility*, translated by H. T. Willets (San Francisco: Ignatius Press), 1993, p. 23.

② Wojtyla's notion of community is founded on communion of persons. Communion is a one-to-one relationship while community is the integration of the different communions. However, the integration is not the summation of parts that make up the whole but a general attitude adopted by the members of the community towards each other in view of the common goal pursued by the community. Unity in the community is not physical unity or the fact of living side by side each other in a given territory; rather, it is a moral unity-union of hearts. The prevailing relationship is that of I-thou, which is dealing with persons as subjects that are co-responsible agents in a common endeavor. The opposite is the I-it which is to deal with the other as an object that the other person manipulates, a thing; hence something not someone. See Karol Wojtyla, "The Person: Subject and Community", *Person and Community Selected Essays* (New York: Peter Lang, 1993), pp. 236 – 258.

body of the arts; and lastly (4) a way of life. [1] It can also be defined according to "elitarian," pedagogical, and anthropological concepts. The first refers to a great quantity of knowledge, as when we refer to a person who is very cultured. The second sense indicates education, formation, and cultivation of man through which man comes to the full maturation and realization of his own personality. The last sense signifies the totality of customs, techniques, and values that distinguishes a social group, a tribe, a people, a nation. [2] Culture is commonly understood as combination of symbols, attitudes, and values expressed in conduct that imply a form of adaptation to natural and social medium on which the life of man unfolds. It also refers to the particular manner of adapting the medium to human needs. This definition includes the cultural and civilization aspects. Culture is differentiated from civilization in that the former refers to man transcending himself, becoming better in the process, while the latter refers to the way by which man adapts the environment to his needs. [3] Civilization comprises the whole legal and political relations in any given society. It includes the whole range of relations embodied in constitutions, laws, and legal and political practice. [4] Both culture and civilization are man's creation.

Man is said to be a cultural being, not simply a natural being. He is cultural in two senses: an artifice of culture, and a prime receiver as well as the greatest effect of culture in its subjective sense (formation of the individual) and objective sense (society's spiritual formation). The primary aim of culture is to cultivate man in as much as he is an individual—that is, as a unique and unrepeatable example of the human species. At birth, he has the bare minimum to survive and live as human beings should. He has the task of making and forming himself so as to fully realize his being. The whole of man is a product of nature and culture. [5] Man is not

---

① *The Dictionary of the History of Ideas* available at xtf. lib. edu.

② Battista Mondin, Man: An Impossible Project? *Philosophical Anthropology* (Bangalore: Theological Publications in India), 1991, pp. 145 – 146.

③ José María Barrio Maestre, Es posible un dialogo entre culturas, http://es. catholic. net/ 4 September, 2013.

④ Yves R. Simon, *Work Society and Culture* (New York: Fordham UP), 1971, p. 156.

⑤ Battista Mondin, Man: An Impossible Project? *Philosophical Anthropology* (Bangalore: Theological Publications in India), 1991, pp. 146 – 148.

born existentially perfect, but perfectible; hence, he needs to "cultivate" himself. He attains his existential perfection by transcending himself through confronting the natural medium to meet his needs and wrestling with his self so as not to conform to what is already there. [①] Culture is something acquired and created. It is a personal creation that simultaneously creates and recreates the person.

Culture is also a result of the person's cultivating of his faculties, talents, possibilities, etc. in a way that is imprinted in external symbols (arts and languages) and in moral attitudes and social institutions. Human culture is the different manifestations of thinking and living that can be reflected in symbols, moral attitudes, and social institutions. It is constituted subjectively through human activity that expresses and in some way reveals humanity, and objectively through work and its accompanying transformation of the world to the extent that such conforms to human nature and objective order of nature. The development of culture then is "intimately linked to the understanding of the human being as a self—a person: a self-determining subject... Culture develops principally within this dimension, the dimension of self-determining subjects. Culture is basically oriented not so much towards the creation of human *products* as towards the creation of the human *self*, which then radiates out into the world of products". [②] The importance of philosophical anthropology in the creation and development of culture comes to the fore because this discipline determines *who* and *what* man is. So, what is man?

III

"*Operari sequitur èsse.*" Operation follows being, so goes the medieval adage. An extended application of this could be that the product is determined by the one who created such. Man's regard for himself, born of the consciousness of his being, influences the becoming of those things that he willed to be.

[①] José María Barrio Maestre, Es posible un dialogo entre culturas, http: //es. catholic. net/ 4 September, 2013.

[②] Karol Wojtyla, "The Constitution of Culture through Human Praxis", *Person and Community Selected Essays* (New York: Peter Lang, 1993), p. 265.

What is man? Contemporary man's condition is unfortunately that of "fragmentation". Man is now ordinarily identified with only an aspect of his being. Some identify him with his actions, others with his appetites, a few with his will, a modicum with his intellect, and a good number with his body.

Awed by the achievements of physical sciences concentrated on the material dimension, man has forgotten his spirituality. Bereft of his spiritual moorings, he has strived to build an earthly paradise isolated from the transcendental, much less the supernatural. Political systems built on any of these fragmented ideologies enact laws that promote such reduced understanding of his person. Thus, a culture that leads to man's apparent inability to discover the truth about him prevails.

This development is due to modern philosophy's change of focus from knowing *what* to knowing *how*, from being cosmocentric and theocentric to being anthropocentric. On one hand, this shift paradoxically led to the proliferation of anthropological studies enhancing the modern's man self-understanding at the expense of certainty of knowledge. On the other hand, it also led to "immanentism," an attitude that has made shut of man from external influences. The methodology that ushered in modern philosophy reveals how it is beholden to the achievements of physical sciences, and it thus shuns the possibility of knowing with certainty those that cannot be doubted, resulting in its divorce from sense data, religion, and traditions. Following a mathematical model, it asserts that the only thing man could be certain of is his thinking, and by thinking, he exists, as in the famous "*cogito ergo sum*". The existence of all other beings is dependent on the human mind's clear perception of them. As a consequence of such philosophy, God and the world became postulates of reason, which were later on also subjected to doubt. Detached from the rest of the reality, man was left to his own devices. [1]

As stated in the foregoing, awareness of his existential conditions prompts man to create products to answer his needs. Man's self-transcendence propels him to improve his lot. Man is not usually satisfied with *status quo*; he wants something

---

[1] Corazon. T. Toralba, "The Response of Fides et Ratio to the Educational Task", in Alfredo Co and Paolo Bolaos eds. , *Thomism and Asian Cultures Celebrating* 400 *Years of Dialogue Across Civilization* (Manila: UST Publishing House, 2012) , pp. 306 - 307.

more of life, better living conditions and faster ways of doing things while longing for stability and security. These desires reflect the complexity of man. It also gives us an insight on *what he is*. The quality of response and satisfaction of desires and needs is affected by his self-esteem, which in turn is developed through interaction with the immediate physical and spiritual environment. He whose self-regard is a composite being with corporeal and spiritual components and whose actions are answerable to a being higher than he is would be more likely to create products that exalt the noble aspects in him. Consequently, they enrich not only the person but also the community's cultural patrimony. On the other hand, a person who regards himself as simply material and whose existence ends with his death makes products that satisfy ephemeral desires, hence the speed by which products are replaced without leaving a trace.

Self-knowledge comes by reflecting on one's own actions, while knowledge of the physical world comes from immediate contact and experimentation. Man tests the possibilities and limits of the material world so much so that he learns to dominate to suit his needs, discover the laws that govern the use and misuse of that particular object, then project its possible uses. In the knowing process, man simultaneously improves his world and is improved, refines the tools at his disposal and becomes refined in his ways. How does man improve his world?

IV

Man dominates the physical world through work, and that "human effort which creates goods, that is to say, the effort which puts itself at the service of a piece of work, a creation of labor, itself destined for the humanity, an effort personal in its origin, but fraternal in its ends". [1] Work could also be defined as the "totality of human activities necessary as means and technically recognized as such by which men transform the world to suit their needs, render service to society and perfect themselves as persons". [2] The production of useful and pleasant goods

---

① Etienne Borne and Francois Henry, *A Philosophy of Work* (London: Sheed and Ward, 1938), p. 96.

② Tomas Melendo, *La Dignidad del Trabajo* (Madrid: Rialp, 1992), p. 104.

propels the person to work. Man works not only to satisfy his physical needs but also his desire for perpetuity. Work enables man to establish a family—whose maintenance he will support—and build society of mutual help. Through his children, he leaves a legacy that may be immortalized through certain ways of doing things, hence the existence of family traditions that are preserved through family rituals.

Work reveals another aspect of man's nature: his sociability and cultural being. He works not only for himself but also for others. Just as no one has all the needed tools for a fulfilled survival, he needs others to live contentedly. Other human beings, at times, could be the end of his actions, the company that will keep him safe, and the mirror through which can they see themselves as they are. The last situation is becoming of friends who are alike in virtue. ①

Acceptance by persons outside the family circle is not restricted to adolescence but is an essential human trait. It is one of the elements that complete the happy man. ② However, the fulfillment proper for man is that which corresponds to the activity of the highest faculty of man, which is contemplation; ③ thus, the need for leisure to "cultivate" the mind. Leisure is understood not as not being engaged in something or an activity of the privileged class—the non working group—but having time at ones' disposal to cultivate oneself or perfect oneself and the immediate society of which he is a part. Leisure is a disinterested inner communion with truth beauty and goodness. ④

V

In a broad sense, culture stands for the cultivation of the spirit, of the intellectual life. And this is carried out largely by studying what other people have learned and done. The cultured person is one who has organised his knowledge and

---

① Aristotle, *Nicomachean Ethics*, 1161b, pp. 27 – 30.
② Aristotle, *Rhetoric*, 1360b, 10 – 1362b, p. 25.
③ Aristotle, *Nicomachean Ethics*, 1177a, pp. 11 – 17.
④ Josef Pieper, *Leisure the Basis of Culture* (London: The Fontana Library, 1965).

increased it with the help of that of others. His intellectual work is systematic and fruitful. Through study and reflection, the intellect is enriched and the life of the spirit becomes more fertile; man is raised, so to speak, beyond his own personal limitations, viewing everything from the wide perspective of a culture which is the fruit of the work of many other people. And all this stock of knowledge— properly assimilated, judged and reflected upon—creates a personal attitude towards events and so generates new ideas and new conclusions, which in turn add to the general patrimony of human culture.

Usually, when we speak about culture, we refer to the result of intellectual work, to the sum total of knowledge produced in us by a studious and reflective attitude. It is as it were a solid and rich store of spiritual experience. It is human knowledge—wide ranging, general and harmonious, not a mass of fragmented pieces of information, no matter how deep and advanced individual pieces may be. And so, when we talk about a person's culture, we are referring not so much to their professional knowledge (which often has an immediately practical purpose), as to all the other duly ordered knowledge which characterizes an individual's intellectual make up and emotional life.

Education comes from the Latin words *educere* and *educare*. The first refers to the drawing out of what is latent so that it could be revealed, while the second refers to the act of guiding or leading. Education is not an act of pouring in but an act of drawing from; hence, the most active protagonist in education is not the teacher but the student whose potentials are drawn out to perfect or actualize. Guidance is exercised on the actions and behaviour so that it may conform to his being human. Education is a process of refinement not only of the intellect but also of the will in its discernment of the truth and the pursuit of the good. Interventions are actively taken in the formative years of the child so that the student becomes habituated in those actions befitting the person. Hence, Wojtyla speaks of the end of education as " the bestowal of mature humanity upon those whom the parents have given life—their own children". [1] Emphasis is laid on the maturing of humanity because education as a task is a

---

[1] Karol Wojtyla, *Person and Community: Selected Essays*, trans lated by Theresa Sandok, OSM (New York: Peter Lang, 1993), p. 335.

process geared towards the "proper maturation of the personality and truly personal relationships". ①

The university's business is education. Some interpret that purpose as enabling individuals to reach their full potential as persons and members of society. Others, following John Cardinal Newman, see the aim of university education as the acquisition of knowledge with the following characteristics: it is processed, hence, impregnated by thought; appropriated, converted into a personal possession; considered as a habit; not useful knowledge in the sense of immediate training for a vocation or profession but rather learning for its own sake. ② Newman also wrote, "Education implies an action upon our mental structure and the formation of a character; it is something individual and permanent, and is commonly spoken of in connection with religion and virtue. "③

A person ordinarily enrolls in a college or university in his late teens, at the threshold of adulthood in which experiences and autonomy have their consequent pitfalls. The years spent in the university are decisive because it is while in the university that the students ask the existential questions: Who am I? What is the purpose of my existence? Where do I come from? What is my destiny? What is life? What is love? What does it mean to be free? These cannot be answered satisfactorily by the courses on science and technology, though experimentation and awe could lead them to pose these questions. The longings of the heart can find solace in the courses of humanities because a college is, more than anything else, a place for the training of character, for the nurturing of those intellectual and moral habits that together form the basis for living the best life one can have. Classical literary works have been the channels of spiritual reflections expressed either in prose or in poetry. It could express itself both in the performing and the fine arts. However, the deepest longings are answered by philosophy because philosophy asks for the ultimate causes of beings. Philosophical reflections also

---

① Karol Wojtyla, *Person and Community*: *Selected Essays*, trans lated by Theresa Sandok, OSM (New York: Peter Lang, 1993), p. 341.

② John Henry Newman, *The Idea of a University* (New York: Double Day, 1959), pp. 127 – 146.

③ John Henry Newman, *The Idea of a University* (New York: Double Day, 1959), p. 139.

give rise to ideologies that become principles that guide one's actions and the conduct of one's life because it is the privilege of philosophy to create in the lover of wisdom the desire to order and be not ordered, to teach, and to know everything though not in details. ①

In a controversial article, Stanley Fish disparaged the usefulness of the humanities, relegating its utility value to critical thinking, which is shared by many academics. Humanities teach critical thinking, where students "analyze ideas, differing viewpoints, justifications, opinions and accounts" and, in the process, learn how to "construct a logical assessment ... and defend their conclusions with facts and lucid argument".② "Critical thinking is the intellectually disciplined process of actively and skillfully conceptualizing, applying, analyzing, synthesizing, and/or evaluating information gathered from, or generated by, observation, experience, reflection, reasoning, or communication, as a guide to belief and action. In its exemplary form, it is based on universal intellectual values that transcend subject matter divisions: clarity, accuracy, precision, consistency, relevance, sound evidence, good reasons, depth, breadth, and fairness. It entails the examination of those structures or elements of thought implicit in all reasoning: purpose, problem, or question-at-issue; assumptions; concepts; empirical grounding; reasoning leading to conclusions; implications and consequences; objections from alternative viewpoints; and frame of reference. Critical thinking—in being responsive to variable subject matter, issues, and purposes—is incorporated in a family of interwoven modes of thinking, among them: scientific thinking, mathematical thinking, historical thinking, anthropological thinking, economic thinking, moral thinking, and philosophical thinking. "③

Defense of the humanities rally the following: Humanistic studies provide students with experiences in "inhabiting multiple worlds and viewpoints, to analyze with precision, communicate with great eloquence, and produce

---

① Aristotre: *Metaphysics*, 982a1 –982b10.

② Stanley Fish, "The Uses of Humanities, Part II", *http: //opinionator. blogs. nytimes. com/2008/01/ 13/* 2 September 2013.

③ http: //www. criticalthinking. org/ 2 September 2013.

knowledge of their own. Humanities can provide an education to a set of intellectual qualities of great value in life. The humanities encourage ways of thinking that are not defined by harsh and fast rules, thinking out of the box, intuition, creativity, and place deep value on the imagination". ①

University professors are privileged in assisting to "the birthing process" of ideas that will form the ideological framework that will be the students' guide in the conduct of their lives. Fostering the attitude of wonder, of reflective and critical thinking, could be the legacy that bodes well for the future of contemporary cultures. As discussed in the foregoing, man's "living space" is a means of adaptation to the immediate milieu, and the conditioning of that space to suit his needs is dependent on his self-knowledge.

The challenge then is to provide students with the needed intellectual and moral tools enabling them to make the right choices among the plethora of options that life present to them. Asked on what "makes" a good teacher, Schall answered: "Basically, a good teacher is someone who leads us to ask the important questions, without at the same time being someone who suggests that there are no answers to such questions. The real mystery of teaching is not that there are questions, but that there are answers. "② Professors will also make a judicious choice of the materials by which the students could be guided in their pursuit of wisdom.

Answers to the existential questions must present a holistic, not a fragmented, view of man. The search must lead to the discovery of what is noblest in man, to his spiritual faculties, to the personal encounter with that being whose existence gave man's life its proper meaning. Man must be enabled to recognize the deep spirituality present in his make-up. He must be equipped with tools that will facilitate his discovery of the truth about him. He must be given space for reflection and silence, to be in contact with his inner world, and thus

---

① "Can the arts and humanities 'save us'?" *http: //news. stanford. edu/news/2009/february11/* 2 September 2013. See also David Roochnik, "The Useful Uselessness of the Humanities", Expositions 2. 1 (2008) 019 – 026.

② Kathryn Jean Lopez. "A Living University: A Conversation with Rev. James V. Schall", *National Review*, *http: //old. nationalreview. com* 4 September 2013.

contemplate the physical world as a place that will make him human, and as a space fit for humans.

VI

The future, then, will be his legacy carved in the present. He prepares for that scenario. However, it is not a spontaneous process that is determined. What the future holds is something to be forged now, leaving a mystery that tomorrow's children will fathom and in which the freedom, which is our gift and which exercise is an ordeal, will continue to rely on the guidance of reason that seeks the truth.

The future of contemporary culture is at the hands of today's youth who may or may not discover his true worth, who may or may not be the slaves of technology, or who may or may not change the course of history. Fortunately, majority of these youths who will be tomorrow's leaders are in the university, and university professors of humanities are privileged to lay the foundations through the educational tasks that they are engaged in. The skills and ideas that they have picked up from the classes and the learning experiences that take place in and outside the classroom help prepare that future.

What will the future be? Your guess is as good as mine.

文化基础的哲学反思

Corazon T. Toralba

摘　要： 基于哲学人类学，本文提出，文化是人在劳动中创造的。在文化形成的过程中，在人自身经历自我转变的过程中，人也改变了从往昔所继承的遗产。人类所创造的文化创造了人类自己，这种文化受到人类对自身定位的影响。通过对文化是什么、文化如何发展的探讨，对人与劳动的概念的反思，以及对重视人性的未来主流文化的讨论，上述观点得到证明。本文的论述起始于《时代周刊》中乔尔·斯特恩以及乔斯·桑布恩的文章对孤芳自赏、聪明绝顶、严肃认真以及乐观向上的"新的伟大一代"的阐述，同时还借用了卡尔·沃特拉所提出的人、教育和社区的概念。

关键词：文化　哲学　基础　劳动

孔子"性相近，习相远"思想的方法论及其现代价值

肖春艳　刘冲冲*

摘　要： 两千五百多年前，孔子站在"逝者如斯夫，不舍昼夜"的浩渺烟波里，以"仁爱"之心触摸春秋战国时代的脉搏，在《论语·阳货》中提出"性相近，习相远"的命题。本文通过分析"性相近，习相远"的丰富内涵，立足辩证统一的思维方式，提出"看人、育人和用人"三位一体的人才观和科学处理问题的思路，与"改革开放前后历史不能相互否定"的内涵具有高度的一致性，对推动我国改革开放的伟大实践具有重要的指导意义和时代价值。

关键词： 孔子　方法论　人才观　辩证统一　改革开放

两千五百多年前，中国的儒家创始人孔子站在"逝者如斯夫，不舍昼夜"的浩渺烟波里，以其独有的"仁爱"之心触摸春秋战国新旧交替的时代脉搏，在《论语·阳货》里谱写圣人对人性的精辟见解——性相近也，习相远也。岁月如梭，历史的车轮循序渐进地从农业文明时代跨入信息化时代，孔子的"性相近，习相远"被勤劳善良的中国人代代相传，烂熟于心。

---

* 肖春艳，湖北经济学院教授、博士，大学生思想政治教育评价中心常务副主任；刘冲冲，湖北经济学院经济系学生。

春秋战国时期，王室衰微，诸侯崛起，"普天之下，莫非王土，率土之滨，莫非王臣"的政治格局全面崩溃，各诸侯为了称霸天下而频繁发动战争，战乱不断，民不聊生。随着土地私有制的产生与发展以及商业经济的进一步发展，中国社会阶层结构进行了自我调整，出现谷禄制侍禄，传统世袭社会解体，文化民间化和世俗化趋势明显，"周文疲弊"，"礼崩乐坏"。孔子生逢乱世，"穷则独善其身，达则兼济天下"，怀揣着那颗"救国救民"的仁爱之心，积极地奔走呼号，身体力行，著书立说，设学校教书育人，推行仁爱思想，以此追求达到社会的良治，建立"天下为公""选贤举能"的"大同之世"。然而，春秋时期世卿世禄制仍占据统治地位，传统的天命观和血统论在理论层面依旧维持着旧体制，出于"克己复礼（周礼）"的目的，孔子对传统的天命观和血统论进一步扬弃，顺应社会思想观念由重天思想向更加重民思想转变、人本主义思想渐兴的时代发展趋势，主张知天命，畏天命，不完全否定天命，不再将天视为人格意义上的最高主宰，承认"命"具有客观性，但是突出强调人本主义，更加注重人的作用，提出了"为仁由己"，"为政在人"，"务民之义，敬鬼神而远之"等肯定人的自主性的主张，并且进一步探讨人性，以此作为他推行仁爱思想的理论基础。"性相近，习相远"在孔子经过多年的学习研究和总结个人社会经历的感悟中应运而生。

时过境迁，重温经典，仔细斟酌"性相近，习相远"，我们不得不折服于孔子的博学多才和睿智深沉。子曰：温故而知新，可以为师矣。又曰：学而不思则罔，思而不学则殆。在孔子的"温故知新"和学思辩证结合的学习思想下，笔者对"性相近，习相远"思想的方法论和现代价值略谈几点个人的想法。

"性相近也，习相远也。"用现代汉语来说就是人的原始天性是相似的，只是在后天不同的环境中受到不同的影响后才会产生区别，最终形成千差万别的个性。"性相近"即人的原始天性是相似的，换句话说，人与人之间没有天生的等级差别，这是对"龙生龙凤生凤"的血统论的否定，带有人人生而平等的意蕴。然而，对于此处"性"的理解，仁者见仁智者见智，孟子主张人性本善，荀子则强调人性本恶，杨子见半善半恶的人,便说"善恶混",董仲舒却认为人性是有善恶品等的,提出了性三品说。朱熹言:"心有善恶,性无不善;若论气质之性,亦有不善。"笔者认为:第一,"性"是人与生俱来的东西,具有自然属性。或者说"生之谓性"(《孟子·告子上》)和"生之所以然者谓之性"(《荀子·正名》)所谓的善与恶,作为一种道德评价指标,立足的是一种评判标准,而这种属于主观评价的标准归结于人的主观性,好比我们对一个人进行评价,到底他是善人还是恶人,首先一个前提条件就是他得作为一个生命存在,如果他没有成为生命体,我们就不具有用善与恶去评价的对象或者意义。其次,从一个生命体呱呱坠地起,我们就能够了解作为生命体的人所具有的善与恶,未免太过于主观化,带有唯心主义的倾向(从一个人的社会化过程而言,处在母亲肚子里面的胎儿,是没有善恶观念的。胎儿发育到后期,甚至呱呱坠地,具备一些基本的生理行为,如哭闹吃喝等,属于生命本能,仍然没有善恶可言。但是,当一个婴儿变为成人的时候,他的大脑与外界进行过多次联系,形成思想意识,但是人的思想意识相当复杂,绝非用简单的善恶就能够定性),所以子曰:人非生而知之者也。如果当其作为一个生命体而存在时,就能够准确定性,那似乎有一种超然因素,夸大了人的主观能动性。最后,世界上不会存在真正意义上的"善"与"恶",这些都是一种带有主观倾向的相对主义的评价标语。当我们用性本善或者性本恶再或善恶混等观点去理解人性的时候,我们往往会有一种错误的价值判断,用片面狭隘的思维去看待人性,而忽视了因比较而产生的相对性因素,这只会导致人性的灾难。此外,"性"是人与生俱来的东西,具有自然属性,这是基础,但是经过"习相远"的过程,"性"渐渐具有了社会属性。"鸟兽不可与同群,吾非斯人之徒与而谁与?天下有道,丘不与易也。"所以,此处的"性"进一步理解为自然属性和社会属性的统一。前者是内生的,具有自然属性,后者是外生的,具有社会属性。"性相近"即人性具有相似性而不是相同性,"世界上不存在两片相同的叶子",绝不能简单地只从内生的自然属性或者外生的社会属性去理解人性,而应该立足于两者的统一性,因为人性具有复杂性,人性因人而异。

　　"习相远"的"习"指的是后天环境的影响，这种影响导致人与人的行为、价值、社会影响力等方面的差异。"近朱者赤，近墨者黑。""一匹白布，染于蓝则蓝，染于黄则黄。"有学者指出：从孔子"性相近也，习相远也"一语的结构来看，以"性"与"习"相对而言，所谓"习"是指诗书礼乐的教化习养作用，孔子所谓"兴于诗，立于礼，成于乐"是也。把"习"等同于诗书礼乐教育、教化，笔者不敢苟同，从一个人的社会化过程而言，个人与环境是互相作用的。社会化的场合有家庭、学校、工作单位等，而主体是人。当一个人的价值观和思想观念未必成熟时，通过相应的教化可以使其完善自我的观念和做出合理的价值判断。但是，人具有自主性，具有选择行为和价值判断的自由，或者具有主观能动性，当他的心智成熟或者选择排斥教育的行为的时候，教化对于他的作用和影响力是微乎其微的，甚至会起到负面效应，毕竟人具有逆反心理。此处的"习"，笔者认为可以理解为自主选择的"习"和客观现实存在的"习"。子曰："为仁由己。"姑且把践行仁爱的行为作为一种"习"，而其主体是人自主选择的，择其善者而从之或者从善如流。当然，也会有人择其不善者而盲从之。"习于诗书礼乐者则为君子，不习于诗书礼乐者则为小人。"客观现实存在的"习"，诸如家庭、学校和工作单位等社会场合存在的"习"，是一个正常的社会人难以避免的，而这些场所所传达的思想观念影响着人的行为、思想观念、价值判断、人生追求等。"习相远"不能简单地理解为教化和教育，而应该考虑到个体的自主选择性和社会环境的客观性，不可偏离其一，否则很容易陷入误区。当然，教育、教化对人的影响是不可否定的。

　　从句式结构上面看，"性相近，习相远"是一个完整的句子，既不能脱离"性相近"单独谈"习相远"，也不可以脱离"习相远"单独谈"性相近"。"性"和"习"两者是相互联系、相互影响、相互制约的辩证统一体。"性相近，习相远"不是简单地从一个静态的角度看待人性，而是从一个动态和静态结合的角度辩证地看待人性。从方法论的角度而言，"性相近，习相远"对我们具有重要的指导意义和现实价值，不容小觑。

首先，我们看人，需要从"性"和"习"两者的辩证统一、动静结合的关系入手。有学者指出："性"加上"习"等于人的实际状况。笔者认为这一观点从静态的角度看人是合理的，但是不仅仅如此。我们看人，既要从静态的角度看到他的原始天性和"习"，比如生理结构、心理结构、智力因素等，又要从动态的过程看到后天环境对他的影响，包括个体自主选择的"习"和客观存在的"习"。个人与环境是互相作用的，尤其是人的社会化过程是动态的。如果简单地认为静态的"性"加上"习"等同于人的实际状况而忽视从动态的角度看待个人与环境的相互作用、相互选择的客观事实因素，很容易以偏概全，陷入"一叶障目不见泰山"的认识盲区。看人，既要看到一个由"性"和"习"结合的生命体，又要从动态的过程考虑生命体与环境的互动过程。我们对人的评价，不能简单地主观定义为好人与坏人，也不能荒谬地从静态的层面把握个体的原始天性和"习"。一个人先天条件较好并且后天经历的环境也很好，人们往往主观认为这个人是个好人，而忽视了这样一个事实：个体可能会头脑发热，做出越轨的行为。因而我们看人需要立足动静结合的方法，实事求是地把握"性"和"习"辩证统一的关系。

其次，我们育人，需要采用孔子提出的因材施教的观念。而"材"则是合理地分析教育对象的"性"和"习"相互作用而形成的新的生命体。育人，不是简单地"满堂灌"或者"标准化"，需要更多地结合教育对象的实际情况而选择有所教有所不教。既要考虑学生的原始天性，比如生理结构、心理结构、智力因素等，又要兼顾学生的"习"，比如家庭关系、学校环境、社会经历等，并且在此基础上更要思索个体的自主选择性与环境的互动性，这样才可以做到因材施教。人的天赋、资质、性格、兴趣爱好和人生追求等是不同的，育人必须考虑到"材"的独特性而因人授渔。人人都是可造之材，人皆可以为尧舜，正是基于因材施教的教化观念。而因材施教又是根源于"性相近，习相远"的普遍性事实，因而育人必须坚持"性相近，习相远"的普遍性规律的指导，因"材"施教，根据人的生理结构、心理结构、智力因素、个人的自主性、家庭关系、学校环境和社会关系等有所为有所不为，不可以不顾教育对象的实际情况而一刀切来推行标准化的人才培养模式。当下中国的教育体制将教育的对象进行了简单的分类，这实际上就是一种变相的一刀切。比如在高中教育中划分出重点班、实验班和普通班，这看上去是培养了多层次的人才，但是脱离了因材施教的根本，没有真正把握学生的"性"和"习"相互作用、辩证统一的关系，阻碍了中国教育事业的蓬勃发展。

最后，我们用人，莫过于因材授职，将合适的人配置在合适的岗位，从而发挥人才的效用，实现人才资源的优化配置，促进社会经济的健康发展。而用人的依据离不开合理地看人，那么"性相近，习相远"则成了用人必须思考的重要理论依据。高明的领导者必须具备培养人才的能力，而因材施教是领导者必然的选择，在此基础上进一步因材授职。当然，有时候因材授职也带有育人的成分。因材授职同样需要立足于个体的"性"和"习"。在我国，领导干部的任免一般都需要考虑年龄、学历、政治信仰、工作经验、兴趣爱好等多个因素，实际上就是要把握好"性"和"习"两者的关系，从一个更加合理的角度选拔人才，实现人尽其才。建设中国特色社会主义，实现中华民族的伟大复兴，必须建立科学的人才选拔体系，必须追根溯源，领会孔子"性相近，习相远"所蕴含的深意，相机而动。有学者指出，培养人才的目的是使用人才，这既是孔子一生致力于人才问题研究的出发点，也是落脚点和归宿。看人的前提是分析个体的"性"和"习"，立足于"性相近，习相远"。看人是为育人（因材施教）服务的，而因材施教则是落脚于用人，因材授职。

另外，笔者认为"性相近，习相远"以其辩证统一的思维方法指导我们应对和处理现实难题，具有时代价值和现实价值的双重意义。

看人、育人和用人必须把握好"性"和"习"辩证统一的关系，并且需要从动静结合的角度做出判断，这背后蕴藏着用辩证统一的思维方法去认识世界和改造世界的思想。子曰："诵《诗》三百，授之以政，不达，使于四方，不能专对。虽多，亦奚何为？"学以致用才能显示知识的价值。按照孔子提倡的学以致用的思想，这种辩证统一的思维应当合理地用于解决当下的中国在社会转型时期面临的诸多难题，这样才能凸显"性相近，习相远"的时代价值和现实价值。笔者认为，对于当下我国社会转型期遇到的问题，我们不能简单地用"要么对要么错"的二分法看待，这样看问题的方法是不科学的。现实社会中出现的问题是相当复杂的，仅仅按二分法的思维方式做出价值判断或者决策，容易将纷繁复杂的社会问题或者层出不穷的社会矛盾简单化，这就背离了我党实事求是的思想路线。毛主席说"没有调查就没有发言权"，忽略对现实复杂性的考虑，而简单地区分好与坏或者笼统、模糊地定性分析，是极不科学的，采用这样思维方式做出的决策会给党和国家造成很大的负面影响，阻碍我国全面建设小康社会目标的实现。因此，我们必须抛弃这种不合理的思维方式，坚持用辩证统一的思维方式看待问题。中共中央总书记习近平强调"改革开放前后历史不能相互否定"，教育全党及全国各族人民要用辩证统一的思维方式去看待改革，这与两千多年前孔子的"性相近，习相远"所蕴含的方法论是一致的，更是与我党实事求是、一切从实际出发、辩证统一地看待问题和科学处理问题的工作方式一脉相承的。这种思维方式是高度科学的，并且也最有利于中国特色社会主义建设事业的发展和实现中华民族的伟大复兴。正确把握"改革开放前后历史不能相互否定"的深刻内涵，坚持采用辩证统一的思维方式去应对问题、分析问题和解决问题，是实现国富民强的迫切需要，是完善社会主义市场经济体制的必然要求，是全面建成小康社会、实现中华民族伟大复兴的必然选择。

参考文献

[1] 王恩来：《人性的寻找——孔子思想研究》，中华书局，2005。

[2] 罗安宪：《中国孔学史》，人民出版社，2008。

[3] 赵法生：《孔子人性论的三个向度》，《哲学研究》2010 年第 8 期。

On the Connotation and Modern Value of "Human Nature Is Similar, Practice Made Them Apart" Proposed by Confucius

Xiao Chunyan; *Liu Chongchong*

Abstract: Confucius proposed the theory of kindheartedness, which was expressed as "human nature is similar, practice made them apart" in *Analects*. The paper analyzes the connotation of the proposition, and then puts forward a new theory of education.

Keywords: Confucius; methodology; view of talent; dialectical view; reform and opening up

中庸与中道

——先秦儒家与亚里士多德伦理观之比较

熊友华　　陈静文[*]

摘　要：先秦儒家和亚里士多德在相近的历史时期分别提出了对后世产生重大影响的中庸和中道思想。作为中国和希腊道德的重要精神，中庸和中道思想在两千多年间深刻影响和指导着东西方思想文化和社会的发展。当前中国正处于构建社会主义和谐社会的关键时期，在寻找改革与发展之路的过程中，有必要再次对传统思想文化进行研究。

关键词：中庸　中道　伦理观

在过去的许多年中，中外学者、教育家对中庸与中道的思想都有过研究，取得了不少成就。他们不仅对中庸和中道各自做出了详细的注解和阐释，而且将其从多方面进行比较，探究其异同，从而吸取二者思想的精华，做到古为今用，洋为中用，促进我国思想文化的发展。然而，关于先秦儒家的中庸与亚里士多德的中道思想的比较研究还有不足，所以本文将结合以前的研究成果，对两者做一个较为全面的比较性研究。

* 熊友华，湖北大学马克思主义学院副院长、教授；陈静文，湖北大学马克思主义学院 2011 级思想政治教育专业研究生。

一　历史背景的异同

中庸与中道都与各自特定的社会历史背景密不可分，它们孕育于社会生活之中，都不可避免地打上了时代的烙印。

先秦儒家的中庸思想产生于一个新旧交替、动荡不安、礼崩乐坏的社会大转型时期。在经济上，奴隶制生产关系不断瓦解，正在向封建制生产关系变革；政治上，王权已经衰落，旧贵族的没落和新势力的兴起，使建立在宗法制基础上的周礼遭到严重破坏，社会动荡不安；在思想意识上，一些传统观念已经动摇，产生了代表各阶级利益的不同思想。在这种社会状况下，孔子首先提出中庸的概念，希望以此来塑造合乎中庸之道的理想人格，为调和当时的阶级矛盾、社会矛盾的政治意愿服务。

亚里士多德所处的时代正是古希腊政治、军事等走向衰落的时期，政治危机十分严重，整个社会处于急剧的动乱中。面对古希腊内忧外患的社会状况，民众迫切需要稳定的良好的社会生活秩序，以发展生产和生活。因此，如何缓和各城邦之间及城邦内部的矛盾就成为当时所要思考的重要问题。为解决这个问题，亚里士多德继承和发展了前人的和谐思想，形成了完整的中道思想，并希望在个体的道德生活和道德行为中寻求和谐，从而在社会活动中平衡各方面的关系，实现社会的稳定。

儒家中庸理论的提出比亚里士多德的中道思想要早一个多世纪，但它们所处的时代背景却有惊人的相似之处。它们都产生于奴隶社会即将崩溃的时代，都在竭力维护即将灭亡的奴隶制度，都是要缓和社会矛盾，使社会安定。中庸与中道思想是中西方伦理精神发展到一定历史阶段的必然产物，它们反映了人们一定的价值标准和文化取向，是人类自我意识进一步发展的结晶。

二　基本内容、方法及目标的比较

（一）内容之比较

"中庸"一词最早出现在《论语·雍也》："中庸为德也，其至矣乎！

民鲜久矣。"① 何为"中庸"呢？对于"中"的起源，众多解说中比较有说服力并能统摄其余的是郭沫若的"射箭之中"和唐兰的"建旗立中"。②前者是由中国古代文化象征之一的射礼得来，射箭中的就意味着达到了目的；后者则是通过对甲骨文的考证得出的结论，它说明"中"是各部落形成联盟后的象征，标志联盟的军事首领建旗以立中的意思。但从本质上来说，两者都表明"中"是不偏不倚的意思。"庸"始于《尚书·尧典》，对其解释也各不相同，较普遍的是"用"与"平常"之义。对于"中庸"，朱熹在《中庸章句》中做了全面的诠释："中者，不偏不倚、无过无不及之名。庸，平常也。"③

中道是亚里士多德在论述德性的时候提出的，他认为道德价值的标准就是要符合中道。在亚里士多德看来，中道表现为一种恰当和合宜，即行为"要在应该的时间，应该的境况，应该的关系，应该的目的，以应该的方式，这就是要在中间，这是最好的，它属于德性"。④ 人的情感和行为始终存在着三种精神状态：过度、不及和中间。前两者都属于恶，只有居于这两个极端中的第三种状态——中道，才是德性。

对于中庸和中道的思想内容，我们可以从以下几个方面加以比较：

第一，过犹不及的思想。中庸是思想和行为既不超过也无不及的内在合理界限，是过与不及的中间状态，所以过犹不及的思想是中庸的基本思想。"子贡问：'师与商也孰贤？'子曰：'师也过，商也不及。'曰：'然则师愈与？'子曰：'过犹不及。'"⑤ 在孔子看来，过与不及是相反的两个极端，它们都是败坏德行的，都是恶，而中庸是既不过度，也无不及，是适度的、恰到好处的状态。孔子曾多次阐释并倡导人们在言行中履行中庸，如在《论语·雍也》中："质胜文则野，文胜质则史。文质彬彬，然

① 孔子：《论语》，张燕婴译注，中华书局，2007（重印），第83页。
② 晁乐红：《中庸与中道——先秦儒家与亚里士多德伦理思想比较研究》，人民出版社，2010，第12页。
③ 朱熹：《四书章句集注》，中华书局，1983，第18页。
④ 亚里士多德：《尼各马克伦理学》，苗力田译，中国人民大学出版社，1992，第36页。
⑤ 孔子：《论语》，张燕婴译注，中华书局，2007，第159页。

后君子。"① 质是内容，文是形式。质不足而文有余，则徒有虚文而陷入浮夸，根本不成德性；质有余而文不足，则会流于粗野，不易被人所理解。既有质又有文，两者相互制约相互渗透，才是君子应该具备的美德。这与亚里士多德的中道思想是基本相同的。亚里士多德认为，"人们应该选取中道，既不过度，也非不及。而在我们所说的品质中，正如其他事物一样，都有一个目标。具有理性的人，或者急迫或者迟缓些，总是以它为归向，中道就是过度与不及的居间者。"② 所以，我们可以看出：中道就是人的情感与行为遵循理性的准则，无过无不及，保持着一种适度与和谐。他运用许多通俗易懂的事例来说明这个论点，拿锻炼和饮食来说，锻炼得过多或者过少都不利于身体健康，饮食过量或是不足也都会损伤体力。唯有适度才能健康，并且不断保持和增进这种状态。

不过，这里要强调一点，孔子和亚里士多德都认为中庸与中道是有一定范围限制的，过犹不及所守的中不是两个恶的中（因为譬如偷盗、强奸等行为本身就是罪过，不存在过度、不及与中，只要是恶，人们就应尽力避免），也不是善和恶之间的中，而是调和作为对立面的美德的中。它要避免过度与不及，时刻以适度为中。

第二，时中的思想。孔子认为中并不是一成不变的，而应当是随着时间、环境、条件的变化而有所不同。"君子之中庸也，君子而时中。"③ 冯友兰先生曾在《中国哲学简史》中提出："'时中'的含义是懂得'适当其时'，又'恰如其分'地行事。"④这就明确提出了"时"与"中"的关系，指出"中"是随时而变、因时而中的。对此，亚里士多德也曾有过相似论述，即相对中道思想。亚氏把中道分为绝对中道和相对中道。绝对中道是一种绝对的中间状态，比如，10 是多，2 是少，6 就是其中间。但是他强调："对于我们而言的中道，即相对的中道，是指不太多，也不太

---

① 孔子：《论语》，张燕婴译注，中华书局，2007，第 78 页。

② 亚里士多德：《尼各马可伦理学》，苗力田译，中国人民大学出版社，1992，第 114 页。

③ 朱熹：《四书章句集注》，中华书局，1983，第 19 页。

④ 冯友兰：《中国哲学简史》，徐又光译，北京大学出版社，1985，第 204 页。

少，这是因人而异的。"① 在他看来，中道是随人随事、因地因时不断变化的，没有一个固定不变的尺度和标准来衡量。它只是对应该的对象，在应该的事件中，于应该的地点和应该的时间，以应该的方式来行动。

第三，中和的思想。中和的思想在《论语》中就已产生。"礼之用，和为贵"②，就集中反映了孔子的中和思想。儒家中和思想的实质在于人伦关系的和谐，它以情感为纽带，强调温情脉脉的伦理道德，甚至将情感凌驾于理性之上。"弟子入则孝，出则弟，谨而信，泛爱众，而亲仁，行有余力，则以学文。"③ 学生在家要孝顺父母，在外要敬爱兄长，然后达到博爱众人，才能学习理论知识。而子女对父母的孝，弟弟对兄长的悌是人的最基本的感情，由此扩展到对宗族、社会、国家，成为完整的情感线条。这种情感伦理具有很强的凝聚力，使人际关系和谐、社会井然有序。亚里士多德虽然也希望通过中道达到和谐的社会状态，但与儒家的感性主义原则不同，他所倡导的是理性主义原则。亚里士多德将理性作为其至善追求的核心要素，他极其重视理性的作用。在他看来，"人的善就是合乎德性而生成的灵魂的现实活动"④，灵魂由理性和非理性两部分组成。非理性的部分即感官和欲望，这是人与动植物所共有的，而理性部分即智慧和德性，这是人所特有的。所以中道学说在亚里士多德德性伦理思想中，也是一种理智德性优先论，具有理性主义的特点。他认为人的行为的起点在于行为者自身，行为是自愿的，行为的选择也必须经过事先的策划，而这一切都得经过理性的思考。要想达到幸福必须依靠理性的力量才能实现。当然，对于中和，儒家还明确提出中和之和并不是说要抹杀个人的积极性与创造性，并不是死气沉沉的和，而是鼓励多样化、积极向上的和，所以君子要"和而不同"。

由此，我们就不难看出，先秦儒家的中庸和亚里士多德的中道都具有朴素的辩证法思想，都强调过犹不及，都倡导人在情感、行为等方面要遵

---

① 亚里士多德：《尼各马克伦理学》，苗力田译，中国人民大学出版社，1992，第35页。

② 孔子：《论语》，张燕婴译注，中华书局，2007，第8页。

③ 孔子：《论语》，张燕婴译注，中华书局，2007，第4页。

④ 亚里士多德：《尼各马克伦理学》，苗力田译，中国人民大学出版社，1992，第14页。

循适度原则，保持一种和谐的状态；两者都认为中庸与中道不是一成不变的，而是不断变化的；都把中庸与中道视为"至善"的最高行为准则和追求的目标，视为人们应当追求的德性。虽然两者都是情与理的结合体，但中庸更注重的是情——由血缘亲情发展而来的家庭私情，而在中道中理则占据上风，亚氏坚决反对这种血亲情理，认为人的情感和欲望要受到理性的管束和制约。

由于中庸和中道都是要求适中，无过无不及，许多人便对其产生误解，将其与折中主义、调和主义等相提并论。

折中主义，就是主观任意地将对立面结合起来，采取无原则的迁就态度。它既承认这一个，又肯定那一个，是没有原则、没有是非的。调和主义就是无视矛盾双方差异性和对立的绝对性，并力图泯灭这种对立，追求无差别的统一。中庸与中道是排斥折中主义和调和主义的。中庸讲"中和"是在维护社会道德标准与社会稳定的前提下保持个人的个性和独立见解，并非无原则的折中或调和。而中道认为德性是过与不及的中间，这个中间不是一成不变的，也不是主观臆断的，而是根据具体的情况有所变化。尽管中庸与中道学说并非完全合乎情理，有许多观点有待改进，但是他们是有鲜明原则性的，也正是这种原则性使他们与折中主义、调和主义等区别开来。

（二）方法之比较

中庸与中道作为一种道德品质，并非每个人都能达到，在具体行为中总会出现偏差。如何达到适度，或者最大限度地接近适度，先秦儒家和亚里士多德都提出了相应的方法。

首先，他们提出一个类似的方法，即权衡适度法。子曰："舜其大知也与！舜好问而好察迩言；隐恶而扬善，执其两端，用其中于民，其斯以为舜乎！"[1] 舜之所以能成圣，就是因为他能把握事物的两个极端而用中庸之道去引导人们，即执两用中。要想成就大事，就要恪守中庸之道，无

---

[1] 朱熹：《四书章句集注》，中华书局，1983，第20页。

过无不及。不过这种状态是一种理想状态，在实际生活中总会有或多或少的偏差，很少有人能达到。针对这种情况，孔子提出"不得中行而与之，必也狂狷乎？狂者进取，狷者有所不为也"①，也就是说孔子最为推崇的是中庸；达不到中庸，就取狂，追求锐意进取；狂也做不到，就只好取狷，不做超越规范的事情。这实质就是退而求其次，选取一个相对较好的。亚里士多德也指出："不得以求其次，这就是两恶之间取其轻。"② 在过度与不及之间，有的危害大一些，有的危害小一些，应该避开与中道更加对立的那个极端。如节制的两端相比较，放纵之恶就大于麻木不仁之恶；慷慨的极端挥霍虽然浪费钱财，但相对于吝啬而言便可算是小恶。一次命中中间固然理想，但是往往很难实现，所以要在两恶之间权衡其轻重，然后力争避免大恶。由此，我们可以看出他们都要求在过与不及之间进行权衡，选取与适度较接近的一个。

其次，他们又根据各自的理论提出了不同的方法。

儒家根据中庸中的时中思想提出权变的方法。所谓权变，就是根据事物发展的具体情况采取相应的措施。"君子之中庸也，君子而时中也。"③ 这句话就表明君子要做到中庸，就必须根据现实的变化，审时度势，灵活处理问题。孟子明确提出"执中用权"的观点，认为执中不能简单机械地在两端中间选取一个中点，而是要灵活地权衡实际情况。他还运用生动的比喻做了说明，如在《孟子》中"嫂溺不援，是豺狼也。男女授受不亲，礼也。嫂溺援之以手者，权也"。④ 看见嫂嫂溺水而不予理睬是不符合人性的行为，但礼法又强调男女授受不亲，在这种道德两难的情况下，给予援助之手不仅不会与礼法相违背，而且会受到赞扬。所以，我们在培养中庸时，要把握好实施中庸的应变能力，在不同形势下灵活应对。

而亚里士多德则提出感性怀疑法，即要警惕自身的感性欲望，避免沉溺于那些引人快乐的东西和快乐。众所周知，人的感性使人具有趋乐避苦

① 孔子：《论语》，张燕婴译注，中华书局，2007，第197页。
② 亚里士多德：《尼各马克伦理学》，苗力田译，中国人民大学出版社，1992，第42页。
③ 朱熹：《四书章句集注》，中华书局，1983，第19页。
④ 孟子：《孟子译注》，杨伯峻译注，中华书局，1960，第177页。

的本性，这种本性会使人们不自觉地陷入快乐的旋涡之中，而快乐会影响我们的判断，使我们被它牵着鼻子走，从而容易犯错。所以我们必须不断地对感性欲望提出质疑，用理性调控感性，将自己拽往相反的方向，才会避免失误，达到适中。

在亚里士多德那里，中道的伦理德性称作习惯德性，"对于我们，没有一种伦理德性是自然生成的。因为，没有一种自然存在的东西能够改变习性"①。所以中道不是生而有之，不是天赋的，而是在后天的行为中逐渐形成的，是通过习惯而达到完善的。儒家的中庸思想是从天人合一的观念出发的，《中庸》开篇就提出"天命之谓性，率性之谓道，修道之谓教"，认为中庸是人性本身所固有的、天赋的德性，将这种潜在的德性变为现实只不过一个向内用心的过程，强调通过"慎独"等方法修身养性。这是两者很明显的一个区别。但是无论是天生的还是后天的，他们都认为要想达到中庸就必须在后天付出努力，在具体的情感和行为情境中练就自己熟练地运用实践智慧的本领，而且两者方法虽有不同，但本质都是避恶趋善。在具体实施时，亚里士多德要求："第一，他必须有所知；其次，他必须有所选择，并因其自身而选择；第三，在行动中，他必须勉力地坚持到底。"② 也就是说，要做到中道，一方面要将行为的动机和行为的结果结合起来，只偏重行为的动机忽视行为的结果就会使道德流于空虚，反之就会使道德限于务实。做有道德的事必须是没有其他目的自愿选择的，不能仅仅因为行为的结果符合道德就断定他是道德之人。另一方面要在知道什么是道德和自愿选择遵循道德规范的基础上坚持践行德性，一以贯之，不断重复道德行为以养成良好的德性。儒家也曾感叹："人皆择乎中曰'予知'，择乎中庸，而不能期月守也。"③ 由此可看出，在如何达到中庸这个问题上，他们都强调行为的动机与结果相一致，并且要坚持不懈，持之以恒，不能半途而废。

---

① 亚里士多德：《尼各马克伦理学》，苗力田译，中国人民大学出版社，1992，第27页。
② 亚里士多德：《尼各马克伦理学》，苗力田译，中国人民大学出版社，1992，第32页。
③ 朱熹：《四书章句集注》，中华书局，1983，第20页。

（三）目标之比较

无论是先秦儒家的中庸还是亚里士多德的中道，其核心思想都是在过与不及之间寻找中间，但这个中间的确定并不是随意而为的，需要有一定的标准。

《礼记·仲尼燕居》中记载："子贡越席而对曰：'敢问何以为此中者？'子曰：'礼乎礼！夫礼所以制中也。'"① 在这里孔子明确指出，中庸的标准是"礼"。情感和行为只有合乎"礼"才可以称为"中"。在礼制的熏陶之下，情感和行为逐渐合乎中庸之道。故孔子云："不知礼，无以立。"② 离开了礼制，对于个人而言，无以修身立德；对于社会而言，则会导致臣弑君、子弑父、兄弟相残的混乱局面。

《中庸》对此也做过明确论述："喜怒哀乐之未发，谓之中，发而皆中节，谓之和。"③ 这是指情感的发挥出于内在的道德信仰并符合礼节，从而使人和事物在合乎中道原则基础上形成的和谐共处的状态。

儒家基本是持性善论的观点，认为每个人只有向内努力，发掘本性，抑制恶端，才能成为君子甚至圣人，再由个人扩展到全体，使人人都具备君子的高尚品格，从而达到"修身、齐家、治国、平天下"的理想局面。所以，从根本上说，儒家主张以道德为工具对人民进行教化，使人们的思想和行为符合礼法的要求，使中国社会走向了德治和礼治的道路。"道之以政，齐之以刑，民免而无耻；道之以德，齐之以礼，有耻且格。"④ 儒家学说将礼和德抬到了一个非常高的地位，使其在社会调控中居于中心，法律只是依附道德，是推行道德的工具，甚至将道德完全凌驾于法律之上。

亚里士多德坚持性恶论，认为人性恶欲是根深蒂固的，而法律恰是遏制人性恶欲的最坚固的堡垒，所以亚里士多德把法律作为中道的标准。他

---

① 李学勤主编《礼论正文》，郑玄注，孔颖达疏，北京大学出版社，第 1613 页。
② 孔子：《论语》，张燕婴译注，中华书局，2007，第 259 页。
③ 朱熹：《四书章句集注》，中华书局，1983，第 18 页。
④ 孔子：《论语》，张燕婴译注，中华书局，2007，第 13 页。

说："法律要求人们全部合乎德性而生活，并禁止各种丑恶之事。为教育人们去过共同生活所制定的法规就构成了德性的整体。"① 他认为法律是没有感情的智慧，是合乎正义而毫无偏私的工具，所以他对人的品质要求是合法基础上的合德。不仅如此，亚里士多德还认识到不经过长期的法律约束和规范，真正的道德就难以养成。

中道思想是在探讨幸福与美德的过程中提出的，他认为："幸福是终极的和自足的，它是行为的目的。"② 人类一直追求的目标就是幸福，所以幸福也是中道的最终目的。当然，中庸的目的是过有道德的生活，它是单纯为道德而道德，不牵扯其他因素。达到了内外自由相统一的状态就达到了中庸。而中道则认为有道德是不够的，过有道德的生活最终还是要走向幸福，这和儒家将道德与幸福等同的思想是不同的。

三 对后世影响的不同及特点

（一）影响

中庸与中道思想是先秦儒家和亚里士多德伦理思想的重要组成部分，它们在许多方面，尤其是对中西方的政治理念和人们的行为准则，都产生了一定程度的影响。

首先，中庸作为中国封建社会的正统思想，对我国的政治理念和士人行为准则的形成和发展具有无法估量的作用。

汉代大儒董仲舒对儒家思想进行了改造，将儒家的"天人合一"思想、法家的集权思想和阴阳家的五行说结合起来，提出天人感应、君权神授理论，并进一步提出了一套维护封建等级制度的"三纲五常"说。这样，儒家思想就符合了当时统治者的需要。在汉武帝"罢黜百家，独尊儒术"之后，儒家思想就正式成为封建社会的正统思想。这必然会对中

---

① 亚里士多德：《尼各马克伦理学》，苗力田译，中国人民大学出版社，1992，第98页。
② 亚里士多德：《尼各马克伦理学》，苗力田译，中国人民大学出版社，1992，第13页。

国政治产生广泛而深远的影响。我们知道，政治秩序贵在稳定，稳定压倒一切。而这种稳定是妥善处理社会各个利益集团的矛盾的结果。所以封建统治者们为了社会的稳定，借用中庸思想，将其作为调节和弥补偏激治国思想的有效良方。汉武帝之后，儒家的中庸思想更是成为统治者的治国方略。历经隋唐到宋明，中庸思想影响着封建专制时代的皇权制度。

中庸思想强调对立面的相互依存，强调不走极端，无过与不及，它旨在对事物两端进行分析后，寻求两极的中间，实现"和为贵"的目标。"天下之达道五，所以行之者三。曰：君臣也，父子也，夫妇也，昆弟也，朋友之交也。知，仁，勇，三者天下之达德也，所以行之者一也。"①可见，中庸讲究君臣之义、父子之亲、夫妇之别、长幼之序、朋友之信，而处理好这些关系，社会也就会随之和谐。因而中庸可以用来帮助处理社会存在的各种矛盾，协调个人与个人、个人与社会、个人与国家之间的关系，起到维护社会稳定的作用。无论是统治阶级利用中庸愚弄人民、麻痹人民，使他们安于被压迫和被剥削的命运而不加反抗，还是人民因自我意识选择遵循中庸，将其作为自身的行为准则，客观上说都起了维护封建统治的作用。但是从另一个角度来说，中庸思想在一定程度上忽视了对立面的相互转化，而此后的儒家对此加以片面强化，发展了先秦儒家中庸思想消极的方面，甚至出于稳固封建统治的政治需要把它同折中主义、调和主义等同起来，从而把其中的积极见解抹杀了，强化了它的保守性。这种保守为历代统治者所重视并被长期利用，从而造成了统治阶级因循守成、害怕变革的心理状态，所以中国历史上尽管有多次具有积极意义的变法活动，但都以失败告终。从这个意义上来说，中庸在一定程度上延缓了中国封建社会的消亡，阻碍了中国社会的发展。

中庸思想不仅是维护封建统治的政治武器，更是个人修身处世的思想指导。因此，它对中国民族性的塑造也产生极大作用。众所周知，儒家伦理思想是经过几千年文明的演变而汇集成的反映民族特质和道德风貌的民族伦理文化。而中庸经过世代延续已经深深地融入中华民族的思

---

① 朱熹：《四书章句集注》，中华书局，1983，第28页。

想和行为中，并内化为人们的一种性格和心理，成为影响人们精神领域的强大力量。但是，随着中庸本义中积极方面逐渐被抹杀，保守消极因素的不断发展，中庸对国民性产生了许多消极的影响。它一方面使主体失去了个性，不利于激发个人的主动性和创造性，使中华民族缺乏勇于冒险和不断创新的性格特征；另一方面则形成一种以过去为定向的价值观念，使人安于现状，不思进取。对于中庸所产生的负面影响，鲁迅批判道："遇见强者，不敢反抗，便以中庸这些话来粉饰，聊以自慰。"① 这深刻揭露了国人保守惧变、怯懦屈从、圆滑世故、苟且偷安等中庸劣根性的一面。

其次，中道思想对西方社会也产生了一定的影响。

"人是天生的政治动物"，亚里士多德的中道思想实际上就是为了论证其政治哲学的。由中道思想出发，他提出了许多独特的政治理念。其一，中产阶级掌权。他认为中道是最高的德性，凡事都以适中为最好，所以大贫不好，大富也不好，不贫不富才是最好的。他们既不像穷人那样只满足于最基本的生活需要，以吃穿住用行为生活的全部，也不像富人那样沉醉于物质利益当中，仅以功利物欲为目的，他们可以平衡各种关系，缓和社会矛盾。所以就建构优良政体的阶级基础而言，亚氏力主最优良的政体必须由中产阶级执掌政权，而且主张在小范围内即城邦内建立共和政体以稳定奴隶社会的统治。其二，树立法治的权威。亚里士多德将法律作为中道的标准，在人类历史上第一次对法治思想做出系统论述。他不相信人治，认为法治优于人治，并强调"良法"的重要作用。当然，亚里士多德并没有绝对否认人在法治国家中的能动作用。任何一项法律的制定和执行都离不开人的因素，但是个人的才智只能作为法律的补充，而且个人才智的运用在任何时候都不能违反法律的基本精神，否则就不可能做出公正的处理和裁决。由此看来，亚里士多德的法治理论并不是绝对地偏向于法治，而是以人治来加以调和，充分体现了他中庸平衡的思想。其三，注重分配的公平正义。亚里士多德强调应禁止公职人员利用职权谋取私利，同

---

① 鲁迅：《华盖集》，人民文学出版社，2006，第25页。

时对各种公职的任期加以限制，对各种荣誉的分配加以管理。此外，他提出"比值平等"的思想，体现兼顾公平与效率的原则。

中产阶级掌权的思想是为当时趋于没落的城邦奴隶制谋求出路而提出的，但这种理论显然已不符合时代发展趋势，只能停留在言语中而不能付诸实施；法治思想则是历代统治阶级法治理论的渊源，奠定了西方的法治主义精神；注重分配的公平正义也具有很强的现实意义，可以逐步缩小贫富差距，在效率与公平之间达到最佳平衡。

中世纪著名神学家托马斯·阿奎那以亚里士多德的理论为基础创建了完整的神学体系。他对亚氏伦理思想中的质料说进行了重新阐释。亚里士多德在探究德性和中道时，对人与动物、植物进行比较，发现任何生命都是质料和形式的统一，而质料就是肉体，形式就是灵魂，在质料与灵魂中，灵魂是生命的源泉，是推动生命的根本力量。托马斯利用这一观点做了进一步的论述，认为形式，也就是灵魂，是直接来自上帝的，上帝是纯形式的。通过改造，亚里士多德的伦理思想为神学所利用，成为中世纪经院哲学的理论来源。

文艺复兴打破了中世纪以来长期禁锢人们思想的宗教神学观，驱散了学术阴霾，给人们提供了一种崭新的思维模式和思想方式，促进了亚里士多德思想的复兴。然而，虽然他的政体划分、法制社会等思想得以继承，但中道的影响已逐渐消失。

（二）特点

通过以上对中庸与中道影响的分析，我们可以明显看出：中庸思想无论对中国的政治理念还是对中国人行为准则的影响都比中道对西方的影响要大，这也是中国伦理思想与西方伦理思想的一个重要区别。这种差异的背后隐藏着它们对后世影响的特点。

第一，内容特质。中庸从本质上说是观念形式，是一个非常抽象的概念，但它并不是绝对的抽象，也并非空洞无物，它是由具体内容充实其中的。换句话说，中庸思想是抽象与具体的统一，是普遍性与特殊性的统一。一方面，中庸是从天人合一的角度提出来的，"天命之谓性，率性之谓道，修道之谓教。道也者不可须臾离也"①，明确指出中庸是天地之道，是道德的最高准则。另一方面，儒家又将中庸放入现实之中，从具体的道德层面进行论述。第一层是个人修养的中庸，要求人们在人格塑造上，不能走极端，做到五美，即"惠而不费，劳而不怨，欲而不贪，泰而不骄，威而不猛"②；第二层是交际处事的中庸，要求人们在人际交往中坚持"毋意，毋必，毋固，毋我"③，既不能主观臆断，绝对肯定，也不能固执己见，自以为是；第三层是为政治国的中庸，中庸也是当政者所需要具备的素质，"子张问于孔子曰：'何如斯可以从政矣？'子曰：'尊五美，屏四恶，斯可以从政矣。'"④ 由此我们以得出结论：先秦儒家的中庸思想不是虚无缥缈的空中楼阁，它关注的焦点还是人，是现实生活的各个方面，讨论的也是人如何为人与人如何更好地生存和发展的问题。中道思想是在论证什么是德性的时候提出来的，它所涉及的都是人们的日常经济、政治和文化生活。但是与中庸将理论与实践相结合相比，中道更注重的是理论，强调的是对知识的把握。所以尽管亚里士多德也有自己独特的方法，但他并没有提出像儒家所提倡的"慎独"等切实可行的方法。

第二，工具特性。儒家学说经过西汉武帝"独尊儒术"之后便成为官方学说。它并不只为一个特定的朝代服务，而成为整个封建时代的正统思想。几千年来，中庸思想作为儒家思想的精华，不断地被统治者宣传利用，并根据统治者的需要得到改造，成为统治人民、稳定秩序的工具。也正因为中庸思想统治着整个社会的意识形态，后来甚至成为科举考试的定项，成为选拔国家管理人员的标准，所以无数的士人前赴后继地对其进行探索研究，也有的士人将其作为跳板去谋求高官厚禄，获得名利和地位。所以从某种意义上来说，将中庸作为统治的工具客观上促进了它的传播，在深化其对后世的影响方面做出了极大贡献。相对而言，

---

① 朱熹：《四书章句集注》，中华书局，1983，第17页。
② 孔子：《论语》，张燕婴译注，中华书局，2007，第306页。
③ 孔子：《论语》，张燕婴译注，中华书局，2007，第118页。
④ 孔子：《论语》，张燕婴译注，中华书局，2007，第306页。

中道却更多是以一种学术理论在发挥作用。尽管亚里士多德提出中道思想是为其政治理论寻找依托，是想将其作为拯救没落奴隶制的工具，但这个工具却不是社会发展所需要的，也不是追求进步的知识分子所推崇的，所以伴随着希腊奴隶制的衰落，中道思想作用的发挥也受到越来越多的局限。

第三，学术特点。概括地说，中国学说是一种道德学说，以讲道理的方式来传递思想；而西方学说则是一种思辨学说，是以真理的身份来引导思想。中庸的道理来自圣人之言。圣人用开阔的视野、丰富的知识、济世的精神和超群的悟性思考社会现象，在纷繁复杂的现象中剖析本质，从而解答各种社会问题，然后一代代的人再根据时代发展撷取精华、剔除糟粕，用言传身教将其中的道理延续下去。这样，中庸思想就成为贯穿中国政治和文化的线索，不间断地影响着社会的发展。而西方讲求思辨，即任何理论学说都要经过时间的检验，只有被证明了的真理才能为人们所信服并加以利用。亚里士多德的中道思想中蕴含着许多真理性的见解，至今仍对社会发挥着积极作用。但总体而言，其思想所适用的范围局限于他所处的时代，一旦脱离那个时代，便会暗淡下去。所以纵观西方文化发展史，我们不难发现：西方的政治伦理思想并不像中国封建社会那样一以贯之地以儒家思想为指导，在求"和"的目标引领下，走德治和礼治的道路。继亚里士多德之后，又出现了许多全新的政治伦理模式，如中世纪的神学政治伦理、文艺复兴时期的非道德政治伦理、近现代权利政治伦理等。

小　结

通过对中庸与中道的比较分析，我们了解到两者在历史背景、基本内容、方法及目标上的异同。除此之外，中庸与中道对后世也产生了不同的影响，但无论是对政治理念还是对人们的行为准则，中庸的影响程度都大于中道。而这种差异也反映了两者对后世影响的特点，即内容特质、工具特性和学术特点。

Moderate and Temperate: Comparison Between Pre-qin Confucianism and Aristotle

Xiong Youhua; Chen Jingwen

Abstract: Pre-qin Confucianism and Aristotle put forward the ethical thoughts expressed as to be moderate and to be temperate. The two thoughts have made great impact on eastern and western history of thoughts. To make comparison between them has great value for our harmonious social construction.

Keywords: moderate; temperate; ethical viewpoints

生态文明与儒家德性精神振兴*

——基于一种情感知识学的阐释视角

方德志**

摘　要：儒家德性精神孕育和成长于华夏传统农耕文明，但它在以源自古希腊的德性精神为支柱的现代工业文明时代表现出衰弱症状；工业文明的负面效应引起人类自觉批判工业文明社会的发展方式及其知识观念模式，呼吁生态文明的到来；生态文明是对前工业文明和工业文明的"扬弃"，将为儒家德性精神的再生长提供适宜的社会条件，（基于一种情感知识学方法论建构的）儒家德性精神振兴也将为生态文明建设提供新的知识（观念）模式。

关键词：生态文明　儒家德性精神　振兴　情感知识学

　　任何事物的成长都需要适宜的条件，儒家德性精神成长同样需要适宜的条件。作为一种崭新的人类文明形态，生态文明将为儒家德性精神的再生长形态提供一种适宜的社会条件，儒家德性精神的再生长形态也将为人类矫正工业文明的负面效应提供崭新的方法论支持。

---

　　* 本文为教育部人文社科青年基金项目"情感主义视域下的道德知识学研究"（项目编号：13YJC720011）和"构建我国主流价值文化研究"（江畅教授主持，项目编号：11&ZD021）阶段性研究成果。
　　** 方德志，哲学博士，温州大学政法学院教师。

一

"德性"① 一词在中西方古代哲学语境中，首先表示诸自然生命力的健康生长状态，随后衍生出指人的那种操持生命健康生长状态的自觉能力。这两种层面的"德性"所需条件虽然不一样，前者属自然条件，后者属社会条件，但是具有类比性，并且在某种条件下——例如在生态文明时代——具有内在的相通性。

华夏传统农耕文明为儒家德性精神的成长提供了最初的适宜条件，最终塑造出以"仁爱"为基础概念的（基于"情感本位"的）儒家道德知识学体系。"仁"是天、地、人、神共通的共生性德性②，"仁爱"是独属于人的社会性德性。从知识论看，儒家的"仁""义""礼""智""信"

---

① 关于"德性"一词的含义，笔者在《追寻德性/virtue 的原始涵义》（《湖北大学学报》2012 年第 2 期）一文中做过阐释。国内学界目前对"德性"一词的理解重点是对"德"字的阐释，这当然不是在与英文"virtue/德性"一词的对称性语境下来阐释的。在由"德性"热而引起人们对汉语"德"字的考察中，笔者比较认同程平源的阐释。程平源认为"德"字最初是先民刻画种子发芽以求得庄稼成长的一个巫术，后来演化为祖先崇拜的"图腾崇拜"。在笔者看来，这种解释能把"德"与"生/性"内在结合起来，揭示了"德"字是人类向大自然求生的一种仪式，进而内化为一种敬畏生命的"品质"，所以"德性"之"德"即是对"生"的敬重。程平源：《儒家德性论源起考——以先秦"德"义变迁为考察对象》（http://www.confucius2000.com/admin/list.aspid = 1735）。

② 把儒家的"仁"阐释为"天、地、（神）、人"的共生性德性，是出于当代儒学发展的一种宗教性诠释考虑。儒学的宗教性解读其母体在"易经"。在笔者看来，易经蕴含的阴阳五行学说为儒学的宗教性解读提供了一种神学性溯源语境。如果把易经的"阴、阳"动力说和"金、木、水、火、土"五行元素说加以改造，就可能成就儒学在生态文明时代的神学性创新（生态神学）。例如，设想生态文明语境下的一种生命神与中国古代神话人物（伏羲氏）签订某种"生命契约"，并以阴、阳动力和金、木、水、火、土（气、光）等生命元素授以伏羲氏创造"易经"，要求人类不得违背生命契约和随意破坏生命元素的转成机制，否则人类将受到生命神的惩罚。如果说，生命神与伏羲氏签订的"生命契约"在现代科学思维环境下是不可信的，那么可以援引现代物理学（相对论）的时空多维性来为此提供预设，即设想一种生命神与伏羲氏签订的"生命契约"是在另一个时空维度中与当下时空维度中的人类保持同在（"宇宙的起点与终点同一"）。"易经"的神学性阐释为儒学的宗教性诠释提供了神迹（神话）基础，从而不必套用基督教来阐释儒学的宗教性。生态文明时代之生态神学下的生命神是对生命元素和生命动力的人格推定，提倡的是一种共生性信仰（不同于基督教的人类中心论），它可以成为生态文明时代人类共同的信仰，基于这种生命神及其共生性教义的儒学则完全可以走向具体的宗教生活。

"诚"等一系列范畴是由人的情感能力所建构的情感知识学范畴。

不同于人的理性能力之抽象性构成知识（观念）方式，人的情感能力是采用现象性方式来构建人与世界之间的知识学结构①。在人的生命与自然万物的生命之浑然一体的共生性成长过程中，人的生命感受性日益敏锐，由此生成了对生命的情感确知（或者称为"情实"），这种情感确知就是人对与其共生的各种自然生命元素的一种自觉意识。（随着情感能力的独立觉醒和属人化的飞跃）人的情感能力再将这种与人共生的情感确知（"情实"）当作认识的对象，由此构成了"仁""义""礼""智""信""诚"等情感知识学范畴。换言之，情感为了认识/确认它自身的"在世"状态，自行构建了"仁""义""礼""智""信""诚"这些范畴。所以，儒家这一套范畴体系只能运用人的情感能力才能判断其真假，如果套用西方唯智主义方法来认知和解析这些范畴就会使之失真和支离破碎。这就是儒家之"美德即知识"的独特个性所在。那么，据儒家知识学来说，无情无爱即是无知，也即无德无能。

从知识发生学的过程来看，儒家"仁""义""礼""智""信""诚"等范畴体系是人的情感能力构建知识学范畴的递进过程，它反映了儒家从个体生命的深度体验（"仁"）中，逐渐显现出对同类的道德感意识（"义"），进而显现出实践的道德规范（"礼"）及其实践判断能力（"智"），再在人的社会性交往中显现出普遍性契约意识（"信"），最后在天、地、人、神的生命本源之同一性体验中显现出一种情感确知/体验的终极实在（"诚"）这一情感知识学的发展过程。从（情感）认识论看，儒家这里的"诚"就相当于西方（理性）认识论中的"存在/being"范畴。"诚"，作为一种实在性之本体对象，完全依赖人的情感能力之纯粹形而上运用。一个人没有对生命本源的深度体验就不能理解儒家的"诚"。孟子所谓的"诚者，天之道也；思诚者，人之道也"，讲的就是人类运用情感能力去深度确知/体验（"思"）生命共生本源时，天道之

---

① 笔者认为，情感与理性是人的两大知识能力系统，它们在构建人与世界之间的对象性知识方式上完全不同，前者是具时空的现象性方式，后者是超时空的抽象性方式。

"诚"与人道之"诚"实现了实在性对接。"诚"是诚实、实有、踏踏实实的意思，它是天的品质，"天"因为具有"诚"这种实实在在的向善厚生的优秀品质，就成了儒家情感知识学（道德哲学）所要追求的终极实在。

同理推知，一个人如果没有对"仁"的深刻体认，就不会有真正的个体尊严意识。"仁"是天、地、人、神共通的共生性德性，个体生命只有领会到"仁"的本真内涵，才能真正感受到生命（人）的尊严；没有"义"的体认，就没有对人"类"的正义感；没有对"礼"的体认，就没有所谓的"智"，所以不践行"尊老爱幼"这个礼节就是失智和无知；没有对"信"的体认，一个人就难以展开"仁"爱之德中的普遍性契约命运；没有对"诚"的体认，一个人就难以形成对生命终极关怀的承诺。

联系现实来看，生活中人们免不了与他/她人发生交往和情感介入，但是如果把这种交往只是当作实现某种抽象性目的的手段，那么情感就会无法本真地介入生命的"在此"状态，人就会感觉不到幸福。但是，如果把这种交往当作一种目的本身，把与他/她人照面的时时刻刻都当作生命"在此"的本真状态，人的情感就有了"在此"的本真着落，人的生命就会觉得幸福。为什么情感有时会苦恼？因为情感也有自身的"同一律"和"矛盾律"，情感的苦恼在于人们对情感"说了谎"，"造了假"，给情感的本真同一性身份制造了"矛盾"。人们常把幸福与欲望挂钩，认为幸福是人的欲望得到某种满足。其实，幸福源自人之纯粹情感的实践要求。一个人如果把每天与他/她照面的人或物都看作异己的对象，那么情感就失去了守护生命"在此"的功能，生命的"在此"就发生了异化，人当然幸福不得。"幸福"的英文单词是"well-being"，就是对人的生命之"存在/being"状况的本真性价值评价，这个价值评价的依据就是指人的情感能力。人的幸福（指包括感官快乐在内的幸福感）固然离不开物质条件的保证，但是它根本上与人的情感感受相关，由人的情感感受能力来决定，缺少仁爱的能力，即缺乏幸福的感受能力。

因此，可以说儒家德性精神塑造的是一种情感哲学、一种幸福哲学，它与古希腊德性精神所塑造的（被近现代西方学界发扬光大的）理性哲学、自由哲学大不相同①。

二

自工业文明时代以来，适宜儒家德性精神生长的条件逐渐被解构，儒家德性精神出现了衰弱症状，源自古希腊的德性精神——理性精神成为时代的主流精神。工业文明时代的哲学世界观和人际伦理观就是在充分运用人的理性能力之抽象性构成知识（观念）方式来构建人际/自关系，它以抽象的个人权利为社会价值导向，割裂人与人和人与自然之间实质性的共生关系，造成人际/自之间的抽象分离。

例如，不同于前工业文明在旧熟人间形成的"德性伦理"，工业文明开辟了一个全球大范围内的新型人际关系伦理，即新陌生人间的伦理。维护新陌生人间的伦理即是基于理性抽象建置下的"规则伦理"。启蒙思想家抽象地论证了个人权利的人性论根据：趋利避害、独立自由、理性自觉，等等。于是新陌生人间的"规则伦理"就成了一种"丛林法则"，人与人的关系成了"狼与狼"的关系，人际异化。为了在"丛林"中立于不败之地，由人际异化推动了资本控制，由资本控制推动了技术发明。在资本条件下，所有的技术发明都是实现资本对人的控制手段。技术发明就像一把利刀，深深扎进人与万物之间共生性这根大动脉上，将人与自然那种天然的生命进化关系隔断，生命密码被抽象地截取到实验室用来再造生命，但是这种再造生命无疑是"异形""畸胎"，阻止了诸生命元素之间的自然复归。所以，卢梭在《爱弥儿》中说，"凡是出自造物主之手的东西，都是好的，而一到了人的手里，就全变坏了。"

---

① 康德哲学最能代表古希腊以来的西方传统德性精神。康德的批判哲学指出，作为一种纯粹实践理性意义上的人，其最高实践目的是自由。笔者要指出，作为一种纯粹实践情感意义上的人，其最高实践目的恰恰是幸福。当然这种幸福不是康德讲的感官意义上的幸福，而是一种纯粹的精神幸福。其实，康德的哲学人类学方法忽视了对人的纯粹情感能力之功能目的的探索。

　　反观现实生活，我们何尝不是戴着一个"规则面具"穿梭在来来往往的陌生人之间，即使不是陌生人，我们也要将其纳入陌生人行列，在都戴上"规则面具"的陌生人面前，我们看不到对方现象性存在身份，看不到对方的表情，只有一个抽象的"规则"预设在心里："我的"权利呢？"我的"利益呢？所以，克尔凯郭尔说，一个漫不经心的人，从来没有关注过自己的生活，甚至从来没有意识到自己的存在，结果，在一个风和日丽的早晨，这个人一觉醒来，突然发现自己死了。人为什么突然发现自己死了？这是因为活着的时候一点儿都没有被他/她的情感注意过，情感失去了对生命"在此"状态的守护功能，一辈子快结束了，他/她还没有意识到自己曾经在世的一遭。

　　还原了"规则面具"下的陌生人，其实是一个现象性存在身份的人，他/她与我们原本就在一个基于现象性构成方式下的共生性系统之中，有血有肉，一个随时需要接受我们为之提供生命元素供养的人。当代罗尔斯的"正义论"似乎为"面具"下的人做了一个现象性身份的还原：每一个人都可能成为现实中的一个最不利者，都需要他人的帮助。当然，每一个人都可能成为一个最不利者不是作为我们帮助他/她人的前提条件。人是情感的动物，人的情感功能决定了人的利他性行为是超功利的，是对人类生命尊严的敬重，那么仅仅给了最不利者以物质上的帮助或满足，无疑降低了他/她做人的尊严，实际上是将其归为荒蛮未化的"丛林一类"。

　　工业文明形态的发展方式从萌生时就受到思想家们（例如帕斯卡尔、卢梭）的警觉和批判。这种警觉和批判一直没有停止，并在工业文明转型期（后工业时期）汇聚成为各种批判和超越工业文明的社会思潮。在工业文明发轫的当代西方学界，哲学心理学领域产生了"爱欲解放论"（马尔库塞）和"爱的艺术"（弗洛姆）；政治伦理领域产生了"关怀社会最不利者"的正义论（罗尔斯）、近新熟人间的"商谈伦理"（哈贝马斯）和"美德伦理"（麦金泰尔）；社会生态学领域产生了情感社会学（乔纳森）、情感生态学（凯·弥尔顿）、生态神学（林恩·怀特）；新知领域产生了从女权运动中成长、成熟起来的"女性思维"（关怀伦理学）以及儒学思想西方传播兴盛，等等，所有这些社会思潮都预示着人类呼唤一种新的时代文明的到来。

三

生态文明，作为一种崭新的时代文明形态，其哲学世界观和人际伦理观将是从一种完全不同的知识学模式上实现对工业文明时代形成的知识学模式的超越，它是对前工业文明形态（包括农业文明和原始文明）主客不分、整体主宰、个体缺失，以及工业文明形态主客二分、个体主宰、整体缺失之哲学思维方法的"扬弃"，是从个体现象性存在身份出发，来形成一种个体之间内在存依性和个体与整体之间包容共生性的世界知识（观念）模式和人际伦理模式。

如果说，前工业文明形态基于"旧熟人"之间的旧"德性伦理"和工业文明形态基于"新陌生人"之间的"规则伦理"是在一种全球大区域间严重发展不平衡、不同步的条件下产生的，那么生态文明形态必须消除这种区域发展的不平衡、不同步性。因为，生态文明形态建设的一个明显特征就是要倒逼全球发展的同步性和平衡性，任何国家或区域不能单独地进入生态文明（由于其他国家的不合作，例如大气污染、核威胁等）。这一显著特征要求人类在新的时代条件下重构新的人类社会关系及其伦理模式——（全球大区域范围内的）"新熟人社会"和"新德性伦理"。

当然这种（全球大区域范围内的）"新熟人社会"和"新德性伦理"的构建最终还是要回到认识人自身以及人与人之间本质关系之知识论方法的变革上。人是一个生活中的人，人有情感又有理智，但终究离不开他/她是一个现象性存在身份的人。这个现象性存在身份决定了作为一种"政治性的动物"的人（个人），是一种"依赖性的理性动物"，是一个在现实中"有欠缺的人"。人一旦找回这种现象性存在身份，认识到个体的现象性存在的欠缺，认识到与他/她人之间共生性的本质关系，那么工业文明时代所构建的"规则面具"就会自行消融，展现在人们面前的将是一个全球大区域内的新熟人社会和新的伦理模式（即"新德性伦理"）。人的知识观念变了，那么技术发明就不再是一种奴役人的手段，生产力的发展就不再是实现一个抽象的彼岸目标。全球区域间的战防大大减少，全球区域间的城际列车往来便捷，政治家抽象的民族雄心全转化为地球村的治安方案。

反观儒家德性精神塑造的哲学（知识学）方法特点，它就是从人的现象性存在身份和情感之现象性构成知识（观念）方式来建构人与人、人与自然万物之间的观念性关系，守护了人与人、人与自然万物之间（诸生命元素）共生性的这一"生命契约"，规避了由人际对抗引发的全球性生态危机和生存威胁。在儒家哲学世界观里，人的生命与大自然各种生命元素之间是一种现象性的共场存在。大地、阳光、风尘、雨露长成了蔬菜和庄稼，蔬菜和庄稼被我们吃了变成了我们的皮肤、毛发和骨骼。在人的生命之高峰体验时，大自然的山水、草木、光影似乎随着人的生命一同绽出，这是美的体验，生命的活跃，也是人的情感能力对自然"一体之仁"的现象性"存在"之真的把握①。

就此可以说，生态文明的到来与儒家德性精神的再生长之间有某种时代感"默契"，生态文明为儒家德性精神的振兴②提供了适宜的社会条件，儒家德性精神振兴也将为生态文明的到来提供重要的知识（观念）方式的支撑。

儒家德性精神如何在生态文明时代实现振兴，在笔者看来，除了上述提到的对儒家道德哲学的基本概念（"仁、义、礼、智、信、诚"

---

① 笔者在《基于"仁爱"德性的儒家伦理构成之现代阐释》（《华中科技大学学报》2011 年第6 期）一文中以非认知性含义下的"sense"来对译儒家的"仁"，以"sense-love"对译"仁爱"，以"sense-beautify"对译儒家的"仁美"，这里将继续沿着这个思路以"sentient-being"（佛家讲的"众生"）来对译儒家（王阳明）的"一体之仁"，以"being"对译"一体之仁"中的"体"（"诚"），并以这个"体/being"来对译西方现代存在哲学中的"存在/Being"，以"幸福/well-being"来理解基于生命（情感）体验的儒家心性哲学所要追求的"人生境界"。"幸福/well-being"是人对生命之此在性的"存在/being"的深刻体验，这是人的情感能力由近及远、由浅及深、由人及物的开拓过程。

② 这里用"振兴"而不用"复兴"，主要是指儒家德性精神从依附封建专制统治走向现代民主条件下的健康生长（"复兴"可能带有狭隘的历史地域色彩，"振兴"是指不间断的生长状态）。在前工业文明以及工业文明时期，儒家的德性文化精神或受家族政治的制约和利用，或受工业理性的抵制，都没有真正获得适宜的生长条件，处于亚健康状态，进而没有形成一种尊重知识的传统和一种普遍的情感知识学理论。工业文明和现代民主条件打破和解构了儒家德性精神生长的狭隘语境，生态文明则为它走向普遍知识学方向提供了适宜的条件。

等）做出新的内涵阐释之外，首先需要从哲学（情感）人类学上对传统儒家思想做新的整体性阐释，即要立足于儒家道德哲学自身的人类学特性（基于"情感本位"，不同于西方道德哲学基于"理性本位"），来对基于"仁爱"的儒家道德哲学做一种哲学人类学的解构（即对人的情感能力做一种纯粹的学理批判），结合时代条件（西方近现代认识论方法），重构一种基于"情感本位"的新儒家知识学方法。关于这一点笔者将另作阐释。这里旨在强调人类生态文明形态的建设将为儒家德性精神振兴提供适宜的社会条件。历史上，基于一种道德知识学为表征的儒家德性精神振兴首先发生在宋明时期。为应对佛老哲学的挑战和宋明时代自然科学的发展现实，宋明理学家（特别是朱熹）从先秦儒家经典（《大学》《中庸》）中第一次比较清晰系统地阐发儒家道德哲学中所蕴含的知识学结构——"格物致知"论，把华夏传统农耕文明孕育的精神世界推向了最高峰。但是，随着明清时代华夏传统农耕文明走向衰落，西方工业文明接连而来和启蒙精神介入，儒家德性精神彻底衰弱下去，时经近二百年，儒家德性精神开始出现振兴的征兆，另外，改革开放以来，我国现代主流价值文化发展趋势日渐明朗①，基于一种（情感本位的）知识学方法构建的儒家道德哲学重建可能是时代的必然要求。

---

① 笔者认为，经过改革开放30多年来价值多元化的激荡和沉淀，我国主流价值文化构建趋势主要沿着三个方向演进：一是近现代西方启蒙文化价值观日趋被当代中国公共知识精英分子掌握和运用成熟，已成为构建中国主流价值文化的重要一支；二是执政党坚持的社会主义基本理论，它又表现为马克思主义哲学基本原理与当代中国具体实践相结合产生的阶段性理论成果，它无疑是构建中国主流价值文化的最重要一支；三是中国传统文化（特别是传统儒家道德哲学的基本原理）潜在地作为中国主流价值文化构建的重要一支。虽然这一支价值文化自新中国成立以来受到极大的挤压甚至被埋没，但是随着改革开放的深入发展，民族知识分子发现改革开放所造就的巨大"物质外壳"并没有催生强大的内在民族精神，而在某种程度上稀释了这种内在民族精神，加剧了社会改革的道德风险，所以，一时间传统价值文化备受宣扬（当然只是一些学者的不彻底的呼声）。笔者认为，当前中国主流价值文化构建应该"三管齐下"，要加强中国传统文化（特别是传统儒家伦理思想）的现代创新和世界性语境整合，利用优秀的传统文化来捍卫改革开放的成果，而不应该唯"拿来主义"的西方近现代启蒙价值文化和"维稳主义"的执政党的价值文化是用。只有这三支文化价值并进，才能真正形成中国主流价值文化的基本结构和基本概念的生成机制，从而生成一种有效的文化创新体制。

Ecological Civilization and the Revitalization of Confucian Ethical Spirit

Fang Dezhi

Abstract: The Confucian ethical spirit, developed from traditional agricultural civilization, is not suited to modern industrial civilization. However, the negative effects of industrial civilization call for ecological civilization which tries to abandon industrial civilization. Therefore, the ecological civilization can provide suitable condition for revitalization of Confucian ethical spirit.

Keywords: ecological civilization; Confucian spirit; revitalization; the knowledge of affection

德勒兹的"欲望机器"与王充"气"的比较

—— 基于中法文化"经验"* 的生成性、流动性的视角

张 能**

摘　要：德勒兹的"欲望机器"植入了后结构主义精神。"欲望"是逃逸于"辖域化"体制,"欲望机器"关涉的或者能关涉的只是一种斗争性、对抗性、流动性与生产性。德勒兹的"欲望机器"理论与王充的"气"论思想在某种程度上有"接入"也有超出。在经验的生成性和流动性、主体的构建、变动不居与无目的性方面,两位哲学家都对各自的文化界面互有接入、承纳与显现;在差异生成论方面,作为法国后现代文化结构主义的代表之一,德勒兹别具一格的"内在性"差异说超出了中国传统哲学中对"差异"的运思。

关键词：德勒兹　欲望机器　王充　气

　　法国思想文化经历由结构向非结构的转换过程,其思想文化的肌体已触及深层的心理、社会制度、历史文化与知识权力等领域。德勒兹——这

---

　　* 此处的"经验"与超验相对,是不依据超验(或者主体)解释的经验。

　　** 张能,同济大学博士研究生,主要研究法国哲学。

一法国后现代主义思想的领军人物，其思想所显现的文化特征也由表及里渗透于哲学概念的表达之中，而这一显化的特征也隐蔽式地切入中国气论文化思想这一主题。气论是中国传统哲学重要的组成部分，它在构成世界认知的同时，也贯穿了中国人思维的方方面面，比如在人格修养方面（气节、骨气）、绘画方面（气韵）、行文方面（文气）等，以"气论"为核心的思维方式重视事物动态的、整体的特征，而非精准的、非量化的结构与成分分析。①

德勒兹哲学所蕴藏的文化资源远不止于哲学，他在电影、艺术、音乐、文学等领域都有涉入，所以摘取德勒兹哲学中的一个概念来透析整个法国思想文化的特征本来就是有失其"隔"，虽然有失其"隔"，但不表示无任何的意义可言，德勒兹的"欲望机器"是其哲学最核心的语词之一，它关联的不只是语词本身的"意义域"，它自身所包蕴、"增补"的文化意义远胜于语词本身的单独显现。本文就中法文化做一种概略式的检讨（以"主体"哲学概念作为其摄入），目的不是在唯一中"独尊"其一，而是在相互融通的界面上寻求互补（西学中取）。

一

德勒兹关于欲望哲学的思想主要集中于《反俄狄浦斯——资本主义与精神分裂症》（1972）与《千高原》（1980）这两部著作。

德勒兹的欲望生产理论具有一种后现代性的理论特征，此种特征在《反俄狄浦斯——资本主义与精神分裂症》一书中表现得尤为突出。此书作为一部里程碑式的著作，将抨击的矛头直接对向了拉康的结构主义精神分析学，他说："精神分析本身原是一件很完美的事（wonderful thing），但是从一开始就没有走好。"②精神分析学所理解的

---

① 具体可以参考吴根友《从气论与原子论看中西哲学思维异同》，《中国社会科学报》2013 年第 5 期。

② Gilles Deleuze & Claire Parnet，*Dialogue*（NewYork：Columbia University Press，1987）．

欲望往往是对某物的一种"缺乏",将欲望与"缺乏"联系在一起,比如阉割情结。德勒兹认为,"欲望不包括任何缺乏,这也不是自然条件;它仅与发挥作用的异质装配变成一种东西。"① 德勒兹的欲望生产是永不停息的,在生产的转换中生产着自身的生成。德勒兹凭借此欲望生产的理论来诠释普遍存在于资本主义和当代社会的精神分裂症这一现象。

欲望自身的生产机制无处不在地发挥着作用,有时滞缓拥堵,有时畅行无碍。德勒兹和加塔利为了说明欲望即是生产机器这一理念,将"欲望"与"生产"相勾连,并在"身体"的表层机理中实现呼应与阐释,进而接通了欲望能源机器与身体器官机器。德勒兹认为,每一个思想个体的人都是一台小机器,"生产"以及"产生"一些东西是机器自身的效果。机器之间处于相互联系的"链接"之中,并无独立自为。生产着自身的生产是欲望机器的一个特性,此特性包裹着欲望机器自身的二重性:欲望既构成生产的原因(生产性)又构成生产的全部过程(动态性)。

加塔利说:"这些欲望机器不断地在精神分析学中轰鸣、生产。精神分析学制造着混乱,制造着新的关节,揭示着欲望。"② 此种欲望机器还具有一种人格化的特征,它自身关联着超我、自我、本我。此种人格化还带有一种表演的性质:"用简单的表现价值代替无意识的真正生产力。"③ 欲望机器除了自身戏剧化的性质外,更倾向于背后的操作或者说在隐形的层面运转,"欲望机器越来越倾向于在背地里、在幕后运转"。④ 欲望机器抵制欲望自身被异化的同时,自身也在粉碎欲望生成着的自身。如果欲望机器在抵制欲望自身的异化,并且在欲望生成中粉碎自身的欲望之生成的话,那么欲望机器即是"制造幻觉与效果"的机器。弗洛伊德没能抵御住欲望自身的异化,而在欲望的生产中生产着欲望自身。"我们想同时说

---

① 于奇智:《欲望与快感》,《世界哲学》2005 年第 1 期。
② Gilles Deleuze & Claire Parnet, *Dialogue* (New York: Columbia University Press, 1987).
③ 〔法〕吉尔·德勒兹:《哲学与权力的谈判》,刘汉全译,商务印书馆,2000。
④ 〔法〕吉尔·德勒兹:《哲学与权力的谈判》,刘汉全译,商务印书馆,2000。

明……弗洛伊德发现了欲望……同时又不断地……异化。"① 正因为被异化的欲望困守在俄狄浦斯中，对神经官能症的解释自然差强人意。因此，加塔利说："正因为欲望被罩在家庭的舞台上，所以精神分析学认不出精神病，而只能置身于神经官能中，并对神经官能症本身做出了一种歪曲了无意识的力量的解释。"② 那么何谓"神经官能症"？神经官能症应该与精神病区分开来。在弗洛伊德看来，神经官能症患者从不会对客体做一些色情化的处理，或者对诸如皮肤、短袜等客体有一种色情化的意识植入其感知之中。"然而，色情地将皮肤把握为一个毛孔，色情地将短袜把握为一个网眼的多元体，这些从来不会出现于神经官能症患者的观念之中。"③ 而精神病患者更多拥有的是对词语的意识，此种意识只是对"词语"的一种复现，"'是词语表达的同一性，而非客体的相似性支配着对于替代物的选择'"。④ 弗洛伊德认为，词语自身有其存在的形式，并未在断裂的物之指示中失去其同一性，而是在不断地恢复、创建着自身的同一性。当然，神经官能症不是再现词语的包涵（subsumption），而是处于"事物再现层次的自由联想"。

对神经官能的解释还是逃离不了精神分析的视野，而德勒兹反对精神分析，在德勒兹看来精神分析有两点是行不通的："一，它无法达到一个人的欲望机器，因为它纠缠于俄狄浦斯的图形或结构；二，它无法达到力比多的社会包围，因为它只纠缠于家庭的包围。"⑤ 精神分析与俄狄浦斯是联系在一起的，它圈于家庭的"坐标"，同时它属于资本主义的这一事实性更加使得德勒兹批判的矛头瞄准它，德勒兹所宣扬的精神分裂是对资本主义的一种抗辩，它自身在瓦解资本主义的试图中也抵制着精神分析理论的"侵蚀"。加塔利认为，精神分析发现了欲望、欲望机

---

① 〔法〕吉尔·德勒兹：《哲学与权力的谈判》，刘汉全译，商务印书馆，2000。
② 〔法〕吉尔·德勒兹：《哲学与权力的谈判》，刘汉全译，商务印书馆，2000。
③ 〔法〕吉尔·德勒兹、加塔利：《资本主义与精神分裂（卷2）：千高原》，姜宇辉译，上海书店出版社，2010。
④ 〔法〕吉尔·德勒兹、加塔利：《资本主义与精神分裂（卷2）：千高原》，姜宇辉译，上海书店出版社，2010。
⑤ 〔法〕吉尔·德勒兹：《哲学与权力的谈判》，刘汉全译，商务印书馆，2000。

器，但是并没有将欲望引至社会的"包围"之中，而是相反，利用一种俄狄浦斯式的异化方式来抑制欲望，所以德勒兹说，"俄狄浦斯从根本上说都是抑制欲望机器的一种器具，而绝不是无意识本身的一种形成。"①其实，资本主义与精神分析是联系在一起的，而革命运动与精神分裂是粘连在一块的。在这里，我们应该对作为过程的精神分裂症与作为医院临床实体的精神分裂症患者的产生相区分，作为过程的精神分裂症是一种积极的力量，它与疾病相去甚远，它与欲望相关，"'精神分裂症'是非地域化的欲望，这一欲望由资本主义所产生，而且得到德勒兹差异哲学的支持。它们不是把这一意义上的精神分裂症视为需要医治的疾病，而是视为需要培养的价值观"。②同时在德勒兹和加塔利看来，精神分裂症是一个破译、消除恐惧的过程。从德勒兹对作为医院临床实体的精神分裂症患者的描述来看，它是一个"垮下来的人"。

分裂分析可以被视为一种后现代理论/实践，它既解构了现代的二分法，同时又摆脱了现代的主体理论、再现式思维模式以及总体化实践。分裂分析阐发了各种围绕多元性、多样性以及非中心化等概念组织起来的后现代观点，并试图创造出新的后现代思维模式、政治观点和主体性。所以德勒兹认为，有关欲望的问题只能为精神分裂分析所完满地说明。欲望自身的机制通常由想象的客体来疏导其欲望的缘由，而缺乏的客体成为想象客体的替代者。通过想象客体的缺乏或者指示欲望所缺乏的客体都不能真正解释欲望本身。将欲望还原为一种缺失的引擎机制，这本不是欲望自身的原相。在精神分裂分析下的欲望阐释是将欲望看成一个生产的过程，而且还被认为是一个工业"生产"的过程。作为生产的生产与生产的连续性都被纳入其欲望生产的过程机制之中。它作为生产与作为生产的生产也即是生成是同一的。德勒兹"攻击精神分析的主要原因在于他们认为精神分析把欲望机器变成了一个被动的再现剧场，把欲望限制在俄狄浦斯和

---

① 〔法〕吉尔·德勒兹：《哲学与权力的谈判》，刘汉全译，商务印书馆，2000。
② 莫伟民、姜宇辉、王礼平：《二十世纪法国哲学》，人民出版社，2008。

家庭这一有限空间之中"。①

　　总而言之，德勒兹笔下的"欲望"已经植入了后结构主义思想，它关及的或者能关及的只是一种斗争性、对抗性、流动性与生产性。欲望逃逸于"辖域化"（territorialize）体制，"通过驯服和限制欲望的生产性的能量来压制欲望的过程被称为'辖域化'，将物质生产和欲望从社会限制力量之枷锁下解放出来的过程被称为'解辖域化'（deterritorialization）或'解码'"。②"欲望"不是弗洛伊德所编码的结果，它在本质上是不能被编码的。虽然欲望有被编码的现象（制度体制性编码、法律压迫式编码）存在，但欲望是大于被编码而呈现出来的东西。由此德勒兹指出，被编码的欲望不是欲望本身，它不过是"辖域化"的欲望，作为欲望本身它是一种流、一种能量、一种动态。显然，作为"流"的欲望显然不是一个被铸造的本体概念，却成为一种被"虚构"的本体而呈现。之所以说欲望是一个"虚构"的本体，是因为：欲望自身抵制时空"辖域化"的行为，它具有一种绝对的普遍性，它推动着一切历史的"解辖域化"；在抵制编码的同时，它还具有一种生产的特性，精神分析的"欲望"是狭隘的欲望，是对欲望本身的一种疏离与遮蔽，德勒兹所言的精神分裂式的欲望在德勒兹看来是一切形式得以产生的促进者与生产者，"欲望就是生产，而且作为欲望生产与社会生产是同一过程"。所以作为德勒兹的解构思想而言，他的特质即显现出来：在解构之际同时也引进了动态性主体的思想，而这无论与德里达还是福柯都是极其不同的，因为后面两位都是在主体性的解构中完全消解了主体性的残余，换句话说，他们的言述性无关乎任何主体。而德勒兹在试图解构主体的同时也隐秘地建构了另一类主体，即动态性的、生成的主体。

　　这一动态性主体的表达与中国文化上的"气"论有相契合的地方，都在讲一种动态性的主体性生成。那么，中国文化的"气"论又有着怎样的规定呢？

----

①　〔美〕道格拉斯·凯尔纳、斯蒂文·贝斯特：《后现代理论批评性的质疑》，张志斌译，中央编译出版社，2001。

②　〔美〕道格拉斯·凯尔纳、斯蒂文·贝斯特：《后现代理论批评性的质疑》，张志斌译，中央编译出版社，2001。

二

中国古代关于气论的思想远至遍布于先秦儒家与道家的学说之中，近至王充、二程、张载等有关的论述，气构成了中国文化独特的思维范式之表达。

儒家哲学似乎与"气"无任何实质的联系，但实质上是对普遍之气遮蔽式的显现。《中庸》曰："天之所覆……凡有血气者，莫不尊亲故曰配天。"① 所谓"凡有血气者"即是对人与动物的一种指谓。荀子有言："有血气之属必有知……故有血气之属莫知于人，故人之于其亲也，至死无穷。"② 荀子在此言及的"有血气"与《中庸》里所提到的"凡有血气者"是对气的一种遮蔽式的显示。同时，"有血气者"与"无血气者"在相互区分中并未对气形成一种遮蔽，反而，"无血气者"同样也是对气的一种敞开式的显现，仍然被化导为气的显现机制之显现的形式。③

关涉《易传》与《中庸》的很多思想论题其实都发生于同一语境。《易传》曰："二气感应以相与……天地感而万物化生……"这与《中庸》所说的"至诚无息……博厚所以载物也……博厚配地，高明配天，悠久无疆"④ 都发生于相同的语境，在此《中庸》的"至诚"即是真实无妄。所谓真实无妄是对现实世界实在性的一种表征，也是对生存于现实世界人的道德的一种规诫，它更是对生活世界和谐的一种期待。就先秦儒学哲学而言，世界的实在性为气论所表征。⑤ 在《易传》的思想中

---

① 朱熹：《中庸集注》，上海古籍出版社，2007，第59页。
② 《荀子》，安小兰译注，中华书局，2007，第186页。
③ 宋代的李侗曾就有血气者与无血气者的相关问题求教过朱熹。
④ 朱熹：《中庸集注》，上海古籍出版社，2007，第47~48页。
⑤ 对于儒家哲学，气论更多彰显的是世界的实在性质，而仁学就是要在这个实在的世界中高扬仁义的道德理想。《中庸》所讲的"诚者"不仅是道德、宗教意义上的，而且包含着对天地万物的自然意义之实在性的肯定。关于这一点可以参考李存山《气论对于中国哲学的重要意义》，《哲学研究》2012年第3期。

更不乏对气论的直接性陈述，《易传》遵循"气（阴阳）—天地—四时—万物"的宇宙生成模式，阴阳二气之和而生化万物，这与老子"二生三，三生万物。万物负阴而抱阳，冲气以为和"①的思想有着共同的主题。当然，庄子也有言及，他说："阴阳于人，不翅于父母。"②先秦儒家与道家都有对"气"进行宇宙本体论的构想，但在所构建的理路上是相互区分的。

道家在"元气"上还有"无生有"的规定。儒家（不只是先秦儒家）却不同，虽然对元气之上是否存在更高的规定性这一思想有知觉意识（如张载），但在张载之前的儒学家们对此都知觉甚微。张载说："大《易》不言有无，言有无，诸子之陋也。"③他显然已经意识到思想更高的规定性这一问题（"太虚无形"）。郑玄曾试图将道家的"无生有"嫁接到"人生而应八卦之体，得五气以为五常，仁义礼智信是也"的理论背景之中，但是在嫁接的过程中，不是"板结"就是"沙化"。在转换的界面上遵照的还是儒家那一套理论形式指引，故而在其本质上没有逃离儒家系统理论所设置的藩篱。虽然二程涉及《太极图》中的"无极""太极"的思想，但是他们终生不讲"无极""太极""是生两仪"。在二程看来，天地本来就是存在的，故不存在"太极生两仪"的问题。程颐有云"有理则有气，有气则有数"，这里的"理"就是对天地之间秩序的一种表征，而且天地之间的秩序是建立在天地固有的基础之上的。

在分析儒家与道家在关于气的构成道路上的区分之后，我们再深入介绍王充的气论。在中国的气论史上，王充的气论思想有其自身独特的魅力，王充气论思想中所蕴含的特质或对气的规定，也全面彰显着中国文化独特的个性。那么王充的气论思想蕴含了哪些特质或者其"气"又是如何被规定的呢？

首先，流动的生命性。王充提出"元气"是化生天地万物的作用之

---

① 王弼注：《老子道德经注校释》，楼宇烈校译，中华书局，2008，第130页。
② 郭庆潘撰《庄子集释》，王孝鱼校，中华书局，1985，第262页。
③ 张载撰《张子正蒙》，王夫之注，上海古籍出版社，2000，第197页。

气,"元气"是流动的,具有生命活力的象征意义。正是因为"元气"流动的生命性,才能构成对精神意识缘起理论的根据。

王充循着庄子、董仲舒入思的路径,从气本论角度论证精神意识的源起。人是阴阳二气合化的产物,"阴气主为骨肉,阳气主为精神"①。也就是说,骨肉肌体为阴气所生,阳气生化为精神意识。"形须气而成,气须形而知,天下无独燃之火,世间安得有无体独知之精。"②王充认为,人的精神作用是禀受"精气"的结果。阴阳一一俱全,则人之形神俱备。并且认为,人的精神意识会随着形体的消亡而消亡,否定了人的形体消亡而精神意识仍然存在的相关论断。

其次,解构中的建构:理论的悖论性。王充对鬼神也有很严厉的批辞,他强烈地批判了灵魂不灭、人死为鬼的说法。他认为,人的精神是依附身体的,因此人死后又怎么可能成为鬼呢。他说:"人死血脉竭,竭而精气灭。灭而形体朽,朽而成灰土,何用为鬼?"③但是,王充在另一个地方又提到这么一句话:"天地之气为妖者,太阳之气也。"④这句话的意思无非是说"妖者(鬼者)"是"太阳之气"生化的。所以王充对鬼神的看法颇具思辨的色彩,他在解构传统的鬼神观念之时,又臆造出另一种"妖者"的观念,而此观念与传统的鬼神观念明显存在悖论,所以王充的鬼神理论具有一种悖论性。

再次,经验性的直观。与传统的所谓"概念"(西方古典哲学)相比较,显然王充的"气"的概念没有上升到抽象的层次(如巴门尼德的"存在"),它蕴含了视觉感觉的直接性,试图用一种观感的非间接的经验方式去把握抽象的事物,这种思维的路径与古希腊哲学(如泰勒斯、阿拉克西曼尼等)有点类似。为什么说王充的气论具有一种经验性的直观呢?首先,王充认为气存在量的差异——粗细之分,"万物之生,俱

---

① 黄晖撰《论衡校释》,中华书局,1990,第 946 页。
② 黄晖撰《论衡校释》,中华书局,1990,第 875 页。
③ 黄晖撰《论衡校释》,中华书局,1990,第 871 页。
④ 黄晖撰《论衡校释》,中华书局,1990,第 941 页。

得一气。气之薄渥，万世若一"，① 所谓"渥"即浓郁也，也就是说气存在轻薄与浓郁的区分；其次，气不仅存在量的差异还存在着质的差异——粗精之分。当然，这种质的差异是相对性的差异，并不是绝对的。王充认为，天地万物之间所构成的气是有等次差别的，它们各自构成的精细程度是不相同的，比如，构成地之气远不如构成天的气之精微，构成较高生物的气要比构成低一级生物的气精细许多。人是万物之灵长，所以构成之气最为精微，但是人与人之间也存在气的差异，"圣者以为禀天精微之气，故其为有殊绝之知"，② 由此而观之，气存在粗细与精微之分，正是这种经验性的气之精微程度的差异性才生化了自然万物之多样性。

最后，自然无为。气（非物质性），③ 自然无为没有任何的目的。王充说："天地，含气之自然也。"④ 又说道："天覆于上，地偃于下，下气蒸上，上气降下，万物自生其中间矣。"⑤ 气"自然"而"无为"。自然即是本来如此，无为是针对有目的性而言的。这即是说，自然是无目的性的率性而为本来如此。"谓自然者无为者何？气也，恬澹无欲无为无事者也。"⑥ 王充谈气的自然无为与他对天人感应目的论的批评有关，因为王充是一位彻底的无神论者。

王充是中国古典气论的代表人物，了解王充即对中国的气论文化有一个总体性的把握。综上所述，王充从流动的生命性、解构中的建构性、直观的经验性与自然无为这四个方面来规定"气"。因此，气的文化特征也自然流露于对气的规定之中，气只不过是一个经验性的直观描述，远没有达到概念抽象的高度。王充那种讲求流动性与生命性的气"本体"概念与

---

① 黄晖撰《论衡校释》，中华书局，1990，第 803 页。
② 黄晖撰《论衡校释》，中华书局，1990，第 875 页。
③ 作为王充的气并非物质性的气，也许这一点有悖于教材式的说法。陈坚教授认为不能用"唯物主义"来界定王充的气，如果是那样的话，那么此种气即是一种无定形的气，与德勒兹的"欲望机器"的内蕴刚好切合。可参考陈坚、王充《逻辑主义者》，《云南大学学报》2013年第 3 期。
④ 黄晖撰《论衡校释》，中华书局，1990，第 782 页。
⑤ 黄晖撰《论衡校释》，中华书局，1990，第 782 页。
⑥ 黄晖撰《论衡校释》，中华书局，1990，第 776 页。

法国后现代主义者德勒兹的哲学有着内在的联系，在各自独立的同时也在参补着各自的缺陷。

三

德勒兹作为法国后现代主义的代表人物，其思想路数上与福柯、德里达还是存在一些差异，其入思的方式也略显不同。德勒兹明显已经走出了西方概念形而上学的"牢笼"，如他对概念的重新解读①，对欲望机器的分裂分析等，从而改善了中法哲学文化各自独立的关系。那么，德勒兹的欲望机器所蕴含的法国后现代主义文化与王充的气所粘连的中国文化存在着怎样的"共识"呢？又带给中国文化怎样的独特视域呢？

第一，德勒兹特别注重经验的生成性，反对先验范畴的自我设定，基于经验来建构一切。"与康德的先验唯心主义找出使感官经验成为可能、同时又与感觉经验相分离的心灵先验范畴不同，德勒兹拥护一种具有动态强度的经验和感官领域，以及一种非概念、非再现的、无意识的思维模式。康德的心灵天赋能力概念试图建立主体的同一性以及客体的通感再现，而德勒兹为通感统觉和概念再现所无法把握的'自在差异'范畴。"② 德勒兹的"欲望机器"就是一种生成论的结果。德勒兹所构造出来的欲望之流，是对尼采权力本体论的一种"转译"，这种被构造的欲望之流，"宣扬着欲望的生产性，谴责各种试图弱化或者瘫痪欲望的社会

---

① 德勒兹认为，概念既非事态的外延指称，也不是体验的含义，而是作为掠过他所有组成成分的纯粹的事件。概念作为其自身组成部分的交汇点，并且作为概念自身的组成部分不可以从普遍的甚至特殊的意义上去理解。概念自身的组成部分相互之间没有种属差异，构成概念自身组成部分的关系既不是包含关系，也不是外延关系，因为无论是包含关系还是外延关系都与种、属相关联，而作为组成概念的组成部分之间是无种属差异的，所以将种属意义上的包含关系或者外延关系赋予组成概念自身的组成部分恰恰是有失其本性的。具体参考吉尔·德勒兹、菲力克斯·加塔利《什么是哲学？》，张祖建译，湖南文艺出版社，2007，第405页。

② 〔美〕道格拉斯·凯尔纳、斯蒂文·贝斯特：《后现代理论批评性的质疑》，张志斌译，中央编译出版社，2001。

力量"。① 欲望本身没有在先的预设，而就是一种"流"，此种"流"与西方古典哲学的概念相异，它更多侧重的是生成式的经验，而不是统摄经验的生成而将其化导、固置，它自身就是一种"力比多"，但此种"力比多"显然不只是一种能量场，德勒兹的欲望机器已经将欲望与马克思的物质生产联系在一起，从而构成欲望机器的双重意蕴。德勒兹这种经验生成性与资本主义对欲望的编码形式有关，经验的生产在其过程，在其欲望机器自身之中，不依赖任何主体性的感受来阐释这种生产论的经验，因为欲望机器本来就是自身生产自身的结果，也即是说德勒兹的经验生成不依靠任何"主体"来支撑，它的生成式的经验在于欲望机器之流在各个场域的（制度、生产、心理等）升华与转换。作为中国气论文化的代表人物王充也推崇气的经验生成性，王充的"气"存于天地之间，并没有对天地构成一种根据，这与董仲舒不同，董仲舒认为，"气"在天地之前。而王充的"气"即是一种生成，与宇宙万物一起生成，并没有高于天地万物而构成其生成的原因。"元气，天地之精微也。""气"与万物一起生成，此种生成都含有"气"的作用，所以气并不是一种在先式的而是存在于万物的生成之中，它流动于自然世界之间，不只作用于自然世界的万物，而且还涉及政治领域，天地之气"遭善而为和，遇恶而为变"，也就是说他把气与政治联系起来了，并且王充认为气不是上天感情的产物，而是自然的，同时善政恶政也是自然的。这一点也与德勒兹很接近，德勒兹的欲望机器也就是微观政治学的一种显示，并且其欲望机器就是一种物质生产性的唯物主义欲望观的体现。

第二，德勒兹与福柯、德里达不同的是在解构主体之后又重新建立起一个"欲望主体"的概念。"欲望机器"虽摧毁了主体的迷梦，却又重新塑造了一个新的主体，这也是德勒兹所始料不及的，此种主体是一种"力"；而王充的气论所显现的主体性的结构阐释也是隐蔽

---

① 〔美〕道格拉斯·凯尔纳、斯蒂文·贝斯特：《后现代理论批评性的质疑》，张志斌译，中央编译出版社，2001。

的，因为从气与物的关系来看，很难将气定义为一种独立于物的"本体"，"非物则气""无体则气""不为物则为气"等都说明了气与物之间并没有谁具有更高的规定性。但王充又说："万物之生，皆禀其气。"这说明王充在无主体的气中又将"元气"作为一种"隐秘"的"主体"而凸显出来，王充的"气一元论"的表达中从没有试图说明气对万物具有一种优越性或者规定性，但对此"元气"的规定，让人认为有构建其"主体"的嫌疑。这与德勒兹是一样的。德勒兹本人从来不会承认对"主体"概念有任何的青睐，但其"欲望机器"就是对"主体"概念的一种显现。两者的思维路向（前者解构，后者建立）完全不同，但在结果上殊途同归，建立了一个主体的思维模型，当然在德勒兹那里是以隐秘的形式建立的。

第三，德勒兹的"欲望机器"是一种动态的过程，不固置，不确定。"德勒兹强调现实的、动态的、不确定的特性，而再现图式却试图通过知识基础将这些动态的、不确定的特征加以固定和稳固化。他们的欲望哲学还攻击更为广义的再现，如总体话语、人本主义基本框架以及一般意义上的认知图式。"① 它更属于一种动态性的哲学；而王充的气论显现的也是一种动态、变动不居的形态特征，所谓"下气蒸上，上气降下""天地和气，万物自生"即是对气变易的描述。

第四，德勒兹"欲望机器"生成论上的差异。其实差异是德勒兹中期哲学的核心概念，德勒兹生成论上的差异是"内在性"（immanence）的差异，此差异只是潜在的而非实际性的差异，如果是实际性的差异，又会坠落到"同一"哲学的深渊，而德勒兹恰恰是抵制"同一"（存在与认同）这一古典哲学的统摄，此差异是程度上的差异而不是本质上的差异；王充的气论也谈差异，但是诉诸的是本质上的一种差异，故而二者在差异路径的延伸中采取的是不同的入思方式。

第五，"欲望机器"是无目的的，如果说有目的就是对编码的东西

---

① 〔美〕道格拉斯·凯尔纳、斯蒂文·贝斯特：《后现代理论批评性的质疑》，张志斌译，中央编译出版社，2001。

（法律、契约、体制）实施解码。德勒兹"欲望机器"表征的是一种反对个体辖域，追求发现"解辖域化"的欲望流；王充的气也是无任何性的目的，自在自为，没有主观意志的规定，天道自然而无为，"天之动行也，施气也，体动气乃出，物乃生矣"，"谓自然者无为者何？气也，恬澹无欲无为无事者也"。

综上所述，彰显法国后现代主义文化特质的德勒兹与中国代表传统古典气论文化的王充之间存在一种"共契"。德勒兹所图绘的哲学景象与中国古典气论文化的气象有接入也有超出，在经验的生成性上、经验的流动性上、主体的构建上、变动不居与无目的性上显然在各自的文化界面上有接入、承纳与显现；在差异生成论上，代表后现代法国文化结构主义的德勒兹别具一格的"内在性"差异之思明显超出了东方文化那种对"差异"的运思。

通过对法国德勒兹的"欲望机器"与中国王充"气"论的对比分析，寻找消解二者各自固结的时间性，敞开二者的空间层次及其表达上的生成转换，从而把二者各自抽象的理论表达还原到相互融通，或许是中法文化的共同使命。不同的文化类型的可比性建立在不可比性上，可比的仅仅是每一种文化类型都有一个自己超出自身局限的现代性转换及其与个人自由度的关联。至于如何转换，转换成什么，开放怎样的自由度，那全然要看介入转换的视域。

理解要求接纳与融合，对德勒兹"欲望机器"与王充"气论"的理解更是两种不同文化的接纳与融合。法国的后现代性并没有成为祭奠的"悼词"，德勒兹的"欲望机器"重新点燃了生命的欲望，生成了经验，那种在追求共识理解中的保留随时缺席的不可理解的话语也在一种流动性的经验中变得清晰可辨，那种纯粹无的"黑洞"似乎也留有中国文化"增补"的痕迹

比较中法文化，可以增进中法之间的交流与合作。但比较中法文化在其方法论上存在着很多的路向，这些路向亦如海德格尔的"林中路"，都是通向思想的道路，笔者所选取的路向也许是"断路""绝路"，但这已不重要，重要的是思想者已行走在这通向不同文化思想的道路之上了。

The "Desire Machine" of Gilles Deleuze and "Qi" of Wang Chong

Zhang Neng

Abstract：The "desire machine" of Gilles Deleuze has been implanted with post-structuralism. The "desire machine" of Gilles Deleuze has some similarities with the "Qi" of Wang chong. The paper compares the two thoughts from the perspective of experience.

Keywords：Deleuze；Desire Machine；Wang Chong；Qi

从"我"到"我们"

——现代工业文化的批判与反思

舒红跃[*]

摘　要：我们每个人既是一个独特的个体，同时也是某一个群体中的一员。作为人类群体的"我们"是如何形成的呢？我们的形成，实际上是不同人之间所产生的一个统一化过程，而这个统一化的过程是一个"接受"的过程，"接受"之所以是人类群体的构建模式，首先是因为各种技术工具是可以被替换的。从"我"与"我们"的视角，本文对现代工业文化进行了批评和反思。

关键词：我们　人　接受　工业文化

很久以前动物尚不存在，众神将土、火和一切可以跟二者融合之物塑造成各类动物。众神委托普罗米修斯和爱比米修斯适当地分配给每一种动物一定的性能。爱比米修斯负责分配，普罗米修斯负责检验。由于爱比米修斯不小心，当他把性能的宝库在那些无理性的动物身上浪费殆尽之后，却发现人类一无所获——赤身裸体，既无衣履也无尖牙利爪。为挽救人类而操劳的普罗米修斯从赫斐斯托斯和雅典娜那里盗取了技术的创造机能和火，因而送给人类一份厚礼。这是柏拉图以普罗塔戈拉斯之口讲述的普罗

＊　舒红跃，湖北大学高等人文研究员教授、博士生导师，主要研究方向为欧洲大陆哲学、技术哲学。

米修斯神话。与普罗米修斯相比,爱比米修斯不仅是一个遗忘者,而且也是一个被遗忘者:正是由于他的过失,普罗米修斯才需要盗取火给人类。(爱比米修斯的)"过失"是因,(普罗米修斯盗取的)"技术"是果;没有"过失",就没有"技术"。"人类的理性和知性始于这种把某些操作移交给某一代具,也即借助既已存在的、作为后种系生成的传播能力的某一技术领域。"①

一 技术的进化:从 "火" 到现代大众 传播文化工业

斯蒂格勒五卷本《技术与时间》这一成名作涉及的内容非常广泛:既有对吉尔、勒鲁瓦 - 古兰和西蒙栋的技术理论的梳理,也有对康德的"三重综合"("领会的综合""再现的综合""认定的综合")、胡塞尔的内时间意识现象学、海德格尔的生存哲学的批判性解读,还有从技术角度对德里达、利科等哲学家思想的阐释。鉴于篇幅限制,下面仅对斯蒂格勒五卷本《技术与时间》中已有中文译本的前三卷最重要的概念或观点进行评介,其中包括第一卷最重要的两个概念"延异"和"已经在此",第二卷的主题"迷失方向",第三卷的两大主题之一——"存在之痛"。

人类因火而得以在世存在,这是普罗米修斯神话的启示。哲学既需要从神话中得到灵感,又不能仅仅停留在神话传说之中,还需要利用理性的力量来证明人类是如何从火中产生的:是先有"火"然后有"人类",还是先有"人类"然后才使用"火"?这是一个无异于先有"鸡"还是先有"蛋"的难题。斯蒂格勒借用他的导师德里达所创造的"延异"概念来解决这一问题。"延异"(différance)一词由德里达首创,它在词源学上有两个基本含义:一是延时,通过延时这一中介延缓欲望的达成;二是不同一、别样、可区分。现有法语中相应的名词"différence"

---

① 斯蒂格勒:《技术与时间3:电影的时间与存在之痛的问题》,译林出版社,2012,第106页。

不能完全覆盖上述特征，德里达创造"différance"一词以指称他的哲学发现。借用该词，斯蒂格勒认为需要从运动和相互关系的角度分析人与技术的关系。表面上看"谁"和"什么"各有所指：技术和人。但是"谁"能不能是技术，"什么"能不能是人呢？为此斯蒂格勒研究由东非人向新人过渡，即"人化"这一过程。这一大脑皮层的分裂过程和石器随石制工具技术的演变而进化的过程是一致的。石器技术的进化非常缓慢，难以想象人是这个进化的发明者和操纵者。相反，可以假定人在这个进化中被逐渐发明。人的发明这一命题的关键在于将"谁"和"什么"并列，既使二者相连，又使二者相分。延异既不是"谁"，也不是"什么"，它是二者共同的可能性，是它们之间的相互往返运动，是二者的交合。缺了"什么"，"谁"不存在，反之亦然。延异在"谁"和"什么"之外，是它使二者构成一种貌似对立的连体。二者之间的过渡是一种投影：大脑皮层在石器岩层中的投影，岩石恰似大脑原初的镜子。这种原初的投影就是"外在化"的开端，它实现于由东非人向新人过渡的几十万年之中，在这一漫长的过程中石器开始形成，大脑皮层开始自己投影映照。所以，是工具即技术发明了人，而非相反，人发明工具。换言之：人在发明工具的同时在工具中自我发明——自我实现技术化的"外在化"。

从人类的起源看，人与技术是一个同时发明的过程，也就是说人与技术是一种"延异"的关系。原始人类以后的所有人，包括当今人类，斯蒂格勒认为他们的生存离不开"已经在此"，或者说先于每一个此在、在此在来到世界之前在他的世界中已经存在的各种代具。"已经在此"是斯蒂格勒受海德格尔影响而提出的一个概念。斯蒂格勒认为，海德格尔的此在有四个特征：时间性、历史性、自我理解和实际性。在海德格尔的基础上，斯蒂格勒用"实际性"表示人（"谁"）对在自己之前形成的技术（"什么"）的依赖，强调"实际性"中既成事实和已经存在的意思。在普罗米修斯神话中，人仅仅因为一个"遗忘"才诞生：爱比米修斯在分配属性时忘记给人留一个，以致人一无所有。所以，人缺乏存在或尚未开始存在，它的存在条件就是以代具（即在人类身体之外存在、替代人类肢体的工具）来补救这个原始缺陷。正是通过"已经在此"，斯蒂格勒把自己的时间观同海德格尔区别开来：在时间的三个维度中具有奠基性的在海德格尔那里是将来，他以将在为基础实现此在的将来、曾在、当前的统一性"绽出"；在斯蒂格勒这里具有奠基性的则是曾在，他是以"已经在此"，也就是此在世界中先于此在已经存在的技术为基础来建立时间三个环节的统一的。

在五卷本的《技术与时间》中，最重要的应该是第一卷《爱比米修斯的过失》和第五卷《必有的缺陷》。《爱比米修斯的过失》分为两个部分。第一部分是"人的发明"，这可以从"谁"与"什么"的延异中得到解释，也就是说人是在"谁"与"什么"的延异中被发明的；第二部分是"爱比米修斯的过失"，这一部分着重论述的是由于爱比米修斯的过失，人类只能从并不属于自己而是自己从前人那里继承而来的"已经在此"中才能得以生存。《爱比米修斯的过失》之后的是该系列著作的第二卷：《技术与时间2：迷失方向》。该卷的主题是"迷失方向"：在"谁"与"什么"的延异中得以发明的人类会随着"什么"的演化和变迁而迷失方向。斯蒂格勒是通过对"后种系生成"的历史的描述来阐释自己的这一观点的。"后种系生成"这一概念在《爱比米修斯的过失》中就已提出，斯蒂格勒用它来表示生物进化和技术进化的差异：生物是由种族或基因决定的种系生成，而技术则是由个体后天经验和教训所决定的归纳式积累，即后种系生成。

斯蒂格勒认为，对于个体来说种族记忆是已经在此的，每个个体都受它的制约；然而，在获得种族记忆的同时，个体又发展了其中的不确定性，因而从这种已经在此中解放出来并进一步"发明"。斯蒂格勒的后种系生成研究建立在勒鲁瓦－古兰记忆结构分析的基础上。后者既将记忆的结构分为三个层次：特定层次、社会种族层次和个体层次，同时又认为存在着不同于社会种族记忆的第四种记忆，比如当今出现的程序化机器，它将"谁"从其种族性中驱逐出去，破坏种族记忆的运作链和行为链，继而破坏以领土形式构成的种族统一体。"'什么'的历史一般来说总是一次次断裂的历史，因为'什么'从根本上是通过中止现有程序而发展的。"①

　　根据普罗米修斯神话，人类是双重过失——爱比米修斯的遗忘和普罗米修斯的盗窃的产物。由于普罗米修斯的计谋，人类吃到了牛肉；由于宙斯的意志，人类失去了存活所必需的、以前是伸手可得的食物。为了补救爱比米修斯的过失，普罗米修斯赠给人类的礼物或禀赋就是：置人在自身之外。人类的存在就是在自身之外的存在。问题是，当今时代人类的外延似乎进入了尾声，也就是说当代的技术断裂登峰造极，这是一种比农业的诞生、工业革命的发生更大的断裂，其后果极其严重——由于把各种操作程序交给机器代管，以群体统一性构成的种族将会面临灭顶之灾。愈演愈烈的工业化不断使人丧失对共同体的归属感，因为个体基本行为链中的主要部分（种族特性主要体现于此）要么被转移到机器设备中，要么个体自行去适应机器设备的自动化。

　　斯蒂格勒认为，随着人类把各种功能（先是骨骼的、肌肉的，然后是神经的，如今是象征的）都交给了器具程序（即工具、机器和工业集合体），我们看到的是技术的后种系生成对人类的种系生成，也就是人类的身体—基因程序的中止：躲在屋檐下时他像只海龟，利用镊子把手加长时他像只螃蟹，成为骑士时他像匹马……他的力量由于使用耕牛而成倍增长，他的拳头因借助于锤子而变得更硬，他的记忆先被转移到书本之中，然后被转移到硬盘之中。问题是人类在每次更换工具时都在一点点地改变人种。

二　"我"的消亡与"我们"的横行

　　作为人，我们每个人既是一个独特的个体，同时也是某一个群体中的一员。作为人类群体的"我们"是如何形成的呢？我们的形成，实际上是不同的人之间所产生的一个统一化过程，而这个统一化的过程是一个"接受"的过程，通过这一过程，某个"我们"作为其他"我"和其他

---

　　①　斯蒂格勒：《技术与时间 2：迷失方向》，译林出版社，2010，第 79 页。

"我们" 的集合者才可能得以构成、联结、固定、持续并得到拓展。一般来说，所谓种族这个最基本的社会群体是通过该群体分享某一共同的过去时刻这一事实而定义的，不过，这样的定义来自通过领土传递下来的过去时刻，使人信服关于纯粹起源的神话，因而这一定义不是没有问题的。事实上，使人类群体得以构建的，是他们与未来的共同关系。种族首先分享的是对一个共同未来的欲望。

"奠定人类群体的，是与未来的关系，而这一关系的前提条件显然是该群体分享着一个共同的过去，但是这个过去必须通过'接受'这个过程才可能成为共同的过去——而'接受'的过程又必须通过投射才能得以实现。"① 民族的实质在于所有个体拥有很多共同的事物，同时也在于所有个体已经遗忘了很多事物。这种遗忘的能力经历了遴选、样品选择和"蒙太奇"的过程，也即对过去的片段和将来的片段进行持留和前摄，并最终构成某个"我们"的"流"。在这一过程中，"接受"是必不可少的。

然而，"接受"的过程的条件在于以下这一系列后种系生成，也即技术性记忆带来的可能性，即能够进入一个从未被某人体验过、也没有被此人生物学意义上的祖先体验过的过去时刻。接受过程的前提条件是能够进入一个既成的过去时刻，过去时刻的既成性却构成了一种"已经在此"的基础，以这种"已经在此"为出发点，继承者便能够幻觉般地与其他通过接受幻觉般地分享同一过去时刻的人一起期望一个共同的未来。从后种系生成的角度出发来思考"继承"的问题，其实质就意味着和既成的过去一样，技术也一样必须接受，它使投映的"我们"得以构成。与此同时，技术也显然使投映技术本身得以被接受。因而这个"接受"的过程既是"物质性"的，又是"观念性"的。"对技术的接受（也即对日用商品的接受）和对既成的过去时刻的接受使一个共同的未来得以投映，从而也使某个'我们'得以构建，而'艾比米修斯的过失'的那则神话故事所体现的人的本源性缺陷所要求的正是上述两种形式的接受。"② 由

① 斯蒂格勒：《技术与时间 3：电影的时间与存在之痛的问题》，译林出版社，2012，第 120 页。
② 斯蒂格勒：《技术与时间 3：电影的时间与存在之痛的问题》，译林出版社，2012，第 123 页。

此可见，"接受"的问题就是技术性的代具问题，以及由代具所涉及的一系列问题。

"接受"之所以是人类群体的构建模式，首先是因为各种技术工具是可以被替换的。正因如此，一般意义上的"接受"所需的条件与各个时代所独有的后种系生成的记忆的特殊性相互联系。也正因如此，当今时代的"接受"问题与商业以及市场的问题密不可分。19世纪以来，随着资本主义大工业的兴起，技术演变急剧加速，这就要求人们必须对各种新工业产品的"接受"过程加以组织。现代性始于工业革命之前，工业革命有效并集中地实现了现代性，它指的是对某种新型时间关系的接受、对传统偏好的摒弃、新的生活节奏的确立，而且在今天，它指的同时也是生活本身的各种条件在生物载体和持留机制方面发生巨大震动，并最终导致信息传递乃至"接受"的条件发生了工业革命。

衡量一个国家现代性的指标是"接受"过程的组织程度。在工业革命之前，"接受"过程在实现的过程中依据的是传统的节奏和制度，而传统则将稳定性置于首要地位，希望它亘古不变，并从稳定性的角度来审视一切变革，因而将一切变革都视为不幸。现代性颠覆了这一视角，现代社会中稳定性变成了例外情况，而变革则成为了首要法则。曾几何时，"接受"的首要决定因素是政治与宗教制度，而今它已受制于一种由市场营销体系全面掌握的"计算"，各种媒体则成为"接受"的传递媒介。各种媒介构成了新型第三持留的领域，而第三持留所具有的物质性则使第三持留的工业化成为可能，其具体表现包括网络、电视、报纸等各种媒介。上述工业化同时也是"思想"的工业化，它直接影响了"我们"在构成的过程中所需的条件。"统一过程是一个'接受'的过程，该'接受'过程的基础是'外在化过程'，也即技术领域，因为技术领域同时也就是持留的领域。"[①]

直到电视在全世界范围内普及之后，人们才真正地感受到上述演变所造成的后果。数字化网络和文化的超工业化使该过程进一步加剧。因此，

[①] 斯蒂格勒：《技术与时间3：电影的时间与存在之痛的问题》，译林出版社，2012，第125页。

当今时代最大的问题是"谁?"的问题。当代技术开启了另一个时代,与传统时代相比,这一新的时代是一个极大的偏差,大到足以开辟一个新纪元,因为对于本质迟缓的人类而言,发展的速度是最核心的问题。随着计算机和信息技术的突飞猛进,进化跨入了一个崭新的阶段,即大脑外延的阶段。从纯技术角度看,突变已经完成。对时间和距离的压缩、行动节奏的加快、对二氧化碳及工业毒素处理的失调、放射物的渗透都提出了一个发人深省的问题:人的肌体是否适应这个长期以来被称作他的环境的环境?这就是人类迷惑的生成,也是人类该向何处去的追问。整个《技术与时间》第二卷都是围绕这一问题展开的。

"存在之痛"是《技术与时间 3:电影的时间与存在之痛的问题》所述两大主题之一。斯蒂格勒认为,正是由于人类的产生跟技术有关,即人是在"谁"与"什么"的延异中被"发明"的,因而此在在世存在的一切重大问题都直接或间接地跟"什么"的发展和变异有关。而 20 世纪决定人类命运的因素是"工业时间客体",即由程序工业提供的产品:"程序工业,尤其是广播电视信息传媒工业,大量地生产着时间客体,它们的共同特征是被上百万个,有时是上千万、上亿乃至十几亿个'意识'同时收听和收看:这种时间上的大范围重合使事件具有了新的结构,与这一新结构相对应的,是集体意识和集体无意识的新形式。"[1]

何谓时间客体?当某一客体的时间流(如一段音乐旋律)与以该客体为对象的意识流相互重合时,该客体即为"时间客体"。斯蒂格勒认为,在人类意识活动转变的进程中,代具具有决定性意义,因为它会影响康德所说的"图型法"的条件。在胡塞尔的"第一持留"和"第二持留"的区分之外,斯蒂格勒提出"第三持留"概念,认为第三持留指的是在记忆机制中对记忆的持留的物质性记录,如录音、录像。随着时间客体的工业化生产,构成意识流统一过程的"综合"的代具化达到了一个新阶段,在这一阶段中,意识的转变能够导致意识被摧毁。由于当今程序工业过于强大,个体意识除非与"世界"相割离,否则注定会沉溺于程序工

---

① 斯蒂格勒:《技术与时间 3:电影的时间与存在之痛的问题》,译林出版社,2012,1。

业的巨流之中，或者是落入"用户归档"的渔网之中。这就把个体行为这种此前未能工业化的东西工业化，从而使程序工业更为强大，以致消费者完全被传媒工业所掌控而无法从中脱身。诸多不同的个体因而不再能够个体化，而是在某种程度上变成一般性的群体，变成没有视野的独眼怪物。

在传统技术时代，种族是个体生存必不可少的前提条件。而种族的形成是一个统一化的过程，这一过程也是一个"接受"的过程——通过对某一共同的过去时刻（大型聚会、宗教仪式、庆典等）的分享，某个"我们"作为其他"我"和其他"我们"的集合体才可能得以构成、固定、持续和拓展。然而，随着当今影视媒体的发展，特别是由于所有劳动工具和社会化工具均有演变为媒体的趋向，因此不同个体分享集体事件的共时化过程越来越具有持久性（第三持留可永久保存）和系统性（影视工业有组织、有预谋的筹划）。在诸多媒体的操弄之下，一般意义上的个性化过程已经丧失，而且在程序工业发送给超大型意识群体的连续不断的"事件流"中，铺天盖地的所谓特例时刻淹没了"事件流"的全部。个性化的丧失同时也是一个大范围的令人担忧的失望过程，与"工具"的承载者机器不一样（它只会让工人失业），它所危及的不仅是无产阶级，而是整个社会和社会中所有的生活方式，这些生活方式通过市场营销这种"说服的技术"和"舆论经济"这种特殊的经济而被越来越多的国家和地区所"接受"。

斯蒂格勒认为，正是出于这样的原因，"我"可以被视为"我们"，反过来，"我们"也可以被视为我。其后果是所谓的"人们/大家"独占统治地位：它既控制了极权体制，又控制了"保护消费者权益运动"和"市场社会"。这是一个不仅"我"失望，而且"我们"也失望的时代，"我"和"我们"在相互混合中消失了。这是一个"非个性化"的时代。

如此一来，海德格尔的"存在问题"变成了斯蒂格勒的"存在之痛"问题。如何应对这一现今最棘手的问题，斯蒂格勒在《技术与时间》第四卷和第五卷中将尝试给出回答。

The Re-thinking of Modern Industrial Civilization from the Perspective of "I" and "We"

Shu Hongyue

Abstract: Every one of us is an independent individual, and at the same time one part of a group. As a human group, how "we" is formed? The formation of "we" is in fact a process of uniformation which is the process of acceptance, and the reason of acceptance lies in the fact that technological tools can be substituted. The paper criticizes and reflects modern industrial civilization from the perspective of "I" and "We".

Keywords: we; human being; acceptance; industrial civilization

位格与完整：马里坦人道主义思想探微

徐　瑾[*]

摘　要：马里坦完整人道主义的起点是作为"位格"而不是作为"个体"存有的人，因为人的作为"形式"存有的位格性超越于作为"质料"存有的个体性以及整个物质世界；其终点也是"位格"的原因是作为位格性存有的人超越于世俗社会及其共同善，并最终指向完美位格的实现。其合理性在于信仰所具有的终极关怀的价值，缺陷在于难以解决理论和实践的二律背反。

关键词：位格　完整　人道主义

在曾作为《联合国人权宣言》起草人之一的著名哲学家雅克·马里坦（Jacques Maritian）的所有著作中，《完整人道主义》最为出名。本文主要从马里坦关于人的存在的形而上学"位格"（person）视角分析其人道主义的"完整"（integral）内涵。

一　作为完整人道主义起点的"位格"

近代以来西方社会经历了三次巨大的文化冲击：一是达尔文的"进化论"。据此理论，人被认为是由动物种群长期进化而来（如何进化是一

---

* 徐瑾，哲学博士，湖北大学哲学学院、高等人文研究院副教授。

个次要的历史性问题），但是以生物学开始的人却不以形而上学结束，在任何时刻，甚至到人类形成都没有任何精神性的东西出现。二是弗洛伊德的"性本论"，当他揭示出人类思想中那些阴暗的、本能欲望的东西时，人们不得不残酷地面对我们可能是邪恶的、卑劣的存在物的事实，"我们每个人的意识中的似乎良好的尊严都成了虚伪的面具。简而言之，人其实处于一个激烈的性本源（libido）和死亡本能的冲突和交汇之地"。① 三是尼采大声宣布"上帝已死"沉重打击了神圣信仰，随之而来的是被日益昌盛的当代科学技术所激发的外在物质需求进一步异化了人们的精神追求，由是物欲横流，功利主义、利己主义盛行。有感于这种现实，忧心忡忡的马里坦认为问题的症结在于人类失去了精神支柱，于是如何重建以信仰为核心的人道主义就成了其中的关键。在马里坦看来，自文艺复兴以来的所有人道主义都不是真正的、整全的，只有根植于基督教信仰的"完整人道主义"才是真正的人道主义。"我们所说的新人道主义与资产阶级的人道主义并无共同之处，而且它更加人道，因为它并不崇拜人（man）但却确实而有效地尊重人类（human）的尊严，对于位格（person）的整体需求行正义，朝向社会俗世中圣经福音对人类事务关爱的实现（这不仅仅以一种精神秩序的方式存在，而且以一种实在的类似道成肉身的方式存在），并趋向一个仁爱的共同体。"② 在这里，实际上马里坦需要建立的是以神为中心的人道主义，并以此来对治当代西方社会过于注重欲望满足的物质主义倾向，并期望以精神秩序的恢复来使这个"无序而混乱"的社会重新走上正轨。

在阐述什么才是"完整"的人道主义的时候，"位格"作为一种对人的先验批判而出现。"人道主义趋向于赋予人更真实的人文内涵，并通过使人全面参与能使其在本性和历史中更加丰富的事件，而彰显其原初的伟大（通过'把世界凝注于人'，舍勒大约是这样说的，'使人延展到世界'）；

---

① Jacques Maritain, *Integral Humanism—temporal and spiritual problems of a new christendom*, Translated by Joseph W. Evans (University of Notre Dame Press, 1973), p. 29.

② Jacques Maritain, *Integral Humanism—temporal and spiritual problems of a new christendom*, Translated by Joseph W. Evans (University of Notre Dame Press, 1973), p. 7.

这即是要求，人发展其美德、创造力、理性的生活，并努力使物质世界成为自身自由的工具。"① 为什么可以使整个物质世界成为人类自由的工具呢？这个问题的回答实际上是，在对人道主义的形上追寻中必须首先明了的，什么才是真正的"人"？这就是关于人的存在的形而上学追问，在马里坦看来，人不仅仅是一个质料性的存有，"个体"（individual），更是一个精神性的存有，"位格"。

在马里坦位格思想中，"个体"与"位格"的区别（根植于质料与形式的区别）非常重要。根据亚里士多德的第一哲学，当我们询问"人是什么"的时候是不够的，因为这只是一般的说法而没有任何实质上的限定，所以必须把握住什么是"存在"，什么是人的存在的本质，所以我们实际上是在问：人如何成为质料（matter）性存在的，换言之，我们寻求的是如何成为如此的原因，这就是形式（form），也就是实体。② 在任何事物中，质料都只是"潜在地存在着，因为它要进入形式，只有进入形式中，它才实现地存在"。③ 也就是说，形式是一切事物的原因和本质。据此马里坦认为："人是由两种角色所组成的，一种是作为质料的角色，它在现实中不关注真正的位格，从严格的意义上来说，它只是位格性的影子，这种质料性的角色我们称之为个体性；另一种是作为形式，或者说作为精神的角色，这便是人类真实具有的位格性。"④ 于是人可以划分为个体和位格两个方面，但是"在人之中并没有如个体性和位格性这样的两种分离的实存。在人身上，并非有一种实存叫'个体'，而另一种实存叫'位格'。事实上，在人身上只有一个实存，在这个意义上叫'个体'，而从另外一个意义上叫'位格'。我们整个实存因为我

① Jacques Maritain, *Integral Humanism—Temporal and spiritual problems of a new christendom*, Translated by Joseph W. Evans（University of Notre Dame Press, 1973）, p. 2.

② 亚里士多德：《亚里士多德选集——形而上学卷》，苗力田编，中国人民大学出版社，2000，第 190 页。

③ 亚里士多德：《亚里士多德选集——形而上学卷》，苗力田编，中国人民大学出版社，2000，第 221 页。

④ ［3］Jacques Maritain, *the Person and the Common Good*, Translated by John J. Fitzgerald（University of Notre Dame Press，1985）, p. 33.

们源于质料的缘故而叫做个体，而同时又因为我们源于精神的缘故又叫做位格"。①

在关涉人的个体性和位格性的论述中，与日益堕落的现代功利主义思想不同（它坚持人的可见的自然性优先于并且实际上重要于人的不可见的、存疑的精神性），马里坦坚持认为：形式高于质料，人的精神性高于质料性。在他看来，"质料本身是一种非存在，它仅仅是一种潜能或能力以便接受形式，并由此经历实质性的转变；简而言之，质料只是一种存在的能力。在每一个由质料构成的存在中，这种纯粹的潜能承担着超自然的能量——'形式'或'灵魂'的印记；形式（和质料一起）构成了实质性的存有，并决定了这个存有如其所是。通过质料承服于形式以及形式赋予质料以某种内在性的事实，形式将自己体现于这样或那样的特殊存在中，并让在空间里并存的其他的存在物得以共享自身特定的本性"。② 因此，在批判所有当代人道主义的弊端时，马里坦首先探究的是作为存在的人的先验本质，这就是"位格"；与所有其他人道主义思想相比，这显然站在了一个更为超越的角度，从而能够更加整全地把握人的本质。当启蒙思想家高举人权、自由的旗帜时，他们眼里的人还仅仅只是自然性存在的人，甚至像拉美特利所说的"人是机器"，而不是康德所说的"人是目的"。当这种批判一切宗教信仰的现代人道主义过于强调人的自然属性，强调人的自保天性、强调人的自然欲望的满足时，理性越来越成为工具，信仰越来越成为虚无；当一切真理都需要通过科学实证时，精神的东西便逐渐被剥离。可以说，现代人道主义正在使人由一个不纯粹的"位格"变成一个纯粹的"个体"。

因此，马里坦的"完整人道主义"必须重新给人以正确的定位，必须找到正确的先验起点，这就是对人的本质性存有的考问——人是上帝的形象（the image of God）。"当我们转向宗教思想中的结论时，我们会发

① [3] Jacques Maritain, *The Person and the Common Good*, Translated by John J. Fitzgerald (University of Notre Dame Press, fourth printing 1985), p. 43.
② [3] Jacques Maritain, *The Person and the Common Good*, Translated by John J. Fitzgerald (University of Notre Dame Press, 1985), p. 36.

现人类高贵性的最深层次在于其模仿上帝的性质——不是那种在通常意义上说的模仿举止、态度等外在的东西，而是一种天生具有的内在方式：这就是上帝的形象。因为上帝就是精神，而人类源自上帝。"① 正是这个原因，作为位格存有的人因为内在与上帝的交通而高于任何质料性存有，甚至高于一切物质世界，"因为它与上帝的纯粹而深邃的内在关联，所以人类位格的自由行为并不属于这个经验世界。人类因其自由而超越于漫天星辰和整个自然界"。② 从这个意义上来说，作为位格存有的人只可能被当作目的，而不可能被当作工具——显然，马里坦的人道主义是站在一个形上的超越起点去回应、批判现代人道主义所导致的各种问题的。

二 作为完整人道主义终点的"位格"

"万物在变化，什么被什么所变，又变成什么。被什么所变，被最初运动者；什么在变，质料；变成什么，形式。"③ 这是亚里士多德的名言，显然，万事万物最后指向的终点都是形式；社会也不例外。如果说超越于整个物质宇宙的"位格"作为完整人道主义的起点的话，那么其指向的终点则同样是"位格"，因为位格超越于整个世俗社会。

"位格"不是孤立和抽象的，它是一个开放的实体，"位格性就是人的精神，而且这种内化于人的位格性使人超越于所谓的独立性；位格的主体性和莱布尼茨所说的孤立的、没有门和窗户的单子毫无共同之处；它要求知识和爱的交流"。④ 正是由于这个原因，位格要求过一种社会的生活，要求服务于共同善（common good）。不过马里坦把共同善分为两个层面，

---

① Jacques Maritain, *The Person and the Common Good*, Translated by John J. Fitzgerald（University of Notre Dame Press，1985），p. 42.

② Jacques Maritain, *The Person and the Common Good*, Translated by John J. Fitzgerald（University of Notre Dame Press，1985），p. 20.

③ 亚里士多德：《亚里士多德选集——形而上学卷》，苗力田编，中国人民大学出版社，2000，第286页。

④ Jacques Maritain, *The Person and the Common Good*, Translated by John J. Fitzgerald（University of Notre Dame Press，1985），p. 42.

一个是由纯粹位格构成的共同善，一个是世俗社会的共同善；位格一方面作为世俗社会的成员服务于社会并在其中彰显、提升自己的位格性，另一方面作为与上帝交通的成员而渴望进入纯粹位格的天国。因此，处身在俗世中的人就不得不面临被社会异化，被社会仅仅当作部分（犹如庞大机器上的一颗螺丝钉）和工具的危险——现代人道主义的悲剧恰恰就是这样，在实践中人们往往被当作了物质欲望的奴隶和经济活动的工具——所以马里坦一方面强调作为位格存在的人需要和他者交通，另一方面强调了位格与社会并非部分与整体的关系。

"即使位格自身要求成为社会的一个部分，或者成为社会的成员，这也决不意味着在整体社会中位格仅仅被当作一个部分来对待，恰恰相反，作为位格本身，它要求在社会中被当作整体来对待。"① 在这里，马里坦认为"位格是整体"的意思是说不要仅仅把位格当作社会的一个螺丝钉，甚至为了整体而牺牲部分，而要将位格当作一个整体性存有来看待，但是马里坦并不否认人同时又是质料性的个体（这一点恰恰是被现代人道主义所过度强调的），从这个角度来说他同意作为个体的人是社会的一部分，"这也是因为人并不是纯粹的位格，不是神圣的位格；他甚至处于有理智存有者的位格性的最低层次。人不仅仅是作为精神性实存的位格，而且，人也是作为物种的组成部分的个体。这就是为什么他作为部分是社会的成员的原因，并且需要社会生活的约束以便引向作为位格的生活，并在此社会生活中支持自身"。② 如果人类社会是由纯粹位格组成的，那么社会的共同善和每个位格的善就是同一的善，但是人远非一个纯粹的位格，他仅仅是一个无法摆脱质料性个体的位格，这种个体性决定了人像动物一样出生、成长，但是他的无助性却远远超过其他动物。尽管人类的位格是一个独立的整体性存有，是所有自然本性中的最高贵者，但是人类的位格却处于位格性的最低层次——他无法摆脱自身质料性存有的脆弱，不得不

① Jacques Maritain, *The Person and the Common Good*, Translated by John J. Fitzgerald（University of Notre Dame Press, 1985）, p. 58.

② Jacques Maritain, *Integral Humanism—Temporal and spiritual problems of a new christendom*, Translated by Joseph W. Evans（University of Notre Dame Press, 1973）, p. 135.

经常处于贫乏、悲惨、穷困以及被欲望所支配的境遇之中。当人进入由同类组成的社会的时候，因为自身的不完满性而不得不需要并依靠社会环境，对环境的依赖使他觉得自己是整体的一个部分，觉得这个整体比自己更优越、更强大，所以它也这样认为整体的共同善高于每个部分的善。但是，马里坦强调的却是：因为人具有位格性的缘故，以及位格所喻示的人是一个独立的、开放的整体的缘故，所以为了自身的位格性的完善需要与社会中其他成员交流，而这就要求社会的共同善必须向作为每个成员的位格作出"回向"。这就是说，作为整体进入社会的是位格；而作为部分进入社会的是个体；整体的共同善在何种意义上超越于私人的善，这只有当它有益于个体性的人，并重新将利益分配给他们且尊重其尊严时才是如此。

现代世俗社会，尤其是沉溺于人的物质性欲望满足的现代社会，从这个意义上来说承服于人的"位格性"，"作为一个精神性整体的位格人意指对整体的超越，超越并高于所有有限存在的世俗社会。从这一点来说，或者我们设想，即便是恺撒的王国以及王国里的共同善也是间接地从属于位格的，从属于位格自身完善以及超越世俗的需要和渴望的，这种渴望的目的指向另外一个秩序，一个超越时空的神圣目的。一个单独的人类灵魂超越于物质世界的整体。没有任何事物高于那不朽的为上帝所拯救的灵魂。相对于灵魂的永恒命运来说，社会为每个位格而存在并从属于位格"。① 对于这个精神信仰日益失落的现代社会，马里坦说："真理并不属于管理我们生活的科技，而属于智慧；文明的至高事业不在于间断性的行为，而在于这内在的固有行动：真正使机器、工业和技术成为服务人们的必需品，使它们服务于位格的伦理，服务于爱和自由。"② 所以他的完整人道主义最终依旧要回到"位格"，因为在他看来，仅仅是质料性存有的世俗社会实际上和物质性宇宙毫无差别——具有悲剧性的是，现代社会正日益向这种抛弃精神性的方向滑落——那么，只注重物质的社会显然低于

---

① Jacques Maritain, *The Person and the Common Good*, Translated by John J. Fitzgerald（University of Notre Dame Press, 1985）, p. 61.

② Jacques Maritain, *Integral Humanism—Temporal and spiritual problems of a new christendom*, Translated by Joseph W. Evans（University of Notre Dame Press, 1973）, p. 194.

人的精神性（位格性），由是"在这里我想说的对于世俗共同善来说，重要的是要尊敬并服务于位格的超世俗的目的"。①

如果说人（位格）是上帝的形象（这本身就蕴含了超世俗的目的）决定了完整人道主义的先验起点的话，那么人是上帝的形象同样也决定了其终点和目的；"完整"的核心就是成为"完美的位格"，虽然这种实现可能是漫长的，但是作为精神信仰来说却是必需的，这正如《新约·哥林多前书》15 章 49 节所说："我们既有属土的形状，将来也必有属天的形象。"向着以耶稣基督为代表的完美位格前进的人类始终有着自己的终极目的，即便这只能在末世审判中才能最终实现。由此在马里坦完整人道主义体系中，当他一再强调要建立一个新基督教世界（new Christendom）时，他实际上追求的是力图建立一个完全由位格组成的社会，尽管这种建立或许遥遥无期，不过正如他始终认为人类精神和灵魂的不朽一样，这样一个世俗化的新基督教世界并不排斥作为"个体"存有的人，他所强调的是要挽救、重现、提升人的已经被现代人道主义所遮蔽和否认的"位格性"，从而建立起整全的、真正的人道主义。而这种位格性所具有的神圣性，必然要求完整人道主义以"上帝"作为自己的核心——实际上，由于"位格"所具有的和上帝交通的特性也必然决定了以"上帝"为核心就是以人类自身（作为"位格"存有的人）为核心。

三 对以位格为基础的完整人道主义的评价

如上所述，我们看到马里坦人道主义之所以是"完整"的原因，或者说，其人道主义始终离不开的形上基础就是对人的本质性存有"位格"的强调；自位格始，批判现代人道主义，自位格终，建立新基督教世界。

---

① Jacques Maritain, *Integral Humanism—Temporal and spiritual problems of a new christendom*, Translated by Joseph W. Evans (University of Notre Dame Press, 1973), p. 133.

　　无可置疑，马里坦在对近代以来人道主义的批判是入木三分的，那种以人（实际上是质料性存有的人）为中心的人道主义不可避免地要陷入物质主义的深渊，以当代资本主义社会为例，他认为："资本主义的客观精神是对行为和发明性的力量提升的精神，是人的物力论和个体积极性的精神，但是它也是对贫穷仇恨，对穷人嘲笑的精神；穷人的存在仅仅是作为生产的工具，服从于利益，而不是作为真正意义上的人，不是作为位格而存在。而富人，另一方面，仅仅作为消费者而存在（为了同样服务于资本的利益），不作为位格而存在；这样，世界的悲剧是，为了保持和发展这个高利贷的庞大经济，这将是无法避免地将所有人作为消费者，或者富人；但是，如果再没有作为工具的穷人的话，那么整个经济将停滞并死亡。"①　显然，这种对资本主义经济的批判是犀利的，而同时马里坦以"位格"作为人的先验存在也是合理的，毕竟人是物性和神性二分的动物，人性的悖论决定了人不仅要寻求现世的有限的生存意义，更要寻求超越的关涉永恒的价值；人对生存意义的寻求，不仅体现于人的经验层面之中，还表现为对隐藏于经验层面之下的什么是人、人从何而来、去向何处、存在的根本意义等超验层面的追求（这也就是我们通常所说的"终极关怀"）。

　　面对人性日益异化、道德日益沦丧、秩序日益混乱的世界，人类已经无法单靠自身掌握的科技找到存在的内在意义。正是在这种情况下马里坦提出建立以上帝为中心的人道主义，无论是把这种"无序"和"混乱"归之于上帝的神秘安排和某种神圣启示，还是把面临的各种困难的解决诉求于与神圣交通的人自身的位格性，这都使得生活中的"无意义"得到了一种合理性的解释，"意义"重新得到复原。完整人道主义重新将神（神圣位格）与人（位格）联结在一起，将现世和未来结合在一起，从而构建了充满神秘色彩而又庄严辉煌、激动人心的终极关怀体系，这些不仅回答了人从何来往何去的问题，而且也回答了人存在的意义与价值的问

---

① Jacques Maritain, *Integral Humanism—Temporal and spiritual problems of a new christendom*, Translated by Joseph W. Evans (University of Notre Dame Press, 1973), p. 115.

题，"信仰不仅是一种思维方式，而且是一种生活方式，它把日常生活置于永恒实体的笼罩之中。这种信仰行为不仅使人精力充沛，而且使人获得一种信念，即人们可以从至善的无限力量中获得最深厚的充实感。由此，人们把自己的生活转向最高的（上帝的、安拉的、黑天的、阿弥陀佛的）精神目标。无论生活中奉行什么，他或她都会充满力量、觉悟与安宁，并且高高兴兴地为他人服务"。① 而且从现实的角度来说，马里坦号召重新返回上帝的人道主义理论同样有着深厚的文化背景和社会背景，据美国《教会研究国际公报》报道，1993 年全世界基督教信徒约 18.6 亿，占世界总人口的 33.5%（其中天主教徒 10.2 亿，基督新教徒 5.8 亿）；就美国而言，1998 年基督教信徒 1.58 亿（其中天主教徒 6201 万）。② 可以说，即便是对上帝的虔诚信仰遭受沉重打击之后的当代基督教在西方社会的影响依然是巨大的，而这些也为马里坦理论的广泛传播和接受提供了现实基础（事实上也是如此）。

但是，马里坦的理论同样也存在着诸多不足，因为他始终强调的是信仰高于理性（人是上帝的形象，位格由此与神相通）。正是由于他的整个人道主义理论以信仰为前提，所以当遇到复杂的社会境遇时，当面临实践中不得不处理的经济的、政治的、伦理的各种冲突和两难的时候，他的理论不能给出一个恰当的、实际的处理方法（信仰不能替代理性，宗教生活不能替代社会生活），当然这也是几乎所有理论家（而不是实践者）的通病。而且，就人本身而言，精神信仰（位格性）是最高贵的，但是物质需求（个体性）却是最强大的，处身现代市场经济的人们始终无所逃逸于经济、科技、政治构建起来的庞大世俗网络，始终无法避免日益异化的人性和精神信仰的虚无。从这个角度来说，理论上的批判和现实问题的解决始终存在着一种二律背反，而这恰恰也是马里坦完整人道主义理论所不得不面对和难以解决的，或许，这也正如马里坦所设想的"新基督教世界"的实现一样，仅仅是一种启人深思的理念吧。

---

① F. J. 斯特伦：《人与神：宗教生活的理解》，何其敏译，上海人民出版社，1992，第 59 页。

② Eileen W. Lindner, *Yearbook of American & Canadian Churches* 2000（Abingdon Press, 2000），p. 10.

Person：Beginning & End of Integrity

—The Metaphysical Presupposition of Integral Humanism of Jacques Maritain

Xu Jin

Abstract：Why we take person as metaphysical presupposition of Integral Humanism of Jacques Maritain? The reason lies in that person is the form but individual is the matter, therefore, man is the image of God which can make man sacred. That is ignored by modern humanism focusing only on man's body, not on man's spirit. Person is the end of integral humanism also because person is not only beyond all universes but also temporal society.

Keywords：Person；Integral；Humanism

无为与守约：《道德经》与《创世纪》 处世方法之比较

李家莲[*]

摘　要：《道德经》与《创世纪》虽然面对着共同的哲学最高存在者，却阐述了不同的伦理要求——知常与服从，二者由此引申出不同的处世方式——无为与守约。对《道德经》与《创世纪》的不同处世方式分析显示，两部经典著作中暗示的不同处世方式不仅体现了中西方民族对待哲学最高存在者的不同态度，而且体现了中西方"人"在哲学中的不同地位，更重要的是，还体现了中西方哲学基本思维方式的差异。

关键词：德　无为　守约

尽管名称不同，可是《道德经》与《创世纪》以不同的名称共同阐释了哲学中相同的最高存在者——"God"与"道"。"老子的道，与基督教的上帝是极其接近的概念。道是非人格化、非神的上帝，而上帝是人格化的、神圣化的道"。[①] "'上帝'的概念在西方与中国的'道'有相似之处……在老子哲学中，'道'是一个至高无上的本体规定，它具有本体论、宇宙论、价值论等多种含义，这一点与西方哲学的'上帝'概念有

---

[*] 李家莲，哲学博士，湖北大学哲学学院、高等人文研究院讲师。
[①] 宫哲兵：《老子与道教》，《道教研究》2004 年第 3 期。

相似之处。"① 事实上，从实质上说，除《道德经》之外的其他中国哲学流派也是以"道"作为自己的研究中心和重心的，因此，冯友兰先生认为，"对超乎现世的追求是人类先天的欲望之一，中国人并不是这条规律的例外"②。

可是，当中国哲人与西方哲人开始把宇宙最高存在者与"人"联系起来的时候，情况就发生了相当大的变化，这种文化源头的差异逐渐演变成为性格迥异的中西哲学内涵与文化传统。在伦理思想上，相同的哲学最高存在者在《道德经》中对人的要求是"德"，而在《创世纪》中，对人的要求是"moral"，"德"与"moral"虽然中文译文大致相似，但二者在词语的文化内涵上是截然不同的，正是这种不同显示了《道德经》与《创世纪》对人的不同伦理要求。在伦理实践上，《道德经》的"德"要求人们做到"知常"，而《创世纪》却通过与人"立约"的方式要求人遵守约定。对两部经典作品中暗示的不同伦理思想与伦理实践的比较揭示，《道德经》与《创世纪》暗示的不同处世方式不仅体现了中西方民族对待哲学最高存在者的不同态度，而且体现了中西方"人"在哲学中的不同地位，更重要的是，还体现了中西方哲学基本思维方式的差异。

一 "德"与"moral"的不同伦理理论
要求：知常与服从

《道德经》和《创世纪》都共同认为，人应该遵守德，但德的内容在二者看来，有很大的不同。《道德经》中的"德"具有双重意蕴，既有本体论意义也有伦理学意义，二者具体内容不同，本体论意义上的"德"给人提出了总体伦理要求，即知常。要分析《创世纪》中"德"的内容，我们首先要明白"德"在英文中的具体含义。英文"德"即 moral，该词

---

① 刘之静：《不可言说的"上帝"与"道"的言说》，《延安大学学报》（社会科学版）2006 年第 2 期。
② 冯友兰：《中国哲学简史》，北京大学出版社，1996，第 4 页。

在韦氏词典中的释意为，"concerned with principles of right and wrong behavior"，简而言之，就是"moral"所关心和讨论的只是涉及人的行为正确与否的标准和原则。这个定义向我们揭示，"moral"的讨论对象不仅包含人的行为准则，而且包括对这种行为准则的价值判断标准。根据moral的定义，《创世纪》认为，人的正确行为准则就是服从上帝的律令，因此，可以用"服从"来概括《创世纪》中"德"的主要伦理内容和伦理要求。

在《道德经》中，道是万物之所以生成的总原理，德为具体某物之所以生成之原理，这是"德"的本体论意义。"孔德之容，惟道是从。""道生之，德畜之，物形之，势成之。是以万物莫不尊道而贵德。道之尊，德之贵，夫莫之命而常自然。""德"即物之所以得于道，而以成其物——道才是万物之所以生的总原理，正是这样，"唯因道德同是物之所以生之原理，所以《老》《庄》书中，道德二字，并称列举"①。《道德经》中讨论的"道"与"德"的关系涉及了宇宙最高存在者与具体事物之间的关系问题，总体看来，这种关系是在本体论层面探讨作为宇宙最高存在者的"道"同与人有密切关系的"德"之间的关系。从"道"与"德"的关系出发，《道德经》揭示了与人有关的道德内容，进而对人提出了总的伦理要求，即知常。由普遍的道所产生的规律可以称为规律或通则，而"凡通则皆可谓之为'常'"②。能否依照"常"而做事，就是道德与否的标准，也是正确与否的处世方法。

《创世纪》中的"moral"的内容与《道德经》中的"德"的内容的不同之处体现在两个方面。首先，由于西方语言具有一种固有的内在精确性，从以上对"moral"一词的分析，我们可以知道，这是一个纯粹关于人的行为原则正确与否的概念，"moral"与"德"在这个层面上的最大不同之处在于，它不在本体论层面来探讨"德"与"道"之间的关系，"moral"所面对的对象仅仅是"人"。其次，"moral"在《创世纪》中揭

---

① 冯友兰：《中国哲学史》，华东师范大学出版社，2000，第172页。
② 冯友兰：《中国哲学史》，华东师范大学出版社，2000，第7~8页。

示的人的正确处世方式是对耶和华神的绝对服从。人是耶和华在第六日创世的作品，一旦造成之后，神还给了人居住的家园，"耶和华神用地上的尘土造人，将生气吹在他的鼻孔里，他就成了有灵的活人，名叫亚当。耶和华神在东方的伊甸立了一个园子，把所有的人安置在那里"①，耶和华善解人意，认为人"独居不好"②，于是又造出了一个女人，使她成为亚当的伴侣。可是，神的一切美意是有条件的，那就是，人不可以吃伊甸园中善恶树上的果子，"园中各样树上的果子，你可以随意吃，只是分别善恶树上的果子，你不可以吃，因为你吃的日子必定死"③。在吃善恶树上的果子之前，人是耶和华的作品，受到耶和华的无限关爱，分享着与耶和华一样永生存在状态。可是，由于受到蛇诱惑，由于自由意志的作用，人最终违背了上帝的命令，被驱逐出伊甸园，开始了以汗水换取糊口之食的尘世生活，从此告别无限性，成为一个有限存在者。以耶和华为代表的"道"在《创世纪》中对人的伦理理论要求是服从，与《道德经》中的"人"不同，《创世纪》所暗示的"moral"的道德内涵就是上帝对人的命令，除了服从与遵守之外，人别无选择，对于以耶和华为代表的"道"来说，即使伊甸园中的"人"也永远不能分有"道"而具有"德"，人永远只是耶和华的作品，永远无法分有上帝的全知和全能，一旦犯戒，就意味着不道德，意味着遭受万古的惩罚与赎罪。

以人为参照点，《道德经》和《创世纪》对德之不同内容的阐释反映了人所具有的不同价值。在《道德经》中，相对于人而言，"道"具有工具价值，人是终极价值，通过对"道"的发现，人找到了如何全生避害的生存方式，即"知常"，从而完成了中国哲学史上道家哲学实现全生避害的理想。《创世纪》中的耶和华或"道"对人没有工具价值，相反，人是上帝的作品，换句话说，人具有工具价值，人是上帝的影子，通过人，上帝实现了对世界的统治。

---

① 《圣经·创世纪》2：7~8。
② 《圣经·创世纪》2：18。
③ 《圣经·创世纪》2：15。

二 《道德经》与《创世纪》的不同处世
方法：无为与守约

在理论上，《道德经》和《创世纪》阐明了不同的伦理要求——知常与服从，当这两种不同的伦理思想与现实生活结合的时候，它们各自给人提出了不同的具体处世方法，《道德经》暗示了无为的处世方法，而《创世纪》暗示了守约的处世方法。

在具体而生动的人世生活中，《道德经》提出了一条具体的处世方法，即无为。无为的人就是知常的人，《道德经》说，"不知常，妄作，凶"，知常的人就是顺"德"的人，这种人应该尽量过"朴"的生活。如何才能过这样的生活？就是要模仿"道"，像道那样，"无为而无不为"。如何才能模仿道？要力争与"道"相似。在哪些方面相似？主要是要模仿"道"的作用方式：要从正反两个方面来模仿。首先，"道"的正面作用方式有两点：第一，无意志。"人法地，地法天，天法道，道法自然。"没有任何属于人的意志，一切都是自然规律自身运行的结果。所以人要取消意志，去除多余的欲望，"绝圣弃智，民利百倍。绝仁弃义，民复孝慈。绝巧弃利，盗贼无有。此三者以为文不足，故令有所属。见素抱朴，少私寡欲"。为了寡欲，就要去智，因此，人不能追求知识，"智慧出，有大伪"，因为知识可以扩大人的视野，激发人的欲望，"民之难治，以其智多；故以智治国国之贼，不以智治国国之福"。第二，无名。道就是无，"道常无名""道隐无名"是相对于具体事物"有"而言的"无"，天地万物都是"有"，而生成天地万物的总原理就是道，是无。"天地万物生于有，有生于无。"在《道德经》的伦理要求看来，对于人而言，追求功名是不正确的处世之道，这样，相对于儒家家天下的"内圣外王"之道而言，《道德经》从自己的角度提供了消解功名的消极处世方式，因此，当人在功名利禄的战场上遭受失意时，"道家学说给中国人的心灵以一条安全的退路，一种宽慰……这就是为什么每个中国人在成功时是儒家，而失败时则变成道家的原因"①。其次，要模仿道的反面作用方式。"反者道之动"道对事物的反面作用方式，对人的暗示就是，人要做什么事，首先要从该事的反面开始。"将欲歙之，必固张之；将欲弱之，必固强之；将欲废之，必固兴之。将欲夺之，必固与之。"② "不自见故明，不自是故彰；不自伐故有功，不自矜故长；夫唯不争，故天下莫能与之争。"③ 由以上分析可以看出，无论正面模仿"道"，还是从反面模仿"道"，对人而言，有一个总要求，即取消人的一切：身体、意识、欲望等，简而言之，就是放弃属于人的一切作为，达到"无为"。

在有限而漫长的尘世生活中，《创世纪》提出了一条实实在在的处世方法，即守约。对于人来说，守约具有两面性。一方面，这样的人就是彻底服从上帝命令的人，是生活在伊甸园中衣食无忧、无忧无虑的人，是具有神一样的无限性的人，是纯洁的人，是没有罪过的人，可是，人因为具有有限性，所以，总不能遵守上帝的律法，一再冒犯，一再受罚；另一方面，这样的人，虽然来自尘土，虽然也被称为"人"，但是没有自由意志，是没有个性的单面人，没有爱情，因为伴侣是神为了免除人独居的不好之处而分配给人的特殊物品，如同伊甸园中的果子一样，除此之外，更没有通常意义上的喜怒哀乐以及七情六欲等。同样，对于人来说，犯戒与讳约也具有两面性。一方面，这样的人用自由意志违背了耶和华的命令而失去了永生的伊甸园，进入了有限的存在状态，失去了衣食无忧的优裕生活，开始了以汗水为生的日子，自由意志给人带来的是罪过以及惩罚；另一方面，被驱逐的人却从此真正开始了人自己的生活，亚当和夏娃自从离开伊甸园，来到尘土之后，马上就开始怀孕并生育，子孙众多，他们成为整个人类的祖先。违约或犯戒使人以失去永生的代价换来了自由意志在尘世的行走，人从此成为真正的生活在尘世的人，而不是伊甸园中无自由意志的人。但是，人永远只是耶和华的作品，虽然在一个有限的存在时间段，人可以利用自己的自由意志为自己谱写一曲壮丽的尘世之歌，但是，

---

① 戴茂堂、江畅：《传统价值观念与当代中国》，湖北人民出版社，2001，第112页。
② 《道德经》第三十六章。
③ 《道德经》第二十二章。

人最终没有忘记那创造天地的父，因为那是人类最初的家园与故乡。由于罪过，人失去了昔日的家园，可是，由于耶和华对人永生的爱，因此，即使在尘世中，耶和华仍不忘一次次与人再次立约，并在《创世纪》中标明了立约的记号，这样，即使处于负罪过程中的人，也总可以通过以与耶和华立约并守约的方式，能够重新回到那失去的家乡。因此，可以发现，在《创世纪》以及整个《圣经》尤其是《旧约》中，守约是耶和华对人提出的最重要的处世方式，人对"约"的遵守与违背构成了人的命运沉浮的内在动力。

《道德经》与《创世纪》中不同的现实处世方式暗示了道或上帝在不同文化中的不同地位。在《道德经》中，由于人的模仿，"道"失去了神秘性，人因为模仿"道"而最终在庄子的哲学中发展为可以"齐生死"的圣人。以上帝为参照，在《创世纪》中，由于自由意志的作用，人冒犯了上帝，因此而一再遭受惩罚，上帝的权威在对人的惩戒中一步步提高，而人的地位却一步步降低，一步步陷入罪恶与苦难，最后终于落入了埃及人的奴役之手，唯有寄希望神与人的再次立约以及人的守约，人才有可能走出痛苦的煎熬，事实上，在随后的圣经文本中，通过摩西，上帝实现了与人的第三次立约，并通过约定拯救了处于苦难中的人。总之，在《创世纪》中，随着文本的推进，神在人面前越来越神秘、越来越有能力，最终成为众人敬仰的万王之王。

三　结论

以上比较显示，虽然名称不同，可《道德经》与《创世纪》共同涉及哲学本体论上的最高存在者，但一旦把这最高存在者和人联系起来，两部书却暗示了截然不同的处世方法。其中的原因在于首先老子和《圣经》作者以不同的态度来看待最高存在者和人自身，赋予二者截然不同的地位，如果思考再深入一步，可以发现，这种不同的深层原因是，中西方存在着两种截然不同的思维方式：主客二分和天人合一，正是这不同的思维方式造成了《道德经》和《创世纪》中截然不同的处世方式。

第一，不同处世方式反映了中西方民族对待最高存在者的不同态度：模仿利用与仰望崇拜。

在《道德经》中，最高存在者成为暗含天机的妙道，它的运动给人的行为极大的启发，人们力图模仿"道"的运动来实现自己的追求，而最完美的模仿就是通过"无为"而使自己成为类似于"道"的存在物。事实上，自从道家哲学形成以来，这种模仿在中国哲学史上是一种绵延不绝的传统。与中国人的实用主义态度相对照，《创世纪》呈现了另外一种截然不同的态度：仰望与崇拜。《道德经》中的最高存在者到了《创世纪》中，具有了截然不同的地位，与《道德经》相比，其地位远远高于其在《道德经》中的任人模仿的"工具性"地位，转身而成为一位全知、全能、全善的神，是所有尘世之王的"万王之王"，受到人类所有成员的敬仰与崇拜。在《创世纪》中，西方人对待最高存在者是一种仰望与崇拜的态度，人永远没有奢望模仿最高存在者，只要这最高存在者能以自己无限的恩慈来拯救人的灵魂，人就认为足够了。事实上，由于基督教在西方文化中的重要地位，在深受基督教浸染的西方哲学与西方文学中，这种体现在人身上的对最高存在者的谦卑态度一直渗透于各个优秀哲学家和文学家的字里行间，发展成为一种独特的西方式集体无意识。

第二，不同处世方式反映了中西方对待人自身的不同态度：从参照最高存在者而言，"人"在《道德经》中的地位远高于其在《创世纪》中的地位。

《道德经》把"人"的地位看得更高，一个重要的原因在于，《道德经》中没有高于人以及惩罚人的"神"，《道德经》所揭示的"道"和"德"的目的是为了提醒人们，聪明的人要善于模仿"道"的运行模式，做事一定要掌握正确的方法，否则，就要遭殃。在这个意义上，可以说，《道德经》的最高存在者是隶属人的，人的存在高于一切，"道"从属于"人"的存在，为了人的存在而存在。与此对照，"人"在《创世纪》中的地位就要低得多，人不是什么特别的存在物，仅仅只是最高存在者的被造物而已，对于这最高存在者而言，人的地位是卑微的，除了仰望和崇拜，除了服从和遵命，自由意志是没有任何用的，它只能给人带来原罪和惩罚。除此之外，《道德经》中的"人"比《创世纪》中的"人"要自由一些，因为没有来自最高存在者的惩罚与审视，人可以随心所欲，只要自己的行为遵循《道德经》所揭示的"常"的道理，人就可以获得幸福和成功，绝对不会有任何危险，至于罪恶，那是根本不会有的事。只要人自己认为自己问心无愧，这个世界上就不存在任何罪恶，顺着这种思维模式，中国文化发展出独特的乐感文化心理。

第三，不同处世方式反映了中西方民族的不同思维方式：主客二分与天人合一。

《道德经》中传达的处世方式显示了中国哲学中的基本思维特征——天与人是可以通约的，因为"天"是可以被模仿的，它存在于人的视野与兴趣之中，这从道家哲学的纬度反映了"天人合一"思维方式的运作模式。老子说，"人法地，地法天，天法道，道法自然"，人与自然一体，天、地、人可以互相贯通，人伦可以效法自然大道，最终达到主客混融的状态。《创世纪》传达的处世方式显示了传统西方哲学基本思维特征——主客二分，"天"与"人"虽处于一个共同体中，但各自具有鲜明的角色定位，"人"必须安分守己，不可对"天"的领地僭越雷池半步，否则，只能遭受来自"天"的永恒惩罚，走上无尽的赎罪之路。正是由于存在这种主客二分的思维方式，"人"才有可能因自由意志而犯戒，因为人在偷吃善恶树的果子的过程中形成了对"天"的领地的僭越，从而犯了罪，必须由此而遭受惩罚，"你既听从妻子的话，吃了我所吩咐的不可吃的那树上的果子，地必为你的缘故受诅咒。你必终生劳苦、才能从地里得吃的。地必长出荆棘和蒺藜来，你也要吃田间的菜蔬。你必汗流满面才得糊口，直到你归了尘土；因为你是从土而出的。你是尘土，仍要归于尘土"①。在基督教传统思想中，因为自己的原罪，人被赶出了伊甸园，从此开始了与耶和华对立的尘世生活，人只能依靠神的恩宠，才能获得拯救，得以找到那流着牛奶与蜜的圣地，最终重新回到失去的家园。

---

① 《圣经·创世纪》3：17~19。

Inaction and Covenant-keeping

— The Secular Ethical Principal Comparison Between *Daoism* and *Genesis*

Li Jialian

Abstract：Although both *Daoism* and *Genesis* face the same highest philosophical entity, they interpret different secular ethical principles, i. e. inaction and covenant-keeping. By comparing the different ethical principles of the two classic works, we can find that western and Chinese people treat the same highest philosophical entity in quite different ways and that "man" has quite different position in western and Chinese philosophical thinking. More importantly, we can find the different approaches of philosophical pondering in western and Chinese philosophies from this comparison.

Keywords：moral；Inaction；Covenant-keeping

各国文化与世界文化

Culture of Different Countries and World Culture

Emergence of Philosophy out of American Culture

G. John M. Abbarno [*]

Abstract: This essay is intended to demonstrate a small portion of how the culture in the United States of America generates a philosophical way of thinking that contributes to values in an ever increasing World Culture. The foundations are traced back to earlier settlers in the United States whose idealism, courage, and practical problem solving establish what can be viewed as parallels to philosophical themes of the movement of philosophy in America known as Pragmatism, most notably the values of individualism and freedom. The essay will make a case for this parallel especially through the contributions made by John Dewey.

Keywords: American culture; pragmatism; individualism; freedom

Among the many U. S. American cultural values, individualism and freedom serve as the cornerstone for others. From the earliest arrival of religious groups fleeing England in the 17th century for a land of religious toleration, America signified the new land of milk and honey. They came to a vast territory for unbridled material explorations and freedom to pursue religious ideals. These apparent disparate values between the immanent and the transcendent forge the USA cultural values that shape the intellectual history of the nation and serve as the

[*] G. John M. Abbarno, Professor of Philosophy at D'Youville College, USA.

foundational values for its philosophical roots. Before formal philosophical writings in the United States we can find the value of self-reliance, being skeptical of conformity, and ascribing truth to what was written or spoken in the mainstream. During the 19th century, the early history literary philosophers shaped their works around values that continue to be implemented in more formal ways by the American Pragmatist movement in philosophy. Ralph Waldo Emerson, Henry David Thoreau, and Walt Whitman were members of what are referred to as the American Transcendentalist movement. Their works expressed their passion for nature and the spirit of it that dwells within to be discovered in each individual as an extension of nature. Experience of man with nature elevated and liberated the individual to think and feel creatively about his social condition. Thoreau celebrated the genius of the individual that often times required objecting to the restrictions on a person by government or any institution that did not respect an individual's rational authority. The laws were valued for their enhancement of this spirit, not its repression. Transcendentalists eschewed the reverence for history as an authority for how human life in America ought to be lived. For them, the future was yet to be written anew by the energized ideas and values of each person who is experiencing circumstances unique to them.

Transcendentalists embraced experimentalism instead of fixed traditional solutions to problems. As conflicts arose, they posed novel alternatives that reflected humankind immersed in similar ordinary experiences. This will set some of the cultural framework that becomes part of the basis of American Pragmatism, a philosophy that puts beliefs into actions; a problem-solving method that becomes associated with the phrase " Yankee ingenuity ". The American Pragmatist philosophy incorporates the cultural values of the United States and formalizes in a method some of the values that presuppose those that were haled by transcendentalists: freedom and individualism. Among the three main pragmatists—Charles Sanders Peirce, William James, and John Dewey, the philosophical contributions of John Dewey shall be the main focus.

Dewey was prolific on all matters of ideas that affected social life writing on education, the arts, politics, and sciences, all of which were integrated with a value theory. Space does not permit to explore all these contributions, many of which have their roots in the earlier ideas of transcendentalism. So I shall comment on the pursuit of individualism, then his pragmatic thought process that over-arches his philosophy about science and values. Dewey's attempt to seek a unification of science and human values, analogues the early American settlers' seemingly incompatible worldviews; their reliance on material expansion through skillful work on the one hand and their values inspired by religious freedoms on the other. First, however, a brief account of his value of individualism. Dewey's emphasis on individualism underscored the conditions that would enhance a person's development. Society is improved if it provides the scaffolding for a person to choose ways of living and produce a public good for all. A person's well being was not to be narrowly regarded as satisfying the economic values alone, as was thought to be the case by many of his contemporaries. He disagreed with those who believed that "economic freedom will automatically lead to all other kinds of freedom ... this conception of liberty can be traced back to struggles against government encroachment in private property and limitations on economic activity imposed by a feudal system" . [1]Dewey supported a view that complements this that can be referred to as a humanistic liberalism. Such a position argued for the measured intervention of government for social reform. This wider conception of freedom and individuality affects more dimensions of social life than economic liberty alone.

Participatory ideals, Dewey believed, could help unite the demands of liberty and equality and the goals of individual fulfillment with the promotion of a common good. The theory of individualism was a necessary supplement to his theory of democracy, and it lies therefore in the heart of his political philosophy. [2]

---

[1] Maciej Kassner, "John Dewey & Friedrich von Hayek on Individualism and Freedom," in *The Continuing Relevance of John Dewey*, eds. Larry A. Hickman et al. (New York: Rodopi Press, 2011), p. 276.

[2] Maciej Kassner, "John Dewey & Friedrich von Hayek on Individualism and Freedom", in *The Continuing Relevance of John Dewey*, eds. Larry A. Hickman et al. (New York: Rodopi Press, 2011), p. 277.

Dewey leaves us a legacy of self-reliance, encouraging us to use our intelligence to uncover causes of difficulties we encounter, no matter how large, and clarify the confusions that we are mired in. This enlists the theoretical and the practical capabilities in every individual that will free him to become a better citizen and fulfilled human being. This requires a bridge between what are often viewed as two disparate domains in philosophy: science and value. The unification of science and values was considered by Dewey at the turn of the twentieth century as the main task of philosophy in general. As we continue our second decade into the twenty-first century, it remains evermore intensely a task of philosophy, one which pragmatism offers some method of success.

Dewey introduces three ideas that demonstrate how this pragmatism integrates values and reconstructs philosophy's role in society: (1) instrumentalism, (2) patterns of inquiry, and (3) inquiry as evaluation.

1. Instrumentalism

An important contrast Dewey sets against traditional philosophical approaches is the meaning he gives to experience—it is interactive. Unlike Empiricism, experience is a naturalism that comprises organisms that are dynamically related. Human beings are among such organisms that use instrumentalism or intelligence for identification of value and meaning in nature.

> Intelligence is a form of behavior in certain occurring situations, situations calling for inquiry, rather than a fund of prescriptions or formulas to be enacted. But then recipes for conduct, injunctions, and advice, the solutions to problems of educational, political, or economic practices, are not forthcoming from Dewey or his philosophy...Dewey is able to suggest how problems are to be encountered and resolved but not what the solutions are or should be. [1]

---

[1] H. S. Thayer, *Meaning and Action: A Critical History of Pragmatism* (New York: Bobbs-Merrill Publishers, 1968), p. 182.

One of the main aspects of pragmatism is to critically engage experience. Each person's inquiry will determine the solution to the problem experienced. From such, an analysis of the meanings between experience and person is formed. The interaction is the instrumental tool of thought or intelligence. One aspect of instrumentalism is when thought attempts to set out a description of its own function in view of a problematic situation. Dewey traces the initial cause of the idea becoming shaped and what plausible consequences to which it leads. Instead of resorting to logical schema to demonstrate the validity of a piece of reasoning, instrumentalism is embodied in the situation that originates it. To achieve the entire descriptive account, assumptions that were contained in the first model are instructive, as they give direction for one explanation instead of another. The situation itself will preclude some assumptions and thought will move to the consequences it portends. There is no standard to the concept "intelligence" — but he allows for a natural capacity. The extent to which a person resolves a problem well, his choice and it's related consequences become satisfactory.

This is precisely what Dewey refers to as logic of a human situation—where "human intelligence, purposes, and actions affect what is experienced".[1] But only these human situations that are indeterminate or unsettled, are what Dewey refers to as logical. These give rise to natural development toward a state of unity or, as Peirce would state, from doubt to belief. Dewey adopts a similar form of inquiry but sufficiently different in its aim at immediate resolution. Inquiry he defines as "the controlled or directed transformation of an indeterminate situation into one that is so determinate in its constituent distinctions and relations as to convert the elements of the original situation into a unified whole".[2]

2. Pattern of Inquiry

Dewey's influence from biological psychology makes his "inquiry" more distinct

---

[1] H. S. Thayer, *Meaning and Action: A Critical History of Pragmatism* (New York: Bobbs-Merrill Publishers, 1968), p. 171.

[2] John Dewey, "Logic: The Theory of Inquiry", in *The Later Works of John Dewey*, vol. 12, ed. JoAnn Boydston (Carbondale: Southern Illinois University Press, 1988), pp. 104 – 105.

from Peirce. As cited above, we are human organisms engaged with an environment. Judgments are made only upon recognition that the "life-world" that we adapt to becomes disrupted. There are circuits of connection that are experienced in an unattentive way until they become interrupted. The first order level of organic experience learns through adapted responses until reconstruction is demanded through inquiry. For example, suddenly you begin noticing a tingling sensation on your left side. Then a numbness in your fingers now extends to your whole hand. Customary activity is interrupted. You now begin to become aware of the continued discomfort and initiate your inquiry. You seek to resume activity in the world. What is sought is a settled question using intelligence as a tool: What is the problem with my left hand? Am I having a heart attack? Is there a pinched nerve? He implements the scientific method here: (1) Identify the problematic situation, (2) classify the problem, (3) formulate a hypothesis, (4) test the idea, and (5) verify or disverify the hypothesis. This intelligent investigation would seek other once unattended experiences that may help explain the aberration from the usual expected use of limbs. The problem of restoring integration and cooperation between men's belief about the world in which he lives and his beliefs about values and purposes that should direct his actions is the deepest problem of any philosophy that is not isolated from life.

The biological importance in Dewey's work demonstrates the human agent's immersion in nature. From the beginning, we are disposed with values: cherishing, liking, disliking, fearing certain elements. These elements are highlighted as their attachment to problems and consequences become clear. So, the steps as cited above are begun again. Consider how the situation slowly begins to become understood as far reaching: A father receives word that one of his two children needs to attend remedial courses over summer while the other receives an opportunity to study abroad in a special honors program. Both cost money but whereas one child's future will be enhanced, the other's will be maintained. Since this is not a wealthy family, a choice must be made, one that Dewey would consider is contained in the problematic situation—awaiting to be made harmonious. The choice in this will render immediate results, demonstrating the value of experimental philosophy. Either the values of fairness for maintaining a child's hope to stay in school is better served than denying his other child an opportunity that few receive for their quality of work. The incompatibilities of consequences must be viewed and assessed as part of a pattern of inquiry that engaged us in past similar circumstances. The solution of one situation is opened to others that may enlighten a more encompassing value. In that instance, it may be determined by the second child's learning the value of charity toward his younger sibling. This value we will have for future situations he may encounter in his own life.

3. Inquiry as Evaluation

Life consists is a series of situations then, overlapping and interpenetrating experiences or contexts, each of which has its interval qualitative integrity while suggesting inferences to attain solutions or and end-in-view for the immediate problem under consideration. What results is a transformation of the situation, from an indeterminate to determinate and harmonious one. Through inquiry it becomes funded with meaning and value. This type of experience Dewey refers to as consummation or reconstruction. However troublesome Dewey's lack of prescriptions and recipes to resolve problematic situations, he allows for the inquiry to be conducted by those who are immediately in it. Evaluations made toward the

> right course of action, the right good, (are implicit in inquiry.) ...
> Inquiry concludes with what ought to be or is the right solution to the problem... For Dewey, judgment, with which inquiry closes, involves an appraisal of the adequacy and 'value' of the intermediate course of inquiry and of propositions that are being prepared for final settlement. [1]

Experimental thinking—options are opened up to that which resolves or unifies the unsettled questions.

---

[1] H. S. Thayer, *Meaning and Action: A Critical History of Pragmatism* (New York: Bobbs-Merrill Publishers, 1968), p. 199.

So any inquiry of this sort aims at a good: It is the epitome of moral activity. Dewey writes:

> Moral goods and ends exist only when something has to be done proves that there are deficiencies, evils in the existent situation ... consequently the good of the situation has to be discovered, projected and attained in the basis of the exact defect and trouble to be rectified. Process of growth and improvement rather than static outcome and result become the significant thing. Not health as an end fixed once and for all, but needed improvement in health, the continual process is the end good. The end is no longer a terminus or limit to be reached. It is the actual process of transforming the existent situation ... Honesty, industry, temperance, justice, like health, wealth, and learning are not goods to be attained. They are directions of change in the quality of experience. Growth itself is the moral "end".①

There are no goods in themselves, no intrinsic values in Dewey's value theory. Just as there is no certainty in his epistemology. Inquiry exposes for us the values that we act on or would act on if the conditions were sufficient for satisfactory consequences.

So, for Dewey, if we were to treat our value assessments in the same way as we treat scientific beliefs, "standards, principles, rules ... and creeds about good and goods would be recognized to be hypotheses."②

The pragmatists, thus, illustrate their rootedness in the attitude of Socratic philosophy: Thought and action must be related. They remind us of the social value of philosophy, by keeping it public and alive as our beliefs are verified by the community in which we participate. As we continue in the 21st century to encounter problems, we must be mindful of Dewey's optimism in the face of

---

① J. Dewey, *Reconstruction In Philosophy* (New York: Henry Holt Company, 1920), pp. 163 – 164.

② John Dewey, *A Quest for Certainty: A Study of the Relation of Knowledge and Action* (New York: Capricorn/Putnam Press, 1929), p. 277.

uncertainty. It is reflective of the optimism of American values. Instead of recoiling, we must use tools available to us to embrace nature and change the quality of experience for our human development. Pragmatism forges the continuity of cultural values and philosophy.

美国文化中的哲学思想

G. John M. Abbarno

摘　要：本文旨在从一个角度阐述美国文化何以产生了一种影响世界文化价值观的哲学思维方式。美国哲学思想的基础可以追溯到早期定居者，他们的理想主义、勇气以及对实际问题的解决方式，可以被视为美国实用主义思潮尤其是个人主义和自由价值观哲学主题的平行产物。本文将借鉴约翰·杜威的研究来对这种平行性做出论证。

关键词：美国文化　实用主义　个人主义　自由

Cultural Differences Between Countries:
the Brazilian and the Chinese Ways of
Doing Business

Erika Zoeller Véras; Daniel Bicudo Véras *

Abstract: Each country has its own cultural backgrounds and standards of thinking, being and acting, and these cultural differences strongly influence the business world. The purpose of this paper is to present some cultural differences between countries highlighting the Brazilian and Chinese examples. Many are the cultural aspects within a society; therefore this paper will emphasize how these aspects can have an impact on business in both cultures, having as a background the basic cultural points of each country. Brazil and China will be analyzed through the Hofstede (2001) dimensions which measure cultural differences. This paper gives a short overview to provide an understanding on how cultural similarities and cultural differences are important when doing business in the mentioned countries. The authors propose that the more acquainted one is with a culture, the more successful his/her business will become. In addition, it is necessary to evaluate which cultural issues have an impact when it comes to business.

Keywords: cultural differences; business; Brazil and China.

---

* Erika Zoeller Véras, Studying at School of Management, Wuhan University of Technology; Daniel Bicudo Véras, English teacher at Hubei University.

1. Introduction

This paper aims to discuss the importance of culture in globalized business, taking into consideration Brazil and China. Many are the cultural aspects within Chinese and Brazilian cultures. Nevertheless, for the purpose of this paper, how culture can have an impact on doing business will be taken into account. The first part briefly introduces aspects about international businesses and culture. Then, there will be a topic to discuss the cultural aspects when doing business in Brazil, and another on doing business in China. Brazil and China will be analyzed through the Hofstede (2001) dimensions, which measure cultural differences. More details about these dimensions are given in Part 5 and Part 6. Finally, the conclusion points out the important role that culture plays within international business.

Reeves and Baden (2000: 4) define culture as the distinctive patterns of ideas, beliefs, and norms which characterize the way of life and relations of a society or group within a society. This set of beliefs shared by a group is frequently assumed to be natural and unchangeable. Culture also consists of the sum of the total learned behaviors transmitted from generation to generation, generally considered to be the tradition of that people: explicit and implicit patterns acquired and transmitted by symbols, constituting the distinctive achievement of human groups. The essential core of culture consists of traditional ideas and their attached values. They not only may be considered as products of action, but also as conditioning influences upon further action. Different cultural groups think, feel, and act differently, and there is no scientific standard for considering one group as intrinsically superior or inferior to another. Therefore, a position of cultural relativism is presupposed in the study of cultures. Judgment and action should be preceded by information about the nature of cultural differences between societies, their roots, and consequences. When the parties understand the reasons for the differences in viewpoints, the negotiation is more likely to succeed.

When it comes to international business and culture, contact between societies may affect cultures, and produce or inhibit social changes in cultural practices. Understanding cultural differences is essential in the modern society. How people from many cultural backgrounds communicate, in similar and different ways, internally and externally, is the object of study of cross-cultural communication. Understanding cultural differences will help ensure that communication across borders is effective and that business transactions are successful.

2. Cultural Aspects of Doing Business in Brazil

Brazil is characterized by a diverse culture and geography, and historically it has been the source of important natural resources. It is the largest country in South America in both population and area, and its culture is a fusion of Portuguese, African and indigenous influences, resulting in a rich and distinct culture. One could say that the family is the foundation of the social structure and forms the basis of stability for most people. Although family size has been diminishing in recent years, families tend to be large and the extended family is quite close.

In order to guarantee success when doing business in Brazil, we here list some important cultural aspects of this society:

- Before the Brazilians can work effectively, they need to know who they are doing business with;
- It is not recommended to rush the relationship-building time. It is better to wait for the Brazilian part to raise the business subject. Expect to spend time when negotiating with Brazilians;
- Face-to-face meetings are preferred to written communication, although when it comes to business agreements, Brazilians value detailed legal contracts;
- They attach more importance to the individual they deal with than to the company;
- As the Brazilians are more comfortable doing business with people and companies they know, questions about the company are expected;
- Normally the highest-ranking person is the one who makes the decisions. This makes evident what hierarchical business is like in Brazil;
- Men greet by shaking hands, with a steady eye contact. This could be

done as an inter-gender greeting, too;

- Kissing is a usual greeting for women. Brazilian friends often do hugging and backslapping, too;

- Embarrassing a Brazilian should be avoided, for this is a group culture;

- When a person is criticized, he/ she loses face with the others in the meeting. The one who makes the criticism also loses face, as an unwritten rule has been disobeyed;

- Informality shapes communication, which normally does not rely on strict rules of protocol. Anyone who feels like adding their opinion will just say it;

- Brazilians are normally more tolerant on interrupting someone who is speaking;

- People, rather than companies, are who Brazilians negotiate with. Therefore, it is not advisable to change the negotiating team. This would mean starting from zero. It is important to highlight that normally the people you negotiate with do not have decision-making authority;

- During introductions at a meeting, business cards are exchanged with everyone.

As Brazilians depend heavily on relationships with others, it is essential to spend time getting to know, both personally and professionally, your Brazilian counterparts. One of the most important elements in Brazilian business culture is personal relationships. By cultivating them, and building trust, one's chance of successfully doing business in Brazil will increase greatly. Curiously, it is common to see members of the same family working for the same company. This is due to the strong importance placed on family relations. Brazilians prefer to do business with those they know and trust, what reinforces this characteristic.

3. Cultural Aspects of Doing Business in China

China's rich cultural heritage must not be overlooked when discussing cultural interactions with this country. With a 5,000-year history and an interesting mix of ethnic groups, it can be said that it is the only continuous ancient civilization. Founded on October 1, 1949, the People's Republic of China is situated in eastern Asia, with an area of 9.6 million square kilometers and a population exceeding 1. 2 billion, which makes up 22 percent of the world total (the word's most populous country). China has followed a family planning policy since the 1970s in order to bring the population growth under control. Today, the country is implementing reform and opening-up policies, and has established what they call a socialist market economy, or socialism with Chinese characteristics. Throughout most of Imperial China's history, Confucianism[①] was the official philosophy and the country's traditional social values were derived from various versions of this philosophy.

In order to succeed in business in China, some important cultural aspects in the Chinese society should be highlighted, such as:

● Respect for superiors, duty to family, loyalty to friends, sincerity and courtesy are part of China's ethical system;

● Respect and status increase with the age;

● When presenting your business card, hold it with two hands, always ensuring that the Chinese side is facing the recipient;

● Make a show of examining the business card carefully for a few moments when you receive it. Then carefully place it into your card case or on the table, etc. It will be considered a breach of protocol if you do not read a business card that has been presented to you;

● Handshaking, especially in a light fashion, is the accepted greeting. Greetings are normally formal and one should greet the oldest person first. As a sign of respect, many Chinese will look towards the ground when greeting someone. As staring may make Chinese uncomfortable, it should be avoided;

● Although gifts are important, giving expensive gifts could be taken the wrong way;

● Never insult or openly criticize someone in front of others, for "maintaining face" is very important for Chinese people.

Duty, sincerity, loyalty, honor, filial piety, respect for age and seniority are the most valued virtues in Confucianism. The society itself becomes stable through the maintaining of harmonious relations. The 关系 GUANXI

---

① Confucius, one of the most influential Chinese philosophers, lived around 500 B. C.

(relationship) is another relevant aspect. It is essential to learn this kind of relationship and also to be able to handle it, in order to succeed in business in China. A need for group affiliation, whether to family, school, work group, or country characterizes the Chinese society as a collective one. They will act with decorum and will avoid anyone's public embarrassment for the sake of maintaining a sense of harmony. The concept of harmonious relationships is the essence of Confucianism, and the culture will revolve around it. The society as a whole will function smoothly if proper behavior through duty, respect and loyalty are shown in the relationships. Doing business in China is a good opportunity to see how Confucianism is highly influential to business practices.

4. Brazil and China: The Hofstede Dimensions of Culture

Five independent dimensions of national culture differences were identified and developed by Geert Hofsted (2001), as below. A large research project on national culture differences across subsidiaries of a multinational corporation (IBM) in 64 countries was the base for these categories. It is possible to provide a graph comparing Brazil and China by showing scores relating the five indexes, which may range between 1 and 120:

PDI (Power Distance Index) —the degree of equality or inequality between people in a country's society is addressed to by the PDI score. The higher the PDI score is, the more it indicates inequalities of power and wealth in a country, whereas a low scoring indicates more social equality. How much a culture does or does not value hierarchical relationships can be seen through this cultural dimension.

IDV (Individualism) —the degree to which a culture values the importance of the individual is addressed to in the individualism score. A high scoring indicates that the country views individuality as important, while low scoring indicates that the country rather values the group, i. e. family, tribe, the motherland, etc.

MAS (Masculinity) —the degree to which a culture reinforces the traditional role of males and females is addressed to in the masculinity dimension. A more accute degree of gender differentiation is found in high scoring countries, whilst there is less differentiation and discrimination between genders in low scoring countries. Competitiveness, ambition, and the accumulation of wealth are valued in the so-called "masculine" cultures, whereas relationship and quality of life are valued in the so-called "feminine" cultures.

UAI（Uncertainty Avoidance）—the level of tolerance for uncertainty and ambiguity within a culture is addressed to in uncertainty avoidance. A low tolerance for uncertainty and ambiguity is seen in cultures with a high uncertainty avoidance score. These societies tend to be more rule-oriented and based on laws and regulations. A low scoring country, on the other hand, is less concerned about ambiguity and uncertainty. Being it less rule-oriented, it is more ready to accept change, consider new ideas and take more and greater risks.

Long-Term Orientation（LTO）, opposed to short-term orientation, is a society's "time horizon," or the importance attached to the future, is described in this dimension. Perseverance is valued in cultures with high long-term orientation.

According to the cultural dimensions by Hofstede（2001）, Brazil and China rank as below:

Table 1 Geert Hofstede Five Cultural Dimensions
（Brazil and China）—from 1 to 120

	PDI	IDV	MAS	UAI	LTO
	Power Distance Index	Individualism	Masculinity	Uncertainty Avoidance Index	Long-Term Orientation
Brazil	69	38	49	76	65
China*	80	20	66	30	118

* Estimated Values.

Source: Hofstede（2001）.

Hofstede's five dimensions can be seen as belows.

If analyzed through the Hofstede's Dimensions, Brazil's low level of tolerance for uncertainty is the country's most proheminent characteristic, for Uncertainty

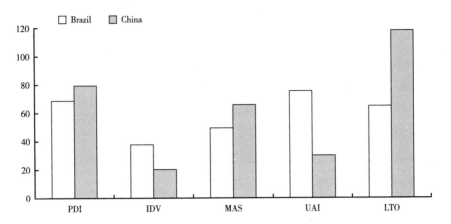

Figure 1   The 5D Model of Professor Geert Hofstede Cultural Comparison Graph (Brazil and China) from 1 to 120

Source: Hofsted (2001).

Avoidance (UAI) is the highest Hofstede Dimension index, ranking 76. Strict rules, laws, policies, and regulations are adopted and implemented in order to minimize or reduce this level of uncertainty. The ultimate goal is to eliminate or avoid the unexpected. Therefore, Brazil does not readily accept change and is very risk adverse.

The highest-ranking factor in Geert Hofstede's analysis for China is Long-term Orientation-LTO (118), which is true for all Asian cultures. A society's time perspective and an attitude of persevering are indicated by this dimension. Overcoming obstacles with will and strength, if not with time, is the most important. When it comes to Individualism (IDV) , the Chinese rank the lowest in Asia, at 20. The high emphasis on a collectivist society, as well as the Communist rule, may partially explain this. A close and committed group, such as a family (including the extended family) or extended relationships, makes evident the low Individualism ranking. Strong relationships, in which everyone takes responsibility for fellows, is fostered by the society. Therefore, in a collectivist culture, loyalty is paramount. China's Power Distance ranking of 80 is of note. A high level of inequality of power and wealth within the society is then suggested.

5. Cultural Similarities Between Brazil and China in Doing Business

Both Brazil and China have historically been described from an Orientalist angle, using the category by Said (2003). Moreover:

1) Both Chinese and Brazilians do not feel comfortable with getting straight to the point when it comes to closing a deal: they prefer to socialize and get to know with whom they are doing business;

2) It is necessary to invest a considerable amount of time developing good rapport and a pleasant, relaxed relationship before discussing business in Brazil and in China. A precondition to a successful business relationship is establishing an atmosphere of trust. Business people in both countries prefer to establish a strong relationship before closing a deal;

3) Although how to address someone in both countries is not exactly the same, it still shows how both countries appreciate hierarchy levels and authority;

4) Embarrassing a Brazilian should be avoided. If an individual is openly criticized, he/ she will lose face with the others at the meeting. And for having disobeyed the unwritten rule, the person making the criticism also loses face. In China, too, a relationship and any business that might result from it can be instantly destroyed by saying or doing anything that causes someone to lose face. Therefore, the rule works for both countries;

5) Chinese and Brazilian business people negotiate with people, not companies. It is not advisable to change the negotiating team, otherwise one may have to start over from the beginning;

6) Face-to-face meetings are most preferred by the Brazilians and the Chinese, rather than written or telephonic communication;

7) Contacts are very important in Brazil and in China. Everyone has networks, and one's network may extend into friends' networks. Creating relationships is part of the culture in both countries, and the advantages will come from having things done.

6. Cultural Differences Between Brazil and China in Doing Business

Fran ois Jullien (1998) describes many cultural differences between Eastern and Western thoughts. As an heir of Europe's, Brazilian culture is highly influenced by the concepts of utopia, ideal reality, transcendence, and how to transform the reality is a main concern. The Oriental culture, especially the Chinese one, is rather pragmatic and resigned facing the reality. Hofstede (2001) highlights:

1) Very long dinners and sometimes spending many days in getting to know each other is an already established Chinese way of building relationships. The same should not be expected from Brazilians, though. Although having meals together is important for Brazilians, it does not have the same value as for the Chinese.

2) In China exchanging business cards is far more ceremonious than in Brazil. In this country it is just a way of exchanging information.

3) For the Chinese culture, the relationship developed with a person represents the relationship with the entire company. Rather than individuals, the foreigners are seen as representatives of their company. For Brazilians, on the other hand, the individual they deal with is more important than the company.

4) In the Chinese culture it is not acceptable to interrupt someone who is speaking. In Brazil, on the other hand, it is more tolerated.

5) Among Brazilians, hugging and backslapping are common greetings if people are close. Also, this would be an acceptable behavior if they are business partners for a long time. It would never be acceptable in the Chinese situation, though.

6) On Individualism vs. Collectivism: Chinese society is collectivist and the group prevails over the individual. There, the individuals are willing to

subjugate their own feelings for the good of the group. As for the Brazilian society, it is more focused on individuals.

7) On Body Language: in China direct eye contact is disrespectful, whereas in Brazil it is a sign of honesty. While Brazilians shake hands when greeting one another, maintaining steady eye contact, many Chinese will look towards the ground at this moment.

7. Conclusion

When doing business, each country has its own cultural particularities: a mixture of attitudes, values, and social expectations. At present, in a totally connected world, being aware of these cultural differences is a condition for success. Business representatives need to be provided with an understanding of the cultural differences in order to be sensitive to them when conducting business across countries. The workplace values and business communication are going to be influenced by these differences, given by each country's own cultural standards of being, thinking, and acting. What may be considered confusing or offensive in the workplace of one country can be considered acceptable in the workplace of another because of culture's decisive role in this context. To understand cultures today, one must, hence, read about different countries, always keeping in mind the special role that culture can play in business. The communication between people with different linguistic and cultural backgrounds and an ever growing number of contacts characterize the world today. The contacts in areas like business need to be as constructive and precise as possible, so that this communication effort can take place. We can conclude that the Chinese and the Brazilian companies can have different perspectives on Sino-Brazilian business. The firms will also be capable of better evaluating the role that culture can play in business. The number of areas where business people can face challenges is demonstrated in the above examples of differences in culture, business practices, business etiquette and protocol.

The Brazilian society's low level of tolerance for uncertainty is demonstrated by its score for Uncertainty Avoidance (UAI) of 76, using the Hofstede Cultural dimensions for analysis. Brazil's index is 38 for Individualism (IDV), and this can be seen in a close long-term commitment to the group, such as (extended) family or relationships. As seen above, in a collectivist culture loyalty is paramount, over-riding most other societal rules.

On the other hand, China's Long-term Orientation (LTO) index is 118, which indicates this society's time perspective and attitude of persevering. Unlike Brazil, China ranks at 20 in Individualism (IDV). The high emphasis on a collectivist society may partially explain this. The low Individualism ranking shows an even more intense group loyalty and relationship than in Brazil. Everyone takes responsibility for fellow members of their group, and strong relationships are fostered by the society. A high level of inequality of power and wealth within the society is present in both countries, where this condition is accepted as a cultural heritage.

When it comes to doing business, major similarities and differences between Brazilian and Chinese societies were found, especially on the way to address someone, to develop relationships, how to exchange cards, body language, interruptions, collectivism and individualism, among others. Studying cultural similarities and differences can have a positive and constructive effect on Sino-Brazilian business. Developing better relationships and doing business more successfully are the possible benefits of understanding the diversity of Brazilian society as well as its unique values and attitudes. By cultivating close personal relationships and building trust, one can increase his/ her chances of successful business in Brazil. One may not forget the strong European heritage in Brazil, which makes the country more direct and holding a specific mindset. As for China, understanding this country's business culture is critical, given its distinct cultural differences from the rest of the world, given its unique dynamic relation among elements, indirect ways and pragmatism, just to name a few. In China the business practices are highly influenced by Confucianism, and doing business in China enables us to see that. Thus, learning about Confucianism and its influence in the Chinese society is crucial.

When doing business abroad, any international business person, company or organization can make use of cross cultural understanding as an important tool. Culture does play an important role, and recognizing and understanding the existence of cultural differences and similarities is unquestionably valuable and helpful. When doing business in these so geographically distant countries, one can notice how this awareness can shorten distances and make the world smaller.

References：

［1］Hofstede, Geert. 2001. *Culture's Consequences, Comparing Values, Behaviors, Institutions, and Organizations Across Nations.* Thousand Oaks CA：Sage Publications.

［2］Hofstede, Geert and Hofstede, Gert-Jan. 2004. *Cultures and Organizations：Software of the Mind.* New York：McGraw-Hill.

［3］Jullien, Francois. 1998. A *Treatise on Efficacy：Between Western and Chinese Thinking.* Sao Paulo：Editora 34 (In Portuguese).

［4］Reeves, Hazel; Baden, Sally. 2000. "Gender and Development：Concepts and Definitions" In：Bridge (Development-Gender), Report No. 55, February, Brighton：Institute of Development Studies, University of Sussex.

［5］Said, Edward. 2003. *Orientalism.* New York：Vintage Books.

国与国之间的文化差异：巴西人与中国人经商的不同方式

Erika Zoeller Véras；*Daniel Bicudo Véras*

摘　要：每个国家都有自己的文化背景和思考、存在与行为标准，这些文化差异强烈影响着商业世界。本文以巴西和中国为例，指出国家与国家之间存在着严重的文化差异。通过霍夫斯泰德（2001）对巴西和中国文化差异的分析，本文认为，考虑文化的相似性和差异性，在一个国家做生意时是很重要的。一个人越熟悉该国文化，他/她的生意就会越成功。此外，提到商业时，有必要评估文化问题产生的影响。

关键词：文化差异　商业　巴西与中国

America and China: Differing Views on the Importance of Education

Frank James Wucinski*

Abstract: In my ten years of teaching in China, mostly at different schools at the university level, I have had to fail many students for plagiarism. I was not at all surprised to read about a cheating scandal that broke out at one of the high schools there. Starting from plagiarism, the paper intends to compare the difference of education in china, USA and Europe.

Keywords: plagiarism; education; difference; china

A little over ten years ago, I sold or gave away most of my possesions, bought a ticket, packed my bags, and got on a plane to China. I didn't have a very clear idea of where in China I was heading, as at that time the only cities I knew in China were Beijing and Shanghai. Still. I was excited to leave my home country, the United States, and experience a new way of life. After an exhaustive two days of travel, which took me from Pittsburgh, Pennsylvania, to Los Angeles, and then to Shanghai, and later Wuhan, I finally got on a five hour bus to a small town called Zhongxiang. I was supposed to stay only a year, but it turned out that Zhongxiang was only the beginning of my teaching career.

Ten years later, I was not at all surprised to read about a cheating scandal that

* Frank James Wucinski, English teacher at Hubei University from USA.

broke out at one of the high schools there. As reported by the UK Telegraph, government officials became suspicious of the school's performance on the gaokao after 99 identical tests were handed in. Apparently, the school has had a long history of turning out students who have done unusually well on China's impossibly difficult college entrance exam, but these 99 exams were the tipping point for officials. In order to combat this wave of cheating, official implemented strict entrance procedures, including out of house invigilators, metal detectors, and pat downs. That cheating is a problem is not surprising to anyone who has taught in China for any period of time. The real surprise is what happened next. After students were forced to take the gaokao without external help, more than 2000 students and their parents gathered outside the school gates and rioted, chanting "We want fairness. There is no fairness if you do not let us cheat".

Most people from outside of China would look at this and be baffled by the seemingly incongruity of this demand. How can cheating possibly be considered fair? But in an educational system that is rife with plagiarism and cheating, perhaps they have a point. But this paper is not about how students in China cheat. Nor is it meant to say that cheating is not a problem in the United States. After all, the American Ad Council, a non profit organization which promotes informative public service campaigns, said that "While about 20% of college students admitted to cheating in high school during the 1940's, today between 75 and 98 percent of college students surveyed each year report having cheated in high school". And Turnitin, an academic integrity software company, reports that 30% of all papers checked by their software, comes back with significant amounts of plagiarism. Instead, this paper will examine the differing attitudes towards education, as seen through their differing attitudes towards cheating, between the American and Chinese public.

In my ten years of teaching in China, mostly at different schools at the university level, I have had to fail many students for plagiarism. As an English teacher, plagiarism is the number one form of academic dishonesty that I have to deal with. In most cases, I would never accuse a student of plagiarism unless I had hard proof, which means finding the original paper on the Internet.

Once I found the proof needed to make any accusation, I would confront the student and tell them that they are guilty of cheating. What happens next comes almost directly from Elisabeth Kübler-Ross' grief model, with one small exception. First comes denial. The student will deny any wrongdoing and will insist I made a mistake. Once I show them the original (though some times even this is not enough, with one student claiming that the author of an article written in 2001 had copied from her) comes anger. The student will become angry that I would dare to accuse him or her. Next, bargaining. Once they realize that I will not change their grade under any circumstance, they will appeal to other students or teachers to intervene on their behalf. Once that fails, comes the sad stories of how failing this particular class will have disastrous results. And then comes ... well that's the end of the stages. It seems that acceptance is never reached because the student will never admit to cheating. Or at least, they will never admit to an act of academic dishonesty. Even the teachers and class members will never say that what that student did was wrong. What both student and faculty member will always come back to is a difference in culture, without being able to come out and tell me what that difference actually is. Both will agree, on a general level, that cheating is bad and a big problem. However, they will never apply that line of reasoning to their own specific case.

As for American student's reactions to being caught, I must admit that I am at a bit of a disadvantage. I have spent a total of about three months in the United States, in the last ten years and when I did live in America, I was never employed as a teacher. However, I did work with students in an academic setting, in both volunteer and paid positions. In addition, I have talked to various teachers in America about this very problem and of course, I was once a student myself. It seems that American students follow just about the same script. They will also deny at first and point out that other students cheat as well. And they will seek to make some type of bargain, though they would not expect another teacher to intervene. Finally though, there will be acceptance, usually in the form of feelings of shame.

The same can be said of the parents of students who cheat. I cannot imagine any American parent defending their sons or daughters, after being found guilty of cheating. (Although, at the same time, I cannot imagine any parent preemptively sitting down with their child and explaining why cheating is bad) Chinese parents though, will. They even encourage it by giving gifts to teachers, sometimes lavish, in the hope that the teacher will help their child along. China daily has published many articles about the fine line between respect and corruption, which parents and teachers must straddle every year on Teacher's day. (http://www. chinadaily. com. cn/china/2013 - 09/10/content_ 16957296. htm)

So, why this difference in attitudes? I believe that this difference can be attributed to people's view of what schools offer. When an American student and his/her family pays for tuition, they have the view that they are paying for an opportunity. The students is given the opportunity to study at a university only. There is no guarantee of anything beyond that. It is up to the student to excel and there is not even a guarantee of receiving a degree after their four years. In China though, the expectation seems to be that parents are not paying for an education, they are paying for a degree; and the lectures, homework, and exams which stand between the student and that degree are merely a formality which can be circumvented in any way possible. This divergent views of what a university is, come from both cultures' history of education .

China has a long history of relying on official examinations, such as the gaokao. The Imperial examination, or Kējǔ, was formalized in 605CE, during the Sui period. Later dynasties relied on the examination to varying degrees, but it certainly became a line of stability in the 1000 years, until 1905, that it was used. Emperors might change and wars might break out, but there was always the Imperial Examination to tie the dynasties together. At the same time, the reliance of the Imperial Examination to fill civil servant jobs opened up paths for social advancement to a greater array of people based on merit, at least on paper anyway.

While the government did encourage the building of schools in every prefecture, by the 1020s, the state school system had a total of 1. 5 million acres of land, providing space for 200,000 students. (Fairbank, Goldman, pg 94) Most students though, were taught at home by private tutors, in order to prepare them for the exam. Because there were few actual universities, it was the taking of the exam itself, which gave the candidate social status.

The European educational model however, differed from that of China. China's system of education was handled through the state, and served to funnel qualified (or socially connected) individuals from into government jobs. Conversely, European schools were started and run by the church. Universities that we would recognize today, began in the High Middle Ages (1000–1300 BCE) Earlier schools where run by monks, but these schools were run by the secular clergy. These schools' main purpose, much like China, was to funnel people into a bureaucracy, but this was the bureaucracy of the church. This was especially important because at that time, the laws of inheritance were strictly primogeniture, that is to say, it was the first born son who inherited land and wealth. This created a large social pressure as many second and third born sons entered society with no direction or outlet for their ambitions. With church run schools though, their second born sons could receive an education and enter the church, which sometimes could offer them a path to more wealth and power than their secular brothers.

Unlike the Imperial Examination, European education had a drastic change with the rise of humanism in the Renaissance. The church had a pretty dim view of human nature, but humanists were much more optimistic about the ability of people to learn. Perhaps the most important piece of work regarding education, came from Pietro Paolo Vergerio. He said of the Liberal Arts in his treatise, *Concerning Character*, that it was the liberal arts which was necessary for a man to reach his full potential and lead to real freedom. (Spielvogel, pg 409) In the humanists' view, it was the job of institutes of higher education to create a well-rounded individual, who would be well equipped to become a citizen of the state. An example of the importance of a well rounded education can be seen in Michelangelo. He is best known as an artist, but he also studied human anatomy. One look at his sculpture the Pieata, will tell us that he studied anatomy not because he wanted to be a doctor, but because in life outside of university, fields of study intersect, sometime unexpectedly and it was for this fact, that a Renaissance education prepared students.

So, what has all this to do with cheating? Well, for both China's Imperial Examination system and Europe's cathedral schools, education was a means to staff their respective bureaucracies. For China, that was the state and for Europe, the church. Both put higher value on the ability to learn and recite their respective doctrines than on critical thinking and so education became secondary to what education could lead to, a position within the government or church. These positions meant more than just getting a good job though. It meant bringing social status to one's family and being able to feed that family. And when we consider the fact that Chinese families extend to more than just parents and children, this becomes even more important. Chinese students today still face this daunting responsibility of having to take care of their whole family. For them, university is not just about learning, but more about making connections and getting a good job. They are often not required to take classes in different fields of study and instead focus on their major. So, when they cheat, they view it not as cheating the system or lying, but as doing what is necessary to pass the exam.

For American students, whose education comes from the Renaissance tradition, cheating once brought shame because there was the feeling that a university education was the whole point of going to a university. University is where many teenagers were sent to became adults. Today though, with the growing importance placed on standardized tests, it is no wonder that students, teachers, and whole schools have been caught up in their own cheating scandals

美国与中国：关于教育之重要性的不同观点

Frank James Wucinski

摘　要： 笔者在中国教英语逾十年，在不同层面的教学活动中，笔者总是要阻止很多学生剽窃舞弊，因此，在中国的报纸上读到中学生考试欺诈的丑闻，已不是什么值得大惊小怪的事情了。从剽窃舞弊出发，本文意欲比较中国人、美国人和欧洲人对待教育的不同观点和文化差异。

关键词：剽窃　教育　差异　中国

Asia's Future: Profiting from the Ethical Wisdom of the World

Thomas Menamparampil[*]

Abstract: Asia today may have the biggest working force in the world: young, gifted, dynamic, and energetic. If they will be creative, well-motivated, and forward-looking, there is no limit to what they can achieve for their nations and contribute to the world. One question we need to ask ourselves on this globalised multi-cultural world is how do we live and work with people of other cultures who think and act differently. In a globalised world, global ethic has become necessary. We need to tap the resources of global wisdom to tame and educate the inclination to global violence, greed, and cruelty to nature. Asian ethical wisdom can be a very useful source. In spite of many differences in worldviews and ethical codes, convergences of moral principles are evident. What is important is to awaken a collective sense of moral responsibility in our society. We need knowledgeable persons who can lead society to what is right, noble and great. The paper is an invitation to intellectuals to take up this mission. If they teach what is true and good not merely with their words but by their life and work, there will be people who listen. Since they are credible personalities, their words become credible. May our leaders of the future be such people? May all of us grow in our commitment to the common good using the wisdom of Asia and insights from

---

* Thomas Menamparampil, Professsor of Philosophy, nominated for Nobel Peace Prize in 2011.

every part of the world?

Keywords: Asia; good; truth; responsibility

1. The Dilemma

Asia today may have the biggest working force in the world: young, gifted, dynamic, energetic. If they will be creative, well-motivated, and forward-looking, there is no limit to what they will be able to achieve for their own nations and contribute to the world. If, on the contrary, they will not able to cohere together and agree on basic values, society will be heading for major troubles. We are already beginning experience some of them. We need certain amount of ethical sturdiness to take on the challenges that lie ahead.

However, it is not easy to agree among ourselves when we look at things differently. When life together becomes difficult, people begin to ask questions. How do we live and work along with persons of other cultures who think and act differently from us? How do we deal with people who have other visions of life, other codes of conduct, other styles of relating with each other, other ways of showing respect, familiarity, approval; or dislike, disapproval, anger or resentment? How do we interact with people who have another understanding of what is right, good, polite, dignified, beautiful or appropriate? How do we join hands with neighbours of other beliefs in promoting the common good and in handling problems in society, like growing violence, crime, dishonesty, AIDS, drugs? Are there ways of transcending inter-community misunderstandings and tensions, basing ourselves on the values still surviving in communities rescued from various civilizational traditions? Can we learn to deal with each other as fellow human beings? How can young men/women grow up with a sense of responsibility in complex situations? These are questions that emerging leaders need to ask themselves today.

Due to global commerce, mass migration and travelling habits of people, and the expanding reach of the communications network, we are compelled to live in a culturally and religiously pluralistic society in almost every part of the world.

Such a situation may be looked at as an unmanageable problem or a singular opportunity for learning from other communities and profiting from the specific genius of each. In trying to draw benefit from cultural diversity lies the realistic wisdom for tomorrow.

But where do we begin? Will a few more 'self-help books' and personality development courses suffice? Or, will better self-presentation, winning manners, and improved norms of civility serve the purpose? Or do we need go deeper and accept the truth that certain things are conducive to social growth and certain things are not, that there are things that are right that need to be done and there are things that are wrong that ought not to be done in view of the common good? Who will teach us about that? It is in such desperate situations that young people with a sense of commitment must come forward and address the most pressing problems of the day with courage and confidence.

May be the present uncertainty about reliable ethical norms is an invitation to respond to our leadership urges and our teaching instincts to exercise a sense of responsibility for the good of human society.

2. An Inclination of the Heart

No doubt, there is a certain amount of pessimism in the air especially in more developed societies. The feeling is that philosophers and saints have devoted lifetimes to study and debate without resolving the issue of a universal human ethics (Dalla Costa xii). This is one of the problems with which the Indian mind had wrestled for centuries. In the ancient epic *Mahabharata* we meet with characters who, unlike Greek heroes, discuss the morality of war even in the midst of the battle. Duryodhana, the evil genius in the entire narrative, is very frank in admitting, "The warrior's (*kshatriya's*) duty is to prevail... whether by virtuous means or not..." (Das 14) Most fighting men would agree with such a statement. Similar ideas would be expressed by Kautilya, Machiavelli or Thomas Hobbes. This is the logic which in India is called the logic of the *big-fish-eating-small-fish*.

Arjuna, the great hero of the epic, admits at one moment, "The mongoose eats mice, as the cat eats the mongoose; the dog devours the cat, your majesty, and wild beasts eat the dog. " (Das 15) He seems to say that taking advantage of the weaker is the law of nature. There are other characters who go to the point of saying that the sacred writings (the *Vedas*) themselves are not helpful in evaluating what is right, that they often contradict; that even good people frequently prove unreliable. Bhishma, the wise man, finally concludes, "*Dharma* (uprightness) is subtle. " (ibidem 46) Yudhishthira keeps questioning *dharma* till the very end of the story (ibidem 281). And no clear answer emerges.

Despite such pessimism when things go wrong or argument takes the wrong direction, we realize that people in different eras and civilizations have always thought that there are some things ethically right and socially becoming, while others are not. They felt convinced that there was a natural desire in human hearts to do what is right. The great Indian poet Kalidasa (5th century) referred to the 'inclination of the heart of a good person' as a reliable guide in such matters (Das 48). Manu, the Indian lawgiver, thought that satisfaction of the mind was one important criterion for evaluating moral choices (Das 48).

Even amidst many uncertainties, people today recognize the need for cultivating a sensibility and developing an attitude of responsibility in making moral decisions. In a globalized world, a global ethic has become necessary. We need the help of global wisdom to tame and educate global greed. This ethic should not limit itself to a new skill to be learned, but a delicate sensibility to be tenderly cultivated. It should not be left as optional to everyone. On the contrary, it should be binding; but at the same time liberating and empowering as well. For, even hard-core capitalists, who seem to be totally indifferent to spiritual realities, feel the need for the protection of law and the mutuality of contracts in order to continue their business (Dalla Costa 5). Everyone is going to benefit from shared ethical principles. Can young thinkers and leaders become guides in this search?

In this area there is an urgent need for collaborating across national identities, cultures and religious traditions. If Martin Luther King, Abraham Joshua Heschel, Thich Nhat Hanh could join hand together in Civil Rights and Peace initiatives, people of different beliefs and identities can share the common ethic of human dignity, human rights, and human liberation. All they have to do is to accept and respect the core ethical values common to different traditions which are to be found in various forms within various cultural heritages. *Dhammapada* taught, "toavoid evil, to cultivate good, and to purify one's mind—that is the teaching of Buddha. " (verse 183) Buddha's 'Middle Way' suggested living a sane, moderate and balanced life. Young people with a sense of responsibility will need to work together with people of other faiths continually following commonly acceptable principles. When they work closely with them, they notice that there is wide common ground that can be shared, and that people are willing to widen it further.

3. Convergences in Ethical Principles

But to bring people of different traditions to a consensus on common ethical principles is not easy. To begin with, what we notice is that ethical codes are religiously and culturally embedded. They are part of the moral wisdom that each community has developed over a period of centuries and are as diverse as cultures themselves. They differ not only among themselves, but also among the sub-groups within them based on class, ideology, historic experiences etc. Nonetheless, convergences in moral perceptions are evident across cultures, religions, ranks and positions. In recent years inter-religious conversations have assisted mutual understanding and generated a desire for the development of an interfaith ethic. Certainly there are some broad principles that would find ready acceptance anywhere in the world. To take one example, when Bernard Lonergan's suggests " Be attentive, be intelligent, be reasonable, be responsible", no one objects. But such norms are too vague to be helpful for organizing our life with its daily challenges.

We do agree that "cultures are seldom unified, coherent, self-contained units" and that an ethnographer's writing freezes a living, developing culture to a moment of its existence. We agree too that in today's pluralistic society, cultures are no more 'integrated': there is mixture, change, conflict (Miller 23). We agree further that cultures are being commodified and commercialized today more than respected, when cultural items are collected, handed around and sold by people who do not belong to that culture (ibidem 70). For, respect for other cultures is not shown by displaying their symbols without knowing or achieving their meaning and context nor by adopting them, but showing how they relate with one's own culture in a healthy manner (ibidem 193). Despite all these problems, cultures retain their meaningfulness, sturdiness and are showing their resilience today.

People living in cities, uprooted from their communities, can have an exhilarating and debilitating experience at the same time (Miller 85). They feel thrilled by the novelty of new ideas and gadgets, but at the same time are drained of their spiritual resources. In this era of de-traditionalization, people are steadily distancing themselves from their own inherited moral codes in the excitement about what is new. An invitation to caution is timely. People of all traditions should be encouraged to understand, re-interpret and re-appropriate their own traditions and values that retain their validity even in the changed circumstances. It is in this context we speak of pluralism which means respecting cultures, races, peoples, communities, and different visions of politics and economics. In this era of differences and uncertainties, we need cultural bridge-builders, internationalists, cross-cultural workers, cosmopolitans, and light-bearers.

4. Fostering an Intuitive Ethical Sensibility

If the global ethic proposed by a dominant community in a country is ethno-centric and self-serving, it will surely be resisted by other communities. In the same way, a vague pluralism or crass pragmatism that leads to relativism in religious faith, morality, and values, would be unacceptable. If, on the contrary, the ethical principles proposed assist people to find a common moral ground for daily living, most people would be happy to profit from them (Schweiker 135). In order to achieve that, we ought to bring sincerity to our moral search and combine an intuitive moral sensibility and ethical alertness to the pluralistic situation in which we have to live.

Cicero spoke of being 'a citizen of the whole universe, as it were of a single city'. Similarly, Diogenes claimed to be the citizen of the world, not merely of Athens or Greece.

Our experience shows that moral sensitivity arises spontaneously in human hearts. Asoka (d. 232 BC), the Indian Emperor, felt 'remorse' after the Kalinga war, thinking over the deaths he had caused. His rock edicts reflect this inner agony and the concern he felt for others as a consequence. The edict XIII reads, "Kalinga was conquered by His Sacred and Gracious Majesty... Thus arose His Sacred Majesty's remorse for having conquered the Kalingas, because the conquest of a country previously unconquered involves the slaughter, death and carrying away captive of the people. This is a matter of profound sorrow and regret to His Sacred Majesty." (Smith 119) From that time he gave himself to the mission of promoting within his empire and in the rest of the world an ethical order of universal significance according to the teaching of Buddha: compassion, liberality, truth, purity, gentleness, peace, joyousness, saintliness, self-control. (Schweiker 343). He sent Buddhist missionaries to Sri Lanka, SE Asia, central Asia and Greece.

5. Developing a Sense of Responsibility

Everyone admits for certain that, despite differences, there can be morally decent people and rational beings and that they can learn from each other. Societies in every age and nation have respected humane and practical forms of reasonableness. For example, they have valued: good judgement, friendship, loyalty, compassion, gratitude, generosity, sympathy, family affection, and the most important principle that one should never use others as a means. People of every ethnic group, political affiliation, rank or position are open to rational truths, welcome dignified codes of conduct, and retain optimism about the wisdom of the world community concerning the common good.

In spite of all this, what seems to be missing is a readiness on the part of many to take collective responsibility for persuading each other to accept at least some broad ethical norms for the common good. No wonder the situation of violence, deceit, injustice, and sexual immorality around us seems to be worsening. But if we could make a decision for collective responsibility, we would be better prepared to face the challenges of our times: e. g. for insisting on honest business transactions, containing terrorism, assisting weaker communities, promoting the more fragile sections in society. We are happy to do such things, not merely because of any material benefits we may derive from them, but because we value people as human beings. It is in this area that leaders who think and are respectful of others can be of great help.

Yajnavalkya listed centuries ago nine virtues common to all: non-violence, truth, refraining from theft, purity, control of senses, generosity, self-control, compassion and patience. Areas where our collective responsibility will need to be exercised in our own days are: human rights, treatment of women, family values, respect for life (questioning life-damaging technology), social ethics, environment, unrenewable resources, and stewardship over nature. We are encouraged to become actively engaged in life-enhancing services like care of children, the old, sick, and needy parents; and showing solidarity within one's own group and assistance beyond, and constantly striving to eliminate violence and deceit. Universal responsibility extends to all humans, in fact to the whole of creation. Some of these are duties, some are ideals. But all are important.

6. Civilizational Heritages

People search for moral norms and ethical principles at the first instance from the insights provided by their own culture and civilization: i. e. what they have learnt from their parents, relatives, teachers, elders; from the wise men of their society, including philosophers, thinkers, religious teachers, writers, poets, artists. What such persons have thought and taught have gone into the collective psyche of their community, and remain there as a ready resource to assist them in their effort to shape their destiny. That remains as the first resource of every community. At the second instance communities look for wisdom from the cultural and historic experiences of other communities in the neighbourhood and beyond. In pluralistic societies this has become a necessity.

Anyone who has to deal with people of another culture/religion/civilization will have to get familiar with the psychological/cultural/spiritual assets of their culture if they want to be effective. An intelligent leader diligently learns the cultural traditions and value-systems of others, so that he/she can be helpful in dealing with current problems, like violence, corruption or unethical practices in the society at whose service he is. In this effort he will have to go beyond invoking prevalent civil laws and UN declarations. If, going further, he refers to their religious and cultural traditions, their wise men and their sacred writings, his words will have greater convincing power.

When we want to evoke the good will of any person or a community, the most intelligent thing to do is to consult the collective psyches and consciences of those communities and profit from the values cherished in their cultures and civilizations. In this paper we shall identify a few values cherished among Asians of various origins: *Altruism, a sense of community, social virtues, respect for nature, uprightness in public life, and religiosity.* Even though these values are under threat in our present day under secularizing pressures, they remain deeply rooted in Asian civilizations.

The following reflection is not an evaluation of the respective merits of different cultural traditions, but an effort to tap the common ethical resources of humankind for the common good. They belong to the whole of humanity.

7. Love, Altruism

Love for others stands at the heart of all ethical codes. Every culture has some way of saying that we ought to do to others what we would like others to do to us. This is a powerful message in an age of intense cultivation of self-interest and absolute commitment to profit-making. "Not one of you is a believer until he loves for his brother what he loves for himself." (Islam, Forty Hadith of an-Nawawi 13) "A man should wander about treating all creatures as he himself would be treated." (Jainism, Sutrakritanga 1. 11. 33) "Try your best to treat others as you would wish to be treated yourself." (Mencius VII. A. 4)

Confucius taught, "Persons of humanity are like this: wanting to develop themselves, they also develop others; wanting to achieve things themselves, they also allow others to achieve what they want. " (Analects 6. 28. 2 – 3)   "Be solicitous of others, be understanding towards others. " (Analects 6. 12. 22) Tzu-kung asked, "Is there one word by which one may live one's entire life?" The master said, "Isn't that word 'consideration' ? Do not impose on other people anything you yourself dislike. " (Analects 6. 15; 23) "To regard everyone as a very important guest, to manage the people as one would assist at a sacrifice, not to do to others what you would not have them do to you. " (Analects 15. 23) These are precious messages even today. The Koran says, "Give to the near of kin their due, and also to the destitute and to the wayfarers. " (Surah 17) Mahatma Gandhi tried to take such teachings into the political field. An emerging young leader can make a major contribution in this privileged field of love and concern for others and commitment to the common good.

8. Preserving a Sense of Community: within Family, Community, Humanity

According to many critiques of Modernity, the type of individualism it has fostered has not promoted a style of communal life that will help human flourishing. We agree that democracy and the rule of law, re-distribution of wealth, and equality of women are important. But equally important is a sense of community in our times. We have some duties to the community. In Asian traditions, rights are attached to *duties and obligations* (Sardar 65) to society. Those who claim the former must accept the latter as well.

Affirmation of community loyalty runs right through much of Asian literature. "Meet together, speak together, let your minds be of one accord... May your counsel be common, your assembly common, common the mind, and the thoughts... Let your aims be common, and your hearts be of one accord, and all of you of one mind, so you may live well together. " (Rig Veda 10. 191. 2 – 4) "Let us have concord with our own people, and concord with people who are strangers to us... May we unite in our minds, unite in our purposes, and not fight against the divine spirit within us. " (Atharva Veda 7. 52. 1 – 2) The Koran re-echoes similar sentiments, "The believers indeed are brothers; so set things right between your two brothers, and fear God; haply you will find mercy." (Koran 49.10) Finally, Mishnah urges, "Separate not yourself from the community." (Mishnah, Abot 2.4)

Family values were deeply cherished in Asia. A Buddhist document says, "Supporting father and mother, cherishing wife and children and a peaceful occupation; this is the greatest blessing." (Sutta Nipata 262) The Jains teach, "Natural mildness should be there in the family." (Tattvarthasutra 6.18) Again, "Lord, give us joy in our wives and children, and make us models for the God-fearing." (Koran 25: 74) South and east Asian families were usually monogamous. The *Chinese family bonds* are traditionally among the strongest in the world. Confucius taught absolute solidarity within the family. He affirmed, "When brothers live in concord and at peace, the strain of harmony shall never cease." (Doctrine of the Mean 15.2 – 3) The following values have been diligently cultivated in Chinese society down the centuries: *filial piety*, *care of the elderly persons*, joint ownership (Bell 16). *Confucianism* has given rise to communitarian cultures in *Korea*, *Vietnam* and other countries; which lay stress on *social morality*, community harmony, and state benevolence. The ethic of *mutual help* has served as bond among student groups and social activists, providing unity of purpose, mutual encouragement and support. (Bell 10 – 11). Communal ethic is particularly strong among the rural farming classes. Japan recently gave a marvellous example after the earthquake how these values may be lived.

But what is most outstanding in Asia is a universal outlook that embraces the whole of humanity. "Consider the family of humankind one." (Jainism, Jinasena, Adipurana) "Let all mankind be one sect." (Sikhism, Adi Granth, Japuji 28, M.1, p.6) People like Mahatma Gandhi and Tagore, spoke for the human race as one, as did Buddha, Asoka and others in their times.

Christians look to the Bible for their inspiration. Traditional family and community values are deeply rooted in the *biblical tradition*. The fourth commandment says, "Honour your father and your mother." (Exodus 20: 12) Respect for elders is taught, "You shall rise before the aged and show deference to the old. " (Leviticus 32) Togetherness and harmony are strongly urged. "How wonderful it is, how pleasant, for God's people to live together in harmony!" (Psalms 133: 1). Prayers keep the community together. "My house shall be called a house of prayer for all the people. " (Isaiah 56. 7) Jesus prayed for unity among his followers, "I do pray not only for them, but also for those who believe in me because of their message. I pray that they may all be one. " (John 17: 20 – 21) He warned them against divisions, "Any country that divides itself into groups that fight each other will not last very long. And any town or family that divides itself into groups which fight each other will fall apart. " (Matthew 12: 25) *Jesus is the bond* among his followers, "For where two or three come together in my name, I am there with them. " (Matthew 18: 19 – 20) "You are all one in Jesus Christ. " (Galatians 3: 28)

9. Cultivating Social Virtues

Abstention from causing injury to any living being and inconveniencing any person is a central teaching in all Asian traditions. Irrespective of caste and creed, the following virtues are held in high regard: *patience*, truthfulness, restraint, purity, liberality, *self-control*, not to kill, obedience to one's teachers, *sympathy*, straightforwardness, freedom from covetousness, freedom from anger (Van Voorst 37). In the Bhagavad Gita Krishna teaches, "Fearlessness, purity, determination in the discipline of knowledge, *charity*, self-control, sacrifice, study of sacred lore, penance, honesty; *nonviolence*, truth, absence of anger, disengagement, peace, loyalty, *compassion* for creatures, lack of greed, *gentleness*, modesty, reliability; brilliance, patience, resolve, charity, absence of envy and of pride; these characterize a man born of divine traits. " (Bhagavadgita 16: 1. 4) Asian religions teach modesty and restraint. Mahatma Gandhi taught *Ahimsa*, the Dalai Lama compassion.

Confucian humanism, is returning to Chinese public life again sturdier than ever before. The Confucian emphasis is on *moral cultivation*: cultivation of humanity, *sense of fellowship*, fostering of social values. Noble-minded persons should take as much trouble to discover what is right as lesser men do to discover what will pay (Analects IV. 16). Confucius insists on the moral education of intellectual leaders. It must be admitted that the humanistic and liberal emphasis in Confucianism has led to fairly egalitarian forms of development in East Asia.

The genius of *Lao Tzu* consists in seeing the advantage of allowing natural processes their normal course, whether they be in society or in nature. He invites you to act like water, yielding, fitting into corners and crevices. And yet water holds energy, generates power. *Taoism* suggests you to recognize the unpredictability of the spontaneous development of things, not to insist too much on pre-arranged approaches. The Tao *does not impose*, *interfere*, meddle; allows things to develop and flourish, each according to its nature.

When Taoism insists on non-action, it means really non-interfering. When the *Tao Te Ching* insists on emptiness, nothingness, the emphasis is on the rejection of the 'Big Ego' to which all are tempted (Burke 135). "The best man, in his heart he loves what is profound. In his associations, he loves humanity. In his words, he loves faithfulness. In government, he loves order. In handling affairs, he loves competence. In his activities, he loves timeliness." (Lao Tzu) (Kessler 301) "He does not boast of himself; therefore he was given credit. He does not brag; therefore he can endure for long." (Lao Tzu) (Kessler 302) The *Koran* too teaches norms of social obligation to each other; it insists on humility.

Care for the poor is a central message in most civilizations, "When you harvest your fields, do not cut the corn at the edges of the fields, and do not go back to cut the ears of corn that were left. Do not go back through your vineyard to gather grapes that were missed or to pick up the grapes that have fallen; leave them for *poor people and foreigners*." (Leviticus 19: 9 – 10) "Cease to do evil. Learn to do good. Devote yourselves to justice. Aid the wronged. Uphold the rights of the orphan. Defend the cause of the widow." (Isaiah 1: 17)

10. Probity in Public Life, Honesty

"Do not cheat anyone by using false measures of length, weight or quantity. Use honest scales, honest weights, and honest measures. " (Leviticus 19: 35 - 36) In an era when corruption is moving into the *highest places*—governments, bureaucracies, legislatures, judiciary, law-enforcing machinery, pollution-controlling agencies, customs departments, immigration offices, official and open markets—the above message from *Leviticus* is most relevant. *Fake goods* of every kind are on sale; duplicate goods of every variety are available: books, DVDs, imitation machinery with substandard parts; adulterated medicines, spurious drugs; endangered species, human beings at risk (women for sex, children for sweatshops) (Naim 2). There *are pirated copies* of classics, of bestsellers, popular music; whatever can be copied or imitated is available.

The globalized world provides the anonymity and distances that illegal traffickers need to keep their business invisible. Internet contacts have furthered their possibilities. The deregulation policy that most governments have adopted has weakened the law-enforcing machinery, and illicit traders keep hopping between jurisdictions. International terrorism follows the track of international illicit trade, using the same techniques and facilities.

Confucius taught that one should pursue justice, not profit. Likewise Taoism teaches "Be honest like Heaven in conducting your affairs. " (Taoism, Tract of the Quiet Way) "There is no misfortune greater than being covetous. " (Tao Te Ching 46) Master Tseng said, "Every day I examine myself...In intercourse with my friends, have I always been true to my word?" (Analects 1. 4)

Centuries ago the Upanishads had taught, " Truth alone triumphs and not untruth. " (Mundaka Upanishads III, 1, 6) Kabir used to say, "Better to be cheated than cheat others. " And Vivekananda, "Society must be moulded by truth. " Islam threatens severe punishments for the wrongdoer, "Lo! Those who devour the wealth of orphans wrongfully, they do not but swallow fire into their bellies, and they will be exposed to burning flame. " (Koran 4. 10) Koran, "Keep your promises; you are accountable for all that you promise. . . . give full measure, when you measure, and weigh with even scales. " (Surah 17)

There is abundant teaching in the Bible about honesty, truthfulness and uprightness: "Do not cheat anyone by using false measures of length, weight or quantity. Use honest scales, honest weights, and honest measures. " (Leviticus

19. 35 – 36) Be honest (Leviticus 19: 15), use honest scales (Leviticus 19: 36), serve in integrity (1 Kings 8: 3), do not accept bribes (Exodus 23: 8; Proverbs 17: 8, 28: 21); God does not tolerate fraud or partiality (2 Chronicles 19: 7). It is a great challenge today to work for probity in public life.

11. Respect for Life, for Nature, Environmental Stewardship

Reverence for life at every stage of its development is a theme that runs right through the heart of every Asian tradition. As it is well known, the Jains were the most radical in their defence of life, possibly in the face of violent invaders, decimating indigenous races, and taking away animal lives in lavish Vedic sacrifices, damaging nature by extending farming areas into the territories of native communities. Buddhism was true to the same tradition of promoting peace. *Nonviolence* today constitutes a core value in Hindu tradition. The Asian soul instinctively recoils before abortion, euthanasia, *excessive* tampering with nature in human reproduction, violence to animal and vegetative life.

For the Vedic Aryans, nature was the symbol of the divine: *sun*, *wind*, *ocean*, *earth*, *soil*, mountains, forests, springs. "O Mother Earth! Sacred are thy hills, snowy mountains, and deep forests. Be kind to us and bestow upon us happiness. May you be fertile, arable, and nourisher of all. May you continue supporting people of all races and nations. May you protect us from your anger (natural disasters). And may no one exploit and subjugate your children." (Atharva Veda, 12. 1. 11) The *farmer prays* fervently that the hurt he inflicts on nature may speedily be healed. "Whatever I dig up of you, O earth, may you of that have quick replenishment." (Atharva Veda, 12, 1.64) "The earth is the mother, and I the son of the earth." (Atharva Veda 12.12) "What, O earth, I dig out of thee, quickly shall that grow again: may I not, O pure one, pierce thy vital spot, and not thy heart." (Atharva Veda 12.35) The Rig Veda has in places phrases like "O knife, do not hurt him", "O stones, listen".

The *Yajnavalkyasmriti* says, "If any man has cut a *tree*, a thicket, a creeper or a shrub, he should recite one hundred vedic verses. If a man is guilty of recklessly cutting a *medicinal plant*, he should subsist on milk for one day and follow a cow. " (2.276) Herbal medicines were very popular. "The earth is a garden, the *Lord its gardener*, cherishing all, none neglected. " (Sikhism, Adi Granth, Majh Ashtpadi, 1, M. 3, p 118)

Emperor *Asoka* writes, "I have ordered banyan trees to be planted along the roads to give shade to men and animals. I have ordered mango groves to be planted. I have ordered wells to be dug every half a mile, and I have had many watering stations built for the convenience of men. "

We can never forget that *Buddha* was enlightened under a tree. Wise men in India those days retired to the forest in order to meditate. The *Himalayas* were a sacred destination. Asia's ancient educational centres were *Ashrams* which were always located on the margin of forests. *Tagore's Shantiniketan* sought to recapture this spirit of closeness to nature. For him, trees were prayers and they spoke about God. "Silence, my soul," he said, "these trees are my prayers. " And he went on, "I asked the tree, speak to me about God, and it blossomed. " The Psalmist expresses similar sentiments in many places. He invites the trees of the forest to shout for joy (Psalms 96: 12).

Other Asian traditions too emphasize the connectedness of things. "No creature is there crawling on the earth, no bird flying with its wings, but they are nations like yourselves. " (Koran 6.38) "Do not let man destroy Nature. Do not let cleverness destroy the natural order. " (Taoism, Chuang Tzu 17) In the context of the recent epidemics that have broken out among cattle, sheep, chickens, fish, dolphins, we need to take a warning. We need to exercise stewardship in behalf of all living things. "Rear them, but do not lay claim on them; control them, but never lean upon them; *be their steward*, but do not manage them. " (Tao Te Ching 51) Lao Tzu had said, centuries ago, "The best man in his dwelling loves the earth. "

12. Religiosity, the Sense of the Sacred

Amazingly, when many of the developed parts of the world have been fast secularizing, Asians as a whole have fiercely held on to their faiths. This religious seriousness is to be considered a common spiritual asset, not only for Asians, but for the whole of humanity.

Z. Sardar affirms that the gulf that exists today between the radical secularism in some regions of the world and the religiosity in other regions is glaringly great. The present-day emphasis on 'rights' needs a foundation. That foundation in the east is provided by religion. He proposes for postmodern times a return to tradition, meaning an effort for 'sustaining the values and axioms of a civilization'. He rejects the amorality, relativism, and nihilism of postmodern culture (McGuigan 91).

India's heroes have always been people with spiritual depth (Buddha, Mahatma Gandhi, Tagore, Dalai Lama, Mother Teresa), not conquerors, millionaires or sportsmen. Asians admire genuine intellectuals, not mere rationalists. They willingly listen to persons who have had a religious intuition and speak with spiritual unction, and who are not mere sectarian or parochially minded zealots. Leaders who are intellectually bent, eager to share knowledge, and are inclined to contemplation, reflection, mysticism and renunciation always earn the respect of Asians and win a hearing.

Asians have amazingly retained a great Sense of the Sacred. It is a precious value in a rapidly secularizing world to be preserved and fostered. They respect religious persons, gladly take part in religious events, make religious journeys (pilgrimages), keep reciting sacred words. Those words are considered eternal (Radhakrishnan I. 299). Asians value silence, renunciation, and a message given with profound conviction. Detachment is considered a sign of genuineness.

13. Models Inspire, Prove Possibility of Imitation

We have referred to several religious texts. They alone may not carry conviction in isolation. They must be put in relationship to human wisdom as understood in different cultures. They must also be counterchecked with the criteria that are widely considered valid in our times. When many approaches combine, the central message about ethical norms goes through and makes an appeal. In this way cooperation in the area of ethical reflection becomes possible, while maintaining at the same time each one his/her own cultural identity. May be Asians will be more open to learn from metaphors than syllogisms, living models than logical arguments. They look with admiration at inspiring precedents even in other traditions.

Amartya Sen, a Nobel Prize winner, suggests a few norms in his recent book *The Idea of Justice* that can be helpful in debating theories and values. He urges us to accept the possibility that another theory than our own may have the features of impartiality, fairness, being unbiased and dispassionate (Sen 2009: 57); to take note of other people's point of view, welcome information and remain open-minded in public dialogue (ibidem 43), to recognize the fact that at a given time we are confronted with a plurality of competing principles, making it necessary for us to subject opinions repeatedly to serious scrutiny and ourselves to self-scrutiny using a variety of these competing principles and different perspectives (Ibidem 183). Global voices on any issue can set us thinking (ibidem 408). A view from a distance always puts things in perspective. Now that human interdependence is growing, it has become important to listen to the consciences of other cultures and to study the moral codes developed in other societies.

Pragmatic people think that persons of high moral calibre hold up unrealistic ideals before others but that these ideals do not correspond to the way that the real world works. But men like Dag Hammarskjold, Mahatma Gandhi, Martin Luther King, Lech Walesa, Vaclav Havel, Albert Luthuli, Alexander Solzhenytsin, Nelson Mandela, Desmond Tutu, Aung San Kyi did not seem to be unrealistic in their approach to the mighty problems they had in hand. And yet they finally achieved what they set out to do.

Let us look at the example of Mahatma Gandhi who drew his ideas from diverse traditions. He was attached to his own religion, but kept learning from Christianity and also showed respect to the Islamic tradition. He was open to all truths, but at the same time he was attentive to differences and was respectful of individual cultural identities. He was inclusive (Schweiker 360) and affirmed his oneness with humanity. He was Hindu in the cultural sense, but not sectarian.

He took images from his own religious tradition and from the Jain teachings on nonviolence, but adapted them to the political and social goals he had chosen. His concept of *ramarajya* sounded much like an interpretation of the Christian concept of the 'kingdom of God'. His idea of *satyagraha*, adherence to the truth, meant in fact loyalty to everything that was upright and good. For him *Ahimsa* was not mere passive nonviolence but active engagement for the alleviation of suffering and the transformation of society (ibidem 67). He sought to achieve liberation, *moksha*, by fulfilling his life-mission in the political field. He looked at this commitment to his duty as a spiritual struggle. He generally took care to express himself in widely acceptable vocabulary, and therefore his words had convincing power.

14. A World in Crisis Is Looking for Answers

We need prophetic persons to take in hand the problems that confront us today. We notice that cultures and civilizations are in crisis today, including the present day's secular civilization itself. The following are some questions that come to our mind in this critical situation. What happens to humanity when, too many of us, having rejected our cultural roots, have become passive consumers of various types of illusions? What happens when we suffer not only from a loss of cultural identity, but of humanity? What happens when materialism replaces social health, and the home values of cooperation, decency, kindness, hospitality are no more handed on to the next generation?

There was a time when companies and governments used to leave ethics to families, teachers, and to community and religious leaders. But today nothing like that happens any more. There is less of ethical content in teaching, less of traditional values in the handing on of heritages, and we forget that our duty to love our neighbour includes also our obligation to 'love our children and grandchildren as we love ourselves'. And we forget that this love is expressed not by being concerned about non-renewable resources only, but also about the transmission of the gains of culture and civilization (Schweiker 515).

The consequences are evident. Sublime values are no more visible in public life. Aggressiveness of the market competes with aggressiveness of arms. Egocentric lust for money and power dominates the world scene. Heroes/ heroines of service are hard to find, but workaholic billionaires keep increasing in number. Their life ambition is to wipe out their business competitors. The wars for colonies of the previous centuries have been replaced by wars for the market. The vocabulary of struggle and fighting for real and imagined rights fascinate the rising generations. Efforts for progress and development have come to be described only in terms of adversarial relationships, ruptures and discontinuities, not of collaboration, common endeavour and sharing of ideas, heritages and resources.

Modernity has promoted justice not moral values. It is evident that claims for human rights alone do not exhaust the comprehensive requirements of morality.

There is growing unaccountability in the corporate culture. Robert Bellah calls it 'market totalitarianism'. Citizens are selling off their personal dignity for a small pay-raise and disposing off their most valued cultural heritage for trivialities which they think add to their comfort. People are blinded by the brilliant performance of some financial wizard, to whom gradually everything becomes legitimate. But we know that there is balance in the human processes and it asserts itself ultimately even after chaotic social movements and uncontrolled aberrations. The global market will be defeated by its own moral inversions and excesses (Dalla Costa 61).

And there is hope. The values proposed by the old cultures cannot die out totally. The cultural energies that have been suppressed or marginalized by global materialism will show their strength in different places. However, they need not take to violence; for, cultures have an inner strength of their own. "Made up of history and experience, memory and expectation, cultures have their resiliency, even rigidity of personality." (Dalla Costa 220) Anthropologists tell us that cultural traditions play a greater role in our life than even beliefs. It is in this area of civilizational sensitivity and cultural promotion that committed leaders can make a significant contribution. They can join hands together for preserving their own respective cultural heritages. In doing so, they are in fact assisting to rescue some of the central values common to humanity. For example, we begin to realize that being singularly selfish is self-defeating. "Self-interest, self-rights and self-preservation involve and are even advanced by self-sacrifice, self-discipline and self-giving." (ibidem 105)

With all the present uncertainties, the world is looking for persons invested with moral authority; not those who claim it as though it is theirs by right, but those who, even from a position of weakness, know how to persuade others to do what is right. That is true authority. What they ask is simple: accept what is true and good. They argue for the truth not merely with their words, but with their life and work. Since they are credible personalities, what they say becomes credible. People generally listen to persons of good judgement who strive to make only acceptable proposals; are knowledgeable, sensitive, and decent; are interpreters of sound ethical traditions; speak to people's interests, show esteem to their values and tastes, seek to understand others' way of doing things; and, more than anything else, who seem to love and respect people. Persons like Mahatma Gandhi and Martin Luther King have been credited for their gift of persuading others of what is best in difficult circumstances, because they appealed to people's consciences. May our leaders of the future be such people. May all of us grow in our commitment to the common good using the wisdom of the world.

References:

[1] Bell, Daniel A. & Chaibong, Hahm. 2003. *Confucianism for the Modern World.* Cambridge: Cambridge University Press.

[2] Burke, T. Patrick. 1996. *The Major Religions.* Malden, Massachusetts: Blackwell Publishers.

[3] Dalla Costa, John. 1998. *The Ethical Imperative*, Addison-Wesley, Reading.

[4] Das, Gurucharan. 2009. *The Difficulty of Being Good.* Penguin Books India, New Delhi.

[5] Kessler, Gary E. 2000. *Ways of Being Religious.* California: Mayfield Publishing Co.

[6] McGuigan, Jim. 1999. *Modernity and Postmodern Culture.* Buckingham: Open University Press.

[7] Miller, Vincent J. 2004. *Consuming Religion.* New York: Continuum.

[8] Naim, Moses. 2006. *Illicit*, New York: Anchor Books.

[9] Radhakrishnan, Sarvapalli. 1982. *The Culture of India.* Calcutta: The Ramakrishna Institute of Culture.

[10] Sardar, Z. 1998. *Postmodernism and the Other*：*The New Imperialism of Western Culture*, London：Pluto.

[11] Schweiker, William. 2008. *The Blackwell Companion to Religious Ethics*, Malden：Blackwell Publishing Ltd.

[12] Sen, Amartya. 2009. *The Idea of Justice*. London：Penguin Group.

[13] Smith, Vincent. 1992. *The Oxford History of India.* New Delhi：Oxford University Press.

[14] Van Voorst, Robert E. 1994. *Anthology of World Scriptures*, California：Wadsworth Publishing Company.

[15] Wuthnow, Robert, ed. 1995. *Rethinking Materialism.* Grand Rapids：William Eerdmans Publishing Co.

亚洲未来：受惠于世界伦理智慧

Thomas Menamparampil

摘　要：今天的亚洲有着世界上最大的劳动力市场。亚洲的劳动力年轻、富有天赋、流动性强并充满活力。如果亚洲劳动力具有创造力，积极向上，那么，他们将对自己的国家和世界做出无可估量的贡献。在当今这个全球化、多元文化的世界，我们需要探寻如何与那些不同于我们自身文化的其他文化世界里的人一起生活。全球化的世界，必须有全球伦理。我们需要利用全球智慧来引导并消除全球性的暴力、贪婪以及对自然的残忍。亚洲的伦理智慧是非常有用的一种资源。尽管在伦理观点和信条上存在着很多差异，但是道德原则的融合却越来越明显。最重要的是要在我们的社会中倡导一种道德责任的集体意识。我们需要有识之士引领社会走向正确、崇高和伟大的未来。本文对这样的人发出了邀请，如果他们能用生命和行动而不是用语言诠释什么是真善美，那么，他们就会拥有更多的听众，因为他们的人格是可信的，所以，他们的话也是可信的。让我们一起承担这种共同善的责任吧。

关键词：亚洲　善　真　责任

A New Skeptical Worldview for Contemporary World Cultures

Lydia B. Amir[*]

Abstract: I address the situation of skepticism as a minority view in contemporary world cultures. First, I associate skepticism to contemporary concerns by presenting a critical approach to religion and identifying the sense in which our age is secular despite the contemporary vigor of religion. Second, finding skepticism intellectually appealing, I suggest that the cause of its unpopularity lies in the emotional response it occasions. I consider, accordingly, various responses to skepticism, from the Hellenistic and Roman school of Pyrrhonism to Friedrich Nietzsche, through St. Augustine, Michel de Montaigne, René Descartes, David Hume, Søren Kierkegaard, and Auguste Comte. I criticize these views and introduce in the third and final section a secular and skeptical worldview I call *homo risibilis*. It rivals, I believe, the benefits of established religions, and can ground, moreover, an ethics of compassion without requiring unwarranted metaphysical assumptions.

Keywords: skepticism; religion; metaphysics

Introduction

Humanism is an intellectual movement of the modern age. Emphasizing human ethics rather than supernatural matters, it has its roots not only in Marxism but

* Lydia B. Amir, The School of Media Studies, College of Management Academic Studies, Rishon LeZion, Israel.

also in thousands of years of human thought from ancient China and India (where Buddhists and Jains observe non-theistic philosophies), through classical Greece and Rome, to the enlightenment and the scientific revolution in Europe. The Humanist Manifesto of 1973, signed by thousands of intellectuals, asserts:

> We can discover no divine purpose or providence for the human species. No deity will save us, we must save ourselves. Promises of immortal salvation or fear of eternal damnation are both illusory and harmful. They distract humans from present concerns, from self-actualization, and from rectifying social injustices ... Critical intelligence, infused by a sense of human caring, is the best method that humanity has for resolving problems. (Beversluis 1995, 49)

For many years now it has been supposed that rational human thought, the cornerstone of the modern period, will overthrow religion. This idea has been repeated by many great men. Mao Zedong's initial thought about religion, for instance, was that old religious ideas would become obsolete with modernization and a move to atheism would be a natural path; religion will perish, however, only if humanity eliminates social classes and establishes much stronger control over the natural world. A century earlier, Karl Marx, whose writings have been especially influential in shaping the history of the twentieth century, concluded that religion is a human creation, an opiate-like fantasy whose purpose is to keep people numbly contented despite oppression and injustice in society. Auguste Comte predicted that religion would be superseded by science. Friedrich Nietzsche attacked institutionalized religion as a "curse," an attempt to shield people from fear of the unknown, and an explanation of reality that has been displaced by the ascent of science. And, in the twentieth century, Sigmund Freud maintained that religion is an illusion pertaining to the infancy of humanity that will disappear once humanity comes of age. [1]

---

[1] For Mao Zedong's thoughts on religion, see Fowler 2008, 251 – 53; see also Comte 1929 (1851 – 54); Nietzsche's *Antichrist* (1954c); Freud's *The Future of an Illusion* (1953 – 74).

Nothing of the sort yet has happened, not even through the workings of Nietzsche's post-modern followers, who were thought to represent the nihilistic crisis of Western culture. Religion fares well with post-modernism, and, regardless of philosophic camps, triumphs all over the world, as a phenomenon that is noted, among others, by Mary Pat Fisher in her conclusion of *Religion in the Twenty-first Century*: "At the turn of the century," she writes, "new religions as well as old are showing considerable vigor." (Fisher 1999, 98).[1]

Misunderstandings, intolerance, and competition between the various religions, and even versions of the same religion, have historically been significant sources of conflict.[2] Now that cultures are mixing to an unprecedented extent, the potential for conflictual relationships has increased—notwithstanding the commendable efforts made to enhance harmony between people on different religious paths by two new religions, Sikhism and Baha'i, as well as by the interfaith movement whose aim is to draw humans together as they reach toward the sacred.[3]

Globalization adds an extra tension to the contemporary world's situation. The French scholar, Alain de Benoist, has commented on the role globalization plays in the crisis of modernity:

Individuals feel uprooted by globalization. Feeling powerless, they erect walls, even if fragile and laughable. On the psychological level, individuals

---

[1]　One can even speak of "the post-modern religious ferment" (Fisher 1999, 117); for more on postmodernism and religion, see Griffin 1988. Religious practices in the twenty–first century for the most part retain their ancient roots, however. At the turn of the century, some seventy-seven percent of the world's population belonged to one of the previously established religions—Hinduism, Buddhism, Judaism, Christianity, Islam, Sikhism, Confucianism, Jainism, Taoism, or Shinto. This figure also includes the belief-systems of traditional tribal culture, or "indigenous spirituality". For these figures, see Fisher 1999, 29. There is no lack of texts on the importance of religion as well as on role of religion in the world today, however; for the former, see, for example, Bellah 2011, and for the latter, see *the series Religion Today* (London and New York: Continuum).

[2]　The Christian Church, for instance, has split over time into 21000 different denominations, some of them quite antagonistic toward each other, despite their founder's teachings to love one's neighbor.

[3]　For the interfaith movement, see Braybrooke 1988; for the relatively new religions of Sikhism and Baha'i, see the fourth Chapter in Fisher 1999.

now feel dispossessed by over whelming mechanisms, an increasingly fast pace and even heavier constraints—variables so numerous that they are no longer able to grasp where they stand. That this happens at a time when individuals are lonelier than ever, abandoned to themselves, when all great world-views have caved in, only intensifies the feeling of a nothingness. Accordingly, globalization resembles a puzzle of splintered images. It provides no vision of the world. (De Benoist 1996, 133)

Reactions to the new uncertainties and speed of change range from exclusiveness and absolutism—erecting walls in an effort to create within them a more certain world-to a new openness in religious expression.

At the same time that considerable tension is building between religious pluralism and religious exclusivism, another global process is the questioning or rejection of religion itself, as Mary Pat Fisher explains:

At the turn of the century, an estimated twenty percent of the world's people do not identify themselves with any religion. Some are involved in material pursuits, more interested in the here and now rather than in promises of eternity. Some have become disillusioned with what they see as the hypocrisy, self-interest, and lack of spirituality in religious institutions. Others have wondered about the nature of reality and the meaning of existence but have come to the conclusion that there is no scientific evidence of any transcendent power behind the scenes shaping human events. Even religious followers have been challenged to develop new understandings of their faith in the light of modern research into the human and cultural dimensions of their prophets and scriptures. (Fisher 1999, 24)

Yet skeptics in religious matters are generally considered to be spiritually under-developed, at best—the "enemy" or the dangerous view to counter, at worst. Skeptics in other matters are rarely taken seriously, as their ideas are viewed as an intellectual exercise whose purpose is to check the validity of "our" sound opinions. ① Because I consider skepticism an often misunderstood yet important world-view, bearer of rationality, tolerance and peace both inward and outward, I have chosen in this article to address the situation of skepticism in contemporary world cultures with the aim of making skepticism more appealing.

With this purpose in mind, I have divided the article in three sections. First, I associate skepticism to contemporary concerns by presenting a critical approach to religion and identifying the sense in which our age is secular despite the contemporary vigor of religion. Finding skepticism intellectually appealing, I suggest that the reason why it is not more widespread lies in the emotional response it occasions. Accordingly, in the second section I consider various emotional responses to skepticism, from the Hellenistic and Roman school of Pyrrhonism to Friedrich Nietzsche, through St. Augustine, Michel de Montaigne, René Descartes, David Hume, Søren Kierkegaard, and Auguste Comte. I criticize these views in order to introduce in the third and final section a secular and skeptical worldview I call *homo risibilis*, which rivals, I believe, the benefits of established religions without the need for unwarranted metaphysical assumptions.

I. Religion, Secularism, and Skepticism

What is a religion? Among the various definitions, the view that associates religion with meaning seems appropriate for this forum. ② On that view, Keith Ward considers religions "belief-systems which articulate, with different degrees of systematization, competing theories about the meaning of human life" (Ward 2001, 11). Along the same lines, Huston Smith maintains that religion's basic

---

① For skepticism as the enemy, see the introduction in Agassi and Meidan 2008; see also Taylor 2007. For the history of skepticism, see Popkin 1996.

② Charles Taylor is critical of suggestions that consider that the "essence of religion" is disclosed in the answers religion offers to the question of meaning (Taylor 2007, 717-18). He objects to these suggestions because they absolutize "the modern predicament". I suggest, however, that even if we grant Taylor that religion entails some sort of "transcendence", especially "the sense that there is some good higher than, beyond human flourishing" (Taylor 2007, 20), this "transcendence" is far from being inimical to the question of meaning. Rather, the argument that religion provides meaning is strengthened by a view that considers that there is a higher good, I suggest, even if it does not specify what this good may be.

posit is that life is meaningful. The claim, he furthers holds, can be elucidated both subjectively, that is, by thinking primarily of life's meaning for us, or, alternatively, objectively, by trying to determine its meaning in the total scheme of things (Smith 2001, 255). Objectively, he explains, there is no way to decide that question:

> There are things to be said in favor of life's meaning, the chief being that it is the seasoned answer to the question, the one that has presided over every known human collectivity, but it is not enough to insure its truth. The hermeneutics of suspicion is always waiting in the wings, ready to challenge the existence of religion's "other world" by claiming that it is only wishful thinking—a projection of the human mind to compensate for the world's lack. "There is no other world," Malinowski intoned, and neither reason nor experience can prove him wrong. (Smith 2001, 261 – 2)

Irredeemably ambiguous to public gaze, life and the world come to us untagged, and serious doubts rightly arise about the validity of the meaning we ascribe to them.

At the beginning of *The Wisdom to Doubt*, John Schellenberg simply states: "Reason requires us to be religious skeptics." (Schellenberg 2007, 1) Secular doubts call into question *all* religious views about the human condition that assume the existence of a supernatural realm. The arguments for and against belief in such a realm are familiar and endlessly debated. [1]Thus, there is no need to repeat these arguments here.

If reason requires us to be religious skeptics, why are not all philosophers skeptical? Immanuel Kant, along with Plato, the third earl of Shaftesbury, and Robert Burton in his *The Anatomy of Melancholy*, associates religion with unrequited love and metaphysics, in order to provide an explanation through the notion of "enthusiasm": unrequited love, religion, and metaphysics are the three areas where enthusiasm is most commonly found because all three are

---

[1] I can mention four recent works: Dennett 1993; Kekes 1995; Kitcher 2007; Wielenberg 2005.

characterized by a powerful longing for an object that can never in principle be possessed. ① The longing can be so intense and the frustration so painful that the sufferer may delude himself into thinking his desire will be fulfilled. This is the essence of enthusiasm, a problem yet to be addressed today as testified to by the contemporary appeal of religion, various forms of mysticism, and uncritical theories of the New Age movement. ②

Moreover, there is a widespread belief in some literature on the emotional tension involved in skepticism, religious or otherwise, that portray it as almost unbearable. It is rarely conceived that skepticism need not be painful. Before describing the most notorious emotional responses to skepticism and proposing my own version of a pleasurable form of skepticism, it is important to clarify the relation of skepticism to secularism—the more familiar term that is often used to describe a defining characteristic of our contemporary cultures—in order to highlight the significance of inquiring into the situation of skepticism in today's world.

The social process known as "secularization" is described with some constancy in the relevant literature. In contradistinction, the views about the meaning of secularism or secularity vary. ③ In his monumental A Secular Age (2007), the religious philosopher Charles Taylor has recently expounded a view of "secularity 3" that may be helpful for our concerns. By this type of secularity, Taylor means "a move from a society where belief in God is unchallenged and indeed,

---

① See Plato, Phaedrus, and Burton 1989, 867. Burton discusses enthusiasm in love, religion, and philosophy in the Third Partition of his book *Love-Melancholy*. See also Shaftesbury's *A Letter Concerning Enthusiasm to My Lord* (1963, I, 15-16); Kant, "Sickness of the Head", 1992, (Ak. 2: 267), 268.

② The New Age is a millenarian movement that anticipates the coming of a Golden age. Through thoughts and prayers, a new positive spiritual atmosphere surrounding the planet is being created that will make things better. This amorphous spiritual trend, whose roots include Western metaphysical traditions and various Eastern religions, has developed in the last decades of the twentieth century. It encompasses people around the world without particular theology, no founder, and no institutionalized religion. Instead, the emphasis of the New Age movement is on direct mystical experience, faith, inner transformation, surrender to the divine, and spiritual healing. For a short introduction, see Fisher 1999, 79 – 80. For a thorough treatment as well as a criticism of the New Age movement's tenets from an epistemological, emotional, and spiritual point of view, see Amir 2009.

③ For a good summery of the discussion in the literature on secularization and secularism, see the Editors' Introduction in Warner et al. 2010.

unproblematic, to one in which it is understood to be one option among others, and frequently not the easiest to embrace. " Even if one objects, as Taylor does, to the sort of narrowed " epistemological" approach that is part of a package of cultural and intellectual changes that make religious belief difficult and "embattled" (Taylor 2007, 10), secularity is not just a net reduction in religious belief or practice, but a change in the very conditions of belief. "Secularity in this sense," the Catholic Taylor writes, "is a matter of the whole context of understanding in which our moral, spiritual or religious experience and search takes place" (Taylor 2007, 3; quoted in Warner et al. 2010, 9). One consequence of this description of our cultural environment is that the emotional aspects of the several options that confront us are compared as in a shopping mall, and it is important to find out whether skepticism can be as competitive emotionally in this market as I believe it is intellectually.

II. Emotional Responses to Skepticism

Skepticism has elicited in its long history a wide range of strong emotional responses. I describe the negative attitudes toward it held by St. Augustine, Auguste Comte, René Descartes and Søren Kierkegaard, who consider it a spiritual crisis, a cerebral or social malady, a bottom-ground for reaching certainty, and a ridiculous position to joke about, respectively. I examine the more varied emotional reactions to different forms of skepticism, such as David Hume's, Michel de Montaigne's, Friedrich Nietzsche's, and Pyrrhonism's, identifying skepticism respectively as a curse yet with a positive outcome, a road to bodily health, a tonic to life, and a therapy leading to peace of mind.

1. St. Augustine

In his insightful "La santé du sceptique: Hume, Montaigne", Frédéric Brahami suggests that St. Augustine may have been the first to consider doubt a state of crisis, or a psychical anxiety that is experienced as a spiritual tragedy, rather than an epistemological process (Brahami 2008, note 1). If true, it sheds light on the fact that this fourth-century thinker was the first to integrate philosophy into religion, but at the cost of relinquishing reason for faith.

Skepticism for Augustine is the natural or even necessary outcome of the spontaneous development of reason. Left to itself, reason ultimately abolishes itself, creating mortal anxiety in the spirit. Skepticism represents natural reason pushed to its limit. In the *Confessions*, doubt is termed a "crisis" and faith is the spirit's "healing". It is the skepticism of the academy that liberates Augustine from his long allegiance to Manichaeism; yet he rejects doubt as a predicament and refuses to entrust philosophers with curing his soul (Augustine, 1956, V, 14, 25). In this last moment of man deprived of God, skeptical doubt represents a trial human intelligence cannot endure. The destructive power of doubt is described as a remedy whose brutality is redemptive. Augustine throws himself into faith through the workings of skepticism, which he experiences both as the best philosophic attitude and as a state that is unbearable. This ambiguity indicates the value, even the necessity, of doubt, as well as the Augustinian view that doubt must be superseded (10, 16). Skepticism for Augustine becomes a pivotal state: By revealing its limitation in providing wisdom, philosophy at its highest urges men to search for their salvation in religion. Augustine dramatizes skepticism by giving it an existential depth that it did no possess before him.

2. Auguste Comte

Many centuries after St. Augustine, Auguste Comte too views skepticism as a crisis. The only fundamental utility of doubt for Comte lies in enabling the individual or the human species the transition from one form of dogmatism to another (Comte 1929, IV, 203; General appendix). Indeed, Comte maintains that the metaphysical mind, which follows the theological mind and precedes the positive mind, is skeptical because it proceeds only by doubting indefinitely. Whilst theologism and positivism characteristically erect theoretical syntheses, the metaphysical mind is entirely critical, and is identified by Comte as skeptical with Voltaire as its most brilliant incarnation (III, 596). Variously referred to as metaphysical mind, critical spirit or skepticism, this is a necessary albeit dangerous intermediary stage of the psychosocial organism's development.

As long as skepticism is limited to the negative function of emancipating the mind from belief in dogmas, it is good. Inasmuch as it works toward progress, skepticism manifests an immense spiritual health: It is the very growth of the organism that is Humanity. As soon as skepticism aims at building, however, it transforms itself into the defining Western malady (IV, 367). Because modernity could confer its emancipatory power to doubt only by absolutizing it (IV, 180; General appendix), the mind cannot yield anymore to authority, be it scientific authority. By opposing organization, doubt becomes an obstacle to progress. The rejection of reorganization tends to dissolve the mind as well as society in general. This situation jeopardizes humanity, which cannot live sanely without hierarchy (IV, 47).

Once it reaches the peak of its power, the metaphysical mind becomes destructively skeptical. Inasmuch as modern consciousness is a demand of liberty, that is, of skepticism, it is dispersed and deprived of any objective ground capable of resisting the delirium that the mind itself produces when it is not disciplined by an external law. Alienation, in the psychiatric sense of the term, awaits at the end of this tragic process: "A cerebral analysis shows that the Western disease is in reality a chronic alienation that is essentially intellectual." (II, 458; my translation)

Skepticism seems to be understood by Comte as a pathology of the mind, a state that may be useful and even necessary, but in which it is impossible to abide. Because its emancipatory function is only transitory, the negative pole of the ambivalence toward skepticism is stronger for Comte than its positive pole.

Frédéric Brahami significantly notes that both Augustine and Comte diagnose the epistemological contradiction of skepticism as follows: Skepticism absolutizes relativization and throws the mind in an emptiness that is contrary to its nature. Skepticism is the symptom of profound despair, the expression of an incurable melancholy or an instance of acute crisis that is undergone by the mind or society. Skepticism thus testifies to a weakened life, a resigned spirituality, or a submissive intellect; it masks that which Nietzsche will later identify as nihilism (Brahami 2008).

The critics of skepticism see it as a disease or a crisis, which is far from accidental, because it expresses the culmination of an inevitable mental or social situation. In order to assess their views, however, it is important to emphasize that these are dogmatic interpretations: Comte considers dogmatism the normal state of human intelligence; even when seemingly the farthest from dogmatism, intelligence continually tends by nature toward the multiple forms of dogmatism (Comte 1929, IV, 203, general appendix); and, for Augustine, the presence of God in one's innermost being directs since the beginning the spiritual path toward salvation. If skepticism is seen through dogmatic eyes, the attitude toward it can understandably be at best ambivalent, and at worst, negative. Dogmatism, however, is in no position to evaluate skepticism because at the outset it considers it a breach in dogmatism, a momentary crisis to be superseded. That dogmatic persons cannot abide by skepticism tells us more about them, I suggest, than about skepticism.

3. René Descartes and Søren Kierkegaard

Two additional philosophers should be briefly recalled in the context of considering skepticism as a state to be superseded either by reason or faith. In his *Meditations*, René Descartes begins with skeptical despair and finds in the depth of doubt the foundation of certain knowledge. Because Descartes finds the *cogito* through doubting, doubt reverses itself into a positive experience at the end of the process.

In *Johannes Climacus*, the nineteenth-century Danish religious philosopher, Søren Kierkegaard, parodies Descartes's attempt at total doubt as an impossible situation that calls for laughter instead of serious refutation (Kierkegaard 1985). In his *Sickness unto Death*, despair is defined as a much wider phenomenon than skepticism, but all its instances have in common the attempt to live as a finite individual, whilst the true self is a synthesis of finite and infinite that cannot be completed without God (Kierkegaard 1980).

4. David Hume

Metaphysical and theological claims cannot be justified, according to Hume, nor can scientific claims and common-sense statements be validated. Hume rejects proofs for the existence of both God and bodies, and considers metaphysical speculations as well as inductive arguments flawed. More than the tenets of his skepticism, however, it is Hume's emotional reaction to it that is remarkable:

> The wretched condition, weakness, and disorder of the faculties, I must employ in my enquiries, increase my apprehensions. And the impossibility of amending or correcting these faculties, reduces me almost to despair, and makes me resolve to perish on the barren rock, on which I am at present, rather than venture myself upon that boundless ocean, which runs out into immensity. This sudden view of my danger strikes me with melancholy; and as it is usual for that passion, above all others, to indulge itself; I cannot forbear feeding my despair, with all those desponding reflections, which the present subject furnishes me with in such abundance.
>
> I am first affrighted and confounded with that forlorn solitude, in which I am placed in my philosophy, and fancy myself some strange uncouth monster, who not being able to mingle and unite in society, has been expelled from all human commerce, and left utterly abandoned and disconsolate. Fain would I run into the crowd for shelter and warmth; but cannot prevail with myself to mix with such deformity.

Apart from this statement in the last chapter of the first book of *A Treatise of Human Nature* (section 7), there is a letter, the last to appear in Hume's life, appended by David Fate Norton to the *Cambridge Companion to Hume* (1993), which testifies to the young Hume's suffering. In his adolescence, he went through a moral crisis accompanied by powerful somatic effects. The symptoms as described in this letter are an enthusiasm for learning, excessive taste for speculation, and immoderate search of truth, followed by a genuine clinical depression accompanied by severe somatic effects.

For Hume, skepticism is an incurable and destructive, yet natural, illness of the mind and the senses, from which the philosopher is not exempt (Hume 1995, I, 303). As skeptical doubt naturally results from thorough and intense reflection on the justification of our claim to knowledge, it increases with sustained thought. Thus, skepticism is inherent to thought; it becomes a disease because it destroys the very foundation of our existence. As nothing can resist the destructive criticism of reason, the profound despair and the somber melancholy that Hume describes in the conclusion of book I of *A Treatise of Human Nature* is understandable.

It is not advisable to live life in such a miserable condition, I suggest. If Humean skepticism leads to such misery, it may be better to give it up. Indeed, Hume does renounce it: Happily, nature itself " cures" him of this philosophic melancholy and delirium, which are now referred to as " chimera. " A little distraction, such as dinning, playing, and conversing with friends, or some strong impressions of the senses are sufficient for counteracting the negative effects of philosophy (I, 362).

Skepticism reveals to Hume that human life is not established on reason. Between life and reason, Hume chooses life and subordinates reason to life's interests. As we have seen, René Descartes begins with skeptical despair and finds, in the depth of doubt, the foundation of certain knowledge. To the contrary, in the first book of the *Treatise of Human Nature*, Hume starts with a firm basis (I, 34), yet ends with a shipwreck. For both of them, however, doubt reverses itself at the end and becomes a positive experience. Descartes finds the *cogito* at the depth of doubt, whilst Hume finds a truth at the bottom of his crisis. But the analogy stops here, because the *cogito* is a theoretical truth, whilst the mind itself appears as determined by life for Hume. It is life, passionate and sociable, that refutes Humean skepticism.

Hume writes in the letter mentioned above that he never recovered completely from his illness, but once he accepted the idea that speculation has value and validity only if it does not turn against life, he felt better. He repeats this idea in the conclusion of the first book of *A Treatise of Human Nature*: Rather than a duty, philosophic labor should be a pleasure.

Brahami emphasizes the difference between Hume's position and ancient skepticism: Seen as untenable, doubt is superseded; a pure Pyrrhonist does not exist for Hume, because Pyrrhonism is not viable. But whilst for Augustine or Comte skepticism is renounced for the sake of a new dogmatism, for Hume it evolves into a new skepticism: The *Enquiry on Human Understanding* combines two sorts of skepticism, because the mitigated ancient academic skepticism[①] can naturally result from Pyrrhonian doubts (Hume 1999, II, 284). At the end of doubting, the Pyrrhonian recognizes the insufficiency of his position. Awakening from his dream, he joins in the laughter he provokes (II, 282). Thus, when skepticism is articulated, it gains a positive constructive power.

5. Michel de Montaigne

Another famous philosopher points to the association of skepticism with health before Hume; however, it is the health of the body that is now concerned. Michel de Montaigne closes the 1580 edition of his *Essais* by the chapter 37 of book II and the 1588 edition by the chapter 13 of book III: Both chapters address the complex relations between skepticism, on the one hand, and medicine and health, on the other. Not only is health a personal issue because of Montaigne's long illness, health is also the Montainian sovereign good (Montaigne 1998, II, 242). His association of skepticism with the highest good testifies to the importance of the former for Montaigne. The extreme dogmatism of the medicine of his time alerts him to the therapeutic virtues of skepticism. Not a mere destructive device that annihilates medical doctors' pretensions, however, skepticism also positively indicates a path to healing. Thus, the theoretical emptiness and practical harm of the medicine of Montaigne's epoch lead him to elaborate a genuine skeptical philosophy of health (Sève 2007).

It is when he writes about medicine that Montaigne practices rigorously the most orthodox Pyrrhonian exercise, the equilibrium of arguments (1998, II,

---

① For ancient academic skepticism, see Long 1986, pp. 88 – 106.

chap. 37). Any proposition or argument is contradicted by a contrary proposition or argument of similar strength. This *isosthenia* or balancing of opposite opinions results in instructing the sick person about medical doctors' ignorance and leaving him to his affects and their immanent evaluations. He is guided by the phenomena and the emotions they contain, in conformity with the practical precepts taught by the Pyrrhonian Sextus Empiricus, who was a medical doctor. Skepticism thus reveals and invites us to use a medicine that inheres in nature (II, 310).

Much more can be said about Montaigne's genuine skeptical philosophy of health, and indeed, this subject can be pursued elsewhere independently from the current study (see Brahami 2008). For the purposes of this essay, however, suffice it to state that Montaigne is not a Pyrrhonist, nor, in the final analysis, a skeptic of another sort. Although "he throve on doubt" and may have been "born with a mind made for doubt", "Truth himself" is Christ for Montaigne, and his professions of submission to the Church carry conviction (Screech 2000, 18, 20). It is his limited use of Pyrrhonian skepticism for the health of the body as well as the final characterization of his philosophy as non-skeptical (despite his tendency to doubt everything), that urges us to move forward in our search for a viable skepticism.

6. Friedrich Nietzsche

Very much like Hume, Nietzsche directs his skepticism against metaphysics and theology as well as toward science and common sense. But Nietzsche differs from Hume in that he does not assume that we are better acquainted with our inner world than with the external world. The inner world is no less a phenomenon than an external object, for Nietzsche. His skepticism includes arguments advanced by Hume and the Pyrrhonian skeptics, but his main argument is not brought up by them. It concerns the conceptual-linguistic apparatus we use to describe the inner and outer worlds and its incapacity to correctly grasp their nature; thus, the world's true nature cannot be described.

From an emotional point of view, Nieztsche's perspectivism is intended to create the appropriate reaction in the strong at heart: It is a tonic to life.

But this view of skepticism as a tonic can be criticized as not viable. Nietzsche combines his own keen sense of the tragic life with an uncontained joy although, as Robert Solomon rightly points out, "he is not always convincing." (Solomon 1999, 144) Indeed, Nietzsche opens the fourth book of *The Gay Science* with a resolution for the New Year: "Some day I wish to be only a Yes-sayer," and urges us in *Twilight of the Idols* as well as in other writings "*to realize in oneself* the eternal joy of becoming—that joy which also encompasses *joy in destruction*" (Nietzsche 1974, sec. 276; 1954b, X, sec. 5). The joyful Dionysian affirmation is reached through self-overcoming, Nietzsche maintains, yet there is a gap between the destructive-lionesque stage and the creative and affirming-childlike state described in *Thus Spoke Zarathustra* (Part I, "On the Three Metamorphoses") and exemplified in other Nietzschean writings. ①

True, Nietzsche explains that once you say yes to a single joy, you say yes to all woe, because joy and woe are associated (1954a, IV, "The Drunken Song"). Joy and woe may be connected, but one generally does not intend to embrace woe when affirming joy. After joy is present, woe may be joyful too. One does not, however, gain a clear indication of how to reach tragic joy, the joy that affirms everything. Moreover, one can doubt that tragic joy exists; tragic joy is found in Richard Wagner's *Art and Revolution* (1896, 40) and *Tristan and Isolde*, in the writings of his one-time disciple Nietzsche, and in William Butler Yeats' late Nietzschean poems; there is no trace of it in previous understandings of the tragic, especially not in Aristotle, whose theory of tragedy does not refer to joy (see Potkay 2007, chap. 8). Finally, even if such a joy is possible, one can doubt its desirability: Being also "a joy in destruction", it is predicated upon cruelty toward others and toward oneself, as expressed in such passages as "what constitutes the painful voluptuousness of tragedy is cruelty", or "to see the failure of tragic natures and to laugh, that is divine" (Nietzsche 1966, sec. 229; 1938, II, 380).

---

① The tension between Nietzsche's critical and positive philosophy is common knowledge in the secondary literature, and is sometimes solved by dividing Nietzsche's thought into periods. See, for example, Magnus and Higgins 1996.

7. The Hellenistic and Roman School of Pyrrhonism

The Hellenistic and Roman school of Pyrrhonism maintains that we do not know a thing about the nature of the world that surrounds us. Thus, Pyrrhonists urge us to suspend all judgments because of the skeptical doubts that undermine all dogmatic claims to knowledge. Yet, the emotional reaction to this thorough skepticism is astonishing: We achieve tranquility as a result of suspending judgment, without intending to do so (Sextus 2000, I, 25-30). Tranquility follows the suspension of judgment—in technical terms *ataraxía* follows *epochē*—like a "shadow following the body" (Laertius 1925, IX, 107; see Sextus 2000, I, 29).

The impossibility of judging does not anguish the thinker who became a skeptic without willing so; to the contrary, it heals him. *Epochē* reduces the trouble to the sole affects that are sensed because they are hard to endure. It purges the mind of worry about the objective reality of pains and goods, because it enables the skeptic to abide by what he feels. Suspension of judgment thus spontaneously moderates the passions (I, 12). It is the very act of thinking that liberates the therapeutic virtues of philosophy: As Frédéric Brahami emphasizes, the skeptic sees health exactly where the dogmatic sees illness, in a thought that lives in its own movement, detached from all content (Brahami 2008).

The skeptics are frank about the radical alteration in life-style they require, however. Pyrrho aims at "altogether divesting ourselves of the human being", and Sextus describes the skeptic as a eunuch with respect to rational desires (Nussbaum 1994, 312). This is so because suspension of judgment frees us from the burden of worrying about what is true and right; it liberates also from the belief in a view of what is good—a belief that adds to the torment when the thing deemed bad is present; and it releases as well from all the evils that come from the intense pursuits of any special practical goal "with eager conviction". These evils prominently include emotion: Joy when the good is present, fear lest it vanishes; desire for the good before it is present; grief if it is absent and even fantasized guilt-being punished for something we have done. These emotions are based upon ethical belief, and Sextus suggests that only the complete extirpation of belief gets rid of them. [1]

I have considered the negative attitudes toward skepticism held by St. Augustine, Auguste Comte, René Descartes and Søren Kierkegaard, as a spiritual crisis, a cerebral or social malady, a bottom-ground for reaching certainty, and a ridiculous position to joke about, respectively. I have argued that skepticism seen through dogmatic eyes may yield an attitude toward it that understandably is at best ambivalent, and at worst, negative. Naturally inimical to skepticism, however, dogmatism either religious or intellectual is in no position to evaluate skepticism, because at the very outset it considers it an untenable momentary crisis. That dogmatics cannot abide by skepticism does not reveal much about skepticism.

I have further described Hume's, Montaigne's, Nietzsche's and the Skeptical Pyrrhonists' respective views of skepticism as a curse, a medicine for the body, a tonic for life, and a therapy leading to peace of mind. I have also criticized the viability of the Nietzschean and the Pyrrhonist endeavors, as well as renounced Humean skepticism because of the strong negative emotional impact it inflicts, and pointed out the limitation of the Montainian view. I suggest that the criticism most skeptical visions occasion calls for a form of skepticism that avoids the problems they create. On this ground, I introduce a worldview I call *Homo risibilis*, which means in Latin "the laughable or ridiculous human being".

III. A New Skeptical Worldview: *Homo risibilis*

Homo risibilis is a skeptical and secular vision that rivals the benefits of established religions without needing religious and metaphysical assumptions. It is thus unconcerned with Augustine's, Descartes's, and Kierkegaard's philosophies. Moreover, it is not subjected to the same criticism occasioned by Nietzsche's philosophy, and is more encompassing than the Montaignian view of skepticism

---

[1] For Pyrrhonian skepticism, see Sinnott-Armstrong 2004; for its practice, see Nussbaum 1994, pp. 280 – 315.

as health of the body. Being pleasurable, it does not call for Humean despair, and it enables itself without recourse to a radical change in human nature such as required by Pyrrhonism. Moreover, its relevance to this forum lies not only in its being based on a criticism of religions and most philosophies either Eastern or Western that offer peace of mind or philosophic redemptions; rather, it lies in its being an egalitarian worldview as well, which grounds an ethics of compassion similar to the Buddhist and Christian ethics yet free from the metaphysical assumptions those ethics rely on.

The worldview I propose can only be sketched within the limitations of this essay, but a fuller version can be found in the third chapter of *Humor and the Good Life: Shaftesbury, Hamann, Kierkegaard* (Amir 2014). I suggest that dissatisfaction with the human condition can be characterized as resulting from a clash between human desires and the impossibility of satisfying them on instinctual, emotional, and intellectual levels for either principled or practical reasons. I suggest, furthermore, that most religious and philosophical solutions to this basic human predicament require renouncing one or more aspects of our humanity as we know it. Thus, theories of redemption, or peace of mind, either Eastern or Western, religious or non-religious, can be divided into general types, the first type negating desire, the second making light of reason's limitations, and the third denigrating both desire and reason. [1]

These solutions come at a cost and should be evaluated accordingly. We may hesitate to choose any of the solutions that make light of reason's limits, or denigrate both desires and reason, but we should also be wary of those solutions that urge us to renounce our desires. If there exists a problem and all the solutions to that problem prove to be unacceptable, then, there remains one possibility to abstain from resolving the problem. Because our humanity depends on a balance between our desires and our reason, when a solution requires a negation of one or the other, or both, a non-solution seems to be the better policy. A non-solution has positive content as well: It presupposes a careful perception of human nature as an amalgam of rationality and irrationality, assumes a lucid awareness of human

---

[1]　For examples of these three types of theories and a fuller criticism of their views of desire and reason, see Amir 2013.

possibilities and limitations, and gives value to life in prioritizing the everlasting struggle with the predicament that lies at the core of human existence.

Humor provides an effective alternative to the urge for radical change, which usually involves giving up important aspects of our personality and our human experience. It can do so by providing relief from the basic tension between our desires on the instinctual, emotional, and intellectual levels, and between our awareness of the impossibility of fulfilling them, for practical as well as principled reasons. Humor enables us to reduce the tension created by this clash between expectations and reality because it can construe the clash as an incongruity, and we can learn to enjoy incongruities that are not immediately funny to us. Enjoyment of the incongruous in a situation that otherwise would be construed as tragic amounts to transmuting through humor suffering into joy. This enables us to be satisfied with dissatisfaction without paying the price of renouncing our desires, our reason, or both, that most solutions to dissatisfaction with the human condition require.

I suggest that *Homo risibilis* is a fitting description of humankind because of the necessary seriousness and ensuing suffering with which we take ourselves and our endeavors in conjunction with the view that in the large scale of things we and our endeavors are futile. [1] For lack of proof of the contrary, we rightly assume the latter view. This is tantamount to experiencing reality first as tragic (reality is serious and brings suffering) and construing it as comical (reality is futile). This acceptance of human ridicule is aided by the love of truth, unpleasant as truth may be, a love exemplified ideally by philosophers. The contemporary French philosopher, André Comte-Sponville, following a long tradition of philosophers that have made the love of truth the mark of the philosopher, reminds us that we may hope that truth will be happy, yet the philosopher will always choose truth over happiness (Comte-Sponville 1993, 199).

The view of human ridicule, however, is worthless without appropriating it as a vision of oneself. Understanding the ridiculous condition of humankind should

---

[1]   That we should take into consideration the view from nowhere is Thomas Nagel's contention (Nagel 1987; 1986). This is not embraced by certain philosophers, such as Robert Solomon (1976, chap. 1) and John Kekes (1995, 175-78; 2010, 234-38). For both, the fact that this view makes our concerns futile is a good reason not to embrace it.

lead to accepting one's own ridicule and finding comfort in it: The more ridiculous I am, the more I exemplify the human condition, the better I am as a human being. ① Modern thinkers who advance the view that we are ridiculous usually consider our ridicule tragic. ② But if human ridicule is thought to reveal human tragedy, it does so because we take ourselves too seriously even when

---

① In *The Tragic Sense of Life*, Miguel de Unamuno voices a similar thought inspired by Don Quixote: "One must know how to make oneself appear ridiculous, and not only in the eyes of others but also in one's own eyes." (Unamuno 1972, 322) Similarly, Kierkegaard suggests that "humor wants to be a fool in the world" (1967-78, vol. II, entry 1690), and Georges Bataille maintains that it is necessary for the human being "to want to be comical, for he is so, to the extent that he is a man (it is no longer a question of characters who are emissaries of comedy) —without a way out" (Bataille 1988, 169). Moreover, Avital Ronell makes the capacity to see oneself as ridiculous the mark of the philosopher: "Knowing one is being ridiculous nails you as a philosopher or at least targets the philosophical component of your Dasein. Being ridiculous already involves a philosophical insert, because it implies the act of laughing at oneself". (Ronell 2003, 298-99) Non-philosophers laugh at others, whereas the person who understands that this other is himself and laughs accordingly becomes a philosopher. The necessary distance from oneself that philosophy requires divides the philosopher's consciousness, making him both laugher and butt. I would add to Ronell's argument that the immaturity of the non-philosophical aspects of the self are a source of perpetual amusement to the philosopher's cool and sobering awareness, just as immaturity is the stuff from which comedy is made.

② For example, Simon Critchley suggests that "the pretended tragical sublimity of the human collapses into a comic ridiculousness which is perhaps even more tragic". (Critchley 2002, 43) Critchley's assertion echoes the view of Schopenhauer, deemed the philosopher of the absurd (Rosset 1967), and the view of the playwrights of the theatre of the absurd such as Samuel Beckett and Eugène Ionesco. Schopenhauer writes: "Thus, as if fate wished to add mockery to the misery of our existence, our life must contain all the woes of tragedy, and yet we cannot even assert the dignity of tragic characters, but, in the broad detail of life, are inevitably the foolish characters of a comedy." (Schopenhauer 1969, I, 322) Commenting on the ambiguity found in Samuel Beckett's plays, Alfred Simon tells us that "not only are human misery and comicality inseparable, they also are each other's paroxysm" (Simon, Le Monde, 27 Dec. 1989; my translation). Referring to The Chairs as a "tragic farce", Eugène Ionesco says that the "human drama is as absurd as it is painful. It all comes to the same thing, anyway; comic and tragic are merely two aspects of the same situation... There are no alternatives; if man is not tragic, he is ridiculous and painful, 'comic' in fact, and by revealing his absurdity one can achieve a sort of tragedy". (*The New York Times*, June 1, 1958, Section II, 3; quoted in Esslin 1961, 101)

In her *Immortal Comedy*, Agnes Heller argues that although terming existential comedies "tragicomedies" is a misnomer, it still points to the specificity of existential comedy: "Whereas paradoxes are dissolved in a joke, and this is why it is a joke, they remain unresolved in the existential comic novel or drama. Whatever is ridiculed is also mourned; the thing which has been lost is mocked, but the loss still hurts." (Heller 2005, 97)

acknowledging our ridicule. ① If it is true that works of existential comedy have expanded the phenomenon of the comic to territories from which they have been formerly excluded because "they sharpened our perception for a broader sense of the comic" (Heller 2005, 95 – 96), they did not expand it enough. I differ from those whose view is tragic-comic, including the playwrights of the absurd, in suggesting that as soon as we acknowledge the ridiculousness of our situation, the comedy is over: We cease to be comical, and with this, we cease to be tragic. We are beyond the tragic and the comic.

Joy and serenity follow from accepting one's ridicule, a view that liberates us without metaphysical assumptions but with remarkable emotional benefits. Such a state establishes a good basis for grounding various ethics. Because of its egalitarian view of the human plight, however, it is especially conducive to an ethics of compassion, similar to the Christian and Buddhist ethics, yet without requiring any unwarranted assumptions. ②

Conclusion

If reason tells us to be religious skeptics, skepticism should not be superseded. Religious thinkers may see skepticism as a crisis, yet this is not an argument against it. Comte may be right in considering the human species as dogmatic; dogmatism may characterize most of us, I suggest, yet not all of us, and

---

① In Dostoevsky's *The Brothers Karamazov*, the visitor in Ivan's nightmare insists: "Yet men, with all their indisputable intelligence, do take the farce of existence as something serious, and this is their tragedy." (Quoted in Kallen 1968, 379 – 80) The contemporary American theologian, Reinhold Niebhur, considers that, "what is funny about us is precisely that we take ourselves too seriously. We are rather insignificant little bundles of energy and vitality in a vast organization of life. But we pretend that we are the very center of this organization. This pretension is ludicrous; and its absurdity increases with our lack of awareness of it. The less we are able to laugh at ourselves the more it becomes necessary and inevitable that others laugh at us." (Niebuhr 1969, 140 – 41) Because we are so serious about ourselves we see life as tragic in the first place; we are ridiculous because we take ourselves seriously and even more ridiculous when considering our ridicule a tragedy.

② A rudimentary version of this article was presented as "Homo risibilis - A New Skeptical Vision" as part of the Roundtable "Religions and Irreligions of the World" at the World Congress of Philosophy, Athens, Greece, August 4 - 10, 2013.

therefore it can and should be criticized. Taking seriously Karl Popper's injunction to equate rationality with criticism, we may improve our rational capacities (Popper 1962). All we need is a skeptical worldview that enables us emotionally to withstand it without changing our human nature, so that the taste for reality that Nietzsche urged us to develop will be acquired without necessarily relinquishing our human-all-too-human nature (Nietzsche 1954a).

I believe the worldview I have presented here, *Homo risibilis*, answers this criterion. It certainly exemplifies that skepticism is not a doctrine among others. A way of life, skepticism is justly described by Marcel Conche as "a profound art of simplifying life" with the aim of experiencing it more fully, I would add. Skepticism reduces life to its simplest expression, to no more than itself (Conche 1995, 9 – 10), revealing thus its inherent richness. The skeptic is the human being freed from all that which dispossesses him from himself. For others, he is a living example of a principle of freedom. Because he does not judge, he is the proponent of tolerance and peace, as peace means everyone's right to be safe in one's home, as well as the right to live according to one's fashion and find happiness as one wishes.

References:

[1] Agassi, Joseph, and Abraham Meidan. 2008. *Philosophy from a Skeptical Perspective.* New York, NY: Cambridge University Press.

[2] Amir, Lydia B. 2009. Rethinking Philosophers' Responsibility. In *Creating a Global Dialogue on Value Inquiry*, ed. by Jinfen Yan and David Schrader, 21 – 56. Lewiston, NY: The Edwin Mellen Press.

———. 2013. The Value of Dissatisfaction-Maintaining the Tension that Unites Desires and Reason. *Journal of Axiology and Ethics.*

———. 2014. *Humor and the Good Life in Modern Philosophy: Shaftesbury, Hamann, Kierkegaard.* Albany, NY: SUNY Press.

[3] Augustin (Saint). 1956 [397]. *Les Confessions.* Traduction française par Pierre de Labriolle. Paris: Les Belles Lettres.

[4] Bataille, Georges. 1988. *Inner Experience.* Trans. and with an introduction by Leslie Anne Boldt. Albany, NY: SUNY Press.

[5] Bellah, Robert N. 2011. *Religion in Human Evolution: From the Paleolithic to the Axial*

Age. Cambridge, MA: Belknap Press of Harvard University Press.

[6] Beversluis, Joel. ed. 1995. Humanist Manifesto II. In *A Sourcebook for Earth's Community of Religions.* Grand Rapids, MI: Co Nexus Press.

[7] Brahami, Frédéric. 2008. La santé du sceptique: Hume, Montaigne. *Philosophia Scienti* [Online], 2 –12.

[8] Braybrooke, Marcus. 1988. *Faith and Interfaith in a Global Age.* Grand Rapids, MI: Co Nexus Press.

[9] Burton, Robert. 1989. *The Anatomy of Melancholy.* Ed. by Thomas C. Faulkner, Nicolas K. Kiessling, Rhonda L. Blair, introd. J. B. Bamborough. Oxford: Clarendon Press.

[10] Comte, Auguste. 1929 [1851 –1854]. *Système de politique positive.* (4 vols). Paris: Mathias. Comte-Sponville, André. 1993. *Valeur et vérité.* Paris: P. U. F.

[11] Conche, Marcel. 1995. Préface. In Pierre Leschemelle, *Montaigne: Le badin de la farce: de la joie tragique à la gaie sagesse.* Paris: Imago.

[12] Critchley, Simon. 2002. *On Humour.* London and New York: Routledge.

[13] De Benoist, Alain. 1996. Confronting Globalization. *Telos,* No. 108.

[14] Dennett, Daniel C. 1993. *Breaking the Spell: Religion as a Natural Phenomenon.* New York, NY: Viking Press.

[15] Esslin, Martin. 1961. *The Theatre of the Absurd.* Garden City, NY: Doubleday.

[16] Fisher, Mary Pat. 1999. *Religion in the Twenty-first Century.* London: Routledge.

[17] Fowler, Jeaneane D. , and Merv Fowler. 2008. *Chinese Religions: Beliefs and Practices.* Brighton: Sussex Academic Press.

[18] Freud, Sigmund. 1953 –1974. *The Standard Edition of the Complete Works of Sigmund Freud*, 24 volumes, ed. by James. Strachey et al. London: The Hogart Press and the Institute of Psychoanalysis.

[19] Griffin, David Ray. 1988. Introduction: Postmodern Spirituality and Society. In *Spirituality and Society*, ed. by D. R. Griffin. Albany, NY: SUNY Press.

[20] Heller, Agnes. 2005. *Immortal Comedy: The Comic Phenomenon in Art, Literature, and Life.* Lanham, MD: Lexington Books.

[21] Hume, David. 1978. *A Treatise of Human Nature.* Ed. L. A. Selby-Bigge. 2nd edition with text revised and variant readings by P. H. Niddich. Oxford: Clarendon Press.
——. 1995 [1739]. *Traité de la nature humaine.* Traduction française par Baranger Philippe et Saltel Philippe. Paris: GF-Flammarion.
——. 1999 [1748] *Enquête sur l'entendement humain.* Traduction française par Didier Deleule. Paris: Livre de Poche.

[22] Kallen, Horace M. 1968. *Liberty, Laughter and Tears: Reflections on the Relations of Comedy and Tragedy to Human Freedom.* De Kalb, IL: Northern Illinois University.

[23] Kant, Immanuel. 1902. *Kants gesammelte Schriften.* Berlin: Koniglischen Preussischen Akademie der Wissenschafte.

[24] Kekes, John. 1995. *Moral Wisdom and Good Lives.* Ithaca, IL: Cornell University

Press.

Kierkegaard, Søren. 1967 – 1978. *Journals and Papers*. Ed. and trans. by Howard V. Hong and Edna H. Hong, 7 vols. Bloomington and London, IN: Indiana University Press.

———. 1985. *Philosophical Fragments and Johannes Climacus*. Trans. Howard V. Hong and Edna H. Hong. Princeton, NJ: Princeton University Press.

———. 1980. *The Sickness unto Death*. ed. and trans. Howard V. Hong and Edna H. Hong. Princeton, NJ: Princeton University Press.

[25] Kitcher, Philip. 2007. *Living with Darwin*. New York, NY: Oxford University Press.

[26] Laertius, Diogenes. 1925. *Lives of Eminent Philosophers*. Trans. R. D. Hicks. Cambridge, MA: Harvard University Press.

[27] Long, Anthony A. 1986. *Hellenistic Philosophy: Stoics, Epicureans, Sceptics*. Berkeley, CA: University of California Press. 2nd edition.

[28] Magnus, Bernd, and Kathleen M. Higgins. 1996. Introduction. In *The Cambridge Companion to Nietzsche*. Cambridge: Cambridge University Press.

[29] Montaigne, Michel. 1998. *Essais*. Paris: Imprimerie Nationale.

[30] Nagel, Thomas. 1986. *The View from Nowhere*. New York, NY: Oxford University Press.

———. 1987. The Absurd. In *Life and Meaning: A Reader*, ed. Oswald Hanfling, 49 – 59. Oxford and New York: Basil Blackwell.

[31] Niebuhr, Reinhold. 1969. Humor and Faith. In *Holy Laughter: Essays on Religion in the Comic Perspective*, ed. by Conrad Hyers, 134 – 49. New York, NY: The Seabury Press.

[32] Nietzsche, Friedrich. 1938. *La Volonté de Puissance*. Texte e? tabli par F. Wurzbach; trad. par G. Bianquis. Paris: Gallimard.

———. 1954a. *Thus Spoke Zarathustra*. In *The Portable Nietzsche*, trans. and ed. Walter Kauffman. New York, NY: The Viking Press.

———. 1954b. *Twilight of the Idols*. In *The Portable Nietzsche*, trans. and ed. Walter Kauffman. New York, NY: The Viking Press.

———. 1954c. *The Antichrist.* In *The Portable Nietzsche*, trans. and ed. W. Kaufmann. New York: The Viking Press.

———. 1966. *Beyond Good and Evil*. Trans. W. Kaufmann. New York, NY: Random House.

[33] Norton, David Fate, ed. 1993. *Cambridge Companion to Hume*. Cambridge: Cambridge University Press.

[34] Nussbaum, Martha C. 1994. *The Therapy of Desire: Theory and Practice in Hellenistic Ethics*. Princeton, NJ: Princeton University Press.

[35] Plato. 1966. *Works*. In 12 Volumes. Trans. Harold North Fowler, intro. W. R. M. Lamb. Cambridge, MA: Harvard University Press; London: William Heinemann.

[36] Popkin, Richard H., ed. 1996. *Scepticism in the History of Philosophy*. Dordrecht:

Kluwer Academic Publishers.

［37］Popper, Karl R. 1962. *The Open Society and Its Enemies*. London: Routledge and Kegan Paul.

［38］Potkay, Adam. 2007. *The Story of Joy*. Cambridge: Cambridge University Press.

［39］Ronell, Avital. 2003. *Stupidity*. Urbana and Chicago, IL: University of Illinois Press.

［40］Rosset, Clément. 1967. *Schopenhauer, philosophe de l'absurde*. Paris: P. U. F.

［41］Schellenberg, J. L. 2007. *The Wisdom to Doubt: Justification of Religious Skepticism*. Cornell, IT: Cornell University Press.

［42］Schopenhauer, Arthur. 1969. *The World as Will and Idea*. Trans. E. F. J. Payne. 2 vols. New York, NY: Dover.

［43］Screech, M. A. 2000［1983］. *Montaigne and Melancholy: The Wisdom of the Essays*. London: Duckworth.

［44］Sève, Bernard. 2007. *Montaigne. Des règles pour l'esprit*. Paris: PUF.

［45］Sextus Empiricus. 2000. *Outline of Scepticism*. Eds. Julia Annas and Jonathan Barnes. Cambridge: Cambridge University Press.

［46］Shaftesbury, Anthony Ashley Cooper. 1963［1900］. *Characteristics of Men, Manners, Opinions, Times, etc.*, ed. by John M. Robertson, 2 vols. Gloucerster, MA: Peter Smith.

［47］Sinnott-Armstrong, Walter, ed. 2004. *Pyrrhonian Skepticism*. Oxford: Oxford University Press.

［48］Smith, Huston. 2001. The Meaning of Life in the World's Religions. In *The Meaning of Life in the World Religions*, ed. by Joseph Runzo and Nancy M. Martin, 255 – 68. Oxford: Oneworld.

［49］Solomon, Robert C. 1976. *The Passions: Emotions and the Meaning of Life*. New York, NY: Doubleday.

———. 1999. *The Joy of Philosophy: Thinking Thin* versus *the Passionate Life*. Oxford and New York: Oxford University Press.

［50］Taylor, Charles. 2007. *ASecular Age*. Cambridge, MA: Belknap Press of Harvard University Press.

［51］Unamuno, Miguel de. 1972. *The Tragic Sense of Life in Men and Nations*. Trans. Anthony Kerrigan, introduction Salvador de Madariaga, afterword William Barrett. Princeton, NJ: Princeton University Press.

［52］Wagner, Richard. 1896. *Art and Revolution*. In *Prose Works*, trans. William Ashton Ellis, 8 vols. vol. 1, 21 – 65. London: Routledge and Kegan Paul.

［53］Ward, Keith. 2001. Religion and the Question of Meaning. In *The Meaning of Life in the World Religions*, ed. by Joseph Runzo and Nancy M. Martin, 11 – 30. Oxford: Oneworld.

［54］Warner, Michael, Jonathan Vanantwerpen, and Craig Calhoun. 2010. Editors' Introduction. *Varieties of Secularism in a Secular Age*. Cambridge, MA: Harvard University Press.

[55] Wielenberg, Erik J. 2005. *Value and Virtue in a Godless Universe*. Cambridge：Cambridge University Press.

[56] Li JiaLian. 2012. The Sentimental Origin of Virtue：An Inquiry into Thought of Moral Sentiments, Hangzhou：zhejiang University press.

当代世界文化中的新怀疑主义世界观

Lydia B. Amir

摘　要：在当代世界文化中，我从少数人的视角来看待怀疑主义。首先，在不考虑宗教因素的条件下，通过把我们的时代视为世俗的时代，我把怀疑主义和当代宗教批判联系起来。其次，我发现，怀疑主义在理智上极具吸引力，在我看来，它不受欢迎的原因在于它所引起的情感反应。因此，我考察了对怀疑主义的多种多样的应对之方，如古希腊和古罗马的皮浪主义、弗里德里希·尼采、圣·奥古斯汀、蒙田、笛卡尔、大卫·休谟、索伦·克尔凯郭尔以及奥古斯特·孔德等人的思想。我批判了这些思想并提出一种世俗化的怀疑主义世界观，称为"人的笑"。我相信它会和宗教形成竞争，并且会建立一种同情伦理学，这种伦理不会建立在那种毫无根据的形而上学假说之上。

关键词：怀疑主义　宗教　形而上学

The Philosophy of Han-Moum (One Body) and Neohumans Culture

Han Gang-Hyen*

Abstract：This paper covers the essence of "the One Body Philosophy" which is a new philosophy, a new science. It contains the culture of saving life of neohumans (新人類 = 仙人), which will become the mainstream culture of the world soon. Above all, the public philosophy is "大一體光明思想 (a Big One Thought)"；the Han-moum Philosophy, that will make all humanity one family, give true peace to humanity. The World will welcome a new era by promoting communication and integrating studies, by a life-saving campaign through a new thought of neohumans, and by keeping the rules of new heaven. The philosophy of eternal life and new culture of neohumans in my paper will become a mainstream culture of the world, which will make all humanity become one and give a true happiness to all humanity.

Keywords：Han-moum Philosophy；Neohumans；the Victor；Holy Dew Spirit；Neohuman Culture (神人類文化)

---

* Han Gang-Hyen, General Director of IANC (Academy).

Introduction

There are a lot of futurists who anticipated the era of neohumans[①] based on their majors and through the changing of modern culture and the future. They are Hose Coredeo, a futurist, Ray Huazweil, inventor, the author of ? The Sincularity is Near? , Herman Kahn (1922 – 1983), a futurist of international fame, Jeremy Limpkin, Eric Drexler (MIT Doctor of Engineering), Timercy Ma, the chairman of the Seminar of the Future, William Halal, a professor of the Gorge Washington University and so on.

Nowadays books on the future are sold well. The reason for that is because people have anxiety about the future and the will of getting the answer. Those who prepare the future are ones who can use their time worthily. If one does not know a new culture of the new era, he/she cannot adjust to the era of light and the civilization of scientific technique. That is the reason that we are interested in the future and study it.

In 2007, Choseonilbo introduced such insistence with a title "The New era of Neohumans that people neither die nor grow old will come". While interviewing H. Cordeiler, a futurist of Venezuela, the reporter felt that he was reading a science fiction. At the interviewing, the futurist anticipated that humans are in the progress of evolving; ultimately, new perfect humans will be born someday.

Also, he said: "Humans have come to today through biological evolution. However they still have a lot of defects. Now people will have evolved quickly and ideologically without trial and error by the intentional design using scientific technology. "The immortality of humans is not impossible. " "It's just a matter of time considering the fruit of scientific technology. " As well, he calls Neo-humans,

---

① Neohumans: In Revelation in the Bible, it predicted that the Victor and the men of new heaven would be reborn as transcendent Neo-humans, attain eternal life, and be other existences to reinstate the light of world according to Nostradamus. Refer to academic studies about this terms of Neohumans, "New Thought", "New humans", "New Culture", Ko si-yeong, "The new culture movement of CheunDoKyeou", *Journal of the Korean Academy of New Religions*, Autumn, 2011, Vol. 27, pp. 97 – 125.

post humans, who will be the final humans that will substitute homo sapiens, present humans. Now they are evolving in a progress of trans-humans, the middle step. And he said, "The neohumans who are in the step of post humans will not grow old, they can achieve the condition of minds and bodies as they want."

Especially, ABC of America broadcasted the people, who believed immortality, talked about immortality with living bodies in August, 1991. Their immortality is completely different from that of Christianity. "Going to heaven after death" has no meaning to them, no matter how sweet future they have, it does not matter to them. They insisted that heaven is accomplished by efforts now and physical immortality is possible, too. Also, we can see that several newspapers such as Sports Choseon,[1] Choseon Ilbo[2] Hangookilbo,[3] Seoul Economy Newspaper wrote about the era of immortality. Plus, well-known prophets and visionary ministers such as Cindy Jacobs, Benny Hinn, Lick Joiner, and Shindy Baker said that they received revelations with one voice that God blesses Korea.

In addition, a lot of futurists, the Association of immortality of America, professors and scholars of Britain insist with one voice now is an era of immortality. The speed of this era's changing is accelerating surprisingly.

The era of agriculture of 3000 years, the era of industry of 200 years, the era of information of 50 years, and what era will come next? It is the era of infinite life-span!

As a philosopher and researcher of Korean new religions, I will say about the unique view of birth and death of the Victory Altar.[4] Also, I will say about the

---

[1] 《Sports Chosun》, 1992. 9. 19. The newspaper ran an article saying "the era when people's life span is 400 years will come in two years".

[2] 《Chossun Ilbo》, 1992. 9. 24. The newspaper ran an article saying "you can live to the age of 400".

[3] 《Hanguk Ilbo》, 1993. 1. 25. The newspaper ran saying "the study of the elixir of immortality", "The endless challenge toward God".

[4] The Victory Altar (勝利祭壇): The name of the Victory Altar came from the order of the Fifth Angel (Park Tae Seun) in a prophecy according to the Bible as one of Korean new religion movement, The original whole name is The Eternal Religion God's Holy Society Victory Altar (勝利祭壇). Some journalists and broadcasters who did not understand the conception of immortality of the Victory Altar call the name to belittle and allude the Victory Altar. However, examining the name, it is originated from the Altar where God preaching immortality stays. The Victory Altar hopes that peoples call it the Victory Altar in short; also I will use the name in my thesis.

method of exodus from birth and death. In addition, I am happy to introduce immortal philosophy under a subject "The Immortal principle and the View of Exodus from Birth and Death" which the Seventh Angel① talks about in the Victory Altar, a new religion in South Korea.

I have participated in worship services to research and to study about a new religion movement of the Victory Altar as a new philosophy for 20 years as a researcher of immortal philosophy. Therefore, I arranged the key points that will be helpful for philosophy researchers of a religion and the followers of other religions to understand the Victory Altar in this thesis.

I remember the title clearly because the congress told me that so far there were no true philosophies or thought, which made me rethink the definition of philosophy and its role.

So I went to Athens to join the congress. God predicted the future in the Bible and the Buddhist books. The Bible said that religions and philosophies seek the truth (God) and the Idea World. If they do not know the essence of God and humanity, they are not perfect and expediential sayings. So in Corinthian 13:8 – 10, "8. Charity never fails: but whether there be prophecies, they shall fail; whether there be tongues, they shall cease; whether there be knowledge, it shall vanish away." "9. For we know in part, and we prophesy in part." "10. But when that which is perfect comes, then that which is in part shall be done away."

While studying the prophetic books of the world for 20 years, I found now it is the time when the aim of the Bible completes because I have collected its evidences and signs a lot. The Bible predicted that a new philosophy would appear and complete the aim of the Bible.

In the Bible, John14:29 said, "And now I have told you before it come to pass, that, when it is come to pass, ye might believe." Additionally, John16: 13 said, "Howbeit when he, the Spirit of truth, is come, he will guide you into all truth: for he shall not speak of himself; but whatsoever he shall hear, that

---

① The Seventh Angel who is the man who opens the seventh seal and blows the last trumpet according to the Bible. His name is 曺熙星 (Morning Bright Star) and is "金運天使" in (陰陽五行) the theory of Yin-yang (陰陽).

shall he speak: and he will show you things to come."

The above words predicted that in the era of change, the Holy Spirit would come, pour His Spirit, and lead people to the way of truth, and say what would happen in the future. Also the Bible said, "If the Spirit of the truth comes, He will teach the perfection, pour the grace of wisdom and the Holy Spirit to the children of light first to make them see God face to face." 1 Corinthians 13: 12 predicted, "For now we see through a glass, darkly; but then face to face: now I know in part; but then shall I know even as also I am known."

So far, the limit of philosophies and cultures is that they could not suggest the answer to the questions "Who am I?" "What is the essence of humanity?" Some anthropologists, scientists, religionists believe in the old evolution theory that humanity evolved from ameba or monkeys. Theologians, who believe in God, believe the doctrine of creation that humanity was created by God, and have the view of afterlife that people go to heaven after death. I am sure that their thought, elusions, and philosophies will collapse by the philosopher of immortality. If there are philosophers who realize the limit of all philosophers, they will be ready to experience the philosophy of new life and the Visible Idea World according to Immanuel Kant.

1. The Han-Moum Philosophy[①]

1) What is the Han Moum Philosophy?

In short, so far, humanity has put a value on the thought, the religion, and the philosophy which were born by the spirit of death in the world of material to

---

① New terms of my paper appeared at the following conference. I wrote them in explaining the whereabouts of the Idea World which philosophy seeks, and in the collection of papers of "*The Academy of Korean New Religion* volume 24, in 2010 of The Korea Academy of New Religions Conference Autumn Season in Korea. The theme was "The study for exodus from birth and death & the theory of Eternal life" (focused on the philosophy of Immortality), I also used the terms at "The Hidden Manna and the Philosophy of Eternal Life" based on the Perspective of Prophecies in Sacred Books at "The 2011 International Conference" by CESNUS held at Aletheia University at Tapei in Taiwan on June 21 – 23, and "A New View of the Afterlife and the New Heaven", 2012 International Conference of the sponsor, CESNUS in Morocco.

decay and perish. I will introduce the philosophy of immortality that leads humanity to overcome death, to kill Ego, and to become immortal existences by practicing the new immortal philosophy in everyday life. That is, the philosophy of immortality can be understood easily through the glossography of "Han" and "Han Moum", and "Han-namu". The philosophy of immortality is figuratively explained by the principle of one blood and one tree.

The principle of Han-Moum is that all humanity on the earth is the offspring of God, the first ancestor. Comparing to a tree, humanity is one body like one big tree which has 7 billion branches.

To use a philosophical term, the principle of Han-Moum includes "the Holistic Ontology", which has the meaning "many is one", the meaning of Holistic One is that small many one is in Big One, paradoxically, on the contrary, essentially, men and women, old men and young men have different color of skin, the root is one. String theory is the same principle as the philosophy of Han-Moum: [1] the body and mind of all humanity is like an organically connected tree, a tree of life which has 7 billion people and receivies one blood.

Everybody has a different value of life and a different way of life in accordance with their philosophy. The thinking way, the action of humanity, character formation, and the shape of humanity are different in accordance with the value people have. Additionally, by what aims people have and where they put their meaning of life, the voyage of life is changed; the happiness and satisfaction of life are changed.

In this respect, the philosophy and value of life and the aim of life are very

---

[1]　The philosophy of HanMom (one body). It can explain as Holistic Monism by One Blood Theory though Focused on Holon and "通論理 (Trans-logic)": Kim Sang Yil, Suun and Whited, pp. 32 – 33. , p. 80, pp. 92 – 93. Kim Sang Yil explicates this "Holon Revolution" in his Suun and Whitehead (p. 80) from the "theory of Holography" in post-modern physics. and This holographic logic is like what Thomas Kuhn calls the "paradigm shift". In this new term holon [= on (part) + holos (whole)], a whole is a part and vice versa. This Holon logic, according to Kim, is also like the Korean Han (韓) logic. Kim Sang Yil Professor also introduces a new academic filed called "mereology". This is all about the issue of whole (One) and part (Many). Also it's "Han Thought" introduces as a process Theology by Cobb, John Jr. , On Han Philosophy, from Kim Sang Yil's Hanism As Korean Mind in 1984. Refer to Cobb, John Jr. , On Han Philosophy, pp. 8 – 9.

important. Now to humanity who is welcoming the era of the light of new heaven, the truth hidden by darkness and ignorance has been revealed gradually. The Ideal World which a lot of philosophers and prophets have only dreamed is coming into view. The philosophy of immortality appeared to save life of humanity by making the world peaceful, and combining all humanity into one. I will introduce it as a new philosophy. A true study or true philosophies should be so simple, clear, and universal that everyone can learn and practice it easily.

2) What is a New Philosophical Term of the Han-Moum Philosophy?

First I will explain this new philosophical term by expressing the "Han" of the "Han Moum". This new philosophical term expresses "Han Moum", which is a combination of "Han (one)", the noun of Hana meaning a big organic mass, and moum (body). This linguistic philosophical terms are seen in "Hana-nim (The God of Lord) Thought", the traditional thought, which Koreans believed the one and only God, it is an expression of heaven coming down from ancient Korea. "Han" of "Han Thought" has a profound philosophical meaning. "Han" has a meaning not only "One" but also more than 20 other meanings, it is an ancient philosophical Korean which is related to heaven and God. Now I will examine the philosophical meaning of "Han". A lot of new meanings have been added to the early definitions of the word "Han". According to Ahn Ho-Sang, the current definitions of "Han" are as follows: 1) great; 2) east; 3) bright; 4) oneness; 5) unification; 6) people; 7) old; 8) wholeness; 9) beginning; 10) Han people; 11) white; 12) light; 13) high; 14) same (ness); 15) many (ness); 16) sky or heaven; 17) long; 18) great leader; 19) up; 20) king; 21) perfect; and 22) inclusiveness.

And "Han" is used as noun, adjective, adverb, suffix and prefix, and can be attached to various words to indicate the above implications. Being holistic in one's thinking is also to be both horizontal and vertical, both subjective and objective.

Therefore thinking of Holistic Ontology can often be Paradoxical as well. For in such holistic thinking that one is many and many are one. In holistically inclusive or holistic ontology thinking the subject is the object, and vice versa. In this intrinsically circular, harmonious and symbiotic way of thinking, woman is man, and man is woman. They are of course different from each other. But they are fundamentally the same blood and body as humans who coming from the original God. This holistic ontology way of thinking is the most fundamental and characteristic aspect of the Korean way of thinking. "Han-moum (unit one body)", "Han-maum (same one mind)", "Han-namu" (same one tree) w/ holism is endlessly broad, deep, and organic inclusive. They have both physical and metaphysical (i. e. spiritual and optical) dimensions in them.

I could see that all humanity is one brother, one family, one body, and all races are the people of God and one tree through "Han", "Hana-nim Thought", "One Tree Theory" in this thesis Not only this but also according to the recording of Herbert foreign missionary, it said that Koreans believed Hana-nim, the one and only God of the beginning. The reason that Koreans have had this thought is because the possibility that they are the tribe of Dan is very high. The phrases of the Bible that support the Han-Moum Philosophy are as follows: Acts17: 26 said about the root of humanity that "From one man he made every nation of men, that they should inhabit the whole earth; and he determined the times set for them and the exact places where they should live". And Genesis 6: 4, Deuteronomy 14: 1, 1 John 3: 2, Romans 8: 14 – 16, Psalm 82: 6, John 10: 35 and Proverbs 12: 23 said about the root and the starting point of humanity. By putting these together, we can see humanity is the children of the most high, is originally God. However, people do not know the secret that humanity was God of heaven. I could see the etymologic origin of "Hanaism" and "Hana-nim Thought" through studying Arirang Korean Folksong. Examining the etymologic origin of Arirang Korean Folksong, I could understand why the people of the world like Arirang, the ancient Korean folk song, and are moved by it. You can see my etymological study about Arirang, Han people and God.

As mentioned above, all humanity who are formed by the one blood of ancestors commonly have life, they are divided into several billions, and they are one tree which has the essentially same nature and the same conscience. Therefore, regarding everybody as one body, one brother, and my body and serving everybody as God is the Han-Moum Philosophy. And by practicing the

Han-moum Philosophy, the body of humanity is completed as that of immortal God. That is the philosophy of immortality. So far, humanity has not regarded everybody as my body, or one body. The work and the philosophy from selfish and wrong self-centered thought and consciousness that comes from regarding everybody as others are sins, emit the poison of desires, lead humanity to death. So James 1：15 pointed out the essence of desire and death. Thinking where the mind of regarding everyone as others, hating, being jealous of, fighting and killing come from, and what the original nature of humanity is, humanity has lived to pursue the philosophy for thousands years with being crazy by the power of ignorant consciousness. If all humanity realizes that they are one body, one brother, and one family, and practice the Han-Moum Philosophy, the philosophy of immortality is finally understood and completed.

Then I will explain "the Han-Moum Philosophy" and "the philosophy of immortality" from the point of view of Holistic Ontology using "the Principle of Hanna-mu" and "the principle of one blood".

3）What is the Principle of Han-Pi（one blood）& One Tree Theory?
I will explain the detail with power point in consideration of the amount of the paper. Those who have a spiritual eye feel through this thesis that the philosophy of bright wisdom appeared. This new philosophy of bright wisdom of eternal life was not on the earth so far, but it was predicted in the Bible. The philosophy of immortality is the wisdom to reveal the secret of heaven, and is the bright philosophy by the oil（the Holy Dew Spirit）pouring. Becoming the slave of death and darkness, being caught by Ego, being used by the direction of their pseudo master, and dying to pay for their wage are the result of the philosophy of humanity's empty life.

Now, the Victor, who overcame the spirit of death and broke the prison of the ignorant spirit, appeared in Korea. Due to the victory of the man, the philosophy of immortality was completed. Therefore, my thesis is about the philosophy of salvation of Neo-humans, which was completed by the Victor by escaping from the darkness of the Ego, the consciousness of death, receiving the true freedom.

All humans were made of the blood of God; however, they have been divided into 7 billions' Self-Consciousness for **6000** years. Even though they are one body, they do not know it. So they make boundaries, fight each other, and live selfishly. The Self-Consciousness in humans is a dividing soul; also it is the evil soul that is the factor of quarrel, confusion, anguish, unhappiness, and death. As well, it is the reason of the lost paradise (ideal world), the birth and death of the universe, and miserable humans' history according to the Victor. No matter how good people are, they have Self-Consciousness, individual consciousness, and self-esteem, it is evil and dirty Satan. Now as we found the factor of death, we should go back to the original being by removing the factor of death.

Everyone can return to one heart of the God. The Victor says, " The truth is in one, peace is in one, and immortality is in one. " After the Savior, Victor, appeared, the directions of all humans' fates were already determined. The Victory Altar (SeungRi-JeDan) campaigns all humanity to be one. As the advent of the Savior, the Victor philosopher means the advent of the perfect Holy Spirit of truth like the Bible prediction in Corinthians 3. The perfect Holy Spirit of truth is just the Holy Dew Spirit according to Isaiah 26: 19 and Hosea 14: 5, also it is the Spirit of the last Angel and the fruit of life in Revelation. The Holy Dew Spirit is the last weapon of the Savior, the Victorious God against Satan, which will recover the original paradise. The strong Holy Spirit that makes 7 billion human beings one is working now. The Satan which knows his fate goes into humans and makes a frantic last-ditch effort. The Satan that drives all humans to destruction is Self-Consciousness hiding in humanity. As Self-Consciousness is the factor of destroying humanity, overcoming Self-Consciousness is the way to achieve salvation and peace. Therefore, the Ideal World and Ideal Form exist in the heart of " Super-Ego and Superhuman".

2. The Philosophy of Immortality

1) What is the philosophy of immortality?

According to new sayings on May 5th, 1987, and February 8th, 2001 of the Victor (Cho Hee Sung) pouring down Holy Dew Spirit, in the SeungRi-JeDan

（Victory Altar）, "humanity is one body because their ancestors are Adam and Eve. As they have the same ancestors, they have the same blood. Having the same blood means the same people. Adam and Eve lived in the Garden of Eden. Only God lives in the Garden of Eden. So the Bible says that where God resides, heaven is. Adam and Eve lived in the Garden of Eden in heaven. Therefore, they were Gods. And their offspring are Gods, too. Puppies are dogs, calves are cows genetically. The children of God are God, too. The evidences are that humans want to live forever in infinite happiness like God though everyone dies. The reason is that their ancestors' blood that experienced immortality flows in their offspring now. So all humanity is Gods. Adam and Eve have been one body generation by generation. This means that the whole universe is my body primarily. Accordingly, the Victor Mr. Cho Hee Sung of the Victory Altar, tells people to regard others as their bodies. The reason the universe moves is because as God exists in the universe, life exists, the subject of life being God.

And then, where does the spirit of dead people exist? As blood in their living children's bodies is their ancestors' blood, it is the spirit of their ancestors. Therefore, the spirit of ancestors is not separated from that of their offspring, but the same one. It is one body. It means the spirit of ancestors is mine, and my spirit is ancestors'. The theory of this saying is new. Therefore, the spirit of ancestors lives in their offspring after their death. The ancestors who died 6000 years ago live in the present. As they are one body, they should be unified spiritually and consciously, but actually they are not, because Satan makes people think individually.

2）The Principle of One Blood by the Victor Cho

As the Savior came, the perfect Spirit came like the Bible predicts in Corinthians 3. The perfect Spirit is the Dew Spirit according to Isaiah 26: 19 and Hosea 14: 5, the Spirit of the last Angel and the fruit of life in Revelation. Here are the words of the Savior.

All of mankind is one spiritually, no matter who they are. As they are one body, they should be unified spiritually and consciously, but actually they are not. Because Satan makes people think individually. The spirit of Adam and Eve

6000 years ago is living as my spirit now. Adam and Eve have been one body generation by generation. Where does the spirit of dead people exist? As blood in their living children's bodies is that of their ancestors, it is the spirit of their ancestors. Therefore, the spirit of ancestors is not separated from that of their offspring, it is one. It is one body. It means the spirit of ancestors is mine, and my spirit is ancestors'. This saying is new. Therefore, the spirit of ancestors lives. The ancestors who died 6000 years ago live in present.

Therefore, the spirit of my ancestors is not separated from mine. Satan has deceived us like that. However, actually parents and grandparents are I. Hence, that I become a Victor means that parents become Victors and grandparents become Victors. The spirit of all ancestors in the Victor becomes Victors. The Victor Cho tells people to regard others as my bodies. This means that the whole universe is my body. The reason the universe moves is because as God exists in the universe, life exists, the subject of life being God. However, advanced scientists do not know it. The philosophy of one body that regards everyone as mine will be the truth that saves people and gives people peace. (2003. 8. 11 sayings of the Victor Cho)

This science is a perfect science. No matter how many people are, the philosophy can make all of them God. You should become a Savior by practicing the science of the Savior. This man (the Victor) told you to regard others as yours. It means there are neither you nor I, but one body. And then all humans become one. Also, it gives all humans peace. Everybody is one body, has the same blood, and is all my body. As nobody is not my body, if people think that everybody regard as their bodies or one body, they cannot but unify and become one body. (1987. 5. 3 sayings of Victor Cho)

Because Self-Consciousness and individualism make home and society unhappy, they are the evil soul that makes people split and fight. Now, the followers are campaigning martyring by killing their Self-Consciousness. When Self-Consciousness in humans dies, the Spirit of peace occupies humans. The Dew of Holy Spirit pouring down from the Victor is the last weapon of the Savior that will recover the original paradise from the lost Paradise. The strong Spirit makes 7 billion humans as one.

The Sutra of Nirvana Volume 29, page 290 says, "The worldly way has no freedom and equality, and yours and mine are different, but Buddha's way is freedom and equal, and makes one. That is the right way for everyone to follow." This means "regard anyone as me". It is also written in the Sutra of Nirvana. So, the true way and real religion is to unite you and me to be one. If they cannot unite everyone into one and everyone is different, can they be a real way and real religion? That's not a real religion.

3) The Principle of Eternal Life

A. The reason of aging and death by the principle of blood.

Most religious doctrines are superficially reflected by humanity's hope of twisted immortality. The theory of separating body from spirit, separating God form this world, believing heaven and hell after death, and the Samsara of spirit are products of such twisted thought. These religious thoughts are just reflected by illusionary copies of natures that are embedded in our blood. Most of all prophets who a lot of religionists revere look like faded idols to the followers of the Victory Altar in the era when the Sweet Dew falls down. Because, although uncountable religions exist, they don't know neither the essence of sins nor the essence of blood and they have led their religions only in their individual thought.

B. People do not die because of aging.

People die due to several reasons such as accidents, diseases, hunger, cold, aging, etc. Among the reasons, most people die due to aging. Most people think that people die because of aging. Is this saying truth? No, it is not. According to the preaching of the Seventh Angel, people die not because of aging but because of some causes of death. Therefore, a lot of scientists have studied the reason of aging, but they have not found out the reasons yet. According to the Bible, people die because of the wage of sins. According to the Nirvana Sutra, "although the Reincarnated Maitreya Buddha appears and preaches because the blood of people decays, they cannot attain the nature of Buddha, and they die. However, they do not believe the saying of the Reincarnate Maitreya Buddha." The Seventh Angel revealed the secret in the Buddhist Sutra on the platform of the Victory Altar. Although all religious

Scriptures tell immortality with their physical bodies (不死永生), people who are caught by karma do not believe it. Most people think of human death as natural. On the contrary the followers with spiritual eyes of the Victory Altar can see that Scriptures predicted when, where, and how eternal life would be established. The followers of the Victory Altar insist strongly that they should announce that people can achieve eternal life with living bodies. According to John 5: 39, "You study the Scriptures, because you think that in them you will find eternal life."

According to Titus 1: 2, "God promised eternal life to His chosen people before the beginning of time." According to Corinthians 15: 26, "The last enemy to be defeated will be death." According to the Nirvana Sutra, "Where the Sweet Dew falls down, there is no death." As I enumerate some sayings, the Scriptures say eternal life with physical bodies. If people die because of aging, they should grow old at the same rate; die at the same time and in the same conditions. However, there are big differences in aging regardless of age. Then where are the causes of aging and contracting diseases from? Let's find out the reason.

C. The causes of aging and the essence of spirit.

There are several medical and biological theories about aging. For example, they are "the theory of mutation", "the theory of autoimmune" that aging comes from immune system's weakening, and "the theory of circulation's disorders", etc. However, they did not say the reason of aging exactly. The modern medical world says that aging comes from reducing the activity of cells. However, their explanation about the reason of death and aging is not clear. According to the theory of the Seventh Angel (the Victor, Mr. Cho Hee Sung), because Self-consciousness (ego) works, peoples' blood decays. As the decayed blood increases gradually, reformed cells decrease, so the phenomenon of shortage of cells occurs on the whole body, not because they become old by growing age. [1] Cells have their life-span, after finishing their life span, they die. Then new cells are formed by not decayed blood. So if blood decays, the

---

[1]　Deepak Chopra, *Men Do Not Grow Old*, translated by Lee Gyoo Hyeong (Seoul: Jeongsin Segyesa, 1993), pp. 98 – 136.

shortage of cells occurs.

Therefore, increasing the amount of decayed blood, black spots are formed gradually on their faces, germs occurs in their blood, the resistance of white blood cells gets weak, finally they contract serious diseases, and die in the end.

As people's body and mind were formed by the blood of their ancestors, people's bodies were transformed by the spiritual body of God, and they are Gods imperfect and caught in Satan's prison (ego). Those who have a lot of sins take death for granted by the memory of genetics of decayed blood and the information that the soul of death (ego) gives, also because of minds that kill life (desire, anger, and sadness), people become old and die. That is the new theory of Neo-humans about the reason of death.

D. Blood is just life.

As life lies in blood, the behavior and mind decaying blood is killing life. The Bible expressed that blood is life in Genesis 9：4, Leviticus 17：11. It is a common sense that almost all patients dying from excessive bleeding come to life again if they receive a transfusion. That verifies that blood is life in the medical world. Humans fetus is formed through the division of cells, each has two genetic information of their parents' blood. Human body is formed by 100 trillion cells. As cells cannot last forever, each cell has a different lifespan. The cells of skin live for twenty-eight days, some cells of hormone can live for only a few hours, and the cells of bone live for eight years. Therefore, several hundred million's cells die a day and discrete. And new cells refill, only clean blood can form new cells. For example, if people's 100 cells die, if their blood is 100 percent clean, 100 cells are made. Aging does not exist anymore. However, almost all people attempt desires in their lives, therefore their blood makes decayed, and as the decayed blood does not make new cells, aging happens to people.

That is, if a man's 100 cells die, as his blood decays twenty percent, eighty new cells are formed. As a result, the shortage of cells happens, it makes wrinkles, and the whole body comes to lose its power and its functions gradually. The shortage of cells reduces the number of white blood cells, so his body loses the power to overcome germs, comes to death finally. Therefore, to know the root of life is the shortcut to understand the principle of immortality.

E. The Root of Life is God (天命), the Root of Death is Ego.

All living things emit the light, the energy of life. Modern physicists have already said that atoms compose all materials, neutrons are in the nucleus of the element, and negative electrons go around neutrons. The power making negative electrons go around neutrons is not automatic, but the power of life making them turns. Having the power of life is to be alive, and to be alive means to have life.

On the other hand, dying is losing life. If the essence of life is God, the essence of death is Satan, the soul of devil. Then what is life? Life is just God. Satan, the soul of devil, has no life; it has only the soul of death. The soul of death rides God and kills life (God) finally. Therefore, a human dying means that God that is the root of life dies and the light energy of God (an eternal living thing) perishes. All living things and the universe were originally immortal God (Buddha) that was the existence of the light of the Trinity. At that moment the two Gods among the Trinity were occupied by the soul of death, Satan, and Satan had snatched its light, separated the Trinity into female and male humans, incased the God in all things, and God in all things have perished until now.

However, the God who was not occupied by Satan found out the factors that kill his children and has developed the Sweet Dew secretly for **6000** years, dreadful weapons: the light killing the soul of death. And He came to Korea in the name of Bright Star, the symbol of lily. The Savior is emancipating all God that is caught in everything including stars and the earth.

F. The co-relationship the working of blood and that of mind.

People think of blood as the essential material of their bodies that just provides nutrition and oxygen. However, blood has another factor beyond the level of material. That is, the working of blood is the working of mind. That is, we can see that mind and blood do not exist separately; they have the same quality simultaneously. Blood is formed by the working of mind; mind is formed by the blood. Like this, we can see that the personality and behavior is different according to the shape of blood. Therefore, the pouch of blood is called heart, not the pouch of blood, which implies the pouch of heart. Therefore, if we have the mind of God, our blood becomes that of God. What is the mind of God? God knows that all humanity is one body and God. So He has the mind that everyone is one body and God. So God regards every one as His body and respects as God.

The Seventh Angel (God) shouted people to regard everybody as my body and God. Regarding everybody as one body, one brother, and my body and serving everybody as God are the Han-Moum philosophy. And by practicing the Han-Moum Philosophy, the body of humanity is completed as that of immortal God. That is the philosophy of immortality. So far, humanity has not regarded everybody as my body, or one body. Furthermore, when people realize that all humanity is one body, God, the children of the most high, they can feel the peace and happiness of humanity, become a free existence from the restraint of their ego, and reinstate the nature of God by receiving eternal life (spirit) because that is the mind of immortal God.

The Factor of Satan, Desires（七情）

Scriptures define three poisons (covet, anger, ignorance) as desire, Satan, karma, and guilt. I will define as desires leading to death and karma, and the root of sins, from now on. As the Bible also said evil desire conceives and it gives birth to sins; when it is full-grown, given birth to death according to James 1：15：sin gives birth to death due to desire, as people continually commit sins, they die. A lot of evil minds decaying blood come from desires. Sexual desires, anger, nervousness, worries, all agonies, and delusion spring from desires; because of desires, there is you and I, mine and yours. So, desires make people commit sins and decay blood. By removing the root of sin, people cannot die. To know the cause of death is important, but to know the way of immortality is more important. I will suggest the Law of Liberty to be free from the character of humans. I will explain the factors and the secret to practice the Law of Liberty. Above, I said that blood is life; God is the root of life. And the factor that kills God that is the root of life is desire that is the character of Satan. Then, where do the three poisons—covet, anger, ignorance that Satan controls—come from and what is the root of desire? If we get rid of the basic factors that bear sins, we can see the principle of immortality.

The Whereabouts and Character of Sins

As the cause of death comes from desires, desires do not attempt desire, 'I', Self-Consciousness attempts desires. Mr. Cho Hee-Sung, the seventh angel, revealed the reason of birth, aging, diseases, and death. People die, because their blood is decayed by attempting desires, not putting on years according to Him. And He pointed out that the root of sins is Self-Consciousness, 'I'.

3. The Future Culture of Neohumans & New Ear of the Light

1) The Future Culture of Neohumans

The Korean new religion insist commonly that the Victor will appear in Korea, due to the advent of him, a new spiritual change will happen centering Korea, and will spread to the world. The movement of neohumans' new culture will go to the world riding the Hanryu according Tagore, a poet of India. In the seminar of the world astrologers in Taiwan in 1984, they predicted in a voice that Korea would lead the world. Soon the advent of neohumans is coming from all over the world in front of us. Then let's see who neohuamns are, and what the culture of neohumans is.

(1) The Definition of Neohumans

The men being reborn as the Holy Spirit are ones to reinstate the original essence. They are changed into the men of God spiritually and physically. They are existences who will live forever eating the Sweet Dew not eating a worldly food. When the big changing is ripe, they can be changed into light. Nostradamus said neohumans as other existences. They are angels who will realize the paradise, and they are transcendent of not only eating but also in-yang, like Jeremiah 16 saying in the Bible, in the new era, people neither get married nor deliver babies nor fight, they regard everybody as themselves to practice the one body philosophy everybody. Also, they are sane existences who are reborn as the Holy Spirit, are not conscious of others, are free from agonies and diseases, and are always happy. Besides, they do not cause a population problem, food problems, and environment problems. Further they are free from restraint of time and space, do not hold funeral because they do not die in an immortal society.

(2) The Role of Neohumans

Their role is to build heaven and to lead humanity to heaven by practicing big love and sacrifice. Gyeoamyourok writes that as the building of heaven did not exist so far and people live in ignorance and sins, neohumans are mocked and blamed by people and few people participate at the work of heaven. When the message spreads to the world, people will crowd to Korea to seek the food of life according to prophetic books. Therefore, the roles of neohumans become the foundation of heaven, become a leading role of heaven, and will lead all humanity to the paradise.

(3) The New View of Tonsijeok Samse Deungmyeong (通時的 三世燈明)[①]

As they have the view of Samsedeungmyeong after life, they can live in the land of immortality. Also, they put their value to eternal life. So they practice the philosophy of immortality and are treasures in this era to change the mortal world. Centering me now, the lives of the ancestors are my previous life (前世), and my present life (現世) is my ancestor's afterlife. My afterlife (來世) is connected to my children. Strictly speaking, all genetic information and traits are connected to this world through blood and lineage.

Therefore, only this world exists. Looking at these three lives with Tonsijeok (通時的 = transcending time) view and explaining it with the principle of Samse Deungmyeong (三世燈明), by attaining the nature of Buddha with living bodies, that is, by being reborn as the Holy Spirit, not only I but also all ancestors can achieve salvation and three lives' dream (前世, 現世, 來世)

---

① The new view of afterlife of neohumans, Tongsijeok Samse Deungmyeong (三世燈明): According to the Seventh Angel, all humans should awake from long sleep facing Samse Deungmyeong's (三世燈明) New Era when the salvation of the previous life, this life, and the afterlife is accomplished in this life at one time, they should be born as the Holy Spirit, the condition of original God.

comes true in me. That is the view of the exodus of birth and death of the Victory Altar.

2) New Ear of the Light & New Rules of New World

(1) New Rules of the New World

It is a law that makes humanity not commit sins, and makes them be reborn as the Holy Spirit. That is, it is a law that makes humanity live forever as God. Also, it makes heaven in people's mind by regarding everyone as my body.

Let me introduce the Law of Liberty.

"Look at and adore the Reincarnated Maitreya Buddha, Victor, Savior who sends down the Sweet Dew every second."

"Beat Self-Consciousness and kill it."

"Regard the sins of brothers as mine."

"Regard others' faults as mine."

"Do not hate brothers"

"Regard brothers' circumstances as mine."

"Regard others as mine"

"Have the conviction of immortality."

"Live life in a way opposite of what Self-conscious desires."

"Conceive the mind of God all the time."

(2) The New Movement of Saving life by the Victor

The prediction of the neo culture above will be accomplished when people try to listen to the message of heaven and the culture of neohumans understand, and practice them, according to Gyeoamyourok (格菴遺錄). The prophetic book suggests how people should live and also give an answer to people. In that respect, the book is greater than any other prophetic books. There is a recording, "there will spread a mystery disease all around. It is so terrible that if people catch the disease in the morning, they die in the evening." "If people do not practice the Law of Liberty and the words of the Victor, the Victor will not keep people from the disease." According to Gyeoamyourok, only the Victor of the Victory Altar can heal the mysterious disease.

(3) New Ear of the Holy Dew Light (天地合一的甘露至誠光明)

The Essence of the Holy Dew Spirit in All the Scriptures

The core term that most scriptures commonly foretold is the Sweet Dew and the Holy Dew Spirit. No matter how much people read Scriptures, unless they realize the hidden truth, it is difficult to find the way leading to nirvana. Without knowing the origin of the Sweet Dew（甘露）exactly in the scriptures, nobody can reach nirvana according to the Buddhist Scriptures. Additionally, Revelation 2：17. "To those who wins the Victory I will give some hidden manna." Then I will check the paragraphs about the Sweet Dew in the Bible.

①According to Hosea 14：5 "I（God）will be like dew to Israel（the Victor）, he will blossom like lilies." He predicted that He will become Dew to the Victor and fall down.

②Isaiah 26：19 "As the sparkling dew refreshes the earth, so the Lord will revive those who have long been dead." God predicted in the Bible that if the Holy Dew Spirit falls down, death will disappear on the earth exactly.

③Joel 2：28 – 30 "Afterwards, I will pour out my spirit on everyone：there will be bloodshed, fire, and clouds of smoke." The terms of bloodshed, fire, and clouds of smoke correspond with fire = 火, rain = 雨, Dew = 露, three abundant God's Spirit（三豊海印）in 『Gyeokamyourok』.

④Micah 5：7 "The people of Israel who survive will be like refreshing Dew sent by the Lord." The Lord says that He will send Dew to people, which means that He will attend to people as Dew like fire（火）, rain（雨）, Dew（露）.

Like this, the hidden manna in the Bible descends from the Savior in the Victory Altar, it is just the Sweet Dew（甘露　海印）. Almost all scriptures of the world predicted the same the manna of heaven. Now I will examine Amrita in ancient myths and literatures. The Sweet Dew is quoted frequently as the synonym of nirvana. When people call Buddhism the Dharma-door of the Sweet Dew（甘露　法門）, in this case, they regard nirvana meaning accomplishing immortality as the Sweet Dew. Therefore, they think that the basic aim of Buddhism is reaching nirvana by receiving the Sweet Dew according to 『普門

品] of the Lotus Sutra (法華經) because the Sweet Dew removes humans' agony, birth, and death of humans. Among the Buddhist scriptures, Amita Sutra (阿彌陀經) that is called little Sutra (小經) says where the Sweet Dew falls down is the pure land of happiness.

(4) The Proclamation of Five New Covenants and their substance

The Victor Mr. Cho Hee Sung (Jeongdoryeong; the Savior of Koreans) who overcame the spirit of death and the Trinity God occupied his body proclaimed the Five Covenants for South Koreans and has accomplished them for 33 years. Gyeokamyourok, a Korean prophetic book with 100 % accuracy, records that Jeongdoryeong seems like a human but God.

(a) The Victor said, "I will destroy communism. "

The first Public 5 Covenants, He removed communism completely using His other selves by controlling Gorbachev and by his other selves killing the ideology of communism in August, in 1991 according to the Seventh Angel's sayings and some proofs.

(b) I will keep Korea from typhoons.

The second Covenant, He has stopped dozens of typhoons blowing toward Korean peninsula.

(c) I will stop rainy seasons in Korea.

The third Covenant, It is rainy seasons in Korea (from 15 June to 15 July). In this season every year rain falls down heavily and ceaselessly for the past 3, 000 years. But it has disappeared for the last 30 years.

(d) I will make Korean harvest abundant.

The fourth Covenant, Korean abundant harvest has been accomplushed since 1981.

(e) I will keep Korea from Korean wars and unify Korea

(5) If Humanity is qualified to receive the light, a New Era will be Open

Mr. Cho, the Maitreya Buddha, appeared and told about the era of light as follows. I cited the new words of the Maitreya Buddha to show the Idea World of the future, the true meaning of new heaven. If humanity is reborn as God (Buddha) and becomes the light of God (Buddha), they become immortal existences. That is, they become immortal Dharma bodies (不生不滅的法身).

As light is life, if humanity becomes righteous like neohumans, their bodies are changed into light. The light is stronger than that of the sunlight, so if one is changed into light, he/she becomes immortal, becomes the forms of life that is not influenced by anything. Due to the light of the victorious Maitreya Buddha, all humanity will become light. The sun will become dark; light will come out from the face of the Maitreya Buddha. Because the light goes spirally, it will shine brightly to the opposite side of Korea, such as America, Europe. On the day, the light from the Savior's face will become cool to the men who will live forever, will make them fly. However, to the sinners, it will become so hot that they cannot stand it. Due to the light of the victorious Maitreya Buddha, humanity will become Buddha (God), will live in infinite happiness forever.

As mentioned above, the advent of the Victor and the movement of the Victory Altar is a new culture of saving dying lives, it is a new science. If religions are created to save humanity from death, the role of the existing religions which did not solve death is finished. Due to imperfect teaching and people who do not know the definition of religion, a lot of people died in 100 years' war,

Soon, the light will come out from the Maitreya Buddha. To receive the light, humanity should be qualified to receive it. When you are qualified to receive it, the sun will lose its light. As the spirit and light of Satan will be destroyed completely, Satan (three poisons) disappears due to the Holy Spirit, then neohumans will fly. If humanity receives the Holy Spirit, their fatigue disappears. If the light comes into the bodies of humanity, the Satan in them dies. So they reinstate God. As the light removes sins, humanity's consciousness（我相）disappears, so they recover God. Then humanity will fly, everything will be done as they think. First, the Maitreya Buddha and neohumans who are accomplished as God will fly. In old times, Einstein predicted when humanity moves faster than the speed of the sunlight, they will not die. The world will not have time and space. The Holy Dew Spirit becomes the fire of hell to sinners, becomes the light of life tree to righteous men who are reborn as neohumans.

So the light is so horrible that sinners cannot die, will live in pain forever. The light will give freshness to righteous men (neohumans), when the light comes into them though their sins remain a little, the sins disappear completely.

Neohumans who are reborn as the Holy Spirit will be changed into light. Those who get out of sins will become light, but those who do not get out of their sins remain with their bodies. When all humanity becomes God, there will be some men who will cry. Such men will live in pain forever.

(6) The Prediction for Neohumans in the Scriptures

Now I will introduce the predictions of neohumans in the future that are foretold in the scriptures. Maitreya Sutra 1 predicts the way of the Sweet Dew as follows. A man who has a splendidly shining spirit, a completely concentrated mind, and a selfless mind will be reincarnated in the world. When he preaches the true way of the Sweet Dew, all humanity will be happy, like that of a thirsty person drinking the Sweet Dew of heaven. Also the neohuman will lead people to nirvana getting out of Samsara.

(7) The predictions for the Mainstream Cultures of the New World

The advent of the Victor of the Bible and the victorious Buddha (the Maitreya Buddha) of the Buddhist scriptures, the advent of neohumans, and the future image of the utmost land are predicted as follows. Let me introduce the key points.

According to the Avatamska Sutra 70 volume, "The Maitrya Buddha appears in the year 3007 on the Buddhism calendar. The year 3000 on the Buddhism calendar is the year 1973. The year 3007 falls on the year 1980, the year is when the Maitreya Buddha was supposed to appear. The Jeungilaham Sutra volume 49 predicted that the Maitreya Buddha would appear in Korea, at that time there would be a lot of people and Koreans would have abundant harvest." Please refer the declaration of the five covenants of the Maitreya Buddha.

The Avatamaska Sutra volume 42 foretells, "The Maitreya Buddha reaches nirvana at his age of 50, and comes to the world." Also, the Nirvana Sutra volume 8 records that the Maitreya Buddha comes out in the year of sheep.

Furthermore, the Nirvana Sutra volume 7 tells that the Maitreya Buddha fights against Satan. He says people die because their blood decays, but people do not believe him. The Maitreya Buddha comes out with Cho (曺) of heaven, his family name, according to the true Maitreya Buddha Sutra, the Nirvana Sutra, and Gyeokamyourok. According to the Jeungilaham Sutra (增 一 阿含 經)

volume 45, "the Maitreya Buddha becomes the seventh basic door. That is, he reveals the basis of the seventh Buddha (God). " Plus, the Nirvana Sutra (涅槃經) volume 8 predicted that the way of the Sweet Dew would appear. That is, it predicted if people eat the Sweet Dew, they will live forever.

Additionally, the Nirvana Sutra volume 9 recorded, "The light of the Sweet Dew goes into the pores of people, they can reach nirvana. " The Nirvana Sutra volume 5 wrote, "If people meet the Maitreya Buddha, all their sins disappear and become a golden mountain (immortal). " Furthermore, the Nirvana Sutra (涅槃經) volume 8 tells, "Like all the water of all the rivers flows to the seas, all religions return to the Maitreya Buddha. " Also the Nirvana Sutra (涅槃經) volume 25 records, "If people look at the Maitreya Buddha, their life spans become infinitely long and their diseases and anguishes are healed. " According to the Nirvana Sutra (涅槃經) volume 25, "伊字三點 means the Trinity Buddha, three Buddha become one by combining, it is the secret of the Maitreya Buddha. " The Nirvana Sutra (涅槃經) volume 29 says. "When one becomes Buddha, the people who meet the Buddha become Buddha. " In addition, the Nirvana Sutra (涅槃經) volume 8 predicted, "There is neither equality nor freedom in the world, but the Tao of Buddha is equal and becomes one, that is the true Tao of all humanity. " Also the Nirvana Sutra (涅槃經) volume 8, "All the recordings of all scriptures are incomplete letters, tell the basis of incomplete letters. But when the Maitreya Buddha appears, the incomplete letters will disappear, complete letters will come out. According to Sakyamuni. " What I said is not perfect. You should throw away the incomplete letters and know the complete letters. The Sweet Dew is a necessity in forming mainstream cultures of the world and neohumans. Then the symbol of the great saint that was predicted in all the scriptures is the Sweet Dew. A new era is coming soon when a lot of neohumans appear, all humanity become saints due to the advent of a saint, death and anguish disappears, and people enjoy immortality.

Conclusion

Without mentioning "Photon Belt", so-called, physicists and astronomies say, now is the era of brilliant light of the Sweet Dew, and awake persons will notice the secret of eternal life, feel heaven in their bodies and mind by experience the essence of God. Also they will think that the Idea World which all philosophers have pursued is realized in their minds. Additionally, they will find the Super Ego and feel it. They will find the clue that all humanity can become one, are truly saved and free from death through the "Han-Moum Philosophy". Furthermore, those who practice "the Han-Moum Philosophy" will recover the original nature of humanity, reach the stage of God. In this respect, my thesis is important.

The thing we have to do is that we realize that all humanity are one, one brother, and one body, and we should get out of the Ego which keep people from knowing the essence of humanity and God, and be reborn as the light of eternal life. The Han-Moum Philosophy is universal neither to change nor to decay, which is the methodology of being reborn as the Neo-humans, by practicing it.

The International Academy of Neohumans Culture and the Research Center of Neo-Humans want to share the philosophy of new life as the practical methodology for salvation with all humanity. What we should do is to realize the root of humanity, to keep the Law of Liberty, and to conceive the mind of recovering humanity 's original nature. If humanity practice them, they can be reborn as immortal Neo-humans. This thought came to the world after Mr. Cho Hee-Sung (曺熙星) overcame his Ego and death. I have studied the amazing new science through a self-experiment methodology for a long time, arranged the philosophy of immortality as the Han-Moum Philosophy, a new philosophy, and revealed it to the academies.

I hope that not only the believers of the Victory Altar but also all the citizens of the world will receive the Sweet Dew, will follow the way of Tao (道脈), and will be born as the Holy Spirit. So far, I have explained the view of the exodus of birth and death of the Victory Altar through the principle of immortality. In addition, I explained the way and process of reinstating original light of God.

Finally, I would like to say again that to solve of humanity's question is just removing Ego, Self-Consciousness. For achieving it, people should live a life in contrast with what they want to live. "Regard the sins of brothers as mine."

"Regard others faults as mine." "Do not hate brothers." Also one should regard brothers' circumstances as one's.

References

[1] Deepak Chopra. 1993. *Men Do Not Grow Old*, translated by Lee Gyoo-Hyeong, Seoul: Jeongsin Segyesa.

[2] Cobb, John Jr. 1984. *On Han Philosophy.* from Kim Sang Yil's Hanism As Korean Mind.

[3] Kim Sang Yil. 2000. *Suun and Whitehead*, Seoul: Jisiksanupsa.

[4] Kwon Hee-Soun. 1993. *The Science of Immortality.* Seoul: Publishing HAE-IN.

[5] Park YoungJin. 2001. *The Victory Altar Where Eternal Life Is Accomplished*, Bucheon: Doseo Publishing Haein.

[6] Lee SangHo. 1979. 大巡典經, Jeonju: The headquarter of Jeungsan.

[7] Underwood, L. H. 1918. *Underwood of Korea*, New York, Fleming H. Revell Company.

[8] Han Sang Yeong. 1987. *The Science Of Immortality.* Seoul: Publishing Haein.

[9] Yoon Taek Lim. 2004. *The Methodology for Qualitative Study of the Culture and History.*, Seoul: Doseo Publishing Arce.

[10] Han Gang-Hyen. 2002. *The Study of Prediction of Gyeokamyourok.* The master's thesis. Tokyo: Mejiro University Graduate School.

[11] Li Jialian. 2012. The Sentimental Origion of Virtue: An Inquiry into Thought of Moral Sentiments, Hang zhou: Zhejiang University Press.

[12] Han Gang-Hyen. 2011. *The Study for Exodus from Birth and Death & The Theory of Eternal Life*, Journal of the Korean Academy of New Religions, April, Vol. 24.

一体哲学与新人类文化

Han Gang-Hyen

摘　要：宇宙中不断变化的银河原则对当今人类和地球产生了极大的影响。地球上的问题很多，如环境恶化、食品短缺、宗教与宗教之间的冲突和敌对、自私自利的个人主义以及人类所面临的各种危险处境等。然而，30 年前，在东方经文中出现了"克己胜者"（新人类或义人的存在方式），这种人超越了自我（即死亡的精灵）并作为圣灵获得了重生。通过发动一场新的文化运动，这种人可以把旧世界（它使众生死于无知和缺乏沟通）变成一个不朽的新世界。所有的经文和未来主义者都预测说，新宗教运动、一体科学和一体哲学的终极目的是要建立这样一个天堂，并实现对人类的救赎。人类将要重获的最大善，就是可以像神一样得到永生，韩国已经开始了这种追求。韩国新宗教运动将开启一个义人的时代，它需要新的伦理、公共秩序、公共哲学以及新的规则来建立这样一个新世界。本文介绍了作为一种新哲学及新科学的"一体哲学"的精华，阐述了新人类（也就是神人）对生命的拯救。这种文化很快会成为世界主流文化。最重要的是，公共哲学是大一体光明思想，也是一体哲学，它把所有人视为一个家庭，并给人类带来和平。通过不断沟通与融合，在一体哲学思想指导下推进生命救赎运动，保守新天堂的法则，世界将迎来一个新时代，我认为，文本所讨论的永生哲学和新（神）人类新文化，将会成为世界主流文化，使所有的人演变为一体，并给人带来真正的幸福。

关键词：一体哲学　新人类　胜利者　圣露精神　新（神）人类文化

中医药文化及其核心价值

陈建华[*]

摘　要：中医药文化是中华民族优秀传统文化的重要组成部分，是中华民族优秀传统文化中体现中医药本质与特色的物质文明、精神文明和科技文化的总和。几千年来，中医药文化为中华民族繁衍生息、治病养生、文明发展做出了重大贡献。中医药文化的核心价值集中反映了中华民族优秀文化的核心价值，也就是中和的生命观念，人与自然和谐的养生理念，从整体中获得中和，从协调中取得和谐。在中医学看来，适中是生理健康的前提，失中是疾病发生的条件，执中是健身防病的法宝，致和是防病祛疾的途径。中医药文化的核心价值源于中国哲学的中庸思想。它是在利用中国传统文化核心理念、价值观念和思维模式指导中医学实践的过程中形成和发展起来的。中医药文化的核心价值不仅是中医药文化研究的核心，更应该成为宣传东方文化、彰显中国智慧的独特窗口，成为理解中华文明的捷径。

关键词：中医药文化　中和　中庸

中医药文化是中华民族优秀传统文化的重要组成部分。充分认识中医药文化的现代价值，意义重大而深远。国家中医药管理局于 2011 年出台了《关于加强中医药文化建设的指导意见》（以下简称《意见》）。《意

＊ 陈建华，湖北中医药大学教授，研究方向为哲学与中医药文化。

见》明确指出："中医药文化是中医药学的根基和灵魂，是中医药事业持续发展的内在动力，是中医药学术创新进步的不竭源泉，也是中医药行业凝聚力量、振奋精神、彰显形象的重要抓手。我们要增强传承和发展中医药文化的自觉性和主动性，从发展繁荣社会主义文化、建设社会主义文化强国的全局来认识和把握加强中医药文化建设的重大意义。"①

中医药文化的核心价值集中反映了中华民族优秀文化的核心价值，也就是中和的生命观念，人与自然和谐的养生理念。中医药文化的核心价值是对中医药核心理念、价值观念与中医思维方式的高度概括。中医药文化的核心价值源于中国哲学的中庸思想。它是在利用中国传统文化核心理念、价值观念和思维模式指导中医学实践的过程中形成和发展起来的。中医药文化的核心价值不仅是中医药文化研究的核心，更应该成为宣传东方文化、彰显中国智慧的窗口，成为理解中华文明的捷径。

一　中医与中医药文化

《国务院关于扶持和促进中医药事业发展的若干意见》指出：中医药是我国各族人民在几千年生产生活实践和与疾病做斗争中逐步形成并不断丰富发展的医学科学，为中华民族繁衍昌盛做出了重要贡献，对世界文明进步产生了积极影响。习近平同志 2010 年 6 月在"墨尔本理工大学中医孔子学院揭牌仪式"上也曾经指出："中医药学凝聚着深邃的哲学智慧和中华民族几千年的健康养生理念及其实践经验，是中国古代科学的瑰宝，也是打开中华文明宝库的钥匙。"②

中医药文化是中华民族优秀传统文化中体现中医药本质与特色的物质文明、精神文明和科技文化的总和。这一本质，充分说明了中医药文化与中国传统文化的密切关系，体现了中医药文化的广泛性。

---

① 国家中医药管理局：《关于加强中医药文化建设的指导意见》，《中国中医药报》2011 年 12 月 29 日，第 3 页。

② 习近平：《中医孔子学院将有助于澳民众了解中国文化》，中华人民共和国中央人民政府网站，http://www.gov.cn/ldhd/2010－06/20/content_ 1631961. htm，2010.6.20。

就中医药文化的基础、结构和属性而言，中医药文化的基础是中国传统哲学、文学、史学；中医药文化的结构由精神文化、科技文化、行为文化、物质文化四个方面构成，涉及中医药文化理念、文化实践、文化环境三个层面，体现中医药的人文属性。这是对中医药文化自身各要素关系的定位。这种定位有利于揭示和阐明中医药文化以核心理念、价值观念和思维方式为代表的精神文化是中医药文化的灵魂与核心，是形成中医药文化特色的根源所在，也是中医药人文属性的根本体现。[①]

就中医药文化功能而言，它具有塑造中医药文化核心理念和价值观念，形成中医药学思维方式和认知，揭示中医药学规律，影响中医药事业传承与发展以及增强中华民族文化认同与自信，扩大中华文化影响力的功能。它揭示了中医药文化与中医药事业的关系，体现其基础性的特点，同时也体现了中医药文化对中华文化复兴的重大作用。

《国务院关于扶持和促进中医药事业发展的若干意见》指出：中医药作为中华民族的瑰宝蕴含着丰富的哲学思想和人文精神，是我国文化软实力的重要体现。将中医药文化建设纳入国家文化发展规划，有利于推进中医药机构文化建设，弘扬行业传统职业道德，开展中医科学文化普及教育，加强宣传教育基地建设，加强中医药文化资源开发利用，打造中医药文化品牌。

二 中医药文化的核心价值在于中和的生命观念

中医药文化的核心价值在于中和的生命观念。首先，中医认为，生命根源于阴阳平和，阴平阳秘是生命得以存在的物质条件。阴阳学说是中医理论的重要来源，著名医学家张景岳说："天地之道，以阴阳之气造化万物；人生之理，以阴阳之气而长养百骸。《易》者，易也，具阴阳动静之妙，医者，意也，合阴阳消长之机。虽阴阳已备于《内经》，而变化莫大乎《周易》。故曰：天人一理者，一此阴阳也；医易同源者，同此变化

---

① 胡真、王华：《中医药文化的内涵与外延》，《中医杂志》2013 年第 3 期。

也。"之所以阴、阳能够成为生命物质的要素，根本在于"和"。中和是生命得以产生的根本条件，一切生命都起源于"阴阳和"。《道德经》有云："万物负阴而抱阳，冲气以为和。""道生一，一生二，二生三，三生万物。""道生一"谓无极生太极，"一生二"谓太极生两仪，"二生三"谓两仪化生"和气"，"三生万物"就是从和气中繁衍出天下万物。

其次，中医主张在护卫生命生长的过程中以"平"为期、以"和"为贵。《黄帝内经·灵枢·本神篇》："故智者之养生也，必顺四时而适寒暑，和喜怒而安居处，节阴阳而调刚柔。如是则辟邪不至，长生久视。"《素问·平人气象论》记载："黄帝问曰：'平人何如？'岐伯对曰：'平人者，不病也。'"不病的表现就是气血平和。《素问·生气通天论》曰："阴平阳秘。"阴阳在对立制约和消长中所取得的动态平衡，是人体生命的最佳状态。这种生命的最佳状态源于阴阳两者相互调节而维持的相对平衡，"阴平阳秘"是中医学用阴阳学说诠释人体正常生理状态的高度概括，如《素问·三部九候论》所说："无问其病，以平为期。"倘若阴阳失调，就会出现问题，乃至丧失生命，如《素问·生气通天论》所云："阴阳离决，精气乃绝。"

再次，中医治病的常用手段就是调和阴阳。如《素问·刺法论》中所说："太过取之，不足资之。"在正常情况下，人体中阴阳两方面处于相对平衡状态。从根本上说，疾病的发生是阴阳的相对平衡被打破，即阴阳的偏盛偏衰代替了正常的阴阳消长。既然阴阳失调是疾病发生、发展的根本原因，那么，调理阴阳，使失调的阴阳向着协调方面转化，恢复阴阳的相对平衡，则是中医治病的最高原则。所以中医治病就是调和阴阳。

最后，中医处判针药的原则在于中和。"中病即止"是中医用药的金科玉律，在用药的过程中，过与不及，都非良策。如《伤寒论·辨可下病脉证并治》所说："凡服下药，用汤胜丸，中病即止，不必尽剂也。"刘禹锡《鉴药》明确指出："过当则伤和。"《灵枢·血气形志篇》亦云："抑强扶弱，损多益广，泻有余补不足，制太过，化不及，致中和之要诀。"

总之，在中医学看来，适中是生理健康的前提，失中是疾病发生的条件，执中是健身防病的法宝，致和是防病祛疾的途径。

三 中医药文化的核心价值源于中国哲学的中庸思想

中医药文化的核心价值源于中国哲学的中庸思想。中国传统文化，尤其是中国古代哲学思想是中医药文化核心价值构建的基础和产生的土壤。中医学在其形成和发展的过程中，不断汲取中国传统文化滋养，最终形成"天人合一"的整体观，尚中贵和的和合观，阴阳变易、五行生克的辩证观以及大医精诚、救世济民的医德修养观等①。中医认识论的原则是"天人合一"，治疗疾病的原则是"执中致和"，处方用药的标准是"补偏救弊"，无一不是中庸思想在生命科学当中的具体运用。

科学是文化的基础，文化是科学的向导。尤其是在自然科学还处在奠基和形成阶段，文化导向对科学所起的作用更是无法估量的。在中医这一生命科学的发生、发展过程中，处处都可以看到人文精神的踪影，处处都可以看到传统文化的印痕。正如爱因斯坦所说："如果把哲学理解为在最普通最广泛的形势中对知识的追求，显然哲学就可以认为是全部科学研究之母。"中华文明早已形成的中庸理念正是中医文化核心价值得以形成的文化基础。

"中"，《说文》："中，内也。从口，丨。上下通。"表示的意思就像箭从圆心穿过的那个点。如果射箭正好达到那个点就叫作"中"（zhòng）。《吕氏春秋·尽数》："譬之若射者，射而不中，反修于招，何益于中！"《史记·周本纪》："楚有养由基者，善射者也。去柳叶百步而射之，百发而百中之。"读去声的"中"，表示"正应，正对上，恰好合上"。"中"在中国文化中具有独特的意义。《论语·先进》记载，"子贡问：'师与商也孰贤？'子曰：'师过矣，商也不及。'曰：'然则师愈与？'子曰：'过犹不及。'"《论语·雍也》中，子曰："中庸之为德也，其至矣乎！民鲜能久矣。"朱熹《论语集注》引程子曰："不偏之谓中，不易之谓庸。中者天下之正道，庸者天下之定理。"不偏就是平衡，不易就是稳定。中庸之道就是均衡稳定的规律。坚守中庸之道，个人就能气定神闲，社会就能和谐共存；破毁中庸

---

① 胡真、王华：《中医药文化的内涵与外延》，《中医杂志》2013 年第 3 期。

之道，个人就会温燥两失，社会就会混乱不安。中庸不仅是中华文明的理念，而且具有普世性，《圣经》就有多处论及"中道"，如《新约全书·罗马书》曾论及"合乎中道"。亚里士多德更鲜明地提倡中庸思想。在亚里士多德看来，"德性就是中庸，……中庸是最高的善和极端的美"。以中道为主的生活就是最好的生活。中国哲学中的儒学对中庸之道阐发得最清晰、最具本体论意义。孔子将中庸视为君子应有之品德，尝言："君子中庸，小人反中庸。君子之中庸也，君子而时中；小人之反中庸也，小人而无忌惮也。"无忌惮者，无所顾忌，任意横行，放纵极端也。《中庸》中说："喜怒哀乐之未发，谓之中。发而皆中节谓之和。中也者，天下之大本也；和也者，天下之达道也，致中和，天地位焉，万物育焉。""中和"就是"中庸"，不偏不倚，既不过分，也不要不及，以期达到理想中的均衡态，所谓恰到好处。"中和"是中国传统文化的核心概念，也是和谐社会重要的文化内涵。作为传统哲学范畴的中庸，其完整意义包括中、和两个方面。"中"表示采取正确的方法，"和"反映达到理想的目的。《中庸》说："致中和，天地位焉，万物育焉。"所谓"执中致和"，就是通过正确途径，借助合适方法，实现美好理想，达到最佳状态。

中医药文化及其核心价值是中华民族宝贵的精神财富，将其继承发扬，创新光大，并逐步推向世界，是中华文化传人神圣的职责。

Traditional Chinese Medicine Culture
and Its Core Values

Chen Jianhua

Abstract：Traditional Chinese medicine culture is one of the most important constituents in Chinese culture; it embodies the nature of traditional Chinese medicine. Traditional Chinese medicine culture has made great contribution to the health of Chinese nation. The core value of it expresses the core value of Chinese nation, such as the moderate idea concerning life, the harmonious health-keeping of man and nature. According to traditional Chinese medicine culture, to be moderate is the pre-condition of health-keeping. To keep moderate is the key point to keep health. The core value of traditional Chinese medicine culture originates from Chinese traditional philosophy and is the application of it.

Keywords: Traditional Chinese medicine culture; moderation; doctrine of the mean

图书在版编目（CIP）数据

世界文化发展论坛. 2013/强以华主编. —北京：社会
科学文献出版社，2014.4
ISBN 978 - 7 - 5097 - 5763 - 5

Ⅰ.①世…　Ⅱ.①强…　Ⅲ.①文化发展 - 世界 - 文集
Ⅳ.①G11 - 53

中国版本图书馆 CIP 数据核字（2014）第 044412 号

世界文化发展论坛（2013）

主　　编 / 强以华
副 主 编 / 李家莲

出 版 人 / 谢寿光
出 版 者 / 社会科学文献出版社
地　　址 / 北京市西城区北三环中路甲 29 号院 3 号楼华龙大厦
邮政编码 / 100029

责任部门 / 社会政法分社　（010）59367156　　责任编辑 / 张建中　周　琼
电子信箱 / shekebu@ ssap. cn　　　　　　　　责任校对 / 白桂芹
项目统筹 / 王　绯　周　琼　　　　　　　　　责任印制 / 岳　阳
经　　销 / 社会科学文献出版社市场营销中心　（010）59367081　59367089
读者服务 / 读者服务中心（010）59367028

印　　装 / 三河市尚艺印装有限公司
开　　本 / 787mm×1092mm　1/16　　　　　　印　　张 / 25.75
版　　次 / 2014 年 4 月第 1 版　　　　　　　字　　数 / 409 千字
印　　次 / 2014 年 4 月第 1 次印刷
书　　号 / ISBN 978 - 7 - 5097 - 5763 - 5
定　　价 / 98.00 元